Gateway to the Confederacy

LOUISIANA STATE UNIVERSITY PRESS BATON ROUGE

New Perspectives on the
Chickamauga and Chattanooga Campaigns, 1862–1863

GATEWAY TO THE CONFEDERACY

EDITED BY **EVAN C. JONES** AND **WILEY SWORD**

Published by Louisiana State University Press
Copyright © 2014 by Evan C. Jones and Wiley Sword
All rights reserved
Manufactured in the United States of America
First printing

Designer: Barbara Neely Bourgoyne
Typeface: Ingeborg
Printer and binder: Maple Press

Maps by Hal Jespersen

Caroline E. Janney's chapter, "No 'Sickly Sentimental Gush': Chickamauga and Chattanooga National Military Park and the Limits of Reconciliation," originally appeared in the *Journal of the Civil War Era*, Volume 2, No. 3. Copyright © 2012 the University of North Carolina Press. Used by permission of the publisher. www.uncpress.unc.edu.

LIBRARY OF CONGRESS CATALOGING-IN-PUBLICATION DATA
Gateway to the Confederacy : new perspectives on the Chickamauga and Chattanooga Campaigns, 1862–1863 / edited by Evan C. Jones and Wiley Sword.
    pages cm
Includes index.
ISBN 978-0-8071-5509-7 (cloth : alk. paper) — ISBN 978-0-8071-5510-3 (pdf) — ISBN 978-0-8071-5511-0 (epub) — ISBN 978-0-8071-5512-7 (mobi) 1. Chickamauga, Battle of, Ga., 1863. 2. Chattanooga, Battle of, Chattanooga, Tenn., 1863. 3. Chattanooga Region (Tenn.)—History, Military—19th century. I. Jones, Evan C., 1980– editor of compilation, author. II. Sword, Wiley, editor of compilation, author.
    E475.81.G38 2014
    973.7'359—dc23

                                                                    2013037866

In Memory of Stephen Innes
Friend and Mentor

Whose example showed that the historian's craft could be an ennobling one.

CONTENTS

ILLUSTRATIONS

Gateway to the Confederacy

INTRODUCTION

EVAN C. JONES AND WILEY SWORD

The 1862 and 1863 campaigns waged for possession of Chattanooga, Tennessee, rank among the most significant of the American Civil War. Located in a narrow valley hollowed beneath the looming Blue Ridge Mountains and Appalachian Plateau to the east and the numerous mountains of the Cumberland Plateau to the west, Chattanooga sat at a transportation confluence where roads, four major railroads, and the Tennessee River converged. Situated in southeastern Tennessee just miles from North Georgia, the diminutive village consequently served as a remote hub, located literally along the border of the Upper South and the Deep South. Between April 1862 and November 1863, Union forces from both the war's western and eastern theaters launched two key offensives to capture this otherwise obscure whistle stop.

While Chattanooga's significance in Civil War historiography has remained largely overshadowed by attention directed by scholars to other events, the region's importance evaded few key players or observers during the war. Writing from Vienna, Austria, in March 1862 for the newspaper *Die Presse,* the politically radical yet astute Karl Marx and Friedrich Engels pronounced, "It is now the task of the Northern generals to find the Achilles' heel of the cotton states." And to that end, locating the transportation nexus of the Confederacy, declared the north–south and east–west hubs of Chattanooga and neighboring Dalton, Georgia, to be "the most important railway junctions of the entire South."[1]

A few weeks later, in April, at the beginning of the 1862 Chattanooga campaign, the now legendary Union saboteur James J. Andrews regarded the city as "the most important strategic point in the Confederacy."[2] The following year President Abraham Lincoln told Major General William S. Rosecrans, the commander of a renewed Union effort to seize the region, "If we can hold Chattanooga, and East Tennessee, I think the rebellion must dwindle and die."[3] Rosecrans himself believed that the city's geographic location made it "the gateway to the heart of the Southern Confederacy."[4] Following the summer of 1863 and the rebel defeats at Gettysburg and Vicksburg, the Confederate high command saw Chattanooga's defense as an opportunity to turn the tide of a war that the South had begun to lose. "I . . . am inclined to the opinion that our best opportunity for great results is in Tennessee," remarked Army of Northern Virginia corps commander James Longstreet at summer's end.[5] After Rosecrans's capture and occupation of the city, the president told his general in chief, Major General Henry W. Halleck, "If [Rosecrans] can only maintain this position, the rebellion can only eke out a short and feeble existence, as an animal sometimes may with a thorn in its vitals."[6] Before the battles for Chattanooga ended, neither the Washington nor Richmond governments spared any expenditure in blood, treasure, men, or materiel to maintain a hold over the city and its gateway through the mountains. For President Lincoln, these campaigns wagered both political risks and opportunities for his besieged administration. A Federal-held Chattanooga meant a lasting liberation of Unionist East Tennessee and an open road to Georgia and the interior of the Confederate southeast. Faced with an ever receding frontier, the prize proved

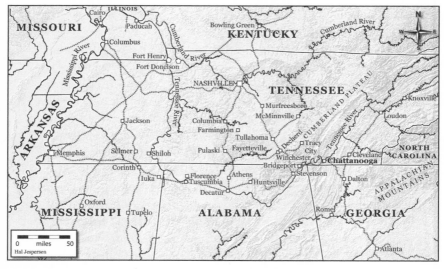

Theater of Operations, 1862–1863.

so valuable to Confederate president Jefferson Davis that he personally traveled to Chattanooga in October 1863 to further his army's likelihood of success there.

The first Federal effort to seize the city came in the spring and summer of 1862. Between April and June of that year, the secretary of war, Edwin Stanton ordered a massive concentration of U.S. forces brought to bear against Chattanooga from various points in the western theater. Following the successful seizure of northeast Alabama by Union brigadier general Ormsby M. Mitchel's division, an almost entirely undefended Chattanooga seemed a prize within easy reach. In June the War Department, acting decisively, ordered that Major General Don Carlos Buell join Mitchel with the rest of the Army of the Ohio by marching overland from Corinth, Mississippi, and unite with Brigadier General George W. Morgan's command, which would push southward through Knoxville from the Cumberland Gap. The combined strength of this massive pincer movement was designed to isolate Chattanooga and overwhelm its few defenders. The Confederate's reactive-offensive strategy, as implemented by the Army of Tennessee's new commander, General Braxton Bragg, however, shifted the Federal focus away from the city almost overnight. By advancing his rebels northward through Chattanooga and into Kentucky, Bragg forced Buell and the entirety of the Army of the Ohio to give chase and ultimately give battle near Perryville on October 8. Though Bragg was ultimately defeated in his failed Kentucky invasion, this move thwarted any Union threat to Chattanooga for some ten months. In many respects, no event of the war provided more colorful figures, nor provoked more daring feats, than the 1862 Chattanooga Campaign. Between the eccentric astronomer-general Ormsby Mitchel; the fiery Maine-born Confederate defender of Chattanooga, Danville Leadbetter; East Tennessee Unionist saboteurs known as the "bridge burners"; and most memorably the twenty-four men of the Andrews's Raid, which resulted in the most famous locomotive chase in history, the 1862 campaign provides a rich tapestry for scholars to marvel. Most important of all characteristics, however, is that the failed expedition marked one of the principal missed opportunities experienced by any Union army during the Civil War.

Then in 1863, along the banks of the meandering West Chickamauga Creek, on September 18–20, the dense scrub forest of northwestern Georgia played host to the largest battle ever fought west of the Appalachian Mountains. Within the ranks of its some 125,000 participants, the slaughter was staggering. The latter forty-eight hours of the Battle of Chickamauga proved the bloodiest two days of the entire war. In what amounted to the most complete Confederate victory and worst Union defeat in the western theater, the "butcher's bill" totaled 34,805 killed, wounded, and missing, amounting to 28 percent of both armies. Among the rebel casualties, one corps commander, one division commander, eight brigade commanders, and fifty-two regimental commanders lay killed or wounded throughout the tangled nest of thickets. No less than twelve Confederate regiments had lost half their total strength. Federal losses were just as bad and included seven brigade commanders and fifty-five regimental commanders.[7] The calculus of the Chickamauga defeat, however, went far beyond the list of killed and maimed. A Yankee stampede from the battlefield would prove the largest rout of any Union army during the war, nearly twice as large as the retreat from Manassas two years earlier. Assistant Secretary of War Charles A. Dana, who rode with the retreating Federals that day, immediately telegraphed the War Department: "Chickamauga is as fatal a name in our history as Bull Run."[8] On the eve of a critical gubernatorial election in Ohio, President Lincoln had to answer to more damning charges of ill prosecution of the war.

In the weeks that preceded and followed the battle, troop trains from across the divided country steamed toward Chattanooga. The railroads created an unprecedented concentration of troop strength in the western theater. Before the campaign was over, elements of all six preeminent Civil War armies would converge on the depot town, numbering more than 170,000 men in total. At Chickamauga, the Federal Army of the Cumberland had sparred with the Army of Tennessee, reinforced with two divisions of the Army of Northern Virginia, most of them Gettysburg veterans under the command of Lieutenant General Longstreet. With a total of 71,491 Confederates to Rosecrans's 60,889 Yankees, General Bragg briefly enjoyed the widest margin of manpower of any rebel commander in the western theater, making Chickamauga one of the few battles of the entire war where the gray-clad troops outnumbered their blue-coated enemy.[9] Following the Union defeat, an alarmed Lincoln consolidated the region's Federal forces under the command of Major General Ulysses S. Grant and marshaled four divisions of Major General William T. Sherman's Vicksburg veterans of the Army of the Tennessee, in addition to two corps of Gettysburg veterans from the Army of the Potomac under Major General "Fighting Joe" Hooker. Major General Ambrose Burnside's Army of the Ohio, in nearby Knoxville, also prepared to march to Chattanooga's relief. Even rebel parolees who had surrendered at Vicksburg in July joined the few post-Chickamauga reinforcements that Bragg welcomed into his army. In differing amounts of strength, it seemed the entire war had been summoned to Chattanooga's gateway.

The slaughter at Chickamauga was followed by the relatively bloodless Union victories atop Orchard Knob, Lookout Mountain, and Missionary Ridge on November 23, 24, and 25 respectively. These series of battles forever swept Confederate troops from the gates of the city. Beyond the Chattanooga battlefields lay the road to Atlanta and prospects for victory that could boost Lincoln's candidacy for reelection in 1864, political and military opportunities that would not be available had Chattanooga remained in Confederate hands. As rebel soldiers retreated into North Georgia that winter, the stage was set for the final campaigns of the Civil War in the western theater. Unequivocal in its military and economic outcome, the 1863 Chattanooga Campaign marked one of the most critical turning points of the American Civil War.

To memorialize the struggle and to remember the dead, blue and gray veterans came together in the 1890s to preserve the battleground as America's first national military park. Now under the protection of the National Park Service, the Chickamauga and Chattanooga National Military Park has increased in size to encompass more than 9,000 acres and today remains the largest protected battlefield in the United States, not to mention one of the most densely monumented battlefields in the world.

⚬⚬⚬

The following collection of essays does not constitute a seamless chronological history of the 1862 expedition or the following year's Chickamauga and Chattanooga Campaigns. Nor does it offer a systematic tour de force of all command decisions involved in those battles. Readers must look to other scholarly volumes for detailed analysis of all of the tactical episodes involved. For the best treatment on the 1862 Chattanooga Campaign, readers will delight in Gerald J. Prokopowicz's *All for the Regiment: The Army of the Ohio, 1861–62,* and be thrilled by Russell S. Bonds's *Stealing the General: The Great Locomotive Chase and the First Medal of Honor.* Peter Cozzens's *This Terrible Sound: The Battle of Chickamauga* remains the most capacious study covering the Chickamauga Campaign yet published. Wiley Sword's *Mountains Touched with Fire: Chattanooga Besieged, 1863,* in addition to Cozzens's *The Shipwreck of their Hopes: The Battles for*

Chattanooga, are widely regarded as the two best single volumes on the post-Chickamauga battles for Chattanooga. For a treatment of both 1863 campaigns, readers should consult Steven E. Woodworth's *Six Armies in Tennessee: The Chickamauga and Chattanooga Campaigns.* A superb book on the founding of the campaigns' commemorative battlegrounds is Timothy B. Smith's *A Chickamauga Memorial: The Establishment of America's First Civil War National Military Park.*[10]

In a field where gallons of ink are spilled every year on "new" studies of the Gettysburg Campaign alone, relatively few monographs have been published exploring these all-important events in Georgia and Tennessee. Lacking the acres of words required to justly demarcate the Chickamauga-Chattanooga battles bequeaths plenty of room for fresh perspectives on the subject. As with all Civil War studies published by the Louisiana State University Press, these ten essays seek to address vacuums in the relevant literature as well as engage controversial issues touching these events in ways beneficial to both professional scholars and lay readers. In this effort to raise new questions and revise older interpretations, our contributors have consulted archives, libraries, museums, and private collections to draw upon a harvest of research found in rare printed materials, unpublished manuscripts, and both obscure and more readily obtainable published sources. Collectively, the contributors aspire to persuade readers to reconsider a few perpetual assumptions regarding these campaigns and to consider aspects of the battles and their aftermath that have received little, if any, previous attention.

The book opens with a scene-setting essay that situates Chattanooga's importance within the greater scaffold of Civil War history. In doing so, Russell S. Bonds explores how the remote village, a place essentially in the middle of nowhere, ended up being in the middle of everything and became among the most coveted strategic targets of the entire war. In his analysis, Bonds focuses on the town's geographic location as the "gateway" to the lower Confederacy and the heartland of the South's industrial war machine. What emerges is the most compelling assessment to date of Chattanooga as a key to the region's vast network of arsenals, factories, foundries, machine shops, mills, mines, navy yards, ordnance works, and railroads, all tied to the town's distribution hub, and its role as a linchpin connecting the western theater to the Virginia front. Bonds's essay also embraces Chattanooga's political significance to both the Davis and Lincoln administrations. In doing so, he elevates the region's importance to Union and Confederate arms in ways that previous scholars have overlooked.

In the second essay, Gerald J. Prokopowicz traces the stumbling advance of Union forces in the largely forgotten 1862 Chattanooga Campaign. Though Federal troops reached the outskirts of an almost entirely undefended Chattanooga in May and June, the city remained in Confederate hands through the early autumn, when Union troops were withdrawn to protect Kentucky. A livid Secretary of War Stanton ordered a formal investigative commission to convene and assess the conduct of the Army of the Ohio's controversial commander, Don Carlos Buell. Yet, as Prokopowicz assesses, the failure of Federal forces at Chattanooga that year was not limited to General Buell. This essay takes a fresh look at the collaborative effort between Buell; his lead division commander, Ormsby Mitchel; the secretary of war; and the new general in chief, Henry W. Halleck, with an eye toward resources and clarity of a vision as provided by the War Department. In doing so, Prokopowicz arrives at some surprising conclusions regarding this failed Federal expedition.

The next essay takes the reader directly to the battlefield and the second major campaign for Chattanooga. The Battle of Chickamauga stands as the most complete Confederate victory in the western theater. Even this success proved dubious, however, for the Confederates failed to exploit it. Historians often fault the rebel commander, Braxton Bragg, for ineptitude or blame subordinates such as Lieutenant General Leonidas Polk. Brigadier General Nathan Bedford Forrest, however, is almost universally portrayed as one of Chickamauga's Confederate heroes, a dynamic battlefield leader with an astute grasp of events, a man whom Bragg foolishly ignored. Modern biographers largely repeat the early legends of Forrest's exploits, tacitly accepting these stories as an accurate portrayal of his performance. Mining a lode of evidence, David A. Powell revises this traditional portrait of the Confederate "wizard of the saddle" in significant ways. In this third essay, Powell examines Forrest's role in a new light and finds that he proved wanting in the days before, during, and after the battle. New to high command and conventional cavalry operations, he repeatedly delivered faulty intelligence and failed to execute the tasks assigned him. Powell uncovers that some of the many failures attributed to Bragg were of Forrest's making. The cavalry legend had not yet grown into his full stature.

The fourth essay, also by Powell, engages the significance of a series of innovations embraced by the Army of the Cumberland under its new

commander, William Starke Rosecrans, in 1863. From the general's use
of "elite units" like mounted infantry, pioneers, and sharpshooters to
repeating weapons, fresh tactics, new methods in supply and logistics,
and even advances in cartography, Powell demonstrates that the Federal
army that set out from Middle Tennessee that summer was unlike any
fighting force the Civil War had hitherto or would ever again see. Powell's
mastery of the sources encompasses some fifteen years spent conducting research on Chickamauga at more than 150 archives. His findings
will, in large measure, reshape what many know about the Army of the
Cumberland during this campaign.

The Battle of Chickamauga is often justly characterized by the lasting
controversies it produced. Two of the most noted incidents occurred
on the last day of fighting, September 20, 1863. The first is the failure
("for reasons now indecipherable," according to the eminent historian
Bruce Catton) of Leonidas Polk to begin the Army of Tennessee's attack
at "day-dawn" as ordered, giving the Army of the Cumberland four precious hours to prepare for the onslaught.[11] The second was the voluntary
withdrawal from the main Federal line of Brigadier General Thomas
Wood's division—a withdrawal that facilitated the Confederate assault
that crushed the right wing of the Army of the Cumberland and cost
Union arms the battle. The two principals, Polk and Wood, are the vic-
tims of historical narratives that verge on caricature. Polk, who did not
survive the war to defend himself, is usually portrayed as an oversleep-
ing buffoon more concerned about getting his breakfast than attacking
the enemy, while Wood's execution of a bad order is ascribed to a fit of
pique or worse. A close analysis of the evidence, which includes a substantial amount of previously unused manuscript sources, reveals that
neither characterization is correct. William Glenn Robertson, the dean
of Chickamauga studies and author of a forthcoming book that will likely
prove the definitive narrative on the battle, carefully deciphers both
controversies and, in doing so, finally sets the record straight.

No victory of the war created more internal divisiveness for a Confederate army than Chickamauga. Following the battle, the army's high
command spiraled into a near self-destructive frenzy. Fury directed
against Bragg by his generals for not following up their triumph with
an immediate advance upon the routed Federals appeared to be fast approaching full-scale mutiny. The crisis became so volatile that in early
October, President Davis personally entrained for Chattanooga to quell
the conflict. In the sixth essay, Craig L. Symonds brings into sharp focus

the anatomy of blame and intra-army politics that brought the Confederate president to Chattanooga. In doing so, Symonds carefully examines both the behavior of the army's key commanders and the leadership style of a president who, in the end, did very little to help improve either the army's internal rapport or the Confederacy's military fortunes in the western theater.

The next essay, the longest in the collection, takes a fresh look at a bitter relationship long known to Civil War historians. It delineates the nearly twenty-three-year rivalry between Union generals Grant and Rosecrans, tracing their complex relationship from West Point; to an obscure battlefield in northern Mississippi, where the rivalry began; to the 1863 siege of Chattanooga and beyond. In doing so, it revisits the intricate events that led to Rosecrans's dismissal from command over the Army of the Cumberland as well as the postwar political sparring between the two that only ended after the death of one and nationally published mutual attacks. What results is the most in-depth analysis of this rivalry and its influence on the Chattanooga Campaign yet published.

The eighth essay shifts focus to the long-term consequences of the 1863 Chattanooga Campaign. From the collapse of the prisoner-exchange program to command shuffles on both sides, the penalties of triumph and defeat are examined in detail. Among its many legacies, the campaign consolidated the winning triumvirate of Grant, Sherman, and Philip H. Sheridan that ultimately swept U.S. armies, east and west, to final victory. Due to events at Chattanooga, George H. Thomas, the "Rock of Chickamauga," stood outside of this clique. As a result, Thomas became increasingly isolated and underutilized by Sherman and underappreciated by Grant in the months to come. Yet that general proved no less valuable to Union fortunes in the latter year and a half of war. Meanwhile, the Confederates found the loss of Chattanooga so reeling that one among them, division commander Patrick Cleburne, offered a staggeringly radical and violently opposed proposal for gradual emancipation of the South's slaves, by incorporating chattel bondsmen into rebel armies as soldiers, in an effort to win the war. This essay makes use of new evidence that adds significant detail to this controversial proposal. The new sources include Cleburne's long-lost 1864 diary, only recently discovered in 2009, as well as another more obscure proposal written by Confederate corps commander William J. Hardee.

The final two essays take the reader far beyond the battlefield to look at how these battles were both remembered and memorialized by the

Civil War generation. Stephen Cushman takes an innovative look at the world-famous author and Chickamauga veteran Ambrose Bierce in a way that few have. While Bierce is most famously remembered for his journalism and macabre fiction writings, Cushman provides the framework to look at him as a historian of his own wartime experience. Bierce's status as a combatant at Chickamauga has mesmerized biographers and historians into an uncritical acceptance of his various representations of the battle. In this penultimate essay Cushman draws upon an impressive cache of materials to subject Bierce's writings on Chickamauga (both fictional and nonfictional alike) to the same rigorous scrutiny that Bierce himself had critically imposed on other historical writings. Cushman's findings shed new light on the noted author's role in the battle and on his literary output.

Caroline E. Janney closes the volume with a vibrant look at the genesis of the Chickamauga and Chattanooga National Military Park. In doing so, Janney reveals a dark side to the postwar efforts of commemoration during the decade of the 1890s. For many veterans, the "gush" of reconciliation gave way to an enduring anger over the war's human cost or military outcome. The park's founding marked a flashpoint between erstwhile Federal and Confederate enemies as a metaphorical brawl between three memory narratives took place: the southern Lost Cause tradition on the one hand, and the northern Union Cause and Emancipationist Cause on the other. For countless survivors of the Chickamauga and Chattanooga battles, reconciliation, in the end, proved impossible.

———◦◦◦———

The completion of this project has proven a tremendous source of happiness. We would like to extend warm thanks to Russ Bonds, Steve Cushman, Carrie Janney, Dave Powell, Gerry Prokopowicz, Glenn Robertson, and Craig Symonds. Our Jedediah Hotchkiss, cartographer Henry "Hal" Jespersen, proved a delight to work with. One could not hope for a better collaborative team. Each contributor brought remarkable talent and patience to this project. Individuals who assisted them are acknowledged at the beginning of the notes in each essay. Collectively, we salute our editors at the Louisiana State University Press, with special cheers to Rand Dotson, who offered encouragement from the start. Amy Andrus, medical librarian at the University of California, San Francisco helped run down many obscure sources. We also thank Gary W. Gallagher,

Michael L. Oddenino, and James Torrance for reading portions of the manuscript. Kevin Brock fastidiously read our work in its entirety and offered an impressive and much appreciated round of corrections. Others who aided our progress include John and Ruth Ann Coski, Gordon Cotton, Peter Cozzens, David A. Friedrichs, Freddy Rickard, Dana Shoaf, Greg Starbuck, Catherine Wehrey, Harold S. Wilson, and Mac Wyckoff. Marion O. Smith, the field's leading expert on the Confederate Nitre and Mining Bureau, meticulously situated all of the region's significant mining operations for our maps. Others had feared that the names and locations of these mines were long lost to history. At the Chickamauga and Chattanooga National Military Park, we offer our gratitude to former superintendent Shawn Benge as well as Jim Blackwell, Doug Briggs, Chris Frasier, John Housch, Patrick Lewis, Hugh Odom, James Ogden III, Todd Roeder, Jim "Ski" Szyjkowski, Denise West, and Christopher Young for their friendship. William Lee White in particular deserves singular recognition for gathering numerous materials from the park's library and archive for most of our essayists.

Lastly, this volume is dedicated to Stephen Innes, formerly the James Madison Professor of American History at the University of Virginia. Mr. Innes enriched the lives of his students beyond measure. This book, a festschrift, stands as a belated yet loving tribute to his memory.

NOTES

1. Karl Marx and Friedrich Engels, "The American Civil War," *Die Presse,* Mar. 27, 1862.

2. Russell S. Bonds, *Stealing the General: The Great Locomotive Chase and the First Medal of Honor* (Yardley, Pa.: Westholme, 2006), 374.

3. Pres. Abraham Lincoln to Maj. Gen. William S. Rosecrans, Oct. 4, 1863, in Abraham Lincoln, *The Collected Works of Abraham Lincoln,* 9 vols., ed. Roy Basler (New Brunswick, N.J.: Rutgers University Press, 1954), 6:498.

4. Rosecrans to Horace Greeley, Jan. 8, 1866, Henry E. Huntington Library, San Marino, Calif.

5. Lt. Gen. James Longstreet to Gen. Robert E. Lee, Sept. 2, 1863, U.S. War Department, *The War of the Rebellion: A Compilation of the Official Records of the Union and Confederate Armies,* 128 vols. (Washington, D.C.: GPO, 1880–1901), ser. 1, 29(2):693–94.

6. Lincoln to General in Chief Henry W. Halleck, quoted in Steven E. Woodworth, *Six Armies in Tennessee: The Chickamauga and Chattanooga Campaigns* (Lincoln: University of Nebraska Press, 1998), 136.

7. We are indebted to David A. Powell for sharing his careful analysis of the *Official Records,* which reveals that Chickamauga casualties yielded fifty-two Confederate and fifty-five Union command turnovers of regimental and battalion commanders, including acting commanders who assumed regimental control in the middle of the battle. This work

will be published in Powell's three-volume history of the Chickamauga Campaign, which is forthcoming from Savas-Beatie. For command-level casualties, see also Woodworth, *Six Armies in Tennessee,* 133. For a detailed breakdown of overall Chickamauga casualties, see David A. Powell, *The Maps of Chickamauga: An Atlas of the Chickamauga Campaign, including the Tullahoma Operations, June 22–September 23, 1863* (New York: Savas-Beatie, 2009), 268–80.

8. Peter Cozzens, *This Terrible Sound: The Battle of Chickamauga* (Urbana: University of Illinois Press, 1992), 479.

9. These Chickamauga combat-strength figures reflect the number of troops that Bragg and Rosecrans had present on the field and available to commit into the fight. The Federal figure of 60,889 includes the 59,650 soldiers Rosecrans counted on the field in addition to Post's brigade of 1,239 men, stationed at Crawfish Spring, the southernmost cusp of the battlefield. The Confederate figure of 71,491 includes the 64,806 men on the field as well as another 6,685 who arrived during the closing stages of the battle and did not meet enemy fire on September 20. If one counts only the troops committed to actual fighting, it would include 124,456 men from both sides, which yields 28-percent casualties from the 34,805 killed, wounded, and missing. Once again, we are indebted to David A. Powell for sharing his forthcoming, fresh statistical analysis of the battle with us.

10. Gerald J. Prokopowicz, *All for the Regiment: The Army of the Ohio, 1861–62* (Chapel Hill: University of North Carolina Press, 2001); Bonds, *Stealing the General;* Cozzens, *This Terrible Sound* (Urbana: University of Illinois Press, 1992); Wiley Sword, *Mountains Touched with Fire: Chattanooga Besieged, 1863* (New York: St. Martin's, 1995); Peter Cozzens, *Shipwreck of their Hopes: The Battles for Chattanooga* (Urbana: University of Illinois Press, 1994); Woodworth, *Six Armies in Tennessee;* and Timothy B. Smith, *A Chickamauga Memorial: The Establishment of America's First Civil War National Military Park* (Knoxville: University of Tennessee Press, 2009).

11. Bruce Catton, *Never Call Retreat* (Garden City, N.Y.: Doubleday, 1965), 248.

CHAPTER 1

"THE FUNNEL OF THE UNIVERSE"

The Chattanooga Country and the Civil War

RUSSELL S. BONDS

War takes places in the middle of nowhere and puts them in the middle of everything. The peculiar priorities of armed conflict—strategic objectives, tactical advantages devoutly wished, and logistical needs of armies in the field, along with mere geographic happenstance—have a way of crumpling the map, transforming locations once isolated and obscure into historic linchpins. Thus do atolls in the middle of the ocean, jungle hills identified only by number, and quiet college towns have their names indelibly inscribed in the annals of history as battlegrounds and, ultimately, hallowed ground. So it was in the American Civil War with a muddy mountain whistle stop in the East Tennessee hills that became the setting and the centerpiece of one of the war's great campaigns—Chattanooga.

There were a number of reasons for the once-insignificant town's rise to prominence apart from its placement at the natural gateway to the heartland of the Deep South. Foremost was Chattanooga's growing importance to Southern transportation—river, road, and rail—across and down the great chessboard of war. Also notable was the late-antebellum growth in the region's industries, with the Mountain City (as some had come to call it) sitting at the capstone of a geographic area that would become the engine, such as it was, of the Confederate war machine. Other causes were political, the local population a mix of old-line Whigs, fire-breathing Secessionists, and ardent, hardscrabble Unionists, their views far removed from the politics of Virginia and the Carolinas and the highfalutin culture of the plantation South. It was, in particular, this pro-Union sentiment that drew the early attention of Abraham Lincoln, who would push his commanders to put considerable emphasis on efforts to capture and occupy Chattanooga and bring relief to the "Tory" loyalists of East Tennessee.

—⊶⊷—

The place seemed destined to be more than a map dot even from early days, a point set apart—almost fortified—by a great river and massive limestone and granite ridges, yet known to generations of drovers, merchants, boatmen, and Indians as the crossroads of prehistoric trade routes between what would become northern Georgia, northern Alabama, and East Tennessee. The settlement that developed into Chattanooga was established by the Cherokees in 1816 and first called Ross's Landing, after Daniel Ross, the Scottish father of the tribe's principal chief, John Ross. The landing itself was unimpressive—hardly more than a "kind of shanty for goods and a log hut for the ferryman"—the surrounding terrain a forbidding wilderness, "with here and there an Indian cabin." But the road and the landing led to prosperity, both for the merchants who set up shop there and for the traders passing through with herds of cattle, horses, and hogs or with creaking wagon trains that were for most the only way to bring their goods to market. Missionaries too were drawn to the region, Methodists, Presbyterians, and Congregationalists "armed with Bible and rifle" and "ready to use either in the effort to win the frontier and the Indians to civilization." Churches, missions, and schools were established, and the Cherokee Nation made great strides forward. By 1826, Cherokees in northern Georgia and eastern Tennessee had not only cattle, horses, and crops but also thirty-one grist mills, ten sawmills, eighteen ferries, eighteen schools, and sixty-two blacksmith shops. With the Tennessee River not just a critical trade route but also the traditional dividing line between white and Indian territory, Ross's Landing was assured of continued prominence both in Indian affairs and in local commerce.[1]

Some early settlers sensed that the little river town's import and influence would be far more than just provincial. In the spring of 1836, an ambitious young merchant named John Pomfret Long came down the Tennessee and arrived at Ross's Landing, which had seen but modest growth despite its twenty years as a trading post. The place still had primitive roads, limited commerce, and only a handful of residents, the town itself "hastily built without any regard for any order or streets."

Land approaches were largely blocked on all sides by imposing mountain ranges. But Long, who was without question a man who was going places, focused not on the walls, but on the door. "Here is the gate," he wrote, "through which the history of nations must pass." Long built a log cabin in the woods, opened a dry-goods store, established a post office, and settled down for life. But he also had a "brighter vision" of what was in store as the "iron rail and the iron horse were looming up into importance."[2]

That vision came to pass two years later, when in the spring of 1838, the Georgia legislature and the commissioners of the new state-owned Western and Atlantic Railroad selected Ross's Landing as the northern endpoint for a planned 138-mile line running up from Terminus (later Atlanta). The board members concluded that the site "combines so great a number and variety of local conditions on which the growth of cities usually depends." It was this addition of the railroad to the already well-established river and overland trade routes that ensured the town's enduring prominence and at the same time doomed the Cherokees who had founded it. The discovery of gold near Dahlonega in North Georgia and the railroad soon to come to East Tennessee made the commercial promise of this recent wilderness irresistible to prospectors and politicians—literal and figurative "gold in them thar hills," indeed. A popular ditty summarized the prevailing envy and clamor for Indian lands:

> All I want in this cre-a-tion
> Is a pretty little girl and a big plan-ta-tion
> Away up yonder in the Cherokee nation.

Hard on the heels of the start of construction on the Western and Atlantic, President Martin Van Buren, continuing the sharp-edged Indian policies of his predecessor, Andrew Jackson, ordered that the Cherokee Indians be removed from their lands in the Chattanooga valley.

Ross's Landing was selected as the staging area for the removal, and Federal troops constructed wooden barracks to house the displaced Indians before forcing them onto flatboats for the first leg of the journey west—the opening tableau of the exodus that would come to be known as the Trail of Tears. In the fall of 1838, more than 13,000 Cherokees departed for the West, many of them leaving their ancestral homeland by way of Ross's Landing. An estimated 4,000 would die in the course of the removal and the nearly thousand-mile trip to the newly created Indian Territory. "It is mournful to see how reluctantly these people go away," wrote H. G. Clauder, a Moravian missionary who witnessed the pitiful scene. "Even the stoutest hearts melt when they turn their faces toward the setting sun. I am sure that this Land will be bedewed with a Nation's tears—if not with their blood." Brother Clauder was surely right about that.[3]

Even as the Cherokees were corralled into stockades and then herded west, white men increasingly saw in this staging area and soon-to-be railroad junction a promising mix of river and road, a boom town in the making. They touted the crisp running water, mountain air, refreshing climate, and beautiful landscape and christened the region "the Switzerland of America." "Why, don't you see?" lawyer and local huckster B. Rush Montgomery proclaimed to all who would listen, and some who would rather not. "The buffalo worked out the line; the Indian followed it; the white man followed the Indian; the wagon road and railroad take the same route." He continued, warming as he went: "The mountains shut in here; the valleys stop here; [the] Tennessee River must pass through here—fact is, don't you see? *This is the funnel of the universe!*" The state legislature promptly authorized the sale of former Cherokee territory, and squatters, merchants, and speculators descended on the valley to register their claims or buy parcels at auction.

In December 1839, a year after the Cherokee removal, the town was chartered as "Chattanooga"—a name whose origin and meaning remains unclear. Place names left by the departed Creeks dotted the southeastern landscape and were as mystifying to the later-arriving Cherokees as they were to white settlers. Thought to be the aboriginal name for Lookout Mountain, some said the word "Chattanooga" was from the Creek Indian phrase *Chadonaugsa,* which means "rock that comes to a point"; others would suggest the name meant "hawk's nest" or "eagle's nest." Similar confusion surrounds nearby Chickamauga Creek, the winding tributary of the Tennessee River that would give its name to one of the great battles of the Civil War. Possible meanings include "good country" (from the Chickasaw language), "dwelling place of the war chief" (*cukko-micco,* from the Creek), or "still water" or "stagnant water" (from the Cherokee). Writers and soldiers eager to give ominous portent to the name after the battle seized on the latter definition but translated it as "river of death." (This enduring confusion over ancient nomenclature is hardly unique to Chattanooga. To this day no one knows what "Tennessee" means, either.)[4]

The new town might have seemed cursed by the departed Cherokees as it struggled in the decade that followed. Construction of the railroad up from the renamed town of Terminus—by then called Marthasville and soon to be incorporated as Atlanta—proceeded very slowly throughout the 1840s, ridges and gorges to the south providing formidable obstacles to engineers and laborers alike. Although the rocky ground held promising deposits of valuable minerals, residents found the soil too thin for large-scale agriculture in staple crops like cotton. Farmers cobbled together respectable harvests of corn and wheat, but much of the surrounding area remained open pastureland or standing timber. Commerce at the river landing was steady—mostly in dry goods, livestock, and produce—but not spectacular, and those with a practiced eye saw that it never would be. The winding Tennessee River provided an avenue for trade but imposed its own natural restrictions, the scale of river commerce limited by obstacles upstream and down—rocky shoals, treacherous rapids, narrow bends, deep gorges. Flatboat pilots bringing their goods to Chattanooga from the west, for example, had to navigate through or past such hazards as the Pan, the Skillet, and the Boiling Pot; a treacherous whirlpool called Deadman's Eddy; the shoals of the Kettle or the Suck; Holston Rock; and Tumbling Shoals before curling around Moccasin Bend to the river landing. These natural hindrances, on both land and water, kept commercial growth well short of explosive, and some investors began to doubt earlier visions of municipal mountain grandeur and prosperity. "We shall soon see," one local entrepreneur wrote, "whether Chattanooga is to be a village or a city."[5]

A city it would be. In May 1850, at long last and after ten years of snail's pace construction, the first train up from Atlanta curled around Missionary Ridge and chuffed into Chattanooga on the Western and Atlantic Railroad. Shortly thereafter, Chattanooga would change from a dead-end terminus to a junction as three other railroad lines—the Nashville and Chattanooga, the Memphis and Charleston, and the East Tennessee, Virginia, and Georgia—were completed and joined with the Western and Atlantic before 1858. The following year a massive freight depot and passenger shed was opened to shelter passengers and handle traffic on the four railroad lines radiating from the Chattanooga valley. The loneliness of the East Tennessee hills was gone forever, and Chattanooga now was the central knot tying together the Deep South with northern markets as well as the West with the eastern seaboard. As Appalachian historian John Alexander Williams has noted, the story of Chattanooga, then, is the story of the roads to and through it. Williams points to the French poet Hilaire Belloc, who wrote that "[t]he Road moves and controls all history." Not only does it "determine the sites of

many cities and the growth and nourishment of all," it also "controls the
development of strategics and fixes the sites of battles." As the Civil War
approached, it seemed that all roads, indeed, would lead to Chattanooga.[6]

⟶ ◦◦◦ ⟵

At the start of the great conflict, the mountains and hills of East Tennessee were a political patchwork, with Chattanooga a stitch in the middle
holding strong for the Confederacy; as one historian put it, "a pocket of
secession in a Unionist county in a disunited section of a factional state
in a country rent asunder by civil war." The stark political differences
in town were made plain before the first shot was fired, as former U.S.
senator Jefferson Davis, returning home to Mississippi in January 1861
after resigning his seat in Congress, stopped for the night at the Crutchfield House hotel. Called on to give a speech, Davis stood upon a chair in
the crowded lobby and made an impassioned argument that Tennessee
should join with the South in secession, "lock shields with her sister
states and meet the vandal foe." But one among the hearers would not
let this go unchallenged. William Crutchfield, the staunchly pro-Union
brother of the hotel's proprietor, gave a blistering response, one both
political and decidedly personal. "Behold your military despot!" Crutchfield cried. "I denounce him as a renegade and a traitor." If Davis wanted
to help Tennesseans, Crutchfield said, he should be in Washington with
Tennessee senators and representatives, defending their rights in Congress. "We are free men, and as such claim the right to think, speak,
and act for ourselves," he continued. "We are not to be hoodwinked,
bamboozled, and dragged into your Southern, cod-fish aristocratic,
Tory-blooded, South Carolina mobocracy!" The ugly confrontation, still
three months before Fort Sumter, embodied the depth of feeling and of
discord that prevailed in Tennessee and particularly in Chattanooga.[7]

Less than three weeks after Davis's journey through their state, Tennesseans voted to reject a convention call to weigh the issue of secession,
apparently considering the election of Abraham Lincoln as president
to be insufficient provocation to sever ties with the United States. Four
months later, after the firing on Fort Sumter and Lincoln's controversial
call for volunteers, the state of Tennessee became the eleventh and last to
secede and join the Confederacy—even then, East Tennesseans opposed
secession by more than two to one. Interestingly, secessionist feeling ran
strongest not in rural villages and hillside farms, but in the newly emerg-

ing industrial areas and railroad towns. "All here are for the Southern Confederacy," a young clerk named John Armstrong wrote from Chattanooga. "There are not more than seven and eight people here who are for the Union." Though only 41 percent of Chattanooga's Hamilton County favored separation, 89 percent of voters in the city itself cast their ballots for secession, apparently motivated by a desire for commercial more than political independence. "The promise of a prosperous future free from Northern meddling was apparently very attractive to the great majority of Chattanoogans in 1861," historian Charles McGehee writes, "and the city's wealthy merchants stood to gain from the impending war as well." Whether driven by politics or purse strings, fractured loyalties would persist as the war got underway. Chattanooga would become a key point and part of the new Southern nation, while the surrounding mountains sheltered thousands of pro-Union citizens whose opposition to the Confederacy in the months to come would range from grumbling disaffection to acts of open rebellion against the rebellion. East Tennessee would remain a house divided throughout the war.[8]

Undersized and isolated as the fighting got underway, Chattanooga was not an obvious strategic prize. The 1860 census put the population of Chattanooga at just 2,545, including 364 slaves and 93 free blacks. Nashville was six times and Memphis nearly nine times as large. Its fledgling neighbor Atlanta, one hundred crowflight miles to the south, was itself only the 99th largest urban place in America—yet even it was nearly five times larger than Chattanooga. The Mountain City wasn't much to look at—a "dirty, nasty, irregular town," one soldier called it; a rough-edged bowl filled with riverbank mud and engine smoke, part ash-heap, part ant-hill. Major General Ulysses S. Grant would later pronounce Chattanooga "one of the wildest places you ever saw." Another, more grammatically challenged witness thought the place "[n]ot verry sightly, being two much scattered Round and two irregular." The imposition of a street grid on the undulating landscape and the haphazard presence of small orchards and gardens contributed to the city's fricasseed look. "Never think you have seen the town at one glance," a Northern visitor wrote. "It is down here and up there and over yonder; the little hills swell beneath it like billows; you will gain the idea if I say it is a town gone to pieces in a heavy sea." Entirely underwhelmed, he took away the impression of "a stinted, rusty-looking market-house subdued beneath a chuckle-headed belfry, four of five churches of indifferent fashion, [and] two or three hotels whose entertainment has departed."[9]

"Chattanooga from the North Bank of the Tennessee."
Harper's Weekly, September 12, 1863.

The scenery surrounding the town was far more impressive—"a grand and glorious view," a Union lieutenant wrote, "Grand and majestic." A witness standing in Chattanooga and turning slowly to take in the terrain around it had the sensation of being surrounded on all sides by ocean waves or perhaps castle walls that made the place as tough to get out of as it was to get into. Three miles to the east of what one might charitably call "downtown" was Missionary Ridge, a north–south wall of granite rising 600 feet above the valley floor. The curve of Raccoon Mountain blocked the approaches from the west, with the sidewinding Tennessee River—between 300 and 500 feet wide as it flowed past Chattanooga—serving as a formidable moat. To the south, some 1,500 feet above the streets of the city and 2,146 feet above sea level, was the dark green-gray frown of Lookout Mountain, with what the locals called its "nose" (or point) drawing "so near as to startle you," an Illinois soldier would presently write, "and you feel as if you were beneath the eaves of a roof from whence drips an iron rain." It was Lookout Mountain—actually the northernmost extremity of a ninety-mile-long ridge—that would give the town its watchtower and make an almost indelible impression on all who saw it, "like an everlasting thunder-storm that will never pass over."

Beyond the immediate mountain walls lay a rugged expanse—Walden Ridge and the Cumberland Plateau to the west, the Great Smokies and the Blue Ridge to the east—mountains beyond mountains on all sides.[10]

Union major general William S. Rosecrans described Chattanooga's great valley surroundings in a letter to his wife. "This is a magnificent valley," he wrote, "not so fertile as the Ohio. But the scenery is grand. The mountains rise on each side of the river something like the palisades, on one side jutting boldly up to the river while on the opposite side they bend away in graceful curves, their craggy edges often softened and rounded while covered with rich dark foliage. The beautiful coves sleeping quietly at them first seem as if the abodes of peace, health, and innocence." However beautiful it was, the place would be far from peaceful.[11]

Of course, it was not the town itself or its impressive surroundings but its resources and rail connections to far-flung places that would make it a particular object of desire. As railroad historian George Edgar Turner put it, "railroad builders extending their trackage in pursuit of trade and commerce unwittingly turned Atlanta, Chattanooga, Corinth, and other places into objectives of major strategic importance." Running out from Chattanooga were four key lines—northeast, northwest, south, and west—which connected with more than a dozen other iron threads that sewed together the South. To the northwest, the Nashville and Chattanooga Railroad slanted up through Middle Tennessee to the state capital. Branching off to the west at Stevenson, Alabama, was the Memphis and Charleston Railroad—the Confederacy's only true east–west trunk line, running to Corinth, Memphis, and the Mississippi River. To the northeast, threading between the Cumberland and Allegheny Mountains on one side and the Blue Ridge Mountains on the other, was the East Tennessee and Georgia Railroad, which passed through Cleveland (via a thirty-mile line known as the Chattanooga and Cleveland Railroad) and beyond to Knoxville.[12] From there the tracks snaked through the mountains to Lynchburg and Richmond in the Old Dominion by way of the Virginia and Tennessee Railroad. To the south was the Western and Atlantic, the line down into the heart of Georgia—a key supply route and, potentially, a highway southward should the mountain gates of Chattanooga be wrenched asunder.

Chattanooga, therefore, became the critical nexus linking the various theaters of war, not only east to west along the Memphis and Charleston but also north to south. For the Confederates, it was an essential connection for strategic movements and supplies; for the Federals, a potential

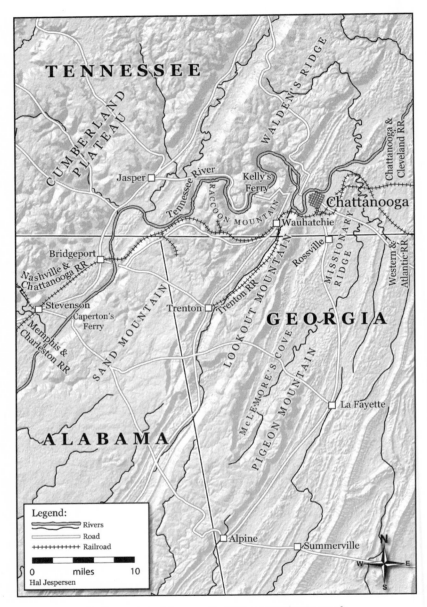

Chattanooga and Surrounding Transportation Network.

base of operations and an avenue for invasion. Its railroads, of course, were not merely important in and of themselves as potential supply routes and strategic assets but also for the industries and resources they connected. Southern manufacturing was comparatively meager and slow out of the gate, but by 1862 the South's railroads linked key factories, foundries, mills, warehouses, and arsenals across Alabama, Georgia, and Tennessee. Railroads running from Chattanooga led south to the factories of Atlanta, then east to the Confederacy's one-and-only gunpowder works at Augusta, or southwest to the industrial centers of Montgomery and Selma and the naval yards of Columbus and Savannah. Other rails stretched westward to the supply route of the Mississippi River, northwestward to the factories and warehouses of Nashville, or northeastward to the great Confederate industries in Virginia and the seat of government at Richmond. The lines running through Chattanooga—particularly the east–west trunk line linking the theaters of war—were essential to provide raw materials to and carry finished goods from these critical industries and to bring forward supplies from the home front to the front lines.[13]

The city itself had hoped to become what one local editor called "the Pittsburgh of the South" as the war brought incessant demand for industrial goods, increased rail traffic, and new investment, the town enjoying a sort of boom as the war began. Citizens chartered a new bank and rolling mill, railroad companies bought new locomotives, and entrepreneurs secured contracts to supply arms to the state of Tennessee. Flour mills, distilleries, furniture companies, tanneries, and packers grew and flourished, and the town grew around them. Busy storefronts lined Market Street between the railroad and the river. By 1860 Chattanooga had six hotels, three newspapers, a billiard saloon, and a marble cutter who offered tombstones "at Northern prices." Most important, however, was the town's iron smelting and manufacturing capability. The Webster Foundry and Machine Works, established fourteen years earlier as the East Tennessee Iron Manufacturing Company, filled orders for heavy machinery, including "steam engines and boilers, mining and mill machines." Among other projects, the foundry produced machinery for the nearby Polk County Copper Company and an iron shaft and gears for the soon-to-be-famous Confederate Powder Works in Augusta, Georgia. Other valuable plants were spread across North Georgia and East Tennessee, most of them serviced by the railroads running through Chattanooga, including such notable facilities as the Cooper Iron Works, a

furnace, nail factory, rolling mill, and flour mill at Etowah, Georgia, and
the Noble Brothers Foundry, a factory and ironworks in nearby Rome,
Georgia, that produced rifled cannon, furnaces, and locomotives.[14]

Also in the surrounding country, and often overlooked by scholars, lay
a fragmented subterranean maze of caves and mines with access to some
of the richest mineral lodes and ore seams anywhere in the Confederacy.
Each earthly deposit proved, in its own way, essential to the South's
military survival. These operations were directed by the Confederate
Nitre and Mining Bureau, established in April 1862, which had its Eighth
District headquarters in Chattanooga. Extensive caves in the region were
mined for saltpeter—including the famous Nickajack Cave near Shell-
mound, described by one reporter as "one of the most remarkable works
of nature in existence. . . . On entering, you begin to think you are in the
deserted residence of giants"—though perhaps even more impressive
was the Long Island Saltpeter Cave near Bridgeport, later surveyed as
more than 13,000 feet long with dozens of high-vaulted "rooms" and pas-
sageways. (In 1863 General Rosecrans, then the commander of the Army
of the Cumberland, would visit this cave and briefly become stuck in a
narrow passage. "For a few minutes," a witness wrote, "it was a question
whether the campaign might not have to be continued under the next
senior general.")[15] The caves provided calcium nitrate, or "cave saltpeter,"
for conversion into potassium nitrate, or gunpowder, and were generally managed by the Nitre Bureau itself or by local contractors. Potash
works were established nearby to accomplish this conversion, including
the Chattanooga (later renamed Chickamauga) Potash Works just east
of town, the Town Creek Potash Works in northeastern Alabama, and
the Cherokee Potash Works near Etowah, Georgia. All of these efforts
helped sustain the enormous gunpowder works in Augusta.[16]

Lodes of precious metals came not from natural caves, but rather
mines blasted by engineers and dug by slaves. Fifty miles due east of
Chattanooga, ore mined from the basin around Ducktown, Tennessee,
produced approximately *90 percent* of the Confederacy's copper used
for artillery projectiles, friction primers, percussion caps for rifles and
pistols, and telegraph wire. Perhaps most importantly, copper too served
as an indispensable ingredient in the smelting of the bronze needed for
cannon barrels.[17] Fifty miles northeast of Chattanooga, slaves mined
lead needed for Minié balls along Chestuee Creek in the Chatata Valley.[18]
Smaller lead mines lay scattered throughout the one hundred miles
between Strawberry Plains in East Tennessee and the Georgia border.[19]

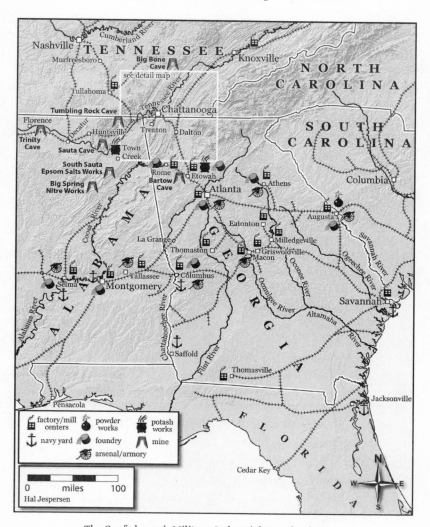

The Confederacy's Military-Industrial Heartland, 1863.

Approximately twenty miles west of Chattanooga sat the high-yield coal veins of the Gordon and Etna Mines. To the southwest, just below the Tennessee River in northeastern Alabama, the Nitre and Mining Bureau operated what historian Thomas Connelly describes as a "nine-county iron belt," which included not only iron mines but also "blast furnaces, rolling mills, foundries, forges, and shops." In all, the region "turned out thirty thousand tons of pig iron and ten thousand tons of bar iron

Chattanooga's Confederate War Industry.

annually."[20] Also nearby, along South Sauta Creek, Alabama, the bureau mined Epsom salts for medicinal uses in Confederate hospitals.[21] In many cases these digs were served by the main railroads or by spurs that curled off the trunk lines to the mines themselves.

All these critical resources were located in and around Chattanooga—yet in the end, despite its importance and success as a rail center, the city would fall far short of its goal as the so-called Southern Pittsburgh. Though private industry in town worked earnestly and in early days thrived, the Confederate government largely invested elsewhere, establishing its most important facilities in other cities. Major arsenals and armories were placed in Atlanta, Richmond, Montgomery, Selma, and Lynchburg, while other plants and mills were built in Macon, Augusta, Selma, and Columbus. Beyond railroad facilities, a small ordnance shop, and its undersized military detachment, Chattanooga itself had little in the way of Confederate-owned industry. This probably had little to do with any lingering distaste Jefferson Davis held toward the city from his recent embarrassment at the Crutchfield House; instead, it may have resulted from worries about potential vulnerability of Southern manufacturing in light of the persistent Unionism and occasional insurgency in the region. Whatever the reason, Chattanooga would remain most important as a link, a gateway, and eventually a "fortified base" for further operations, not as a prize in its own right.[22]

Moreover, the initial optimism and investment in the town soon gave way to unrealized hopes of industrialization and commercial profit, not to mention the simple harsh realities of war. Inflation, shortages, and a slowly strangling river trade all took their toll on Chattanooga, and medical officers seeking empty buildings to commandeer as hospitals soon found plenty of warehouses standing empty of goods.[23] Yet whatever it lacked as a commercial center, the city's importance as a central railroad junction and mountain passageway to Georgia would only increase as Federal advances eroded the Confederacy and removed other Southern rail hubs from service.

By the summer of 1862, former railroad cities like Nashville, Corinth, and Memphis would be in Union hands, with the Memphis and Charleston Railroad severed by Federal forces in northern Alabama. A year later Jackson and Vicksburg, Mississippi, would be gone as well, further crippling the South's ability to move, reinforce, unite, and supply its armies. The loss of these cities and capitals were staggering blows strategically and symbolically, yet perhaps more grievous was the loss of resources and industries in the occupied regions. As the fledgling nation was slowly, persistently whittled down, the heartland industries in Georgia, Alabama, and Tennessee—shielded by mountain ranges, linked by and accessible through Chattanooga—became even more essential to the ability of the South to wage war. Following the Union capture of Nashville, New Orleans, Memphis, and Baton Rouge in 1862, the indispensable war industries from all four cities relocated to Georgia. By 1863 the region's military-industrial complex would reach its full maturity and the height of its wartime production. As the eminent scholar Mary A. DeCredico assesses: "The state had become the Confederacy's economic backbone. . . . It is not an exaggeration to say that Georgia's military centers and its railroads permitted the South to continue the fight."[24]

In brief, the manufacturing facilities to the south of Chattanooga, in

Georgia as well as western Alabama, provided every material requirement needed to sustain the rebellion and would, by 1863, become the
military-industrial heartland of the Confederacy. Commissary factories
cured salt pork and baked hardtack by the trainload. Textile mills loomed
cotton for haversacks, canvas for tents, and wool for uniforms and army
blankets. Clothing depots employed tailors and seamstresses who sewed
wool trousers, jackets, caps, and overcoats by the tens of thousands. Cob-
blers worked in factories to produce shoes and boots in equal numbers.
Leatherworks crafted belts, cartridge boxes, and bayonet scabbards.
Rolling mills made railroad rails, freight cars, and percussion caps. Arsenals cast field and siege cannon, belt buckles, cavalry spurs, uniform
buttons, and iron plating for gunboats and assembled muskets, carbines,
revolvers, swords, and canteens. Under the supervision of the Central
Ordnance Laboratory in Macon, Georgia, munitions works rolled cartridges and cut fuses for artillery shells. Riverside navy yards dry docked
ironclads that, once complete, would guard the watery approaches to
these centers and their railroads. Chattanooga and its rugged gateway
remained the key to all of it. By the spring of 1864, the *New York Times*
would point to the little Mountain City and the East Tennessee hills that
surround it as "the most important strategic point in the Confederacy."[25]

For his part, President Lincoln had felt much the same way about
the place all along. "Chattanooga is as important as Richmond," he is
widely misquoted as having said—and though he never said that *exactly,*
he made similar comments on more than one occasion, recognizing
from the early days of the war that the Mountain City would be crucial
to Federal operations. Moreover, from a political standpoint, he saw in
the region a striking similarity to the mountainous pro-Union area of
western Virginia and had strong feelings for the oppressed Unionists of
East Tennessee. In the months to come, Lincoln would repeatedly press
his generals to move forward to capture Chattanooga and bring relief to
these aggrieved loyalists. In June 1862, writing to Major General Henry
Halleck at Corinth, Mississippi, he urged an "expedition" against Chattanooga. "To take and hold the railroad east of Cleveland, in East Tennessee, I think fully as important as the taking and holding of Richmond,"
he said. The following year Lincoln again emphasized his view of the region's importance, writing to General Rosecrans, "If we can hold Chattanooga and East Tennessee, I think the rebellion must dwindle and die."[26]

The residents of Chattanooga, with their hometown still quite small
and hundreds of miles removed from early clashes of arms in Virginia,

Missouri, and elsewhere, began the war with fervent hopes that the conflict might be resolved quickly and would never breach the natural ramparts surrounding their young city. They "appear to have remained aloof from the mounting crisis," as one local historian put it, and "felt secure in their location, remote, it appeared, from any prospective scene of battle." The confidence of Chattanoogans in their own security quickly became unraveled, however, and by the spring of 1862, pressure was increasing from all directions:

- From the northwest: in February Nashville fell to Union forces under Major General Don Carlos Buell, and Chattanooga was inundated with refugees and convalescing soldiers housed in makeshift hospitals.

- From the northeast: by midsummer, Union forces surrounded Cumberland Gap and forced the evacuation of the garrison there, possibly exposing Knoxville and even Chattanooga to advancing blue columns from that direction.

- From the west: first in the form of hundreds of wounded Confederates brought east from the bloody field at Shiloh, then later that same week, a Union division under Brigadier General Ormsby M. Mitchel captured Huntsville, Alabama; severed the Memphis and Charleston Railroad; and began to push eastward.

- And even from the south, as nearly two dozen disguised Union soldiers led by smuggler James J. Andrews stole a train near Marietta in a daring attempt to sabotage the Western and Atlantic, only to be foiled by a group of determined Georgia railroad men in what would later become known as the Great Locomotive Chase. Andrews's goal had been to destroy bridges and railroad tracks, isolating Chattanooga from the south and leaving it vulnerable to capture by Mitchel's advancing troops.

In short order the war was closing in on Chattanooga, and it seemed unlikely that the city's natural fortifications would be adequate protection after all.[27]

In the summer of 1862, the war arrived in earnest at Chattanooga's door in the form of two incidents—neither a major battle, but both involving early Federal threats that served to emphasize the city's status as a strategic target and its importance as a transportation junction. First, on June 7, 1862, a detachment from Mitchel led by Brigadier General James S. Negley appeared opposite Chattanooga on the west bank of the Tennessee River. Federal artillery batteries unlimbered and began firing shells down into the streets, causing "great consternation" among residents. "Our shells did terrible execution in the town, completely destroying many buildings," a colonel reported, though Major General Edmund Kirby Smith, commanding rebel forces in East Tennessee, disagreed. "[T]here was considerable noise and bursting of shells, but little damage was done," he told his wife. Nonetheless, and at a minimum, the fury of the bombardment rattled the windows and the residents themselves and brought a sudden and arresting glimpse of the horrors of war. "Could experiences of those who live in civil wars be extended to succeeding generations," Kirby Smith continued, "we would not have much need or use of armies." After two days of desultory yet terrifying shelling, Negley's undersized force—lacking support as well as any means of crossing the moat of the Tennessee—withdrew westward beyond the horizon.

Chattanoogans had seen their first Yankee soldiers, had heard shots fired in anger, and had experienced a bombardment's effect. The days of imagined security and indifference to distant dangers were over. Sam Reid, a reporter for the *Mobile Register,* seemed heartened by the incident, pronouncing the city "the New Castle of our country." He believed Chattanooga, with its mountain passes and protective river, could be held against almost any force—all the defenders would have to do is block the passes and "make a Thermopylae of it."[28]

Then, just a few weeks after Negley's half-hearted bombardment, Chattanooga again found itself threatened by a Union force, this one under General Buell, bearing down from the west along the Memphis and Charleston Railroad. "This movement threatened the very heart of our country, and was destined, unless checked immediately, to sever our main line of connection between the East and West," Confederate major general Braxton Bragg reported. In danger of being left holding the bag near Corinth, Mississippi, Bragg instead engineered a massive relocation of most of his Army of Tennessee from Mississippi. In what one historian would call "the finest hour of Confederate railroads," the general moved more than 31,000 gray soldiers by rail via a roundabout, 776-mile route from Tupelo to and through Mobile, Montgomery, and Atlanta to arrive in Chattanooga. The rail movement was rapid for that era and extremely well executed. Soldiers were issued seven days' rations at Tupelo, and the first infantryman stepped off the cars in Chattanooga just six days after leaving northern Mississippi. (Artillery and wagon trains followed more slowly along an overland route through Tuscaloosa, Alabama, and Rome, Georgia.) Consolidating his force with Kirby Smith's paltry

Department of East Tennessee, along with cavalry under Nathan Bedford Forrest, Bragg forced Buell's army to abandon its drive toward the Mountain City; by mid-September he had maneuvered Buell some 150 miles north to near Bowling Green, Kentucky. "Bragg's timely movement saved Chattanooga and eastern Tennessee's invaluable copper and nitre resources for the Confederacy for another year," railroad historian John Elwood Clark notes.[29]

With the bluecoats increasingly earnest in their efforts to take the city, and with Confederate forces equally determined to maneuver by road and by rail to hold it, Chattanooga's evolution seemed complete. Less than a year after the war's curtain-raising battle at Manassas, Chattanooga had been transformed from an out-of-the-way whistle stop—"barren of anything worth having," according to one visitor—to a critical Southern bastion that brought to mind heroic battlefields of old, a vital passageway not only for supplies but also for men with guns in their hands, and a place suddenly threatened from all sides and squarely within the strategic sights of the president of the United States. Whether or not it was truly the funnel of the universe, there could be no question that from late 1862 onward, Chattanooga would be the funnel of the Civil War, the gateway to the Lower South, and the key to ultimate victory. "Next after Richmond and Vicksburg, the mountain fastness of Chattanooga was the most important strategic point in the Southern Confederacy," philosopher and historian John Fiske wrote—and then went on to explain its value, the good and the bad, for each side. "Its possession by the Confederates gave them control of eastern Tennessee, enabled them easily to move reinforcements between Virginia and the West, and was a perpetual menace to Tennessee and Kentucky." Yet, he continued, "[i]ts possession by the Federal army would practically isolate Virginia and North Carolina on the one hand, and lop off Mississippi and Alabama on the other; and by opening the way into the interior of Georgia, would throw what was left of the war entirely into the Atlantic region."[30]

Such were the mortal stakes in the struggle for Chattanooga, a town less than twenty-five years old, a place in the middle of nowhere and yet somehow in the middle of everything—as the essays that follow will presently demonstrate. The everlasting, immovable thunderstorm of Lookout Mountain stood frozen in place—and always will—but as the calendar turned to 1863, the amphitheatric stage was set for the great campaigns of the western theater, and the worst of all possible storms was about to break on Chattanooga and its people.

ACKNOWLEDGMENTS

I owe deepest thanks to William Lee White for providing unpublished primary and secondary sources, to James Ogden III for offering encouragement and suggestions, and to Marion O. Smith for his unparalleled work on the overlooked but critical topic of Confederate mining operations. Cartographer Hal Jespersen did a great job designing the maps. And I am indebted most of all to editors Evan Jones and Wiley Sword for their support and insight as well as for the honor of including me in this distinguished group of authors.

NOTES

1. *Chattanooga Commercial,* Feb. 24, 1878 (article quoting missionary letter from 1817), quoted in Gilbert E. Govan and James W. Livingood, *The Chattanooga Country, 1540–1975: From Tomahawks to TVA,* 3rd ed. (Knoxville: University of Tennessee Press, 1977), 77. See also ibid., 59, 68.

2. John P. Long, "A Historical Sketch of Chattanooga, Tennessee," Long Collection, Chattanooga Public Library, quoted in Charles Stuart McGehee, "Wake of the Flood: A Southern City in the Civil War, Chattanooga, 1838–1873" (Ph.D. diss., University of Virginia, 1985), 13.

3. Report of the Board of Commissioners of the Western and Atlantic Railroad (n.p., 1838), 4–5, quoted in ibid., 15; Joel Chandler Harris, *Georgia from the Invasion of De Soto to Recent Times* (New York: D. Appleton, 1896). For a thorough discussion of Chattanooga's role in the Indian removal, see "The Trail Where They Cried," in Govan and Livingood, *Chattanooga Country,* 75–97; and H. G. Clauder to Theodore Schulz, Moravian Archives, Cherokee Mission, 290, quoted in John Ehle, *Trail of Tears: The Rise and Fall of the Cherokee Nation* (New York: Doubleday, 1989), 363.

4. McGehee, "Wake of the Flood," 15; *Knoxville Whig,* Apr. 17, 1858, quoted in Robert Tracy McKenzie, *Lincolnites and Rebels: A Divided Town in the American Civil War* (New York: Oxford University Press, 2006), 17. For Chickamauga meanings, see Peter Cozzens, *This Terrible Sound: The Battle of Chickamauga* (Urbana: University of Illinois Press, 1996), 90 ("loosely translated" it means "River of Death"); "Origin of Names," in *Society of the Army of the Cumberland, Thirty-Sixth Reunion* (Cincinnati: Robert Clarke, 1897), 121 ("good country"); and Govan and Livingood, *Chattanooga Country,* 20–21. Govan and Livingood are skeptical of the "river of death" translation, suggesting that settlers "invented meanings frequently to suit their fancy." Ibid., 20. Similar gullibility may surround the Yazoo River in Mississippi— its name often translated from the Choctaw as "river of death" instead of more-mundane alternate interpretations like "old ruins." Edward Fontaine, *How the World Was Peopled* (New York: D. Appleton, 1872), 151. On the meaning of "Tennessee," see Paul H. Bergeron, *Paths of the Past: Tennessee, 1770–1970* (Knoxville: University of Tennessee Press, 1979), 3 ("No one knows for certain"); and Nancy Capace, *Encyclopedia of Tennessee* (New York: Somerset, 2000), 2 (possible meanings include "river with a big bend" or "curved spoon").

5. Noel C. Fisher, *War at Every Door: Partisan Politics and Guerilla Violence in East Tennessee, 1860–1869* (Chapel Hill: University of North Carolina Press, 1997), 17–18; James W.

Livingood, *A History of Hamilton County, Tennessee* (Memphis: Memphis State University Press, 1981), 24–25; McGehee, "Wake of the Flood," 24–25.

6. Hilaire Belloc, *The Road* (New York: Harper and Brothers, 1925) quoted in John Alexander Williams, *Appalachia: A History* (Chapel Hill: University of North Carolina Press, 2002), 143. Shelby Foote has observed that ten roads radiated out from the college town of Gettysburg "as if it were probing for trouble in all directions." *The Civil War: A Narrative,* vol. 2, *Fredericksburg to Meridian* (New York: Vintage, 1963), 446. The same could be said of Chattanooga and its railroads.

7. McGehee, "Wake of the Flood," 74; Albert Lawson, "Words of Prophecy," in *War Incidents and Anecdotes of Army Life: Reminiscences from Both Sides of the Conflict between the North and South* (Cincinnati: by the author, 1888), 147–51. Davis's wife, in her memoirs, sought to minimize the incident: "Much has been made of this scene, but it was merely the vagary of a drunken man, for which his brother apologized." Varina Davis, *Jefferson Davis: Ex-President of the Confederate States of America: A Memoir by His Wife* (New York: Belford, 1890), 6–7.

8. John M. Armstrong to R. A. Armstrong, Jan. 8, 1861, quoted in Zella Armstrong, *The History of Hamilton County and Chattanooga, Tennessee* (Chattanooga: Lookout Publishing, 1940), 4n2; W. Todd Groce, *Mountain Rebels: East Tennessee Confederates, 1860–1870* (Knoxville: University of Tennessee Press, 2006), 36, 39; McGehee, "Wake of the Flood," 67.

9. U.S. Census Bureau, "Population of the 100 Largest Urban Places: 1860," June 15, 1998, http://www.census.gov/population/www/documentation/twps0027/tab09.txt; Wiley Sword, *Mountains Touched with Fire: Chattanooga Besieged, 1863* (New York: St. Martin's, 1997), 83; U. S. Grant to Julia, Oct. 27, 1863, in U. S. Grant, *The Papers of Ulysses S. Grant: July 7–December 31, 1863,* ed. John Y. Simon (Carbondale: Southern Illinois University Press, 1982), 334–35; McGehee, *Wake of the Flood,* 41; Benjamin Franklin Taylor, *Pictures of Life in Camp and Field,* 3rd ed. (Chicago: S. C. Griggs, 1888), 21.

10. Chesley A. Mosman, *The Rough Side of War: The Civil War Journal of Chesley A. Mosman, First Lieutenant, Company D, 59th Illinois Volunteer Infantry Regiment,* ed. Arnold Gates (Garden City, N.Y.: Basin, 1987), 82; Taylor, *Pictures of Life in Camp and Field,* 20; Peter Cozzens, *The Shipwreck of Their Hopes: The Battles for Chattanooga* (Urbana: University of Illinois Press, 1994), 15.

11. William S. Rosecrans to My Dearest, Aug. 30, 1863, William Starke Rosecrans Papers, Box 59, Folder 91, Charles E. Young Research Library, University of California, Los Angeles.

12. R. G. Payne, *Report to the General Assembly on the Condition of the Railroads in Tennessee* (Nashville: G. C. Torbett, 1857), 31.

13. George Edgar Turner, *Victory Rode the Rails: The Strategic Place of the Railroads in the Civil War* (Lincoln: University of Nebraska Press, 1992), 18. Christopher R. Gabel has noted that the South's north–south lines were in the wrong place and ran in the wrong direction for military operations; "[w]hat the Confederacy needed were east–west lines linking the major theaters of war." "Rails to Oblivion: The Decline of Confederate Railroads in the Civil War," Combat Studies Institute (Fort Leavenworth, Kans.: U.S. Army Command and General Staff College Press, 2002), 4.

14. Henry Watterson, *Chattanooga Daily Rebel,* Oct. [?], 1862; Govan and Livingood, *Chattanooga Country,* 162–67. Instead of Chattanooga, Selma (and later Birmingham), Alabama, would become known as "the Pittsburgh of the South."

15. Marion O. Smith, *Civil War Tours for Cavers: Sewanee to Chattanooga* (Louisville, Tenn.: Byron's Graphic Arts, 1998), 43–44.

16. For details on Confederate mining, caves, potash works, and other operations, see Marion O. Smith, *Confederate Niter District Eight: Middle Tennessee and Northwest Georgia* (Cookeville, Tenn.: by the author, 2011); *Civil War Tours for Cavers;* and *Confederate Niter Bureau, Operations in Alabama* (Louisville, Tenn.: Byron's Graphic Arts, 2007). Generally, see also C. L. Bragg, *Never for Want of Powder: The Confederate Powder Works in Augusta, Georgia* (Columbia: University of South Carolina, 2007).

17. On the importance of the Ducktown copper-mining district, see Frank E. Vandiver, *Ploughshares into Swords: Josiah Gorgas and Confederate Ordnance* (Austin: University of Texas Press, 1952), 201nn20, 21.

18. Marion O. Smith, "Bradley County Mine Yielded Tons of Lead during Civil War," *Chattanooga Regional Historical Journal* 12, no. 1 (Dec. 2009) .

19. Thomas Connelly, *Army of the Heartland: The Army of Tennessee, 1861–1862* (Baton Rouge: Louisiana State University Press, 1967), 6.

20. Ibid., 9.

21. Regarding the Epsom-salts mine, see generally Smith, *Confederate Nitre Bureau;* and Bragg, *Never for Want of Powder,* 88.

22. Montgomery C. Meigs to Edwin M. Stanton, Oct. 3, 1863, U.S. War Department, *The War of the Rebellion: A Compilation of the Official Records of the Union and Confederate Armies,* 128 vols. (Washington, D.C.: GPO, 1880–1901), ser. 1,30(1):58 (hereafter cited as *OR;* all citations are to series 1 unless otherwise specified). In this communication Meigs described Chattanooga as a "fortified base" that "threatens the south and southwest."

23. McGehee, "Wake of the Flood," 101–102.

24. Emory Thomas initially devised the term "military-industrial complex" in relation to the Confederacy to depict this region's rising war industry. Thomas, *The Confederate Nation, 1861–1865* (New York: Harper Torchbooks, 1979), 210–12. See also Mary A. DeCredico, *Patriotism for Profit: Georgia's Urban Entrepreneurs and the Confederate War Effort* (Chapel Hill: University of North Carolina Press, 1990), 110.

25. "The Present Aspect of the War Causes for Hope," *New York Times,* Mar. 16, 1864. For more on the military-industrial heartland of East Tennessee, western Alabama, and Georgia, see Connelly, *Army of the Heartland,* 3–22. See also, generally, Thomas, *Confederate Nation;* Vandiver, *Plowshares into Swords;* and Harold S. Wilson, *Confederate Industry: Manufacturers and Quartermasters in the Civil War* (Jackson: University Press of Mississippi, 2002). For Georgia specifically, see DeCredico, *Patriotism for Profit.* Historians are virtually unanimous in pronouncing Chattanooga of vital strategic importance in the war. Steven E. Woodworth has described Chattanooga as "a key transportation nexus and gateway to the southern Appalachians," whose capture "exposed the deep South to Union invasion." *Six Armies in Tennessee: The Chickamauga and Chattanooga Campaigns* (Lincoln: University of Nebraska Press, 1998), xiii. Albert Castel declared that the loss of Chattanooga "meant the loss of Tennessee and threatened the loss of Georgia. . . . Without them, victory would be impossible and defeat certain." "Foreword," in Sword, *Mountains Touched with Fire,* x. See also Cozzens, *Shipwreck of Their Hopes,* 7.

26. A. Lincoln to H. W. Halleck, June 30, 1862, *OR* 17(1):53; A. Lincoln to W. S. Rosecrans, Oct. 4, 1863, ibid., 30:79. The secretary of war later wrote Halleck, "The President regards [the Chattanooga expedition] and the movement against East Tennessee as one of the most important movements of the war, and its occupation nearly as important as the capture of Richmond." Edwin M. Stanton to H. W. Halleck, June 30, 1862, ibid., 11:280.

27. Govan and Livingood, *Chattanooga Country,* 159, 183. For an account of Mitchel's advance into northern Alabama and the Great Locomotive Chase in North Georgia, see, generally, Russell S. Bonds, *Stealing the General: The Great Locomotive Chase and the First Medal of Honor* (Yardley, Pa.: Westholme, 2006).

28. Negley's Raid—sometimes hilariously overstated as "the First Battle of Chatta-nooga"—is described in James B. Jones Jr., "Negley's Raid," *North and South* 11, no. 2 (Dec. 2008), 84 et seq. See also Report of Col. Henry A. Hambright, 79th Pennsylvania Infantry, June 8, 1862, *OR,* 10(1): 920; E. Kirby Smith to wife, June 8, 1862, quoted in Joseph H. Parks, *General Edmund Kirby Smith, C.S.A.* (Baton Rouge: Louisiana State University Press, 1992), 82–83; and *Mobile Daily Advertiser and Register,* June 10, 1862, quoted in J. Cutler Andrews, *The South Reports the Civil War* (Princeton, N.J.: Princeton University Press, 1970), 234.

29. Braxton Bragg to George Wm. Brent, May 20, 1863, *OR,* 16(1):1089. The Army of Ten-nessee's movement by rail from Tupelo to Chattanooga is described with admiration in John Elwood Clark, *Railroads in the Civil War: The Impact of Management on Victory and Defeat* (Baton Rouge: Louisiana State University Press, 2004), 28–30; Larry J. Daniel, *Soldiering in the Army of Tennessee: A Portrait of Life in a Confederate Army* (Chapel Hill: University of North Carolina Press, 2003), 29; and Connelly, *Army of the Heartland,* 203–204. Interest-ingly, Bragg had spent time in Chattanooga two dozen years earlier—as a U.S. Army lieuten-ant taking part in the Cherokee removal. Govan and Livingood, *Chattanooga Country,* 92.

30. Sword, *Mountains Touched with Fire,* 83; John Fiske, *The Mississippi Valley in the Civil War* (Boston: Houghton Mifflin, 1900), 247–48. The details of the campaigns for Chat-tanooga and thereafter—the Confederate evacuation and Federal occupation of the city; the Battle of Chickamauga; the arrival of Ulysses S. Grant; the "cracker line"; the Battle of Chattanooga; and the city's second life as a Federal base for Sherman's campaigns in Georgia—are addressed and dissected by other contributors to this volume.

CHAPTER 2

LAST CHANCE FOR A SHORT WAR

Don Carlos Buell and the Chattanooga Campaign of 1862

GERALD J. PROKOPOWICZ

Early in June 1862, Union major general Don Carlos Buell and his Army of the Ohio set out from Corinth, Mississippi, with the objective of capturing Chattanooga, Tennessee. In a war that had already become longer and more costly than most people had imagined, this was the most promising strategic moment yet for the North. On the Virginia Peninsula, Major General George B. McClellan's Army of the Potomac was poised at Richmond's doorstep, while Buell's army marched toward the heart of the Confederate position in the West. By August, after two months of strenuous effort, Buell was within striking distance of his goal.

He never reached it. As the Army of the Ohio toiled across Tennessee and northern Alabama in the hot, dry summer of 1862, a substantial Confederate army was assembling at Chattanooga. When the rebels launched a counteroffensive in mid-August, Buell retreated hundreds of miles, from the Tennessee River to the banks of the Ohio, giving up almost all of the ground he had won since the beginning of the war. Buell turned back the Confederate invasion of Kentucky in a tactically indecisive battle at Perryville on October 8, but he allowed the invading army to return to Tennessee intact. On October 30 the general was removed from command, his military career effectively over. Worse for him, five days later Secretary of War Edwin Stanton directed General in Chief Henry W. Halleck to appoint a military commission to investigate and report on Buell's conduct of the campaign.[1]

Don Carlos Buell was hardly alone among Union generals in failing to win battles or to fulfill his strategic mission, but no other army commander in the Civil War was subjected to inquiry by a military commission. Commissions to review unsuccessful generals were not a traditional part of American military procedure. The first U.S. military commissions had been established during the war with Mexico in 1847, when Major General Winfield Scott created them to try cases of murder, rape, and other crimes committed by soldiers against civilians (and vice versa) that were not covered by the Articles of War.[2] President Abraham Lincoln authorized trial and punishment by military commission for "all persons . . . guilty of any disloyal practice" on September 24, 1862, in the same order that suspended the privilege of the writ of habeas corpus, but there is no evidence that he expected the army to use these to punish some generals *pour encourager les autres* in European fashion.[3]

This was the apparent purpose of the Buell commission. The War Department filed no charges against Buell, so the commission was not a court-martial, nor a court of inquiry, but a unique ad-hoc tribunal created at the behest of the secretary of war. It met from December 1862 to May 1863 and consisted of five officers appointed by Halleck, four of whom were outranked by the general whose conduct they were reviewing.[4] When Major Donn Piatt, who as judge advocate of the commission was responsible for presenting the government's case, asked Stanton for directions, the secretary told him to consult the governors of Indiana and Tennessee, Oliver P. Morton and Andrew Johnson, both of whom hated Buell.[5] Morton told Piatt that he and Johnson had demanded the commission and that the general had committed treason in failing to defeat the rebels. Since no formal charges were ever entered, Buell made a point of wearing his dress sword to the commission's sessions each day to remind onlookers that he was not under arrest and could carry arms. But the fact that he was not formally charged also meant that Buell did not have the rights of the accused, so he had to argue with commissioners first to be allowed to attend the hearings, and later for the opportunity to cross-examine the government's witnesses and to present his own.[6]

Why was Buell subjected to this peculiar proceeding? The commission was specifically directed by Stanton to investigate "operations of the forces under command of Major-General Buell in the States of Tennessee and Kentucky," but based on the historical attention they have received, these campaigns do not seem to merit the distinction.[7] The Perryville Campaign has been overshadowed by Robert E. Lee's simultaneous invasion of Maryland that culminated in the Battle of Antietam so that now only students of the Civil War recognize its importance. Buell's effort to seize Chattanooga has likewise been overshadowed by the climax of the

Peninsula Campaign in June 1862 and the dramatic Seven Days' Battles that ended the Army of the Potomac's march toward Richmond. The Chattanooga Campaign, which fizzled to an end without a major battle, has in contrast faded into almost complete obscurity.

In 1862, however, Buell's drive into Middle Tennessee and northern Alabama represented the Union's best hope for a decisive strategic victory, other than the campaign against Richmond itself. Had he captured Chattanooga, the war might have ended earlier by months, perhaps an entire year, than actually happened, saving tens of thousands of lives.[8] The campaign began with every indication of success but ended as the most convincing strategic defeat suffered by any Union army. President Lincoln spoke for the country when he asked in frustrated bewilderment: "What is the meaning of all this? . . . Don't our men march as well, and fight as well, as these rebels?" To Lincoln, as well as to politicians like Stanton, Morton, and Johnson; to journalists like the Indianapolis editor who wrote that Buell's men should assassinate him; to soldiers like commission member Brigadier General Albin Schoepf, who had plotted against Buell while serving under him; and to many at home in the North who wondered how such a promising campaign could turn out so badly, it seemed that someone had to be held responsible for failing to seize the greatest missed opportunity of the war.[9]

⟤⟤⟤

Don Carlos Buell was a career professional soldier. He was born in Ohio in 1818, graduated from West Point in 1841, and served in the Seminole War of 1841–42 and the war with Mexico, during which he was wounded and twice brevetted for bravery. He was an efficient, dedicated soldier who spent the next thirteen years of his career pushing paper in the Adjutant General's Office, reaching the rank of lieutenant colonel. He was also a conservative Democrat and a slaveholder in the years before the Civil War, but there was no question of his loyalty to the Union. When the war began he hurried east from his post as adjutant general of the Department of the Pacific in California to assist his friend George McClellan in reorganizing the Army of the Potomac after its defeat at Bull Run. In November 1861, when Brigadier General William T. Sherman appeared to be suffering a nervous breakdown, McClellan appointed the calm, methodical Buell to take Sherman's place as commander of the Department of the Ohio.[10]

Major General Don Carlos Buell. Library of Congress.

The forces under Buell's command, later to become famous as the Army of the Cumberland but originally known as the Army of the Ohio, consisted, like all Civil War armies, primarily of volunteer regiments whose men reflected the political cast of the society that organized them. Since the regiments of the Army of the Ohio were almost exclusively recruited in states west of the Appalachian Mountains, including Kentucky and Tennessee, the political leanings of many of their rank-and-file soldiers were similar to those of their leader: conservative, Democratic, and antiabolitionist. The army's officers were more mixed; among the colonels and brigadier generals, some like Mahlon Manson of Indiana, Lovell Rousseau of Kentucky, and George Thomas of Virginia shared a conservative outlook, while others like the fiery Polish revolutionary exile Schoepf were antislavery Republicans.[11] On the critical issue of slavery, the views of both officers and men would evolve in favor of emancipation and against the property rights of slaveholding Southern civilians, while those of Buell would not, with significant implications for the outcome of the campaign against Chattanooga.

From the moment he took command of the department, Buell was

assigned the goal of liberating East Tennessee. Many of its residents had
remained loyal to the Union, and Lincoln was anxious for the Army of
the Ohio to free them from Confederate rule. Economically, this region
was important as a major source of copper and saltpeter, both necessary
to the Confederate war effort. Chattanooga, at the area's southern end,
was the strategic gateway to the Confederacy. It sat at the intersection
of the main east–west and north–south rail lines, forming a vital junction in the fragile Confederate railroad system. A Union army occupying
Chattanooga would interrupt commerce and military transport between
Richmond and Memphis, and by moving south to Atlanta and Macon,
it would cut the Southern rail network in two. As early as October 1861,
Lincoln wrote a "Memorandum for a Plan of Campaign" that included a
drive into East Tennessee via the Cumberland Gap as part of the overall
Union strategic design.[12]

Where Lincoln saw opportunities in the mountains of East Tennessee,
however, Buell the professional soldier saw only obstacles. There were
no waterways or railroads leading into the area from the north and few
good roads, so it would be difficult to transport supplies for an army. Allowing his troops to buy or seize food from local civilians was, for Buell,
not an acceptable alternative, in part because he shared the view widely
held in the North early in the war (including both Lincoln and McClellan) that most Southern civilians were fundamentally loyal and could be
persuaded to abandon the rebellion as long as the government protected
civilian property and limited its violence solely to actions against the
Confederacy's armed forces. Buell also rejected the idea of living off the
land because he valued the order and discipline of the Regular Army, in
which he had spent his adult life, and was unimpressed by the free-and-
easy ways of volunteer soldiers. He had no desire to relax their discipline
further by allowing them to forage for their own food, the supply of
which would be limited in what Buell called the "barren, mountainous
region" of eastern Tennessee. To invade the area with 20,000 men, he
argued, would require another 10,000 to garrison their supply lines.[13]

Buell thus decided that the objective of the Army of the Ohio's first
campaign, in January 1862, would not be East Tennessee but Bowling
Green, Kentucky, which was defended by General Albert Sidney Johnston's Confederate forces. While the main body of the army moved slowly
forward, a detached division under Brigadier General George Thomas
defeated the rebels at Mill Springs on January 17, forcing Johnston to
retreat from his outflanked position. A few weeks later U. S. Grant's victo-

ries at Forts Henry and Donelson caused Johnston to evacuate Nashville as well, allowing Buell's army to swoop in and occupy the state capital on February 25 without having to fight a major battle.

In response to insistent messages from Lincoln and McClellan repeating the importance of a move into eastern Tennessee, Buell dispatched the equivalent of a division under Brigadier General George Morgan toward the Cumberland Gap, but he continued to resist the administration's desire that he make East Tennessee his primary objective. In early March he ordered the army's Third Division, under Brigadier General Ormsby Macknight Mitchel, south into Alabama to sever the Memphis and Charleston Railroad between Chattanooga and Corinth, Mississippi. Under orders from Halleck, whom Lincoln appointed to command all the Union forces in the western theater, Buell left some garrison troops in Nashville and led his remaining five divisions westward to link up with Grant's Army of the Tennessee, which was peacefully encamped along the Tennessee River at Pittsburg Landing.

Three of Buell's divisions reached Grant's camp on the evening of April 6, in time to participate in the Battle of Shiloh. Afterward, Halleck consolidated the armies of Buell, Grant, and Major General John Pope into a single massive force under his direct command and set off in glacial pursuit of the defeated rebels. George Thomas was put in command of what had been the Army of the Tennessee and his division removed from Buell's jurisdiction. Thus at one stroke, Buell lost a good division, his best subordinate, and the opportunity to exercise independent command over what was left of his army.[14]

While Halleck's collection of armies was ponderously inching closer to the Confederate position at Corinth, Buell's Third Division was carrying out its mission in northern Alabama. Mitchel captured Huntsville and Stevenson on April 11 and Decatur on April 13.[15] He had become a famous astronomer before the war, for which he was nicknamed "Old Stars," and was vain, ambitious, and a string-puller who sought favors from Secretary of War Stanton over Buell's head, but Mitchel was also a trained soldier who had not let his West Point education deprive him of energy and imagination.[16] It was a detachment from his division, led by Union spy James J. Andrews, that captured a Confederate locomotive near Atlanta on April 12 and tried to destroy bridges and tracks behind them as they raced northward, with the goal of isolating Chattanooga. Although the raid failed, it highlighted the strategic importance of Chattanooga, if it were not already obvious to Mitchel, Buell, or anyone with a map.[17]

Brigadier General Ormsby M. Mitchel. National Archives.

Mitchel, meanwhile, succeeded in his primary mission of seizing the Memphis and Charleston along the one-hundred-mile stretch north of the Tennessee River from Decatur, Alabama, eastward to Bridgeport, Alabama. Chattanooga, which lay only thirty-five miles beyond Bridgeport, seemed ripe for the taking. The rebel commander there, Brigadier General Danville Leadbetter, had no more than 1,780 troops to defend the town.[18]

Back in Mississippi, the Corinth Campaign reached its anticlimax on May 29, when the Confederate defenders of the town slipped away without a fight, leaving it to be occupied by Halleck's enormous force of 86,000 soldiers. "Old Brains" now faced a moment of extraordinary strategic potential.[19] One option was to pursue the Confederates south and seek a decisive battle, but Halleck had taken a month to cover fewer than thirty miles from Shiloh to Corinth, so rapid pursuit was unlikely. A second option was to keep some forces in Corinth and send most of the army westward to Memphis and then down the Mississippi to Vicksburg to seal off the Trans-Mississippi region. Halleck rejected this as well, explaining later to Stanton that "if we follow the enemy into the swamps of Mississippi there can be no doubt that our army will be disabled by disease."[20] The third option, which he chose, was to hold Corinth and detach a portion of the army to march eastward to Chattanooga. On June 10 Halleck reconstituted Buell's Army of the Ohio as a separate command (but still without Thomas or his division), and the next day he ordered it (now numbering 35,000 troops) to move directly to Chattanooga and unite with Mitchel's 10,000-man division.[21]

This was Buell's moment. He knew that Chattanooga was important, and he also knew that it was essentially unguarded. Three days earlier a brigade of Mitchel's division led by Brigadier General James S. Negley had approached the city from north of the Tennessee River, lobbed a few shells into the town, and retired. There were few Confederate soldiers present, and the ones who were there fled in panic. Negley reported that he did "not consider the capture of Chattanooga as very difficult or hazardous, if we were prepared to do it and then hold the place."[22] Since Mitchel's division already held most of the Memphis and Charleston Railroad between Corinth and Chattanooga, including the points where it crossed the Tennessee River, Buell would have faced no organized opposition until he reached his objective. Grant believed that if Buell had advanced "as rapidly as he could march, leaving two or three divisions along the line of the railroad from Nashville forward, he could have arrived with but little fighting, and would have saved much of the loss of life which was afterwards incurred in gaining Chattanooga."[23] One of the general's own division commanders later testified that the army could have completed such a march in "twenty to twenty-five days [given] a margin for difficulties and troubles."[24]

Mitchel was holding open the door to Chattanooga if Buell was willing to dash through. Had he done so, he could have had rations for his army shipped up the Tennessee River as far as Eastport, Mississippi, the limit of navigation at that time of year. From Eastport, supplies could have been shuttled by wagon six miles to Iuka, then sent by rail eastward as far as Tuscumbia, Alabama. Leaving a division to repair the railway between Tuscumbia and Decatur, where it was in Mitchel's hands, he could have sent at least three divisions ahead with whatever rations the troops could carry. They could have lived on half-rations and foraged as needed, as other invading armies would do elsewhere in the war: General Braxton Bragg's in Kentucky, Lee's in Maryland, Grant's in Mississippi, and Sherman's in Georgia. Once the railway link from Corinth to Decatur was repaired, the army could use the fifteen locomotives and numerous railroad cars that Mitchel had captured at Huntsville, so there would have been no shortage of rolling stock.[25]

With Chattanooga under his control, Buell could then have opened a shorter, more direct supply line from Nashville via Stevenson. He also would have been able to draw on the friendly population of the Tennessee River valley for additional supplies. The 10,000 rebels at Knoxville, under Major General Edmund Kirby Smith, would have been trapped between Buell's force and Morgan's 9,000-man division at Cumberland Gap, forcing them to abandon the state altogether and achieving Lincoln's cherished goal of liberating eastern Tennessee. This would also have secured the Union's long supply line from Nashville back to Louisville by denying the rebels the mountain sanctuary from which they otherwise could launch cavalry raids into Kentucky or upper Tennessee. Chattanooga itself could have been held by a relatively small force because of its natural defenses along Missionary Ridge and Lookout Mountain. Even if the Confederates were to have assembled all the troops available in the western theater to counterattack, it is unlikely that they could have done more than to besiege Buell's army in the city; when that happened to Buell's successors William Rosecrans and George Thomas after the Confederate victory at Chickamauga in September 1863, Union forces were able to hold out for over a month until relief arrived.[26]

At the least, the capture of Chattanooga in the summer of 1862 would have given Federal forces possession of all of eastern Tennessee, including Knoxville, and would have forced the Confederates to attack the Army of the Ohio at Chattanooga instead of invading Kentucky and fighting there, as they were to do at Perryville in October 1862. Even if defeated

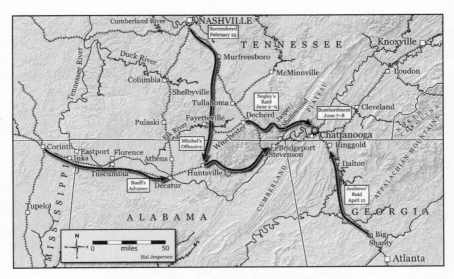

Federal Operations against Chattanooga, 1862.

in such a battle, Buell could have withstood a siege in Chattanooga, which still would have advanced the time line of the war in the West by an entire year. But if Buell managed to defeat a Confederate army at Chattanooga in 1862, it would have put Union forces in position to launch a campaign for Atlanta in 1863 instead of 1864. July 1863 might then have been marked by three great Northern victories—at Gettysburg, Vicksburg, and Atlanta—instead of two, a combined blow that might have sealed the fate of the Confederacy twenty-one months early, without the costly summer campaigns of 1864.

Unfortunately for all the soldiers on both sides who would not survive the bloodletting of 1864, Buell did not dash into Chattanooga. Instead, he attempted to conduct a classic campaign of Jominian maneuver, establishing well-stocked supply depots that would serve as springboards for his army's cautious advances. He had seen this strategy work three times already in 1862, having led his men into Bowling Green, Nashville, and Corinth, each one abandoned without a fight when the defenders had been placed in an untenable position by the irresistible maneuvers of large Union forces—so why not use the same technique to take Chattanooga? This must have appealed to him much more than a reckless lunge deep into enemy territory that would put his army at risk and force his men to antagonize Southern civilians by living off the land.

The march on Chattanooga, as Buell executed it, started with two
strikes against it. The first was self-inflicted. In April, when Mitchel's
division first reached the banks of the Tennessee River, Buell ordered
him to burn the railroad bridges at Bridgeport and Decatur.[27] Doing so
would secure Mitchel's flanks by preventing any rebel counterattacks
from the direction of Chattanooga or Corinth, but it would similarly
prevent him from moving rapidly toward either objective. On April 23
Buell repeated his instructions to destroy the Decatur bridge "without
fail" as well as "the importance of destroying the Bridgeport bridge."[28]
Mitchel thought these orders were absurd. He complained to Secretary
of the Treasury Salmon P. Chase: "I spared the Tennessee bridges near
Stevenson in the hope I might be permitted to march on Chattanooga and
Knoxville, but am now ordered to burn the bridges. I do not comprehend
the order, but must obey it as early as I can. This entire line ought to be
occupied, in my opinion, and yet I fear it will be abandoned."[29] By May 1,
both bridges were destroyed.[30]

The second strike was a lack of clarity in Halleck's orders to Buell. As
soon as Union forces occupied Corinth on May 30, Halleck ordered Buell
to repair the Memphis and Charleston Railroad as far east as Decatur in
order to link up with Mitchel's forces and to gain access to the valuable
locomotives and rolling stock at Huntsville. At a meeting on June 10 to
discuss the capture of Chattanooga, Buell apparently persuaded Halleck to let him march to the northeast; concentrate at McMinnville,
Tennessee; and move over the mountains into East Tennessee to take
Chattanooga from the north. This approach would have the advantage
of a short supply line from McMinnville to nearby Nashville. The next
day, however, Halleck changed his mind. "After carefully considering
the whole matter I am satisfied that your line of operations should be
on Chattanooga . . . instead of McMinnville."[31] He also reminded Buell
of the need to open the rail line from Corinth to Decatur.

Although Halleck did not issue any written orders to Buell specifying
how he was to supply his army, Buell apparently believed that he wanted
him to repair the Memphis and Charleston not only for the purpose of
opening communications with Mitchel's division but also to supply the
army all the way to its objective, writing that "it was his [Halleck's] idea
that I should draw my supplies by that route."[32] Accordingly, he ordered
Brigadier General Thomas J. Wood's Sixth Division to march east to Decatur, "repairing the railroad as you go," supported by Brigadier General
William "Bull" Nelson's Fourth Division, along with eight companies of

the 1st Michigan Engineers and Mechanics Regiment.[33] At the same time, Buell ordered the other two of his four available divisions, Brigadier General Alexander McCook's Second Division and Brigadier General Thomas L. Crittenden's Fifth Division, to cross the Tennessee River at Tuscumbia, Alabama, and march toward Chattanooga along the northern bank of the river.[34] On June 21 Halleck wrote to the army commander: "I repeat, the road to Decatur must be put in running order with all possible dispatch. That being done, supplies can be sent to you in abundance."[35] When Halleck reassigned Thomas and his division to the Army of the Ohio on June 22, Buell directed him to take over the role of railroad guard from Nelson's division, allowing the latter to leave Iuka and follow Wood's troops toward Decatur.[36] The railroad from Corinth to Decatur was finally ready for traffic on June 29, but the labor that Buell's men poured into the project turned out to be futile because Mitchel had failed to execute Halleck's order to dispatch some of the locomotives he had captured at Huntsville.[37] With no engines to operate on the line except for a few broken-down relics, and with frequent raids by rebel guerillas who burned bridges and trestles, Buell complained that despite all the effort his army had put into repairing the Memphis and Charleston, "substantially we derived no advantage from it."[38]

The destruction of the Tennessee River bridges and Halleck's insistence on repairing the railroad were two strikes against Buell, but it takes three to strike out. Neither of these factors forced Buell to let ten days lapse between his initial orders to McCook and Crittenden on June 12 to cross the Tennessee and the commencement of their march toward Chattanooga, nor did they require him to move as slowly as he did. Staff officer Ephraim Otis later described the march that followed as "leisurely" and claimed that Chattanooga "could easily have been reached without forced marches or special effort long before it would have been possible for the enemy to gather up his scattered forces in Mississippi and place them in our front."[39]

Certainly the Tennessee River was a substantial obstacle, but other Civil War generals found ways to overcome such impediments. Brigadier General William Sooy Smith testified in February 1863 on Buell's behalf that it would have taken three weeks for the entire Army of the Ohio to cross the Tennessee at Decatur without a bridge and three weeks more to cross again at Bridgeport or Stevenson, but this was a reflection of Buell's Regular Army mentality, not of the inherent difficulty of crossing a river. Under Buell, building a proper bridge took a long time, as he demonstrated in March 1862, when he spent two weeks crossing his army over the much smaller Duck River en route to Shiloh. In contrast, an Army of the Potomac veteran observed, had Halleck assigned the task to a more aggressive engineer, "the want of a railroad bridge at Decatur would not have delayed [Buell's] march for a single day" because supplies could have been ferried across, a process that was "inconvenient [but] was no serious obstacle."[40] It was the Army of the Potomac that provided the war's most spectacular extemporaneous river crossing, constructing a 2,100-foot-long pontoon bridge over the James in eight hours in June 1864, but Buell's troops (under Rosecrans's leadership) demonstrated their own capabilities in 1863 when they used rough-and-ready methods to cross the Tennessee at multiple locations in one day during the Chickamauga Campaign.[41]

As for being tied to the Memphis and Charleston Railroad for supplies, even if Halleck had expressly ordered this (which he later denied), Buell did not let it stop him from arranging alternate supply routes.[42] On June 11 he wrote to Mitchel, "I wish the Nashville and Chattanooga Railroad put in order at the very earliest possible moment," and the next day told J. B. Anderson, the railroad superintendent at Nashville: "The Chattanooga road is of the most importance now, because it can be soonest completed. Put all your force on it at once."[43] When Buell ordered the Second and Fifth Divisions to cross the Tennessee at Tuscumbia, he positioned them to march on Athens, Alabama, where they could draw supplies from Nashville on the Alabama Central Railroad. Mitchel had put "every available mechanic under my command" to work on that railroad and had repaired it from Nashville to Reynolds's Station, just north of Pulaski, Tennessee; Buell directed him to continue working on both of the railroads running south from Nashville because it was "desirable to open as many channels of communication as possible to depots . . . in this region."[44] On July 1 Halleck conceded that Buell's army could not be supplied via Memphis and asked when it could start drawing supplies on Nashville instead, to which Buell replied that he was already doing so on the Alabama Central (albeit with a twenty-three-mile gap where wagons had to haul the supplies) and that he expected to have the Chattanooga road open in ten days.[45]

Why, then, did Buell take two months to move the head of his army from Corinth to Battle Creek, Tennessee, just north of Bridgeport, while the tail of it remained at Tuscumbia many miles to the west, with the rest strung out in between? It was his determination to accumulate large stockpiles of supplies at the front before advancing, rather than the availability of any one rail line or the absence of bridges, that slowed his progress to a crawl. Just meeting daily needs was a challenge since the Army of the Ohio, like every Civil War army, needed prodigious amounts of food and forage. As of June 10, the army reported some 60,000 men present for duty, with about 30,000 of them in northern Alabama. The soldier's daily ration weighed 3 1/4 pounds, so the army in Alabama required approximately fifty tons of food each day, an amount that could be carried by a five-car train or hauled by sixty army wagons. (A wagon could carry more than a ton of payload, but a substantial portion of it had to be set aside for forage for the six mules or four horses drawing it). Transporting enough food to feed the army for a day was not by itself an insoluble problem, especially if the men were put on half-rations (as they were in July) or if they had permission to forage for additional subsistence from local civilians (which they did not). The problem Buell could not solve was how to transport enough surplus food, beyond the army's daily needs, to build up depots that could supply the army as it moved even farther from its base.[46]

Part of the problem was the distance to that base. The army's lines of supply originated three hundred miles to the north at Louisville, Kentucky, on the Ohio River. From there, supplies were sent to the army's forward base at Nashville. The most efficient way to move cargo from Louisville to Nashville was by steamboat on the Ohio and Cumberland Rivers, but by July 23 the Cumberland was so low that boats could no longer reach the Tennessee capital. The alternative method was the single-track Louisville and Nashville Railroad, which proved inadequate to the task. The army's commissary officers in Nashville requested two million rations a month but received barely half of that. One million rations was enough to feed 30,000 men for thirty-one days but not enough to build up a useful surplus. Even if both railroads leading south from Nashville had been continuously operational, they would not have been able to stock the depots to the levels that Buell wanted. "We are living from day to day on short supplies," the general wrote to his chief quartermaster at Louisville on July 7, "and our operations are completely crippled."[47]

The first location where Buell attempted to establish a forward depot was Athens, Alabama. Before leaving Corinth on June 11, he ordered Mitchel to have five days' rations for two divisions and forage for horses and mules waiting at Athens by June 22.[48] When the first units of Crittenden's and Nelson's divisions arrived on June 27, however, they found nothing. "There is no forage at Huntsville, Athens, Elk River, or Reynolds Station," the army's chief of staff, Colonel James B. Fry, bluntly telegraphed to the harried assistant quartermaster at Nashville, Captain J. D. Bingham. "Why is this? Send forward grain. We expected 150,000 rations of forage at Athens and found none." Bingham replied helplessly that he had ordered 2,500 tons of forage for Athens but had received less than a tenth of that amount from Louisville.[49]

Forage was as difficult a problem as food. The Army of the Ohio did not have much cavalry, but it had thousands of horses that pulled its artillery and carried its officers and even more horses and mules that hauled its wagons. Each animal required more than twenty pounds of forage daily. Not all of this needed to be supplied by rail or wagon from the North—horses and mules could graze and soldiers could buy or even seize hay or green corn from civilians without the same political consequences that attached to confiscating food for troops. Forage nonetheless made up the bulk of the freight that was shipped from Louisville and Nashville to the army. By June 30, the army was requesting 300 tons of supplies daily from Louisville, at a ratio of 3 1/2 tons of forage for every ton of subsistence.[50] The failure to receive forage proved crippling. From Athens, the commander of the Fifth Division reported plaintively on July 1, "I am out of forage"; from Huntsville on July 5, Buell directed Thomas to use his transportation exclusively to send forward forage, "for which we are suffering."[51]

Part of the problem was that Buell's subordinates, particularly Mitchel, were not up to the task of administering a large army. Thomas wrote to Buell that his division at Tuscumbia would be able to send forward as much forage as the army needed if only it had one of the locomotives that Mitchel was supposed to have delivered at Decatur weeks ago. Mitchel claimed that he never saw the order to send any locomotives across the Tennessee, and no one from army headquarters followed up with him until after the fact. He also failed to stockpile supplies for the army at Athens as requested. It was not his fault that the patchwork combination of rail and wagon shipments from Nashville only delivered enough food and forage to support his own division, but it was certainly his fault for not warning Buell that he was unable to provide the requested supplies for the rest of the army. Mitchel created further problems by telling his commander that the Nashville and Chattanooga line was almost operational long before it was, by allowing cotton speculators (of which

Mitchel was one) to use valuable railroad capacity for sending bales of "white gold" to the North, and by communicating directly with Chase and Stanton over Buell's head.[52]

Staff errors at army headquarters also contributed to the frequent supply snafus. For example, after Buell began to build up a new forward depot at Stevenson, units began to requisition their forage from that depot regardless of where they were located so that sacks of oats traveled from Nashville to Stevenson and then halfway back along the same line to their destination in Tullahoma.[53] Instead of delegating authority to local officers to solve this kind of problem, Buell and his staff tried to manage details themselves. The *Official Records* are full of trivial messages issued from army headquarters in the summer of 1862 telling generals everything from which instruments were allowed in evening field music to how to remove stones from a road to make it smooth enough for wagons to use.[54]

Despite all of this, by the second week of July, Buell was at last ready to order the army forward to Chattanooga. After dealing with inadequate supplies, unmanageable subordinates, a dissatisfied general in chief, and a message of patient disappointment from the president, on July 12 the railroad from Nashville to Stevenson was finally ready. The first train left Nashville on July 13 headed south via Murfreesboro. Unfortunately for the unlucky Buell, Nathan Bedford Forrest and 2,000 Confederate cavalry were headed for Murfreesboro the same day. They swept through the town, captured the garrison, destroyed the 200,000 rations that had been painstakingly collected there, and tore up the track for miles. Grimly, Buell absorbed this fresh blow, writing to Halleck, "We will go to work again."[55] The men of the Army of the Ohio went on half-rations on July 13 as they once again turned to repairing bridges, building stockades, patrolling the countryside, starting a new depot at Stevenson, and sawing lumber for pontoons to cross the Tennessee. By the end of the month, there were fourteen fortified outposts guarding the thirty-six miles of track north from Stevenson to the Elk River, with similar deployments elsewhere.[56]

This effort too was of no avail. On August 12 John Hunt Morgan's cavalry attacked Gallatin, Tennessee, north of Nashville. There they collapsed an eight-hundred-foot railroad tunnel, crippling the army's lifeline at its most vulnerable point. With the Louisville and Nashville line out of commission, it became impossible to send enough supplies for the Army of the Ohio to do anything more than hold its position, and soon not even that. As the army sat immobilized, and Union forces in the rest of the western theater remained inactive, Confederate general Braxton Bragg seized the initiative and concentrated more than 30,000 troops from Mississippi and Alabama at Chattanooga. In the middle of August, Bragg's army and Kirby Smith's forces near Knoxville both crossed the Tennessee River and headed north. Buell's objective was no longer Chattanooga but the survival of his army. On August 23 he ordered the commander at Stevenson to evacuate the depot and "quietly prepare the pontoons for burning."[57]

The Army of the Ohio retreated, first to Murfreesboro on August 29, then to Nashville, destroying as they fell back the dozens of railroad bridges and trestles they had painstakingly built over the preceding weeks. When Bragg bypassed Nashville and continued on toward Louisville, Buell followed, leaving almost all of Middle Tennessee except Nashville in rebel hands. By the end of September, the army had returned to its namesake river, where it reorganized and rested in Louisville for a few days before fighting a portion of Bragg's army at Perryville on October 8. The battle ended the Confederate offensive into Kentucky, but the rebels escaped back to Tennessee without further fighting; Buell was relieved of command on October 25. Chattanooga would remain a Confederate mountain citadel for another eleven months.

The Northern public demanded to know why the attempt to take Chattanooga, an undefended city when the campaign began, had failed so badly. An angry Secretary of War Stanton ordered a commission to find out. He expected it to report that it was all Buell's fault, and that the general's political conservatism, his reluctance to seize the property of Southern civilians, and even his loyalty to the Union would be called into question. To Stanton's dismay, the commissioners found otherwise. The slow advance, they concluded, was primarily Halleck's fault for insisting that Buell draw his supplies over the Memphis and Charleston Railroad, and they held that Buell's conciliatory policy toward Southern civilians was not his fault either since it was the policy of the administration through the summer of 1862.[58]

The commission was not entirely accurate in its assessment of Halleck's orders, but its second conclusion at least touched on a more fundamental reason for Buell's failure. Throughout the campaign, he demanded extreme circumspection in dealing with civilians, in part because he believed that it was the best way to convince Southerners voluntarily to resume supporting the government, but even more so because he was a Regular Army man who wanted more order and discipline than his volunteer soldiers could offer. Since nothing unraveled the discipline of an army more than pillaging from civilians, Buell tried to punish violators harshly, even when they were reacting to acts of violence committed by guerillas.

A critical incident occurred on May 2, when Russian émigré colonel Basil Turchin of Mitchel's division allowed his men to pillage the business district of Athens, Alabama. In response to the "sack of Athens," Buell removed the colonel from command and had him court-martialed. Turchin's wife took his case to Washington, and by August, Turchin was not only back in command of his brigade but also held a promotion to brigadier general for good measure.[59] Buell, like McClellan in Virginia, failed to recognize that the administration, the Northern public, and the rank-and-file soldiers were all losing patience with the policy of treating Southern civilians with kid gloves. The war was becoming harsher, on both sides. Turchin did not order the sack of Athens for a lark but to punish the town for the acts of rebel bushwhackers who had fired at his men from civilian houses the day before. In another well-publicized incident, after Brigadier General Robert McCook was shot and killed by rebel guerillas near Huntsville as he lay in an ambulance on August 5, the men of his brigade responded by burning houses for miles around. When soldiers refused to return escaped slaves to their masters, even those who professed loyalty to the Union, it was from a growing recognition that slavery supported the Confederate economy, thus prolonging the war, and that slaveholders could not claim the protection of the Constitution with one hand while using the other to tear it apart. As even the antiabolitionist Midwesterners and border-state men of the Army of the Ohio moved toward a more aggressive war on slavery and the Confederacy, Don Carlos Buell lagged behind. He never accepted what he called "the idea of carrying on a war of vengeance instead of one for the preservation of the Union."[60]

Had he done so, he might have been more willing to lead his divisions across Alabama and Tennessee without so much concern about their supply lines. Had he trusted his volunteer soldiers more, he might have counted on them to fight well and forage too. The ultimate irony is that if he had captured Chattanooga in 1862 and brought the national bloodletting to an earlier end, the war might well have had fewer of the revolutionary results that conservatives like Buell and McClellan feared. One year less of war would also have meant one year less of self-emancipation, one year less of black soldiers shattering white stereotypes, and one year less of the antebellum leadership of Southern society dying in camp or on the battlefield. It was the defenders of the traditional order, like Don Carlos Buell, who helped destroy it by trying to fight the war too traditionally.[61]

ACKNOWLEDGMENTS

Thanks to my colleagues at East Carolina University for providing a stimulating environment during the writing of this essay, to David Powell for a timely research tip that launched this project, and to Evan Jones for his patience.

NOTES

1. Edwin M. Stanton to General Henry W. Halleck, Washington, D.C., Nov. 4, 1862, U.S. War Department, *The War of the Rebellion: A Compilation of the Official Records of the Union and Confederate Armies,* 128 vols. (Washington, D.C.: GPO, 1880–1901), 1st ser., 16(1):6–7 (hereinafter cited as *OR;* all citations to series 1 unless otherwise specified). For Buell's role in the Chattanooga and Perryville Campaigns generally, see below and Gerald J. Prokopowicz, *All for the Regiment: The Army of the Ohio, 1861–1862* (Chapel Hill: University of North Carolina Press, 2001), 83–184; Larry J. Daniel, *Days of Glory: The Army of the Cumberland, 1861–1865* (Baton Rouge: Louisiana State University Press, 2004), 91–177; Stephen D. Engle, *Don Carlos Buell: Most Promising of All* (Chapel Hill: University of North Carolina Press, 1999), 182–320; and James Lee McDonough, *War in Kentucky: From Shiloh to Perryville* (Knoxville: University of Tennessee Press, 1994).

2. Winfield Scott, *Memoirs of Lieut.-General Scott, Ll.D. Written by Himself* (New York: Sheldon, 1864), 543–46, quoting General Orders No. 20, Feb. 19, 1847. See also Louis Fisher, "Military Commission: Problems of Authority and Practice," *Boston University International Law Journal* 24 (Spring 2006): 15–51; and David Glazier, "Precedents Lost: The Neglected History of the Military Commission," *Virginia Journal of International Law* 46 (Fall 2005), 5–78. Procedure under Scott's commissions was to be the same as that of a court-martial, with penalties not to exceed those of state laws for similar crimes.

3. Abraham Lincoln, "Proclamation Suspending the Writ of Habeas Corpus," Sept. 24, 1862, in Abraham Lincoln, *The Collected Works of Abraham Lincoln,* ed. Roy P. Basler, 9 vols. (New Brunswick, N.J.: Rutgers University Press, 1953–55), 5:437.

4. For the names of the members of the commission, see E. D. Townsend, Special Orders No. 356, Washington, D.C., Nov. 20, 1862, *OR,* 16(1):7. Maj. Gen. E. O. C. Ord was the only one senior to Buell. The president of the commission was Maj. Gen. Lew Wallace, who had been promoted to major general later than Buell. The other three members were brigadier generals: Napoleon Jackson Tecumseh Dana, Daniel Tyler, and Albin Schoepf. Schoepf had served under Buell and expressed hostility toward him on several occasions; he and Ord were removed from the commission before it finished its work. See ibid., 542–46, 591–600;

and James B. Fry, *Operations of the Army under Buell from June 10th to October 30th, 1862, and the "Buell Commission"* (New York: D. Van Nostrand, 1884), 110.

5. Buell reciprocated the contempt of Governors Johnson and Morton. He repeatedly disagreed with Johnson over military strategy in Tennessee and believed that Morton tried to undermine his leadership of Indiana troops. "His interference was injurious to discipline but he persisted in order to preserve his influence with the troops, the people, and the Government. The seeds of mischief, always present in his extra-official conduct toward the Indiana troops, were now [in September 1862] being sown with a vigorous but crafty hand, in the counsels at Washington and among the executives of other States, to impair my authority and effect my removal from command." Don Carlos Buell, "East Tennessee and the Campaign of Perryville," in Robert Underwood Johnson and Clarence Clough Buel, eds., *Battles and Leaders of the Civil War,* 4 vols. (1887–88; reprint, New York: Castle, 1956), 3:43 (hereinafter cited as *B&L*).

6. Piatt did a conscientious job of calling witnesses and asking hostile questions about Buell's conduct of the campaign, but in later years he described Morton and Johnson as "scurvy politicians" who unfairly imposed on Buell. Donn Piatt and Henry V. Boynton, *General George H. Thomas: A Critical Biography* (Cincinnati: Robert Clarke, 1893), 177–79; *OR,* 16(1):21–22.

7. *OR,* 16(1):7.

8. Ulysses S. Grant speculated that the seizure of Chattanooga after the fall of Corinth could have prevented the siege of Knoxville and the battles of Stones River, Chickamauga, and Chattanooga. Grant, *Personal Memoirs of U. S. Grant* (1885; reprint, New York: Da Capo, 1982), 199.

9. Donn Piatt, *Memories of the Men Who Saved the Union* (New York: Belford, Clarke, 1887), 38 (quoting Lincoln); *OR,* 16(1):642.

10. For Buell's prewar career, see Engle, *Don Carlos Buell,* 1–63.

11. For the genesis of the Army of the Ohio, see Prokopowicz, *All for the Regiment,* 7–54; and Daniel, *Days of Glory,* 33–42.

12. Lincoln, "Memorandum for a Plan of Campaign," [c. Oct. 1, 1861], in Lincoln, *Collected Works,* 4:544–45. Buell recognized the strategic and political importance of Chattanooga and the Tennessee Valley as "a doorway to the rear of Richmond, and a commanding rendezvous which looked down with a menacing adaptability upon the Gulf and Atlantic States." Buell, "East Tennessee and the Campaign of Perryville," 34.

13. Statement of Major General Buell in review of the evidence before the Military Commission, *OR,* 16(1):24, 32–33.

14. Headquarters, Dept. of the Mississippi, Special Field Orders No. 31, Apr. 28, 1862, Pittsburg Landing, Tenn., ibid., 10(2):138–39; Special Field Orders No. 35, ibid., 144–45.

15. Abstract from "Record of Events," Third Division, Army of the Ohio, *OR,* 10(1):642; O. M. Mitchel to Stanton, Huntsville, Ala., Apr. 17, 1862, ibid., 10(2):111. Three days after the capture of Huntsville, Mitchel was promoted to major general, confirmed on May 2, with rank dated to April 11. John H. Eicher and David J. Eicher, *Civil War High Commands* (Stanford, Calif.: Stanford University Press, 2001), 704.

16. For Mitchel's prewar career, see F. A. Mitchel, *Ormsby Macknight Mitchel Astronomer and General: A Biographical Narrative* (Boston: Houghton, Mifflin, 1887).

17. For an entertaining recent account of the Andrews raid, see Russell S. Bonds, *Stealing the General: The Great Locomotive Chase and the First Medal of Honor* (Yardley, Pa.: Westholme, 2007).

18. Report of E. Kirby Smith, June 5, 1862, Knoxville, Tenn., *OR,* 10(1):905.

19. Many Civil War authors, including Bruce Catton, Allen Nevins, Kenneth Williams, James McDonough, Earl Hess, Donald Stoker, and Ed Bearss, have observed that this was a moment of great opportunity for Halleck, although they are far from unanimous about what he should have done. For the size of Halleck's force, see ibid., 10(2):146–51.

20. Halleck to Stanton, June 25, 1862, Corinth, Miss., ibid., 16(2):62.

21. Special Field Orders No. 90, June 10, 1862, Corinth, Miss., ibid., 3; Halleck to Buell, June 11, 1862, Corinth, Miss., ibid., 9.

22. Ja[me]s S. Negley to Mitchel, 8:00 A.M., June 8, 1862, "Before Chattanooga," *OR,* 10(1):920; Mitchel to Buell, June 10, 1862, Huntsville, Ala., ibid., 288. A veteran of Buell's army later wrote that he had little doubt that if Negley had been supported, "Chattanooga might have been taken, and the whole course of the war in the West would have been changed." Ephraim A. Otis, "Recollections of the Kentucky Campaign of 1862," *Papers of the Military Historical Society of Massachusetts,* vol. 7 (Boston: Military Historical Society of Massachusetts, 1908), 231.

23. Grant, *Personal Memoirs,* 199; see also 209.

24. Testimony of T. J. Wood, Dec. 17, 1862, Nashville, Tenn., *OR,* 16(1):176. I have elsewhere argued that Negley's demonstration in front of Chattanooga in early June compromised Buell's opportunity to take it by prompting the Confederate high command to send reinforcements, but most of these troops did not arrive until July or August. As of June 30 there were only 15,000 rebels defending all of East Tennessee, including Knoxville and Chattanooga. Prokopowicz, *All for the Regiment,* 121; Returns of the Department of East Tennessee, commanded by Maj. Gen. E. Kirby Smith, for June 1862, *OR,* 16(2):715.

25. Report of O. M. Mitchel, Apr. 11, 1862, Huntsville, Ala., *OR,* 10(1):641. In a subsequent report Mitchel claimed sixteen instead of fifteen locomotives captured.

26. For the terrain around Chattanooga and the fight for the city in 1863, see Peter Cozzens, *The Shipwreck of Their Hopes: The Battles for Chattanooga* (Urbana: University of Illinois Press, 1994).

27. Buell to Mitchel, Apr. 19, 1862, "Field of Shiloh," *OR,* 10(2):114.

28. Buell to Mitchel, Apr. 23, 1862, "Field of Shiloh," ibid., 118–19.

29. Mitchel to Salmon P. Chase, Apr. 19, 1862, Huntsville, Ala., ibid., 115. Mitchel's message was forwarded to the War Department and eventually to the White House. Halleck wrote to Lincoln three days later: "No orders, to my knowledge, have been given to General Mitchel to destroy railroad bridges. On the contrary, he has saved some which were fired by the enemy." Halleck to Lincoln, Apr. 22, 1862, Corinth, Miss., ibid., 117.

30. Mitchel to Buell, Apr. 27, 1862, Huntsville, Ala., *OR,* 10(2):134; Mitchel to Stanton, May 1, 1862, Huntsville, Ala., ibid., 155–56. Buell later claimed that he gave Mitchel discretion as to destroying both bridges, but as he admitted in a *Century* magazine piece, "the destruction of the Bridgeport and Decatur bridges was not contrary to my orders under certain conditions." Don Carlos Buell, "Operations in North Alabama," *B&L,* 2:705.

31. Halleck to Buell, June 11, 1862, Corinth, Miss., *OR,* 16(2):9.

32. Statement of Major General Buell in review of the evidence before the Military Commission, ibid., 16(1):30.

33. Fry to Brig. Gen. T. J. Wood, June 11, 1862, "Headquarters," ibid., 16(2):11. Wood's and Nelson's divisions had been working on the railroad since June 1. Fry to Wood, June 1, 1862, "In camp," ibid., 10(2):236–37; Fry to Brig. Gen. [William] Nelson, June 3, 1862,

"Camp near Corinth," ibid., 250–51; Fry to Wood, June 3, 1862, "In camp," ibid., 251; Buell to Halleck, June 1, 1862, "Near Corinth," ibid., 236.

34. James B. Fry [Buell's chief of staff] to Maj. Gen. [Alexander] McCook, June 12, 1862, "Headquarters," *OR*, 16(2):18; Fry to General [Thomas L.] Crittenden, June 12, 1862, "Headquarters," ibid., 19.

35. Halleck to Buell, June 21, 1862, Corinth, Miss., *OR*, 16(2):44.

36. Halleck to Buell, June 22, 1862, Corinth, Miss., ibid., 48–49.

37. Geo[rge] Thomas to Halleck, July 1, 1862, Tuscumbia, Ala., ibid., 86; Thomas to Fry, July 7, 1862, Tuscumbia, Ala., ibid., 103.

38. Statement of Major General Buell in review of the evidence before the Military Commission, *OR*, 16(1):31.

39. Otis, "Recollections of the Kentucky Campaign," 232.

40. George A. Bruce, "Buell's Campaign against Chattanooga," *Papers of the Military Historical Society of Massachusetts,* vol. 8 (Boston: Military Historical Society of Massachusetts, 1908), 114–15.

41. Testimony of General William Sooy Smith, Feb. 9, 1863, Cincinnati, *OR*, 16(1):407. Compare Smith's testimony on February 2, 1863, implying that Buell could have gone straight from Corinth to Chattanooga and could have held the city with 25,000 men. Ibid., 396. For the 1862 Duck River crossing, see Prokopowicz, *All for the Regiment,* 96–98. For the 1864 James River crossing, see Gustav J. Person, "Crossing the James River, June 1864: 'The Real Crisis of the War,'" *Engineer: The Professional Bulletin of Army Engineers* 38 (Sept.–Dec. 2009): 58–64. For the 1863 Tennessee River crossing, see Otis, "Recollections of the Kentucky Campaign," 231: "A year later the Army of the Cumberland, in the advance to Chickamauga, found no difficulty in crossing it at several points without serious delay or difficulty." In November 1863 William T. Sherman's Army of the Tennessee also crossed the Tennessee River at Bridgeport on a pontoon bridge. Cozzens, *Shipwreck of Their Hopes,* 121–22.

42. Halleck, Endorsement to Opinion of the Commission, Washington, D.C., May 29, 1863, *OR*, 16(1):12. On June 12 Halleck wrote to Buell that he should leave his supplies in Corinth, since they "can be taken by rail from here to any point on your line," implying that Corinth would remain Buell's supply base. Halleck to Buell, June 12, 1862, "Headquarters," ibid., 16(2):14–15. Buell replied that he would need wagons "when we get to the limit of the river or railroad communication, say Stevenson, and what we need there will be needed as soon as we arrive if we are to go right on. They ought to go with the troops." Buell to Halleck, June 12, [1862], "Headquarters," ibid., 15. This suggests that Buell at least began the campaign contemplating a direct march to Stevenson, then moving "right on" to Chattanooga.

43. Buell to Mitchel, June 11, 1862, "Headquarters," *OR*, 16(2):10; Buell to J. B. Anderson, June 12, 1862, "Headquarters," ibid., 16–17.

44. Mitchel to Buell, June 12, 1862, Huntsville, Ala., *OR*, 16(2):17; Buell to Mitchel, June 12, 1862, "Headquarters," ibid., 17.

45. Halleck to Buell, July 1, [1862], Corinth, Miss., *OR*, 16(2):82; Buell to Halleck, July 1, [1862], Huntsville, Ala., ibid., 83. See also Buell to Halleck, July 12, [1862], Huntsville, Ala., ibid., 127. Here, Buell calls the "Memphis and Charleston road useless as a channel of supplies for this army."

46. Abstract from Tri-Monthly Return of the District of the Ohio, June 10, [1862], *OR*, 16(2):5; Testimony of Capt. H. C. Symonds, Jan. 19, 1863, Louisville, ibid., 16(1):340

(Symonds was a commissary officer); Testimony of Col. W. P. Innes, Dec. 24, 1862, Nashville, Tenn., ibid., 251 (Innes was an experienced engineer and colonel of the 1st Michigan Engineers and Mechanics Regiment); Buell to Halleck, July 11, 1862, Huntsville, Ala., ibid., 16(2):122–23; Col. Edward M. McCook to Fry, July 10, 1862, Reynolds's Station, Tenn., ibid., 117. For details on army-wagon capacities, estimated by Civil War quartermasters, see *How to Feed an Army, Published by authority of the Secretary of War for Use in the Army of the United States* (Washington: GPO, 1901). See also Lenette S. Taylor, *"The Supply for Tomorrow Must Not Fail": The Civil War of Captain Simon Perkins, Jr., a Union Quartermaster* (Kent, Ohio: Kent State University Press, 2004), passim, esp. 40–79. Perkins served in the Army of the Ohio during the Chattanooga Campaign.

47. Testimony of Capt. H. C. Symonds, Jan. 19, 1863, Louisville, *OR*, 16(1):339–42; Col. Buell to Col. [Thomas] Swords, July 7, [1862], Huntsville, Ala., ibid., 16(2):104.

48. Fry to Capt. [Oliver D.] Greene, June 14, 1862, Tuscumbia, Ala., *OR* 16 (2): 23.

49. Fry to Capt. [J. D.] Bingham, June 29, 1862, Huntsville, Ala., ibid., 73; Bingham to Fry, June 30, 1862, "Headquarters," ibid., 79.

50. Fry to Swords, June 29, [1862], Huntsville, Ala., *OR*, 16(2):73.

51. Thomas L. Crittenden to Buell, July 1, 1862, "Camp near Athens," ibid., 85; Buell to Thomas, July 5, 1862, Huntsville, Ala., ibid., 97.

52. See, for example, Mitchel to Stanton, July 19, 1862, Washington, D.C., *OR*, 10(2):290–95 (with enclosures, defending Mitchel's participation in cotton purchasing); Halleck to Stanton, July 3, 1862, Corinth, Miss., ibid., 16(2):92–93 (requesting an explanation from Mitchel for failure to deliver locomotives); Mitchel to Buell, June 8, 1862, ibid., 10(2):275 ("the road to Stevenson could be very soon opened"); and various messages from Mitchel to Stanton or Chase cited previously. Buell later wrote that he was unaware of Mitchel's involvement in the cotton trade or his correspondence with Washington. Buell, "Operations in North Alabama," 707–708.

53. Taylor, *"Supply for Tomorrow Must Not Fail,"* 71–72.

54. Aide-de-Camp and Acting Assistant Adjutant General. to Mitchel, June 30, 1862, Huntsville, Ala., *OR*, 16(2):78; Fry to Nelson, July 9, 1862, Huntsville, Ala., ibid., 111–12.

55. Buell to Halleck, July 15, 1862, Huntsville, Ala., *OR*, 16(2):151.

56. J[ames] St. C[lair] Morton, Ch[ief] Eng[ineer], Army of the Ohio, "Defences for the Guards of the Railroad between Elk River and Stevenson on the Nashville and Chattanooga R. R.," July 26, 1862, Don Carlos Buell Papers, Filson Historical Society, Louisville, Ky.

57. Fry to Col. [Michael] Shoemaker, Aug. 23, 1862, Decherd, [Tenn.], *OR*, 16(2):398.

58. Lewis Wallace, "Opinion of the Commission," [1863], ibid., 16(1):8–12.

59. After his promotion, Turchin outranked the officers of his court-martial, which meant they could no longer sit in judgment on him. The most complete account of these events is George C. Bradley and Richard L. Dahlen, *From Conciliation to Conquest: The Sack of Athens and the Court-Martial of Colonel John B. Turchin* (Tuscaloosa: University of Alabama Press, 2006).

60. Buell's cross-examination of Speed S. Fry, Dec. 22, 1862, Nashville, Tenn., *OR*, 16(1):228. Mark Grimsley describes the evolution toward harsher warfare in general in *The Hard Hand of War: Union Military Policy toward Southern Civilians, 1861–1865* (New York: Cambridge University Press, 1995). See also Prokopowicz, *All for the Regiment*, 121–27; and Daniel, *Days of Glory*, 97–102.

61. Glenn David Brasher argues in *The Peninsula Campaign and the Necessity of Emancipation* (Chapel Hill: University of North Carolina Press, 2012), which appeared as this was being written, that Northerners attributed McClellan's defeat in 1862 to his deliberate pace and refusal to touch Southern property, especially slaves, in contrast to the Confederates' willingness to use slaves as laborers and (in some contemporary accounts) even as soldiers. The result was a political shift away from a conciliatory policy toward more-aggressive war making, including emancipation. This is a persuasive argument, but like much Civil War writing, it focuses on events in Virginia to the exclusion of those in the West. Buell's conduct of the Chattanooga Campaign paralleled McClellan's on the Peninsula, so that the almost simultaneous failure to capture both Richmond and Chattanooga magnified Northern disappointment beyond the effect of either campaign alone, which hardened Northern attitudes against slavery and the South.

CHAPTER 3

A LEGEND IN THE MAKING

Nathan Bedford Forrest at Chickamauga

DAVID A. POWELL

In Ken Burns's famous documentary on the Civil War, author Shelby Foote called Nathan Bedford Forrest an "authentic genius" of the Civil War. The phrase has the ring of truth. When the war began, Forrest was already a self-made millionaire, a successful planter, businessman, and slave trader who, despite his almost complete lack of formal education or social standing, rose to prominence in antebellum Memphis society. When war came, he proved no less resourceful. Initially enlisting in Confederate service as a private in a local cavalry company, his prominence soon brought him the offer of a commission and authority to raise his own regiment of mounted troops. He had no formal military training, Mexican War or Indian-fighting experience, or even militia service to fall back on. Despite this handicap, by war's end, he was a lieutenant general and one of the most feared of all Confederate leaders. Interest in him has not waned since—a shelf full of biographies and histories relating to Forrest or his command have been published in the nearly one hundred and fifty years since the war's end.

Virtually all of those works echo Foote's opinion. Histories have become tales, grown to legends, all describing Forrest's exploits in larger-than-life terms. A few critical works have appeared, largely centered around his ruthlessness or culpability for controversial incidents like the Fort Pillow Massacre in 1864, but even those authors readily admit his military skills. "What-ifs" abound: What if he had been listened to at Fort Donelson, heeded at Shiloh, unleashed on Sherman's lifeline through Tennessee in 1864? There is no end of speculation about how Forrest could have changed the war had his skills been used more effectively in Confederate service.

In history's haste to engrave Forrest's accolades in the historical record, however, some aspects of his career have been overlooked. Forrest the military genius did not spring forth wholly formed from the head of Mars; like virtually every other officer of the Civil War, he had to learn his trade as he went, and his career was not without tactical blemish. He made mistakes, sometimes costly ones. He was impetuous, had trouble delegating authority, and had a tendency not to believe something until he had seen it for himself. While these traits were not always a handicap when commanding a regiment, where personal bravery and frontline leadership were expected, they proved to be an increasing problem as Forrest rose through the ranks to brigade, divisional, and corps command. Moreover, while he proved to be an excellent guerrilla, understanding irregular warfare and excelling at independent raiding, Forrest had trouble grasping and performing the duties of regular cavalry. Picketing, patrolling, and information gathering were critical needs of a nineteenth-century army operating on campaign. As the cliché notes, cavalry were the "eyes and ears" of an army commander. Forrest did not excel in these areas, especially earlier in the war, and the Confederacy suffered for it.

In 1863 Forrest was thrust into the role of traditional cavalryman virtually overnight. He served as a divisional or corps commander of cavalry during two critical campaigns: Tullahoma and Chickamauga. Both operations faced well-planned Union offensives aimed at avoiding bloody frontal attacks by dint of deception and maneuver, which if anything magnified the importance of the cavalry's role in uncovering those movements. Forrest, commanding half of the Confederate Army of Tennessee's cavalry, did not rise to the occasion. At Tullahoma the rebels were badly deceived, outmaneuvered, and forced into a dispirited retreat. Chickamauga, while a Confederate victory, was won more through luck and Federal bumbling than via timely, accurate intelligence procured by the Southern mounted arm. Both campaigns were marked by extremely poor cavalry performances, and Forrest shares a portion of the blame for that failing.

Forrest's early military career did not reveal any weakness in conventional cavalry duties. Until the spring of 1863, he commanded at most a brigade of partisans, assigned almost exclusively to raiding missions. After the sudden death of Major General Earl Van Dorn in May 1863, however, Forrest was quickly given both additional rank and new respon-

Brigadier General Nathan Bedford Forrest.
Courtesy of the Tennessee State Library and Archives.

sibilities—perhaps too quickly, as it turned out, for 1863 was a critical
year for the Confederacy in the war's western theater, with Union armies
marching down the Mississippi River and through Tennessee. In May of
that year, after tracking down and defeating a Union raiding force under
Colonel Abel Straight, Forrest was promoted to command a division of
cavalry under Van Dorn. Almost immediately, however, Van Dorn's death
thrust him into corps command—and a week later he moved back down
to divisional responsibility when the other division in that corps was
transferred to Mississippi to help defend Vicksburg. Within the space
of three weeks, Forrest had gone from commanding a brigade, then a
division, and finally a corps before returning to divisional command
through transfers. It was a dizzying sequence.

For the first time, Forrest was expected to assume the duties of a
traditional cavalryman. Van Dorn's assignment had been to screen the
Army of Tennessee's left flank in Middle Tennessee. It was a mission well
suited to a West Pointer with cavalry experience in the prewar army.
With that general's untimely death, however, Forrest—the raider and
irregular—was forced to assume that role.

In late June Union major general William S. Rosecrans launched his Army of the Cumberland against the rebels in Middle Tennessee, initiating the Tullahoma Campaign. Rosecrans, who for months had been augmenting his own cavalry force by mounting thousands of infantrymen on local livestock, devised a plan to feint to the west while marching the bulk of his army eastward, around the Army of Tennessee, to capture the Confederate supply depot and base at Tullahoma. Thus, his opponent, General Braxton Bragg, would be severed from his communications and forced to fight or flee. A successful turning movement would visit disaster on the rebel army. Bragg, badly outnumbered, could not afford to fight Rosecrans on anything like even terms.

Outnumbered, that is, except in cavalry: the Confederates possessed a small numerical advantage in horsemen, with more than 13,000 rebel troopers facing Rosecrans's 12,000 or so blue riders. This large force was officered by Forrest on the left and Major General Joseph Wheeler, commanding another two-division cavalry corps, on the right.

Numerical parity did not add up to a similar balance in performance. Instead, the rebels were badly fooled. Forrest, new to the job, interpreted the Union feint as the main thrust. Wheeler, a trained cavalryman who dreamed of being a raider, was in the process of pulling his cavalry completely off Bragg's right flank to launch his own attack on the Union base at Nashville. His bad timing meant that Rosecrans's real offensive went unreported at Confederate headquarters for nearly forty-eight hours. Almost too late, Bragg discovered his real peril and was forced to retreat abruptly. By July 4, the rebels had fled to Chattanooga, shedding prisoners and deserters along the way. Only staggering rains prevented Rosecrans from trapping the Army of Tennessee outright. The Confederate cavalry must bear a lion's share of the blame for the fiasco: the information they provided Bragg during the week's action was usually both untimely and incorrect.

Forrest might be excused some blame: not only was he new to cavalry operations but he was also recovering from a wound. On June 9 he was shot by one of his own officers during a dispute over a transfer. He killed the culprit, and the wound, while troublesome, did not ultimately prevent him from taking the field two weeks later when Rosecrans advanced. The incident does highlight another aspect of Forrest's personality, however: he sometimes lacked a deft touch in relationships both with subordinates and superiors.

Coincident with Tullahoma came the news of Lee's retreat from Penn-

sylvania after the rebuff at Gettysburg and the surrender of an entire
rebel army at Vicksburg. The North celebrated, and in August all eyes
turned expectantly to Chattanooga as Federals and Confederates alike
realized that Rosecrans's next objective had to be that city, gateway to the
Deep South. First, however, the Federals had to stockpile supplies and
prepare, for taking Chattanooga would be no easy venture. Bounded by
mountains and lying on the south bank of the Tennessee River, it was a
natural fortress, not easily captured on the fly.

"I have arrived here and assumed command. My forces are on picket
from this place to Chattanooga."[1] With that terse telegram, sent from
Kingston, Tennessee, on July 30, 1863, Forrest alerted Major General
Simon Bolivar Buckner in Knoxville of his presence on Buckner's flank.
Buckner commanded the Department of East Tennessee, newly subordinated to Bragg's main army at Chattanooga. Knoxville and Chattanooga
were only ninety miles apart, and Buckner, with only about 15,000 men
in his command, had too small a force to adequately defend Knoxville.
Combining with Bragg was the obvious solution, and in early August
his department was redesignated the Third Corps, Army of Tennessee.[2]
Forrest's cavalry division, numbering 3,700 men, would serve as the link
between the two forces.[3]

At Tullahoma, Rosecrans threatened the rebel left but delivered the
main attack on their right flank. Defending Chattanooga, Bragg assumed that Rosecrans would again resort to a turning movement, either
upstream from the city against his right flank or downstream against
his left. Because another Union army under Major General Ambrose E.
Burnside was coming from eastern Kentucky and expected to attack
Knoxville, Bragg thought it most likely that Rosecrans's main effort
would come upstream so that the two Union forces could support one
another. Thus, Forrest's front was where the rebel commander expected
the main Federal force to appear. This assumption overlooked the fact
that the only way to supply an army of any size operating in the region
was via the Nashville and Chattanooga Railroad, and those rails ran
south into Alabama before turning eastward to follow the Tennessee
River through the mountains to Chattanooga. Rosecrans's logical bases
at Bridgeport and Stevenson, Alabama, were both downstream from
Bragg's base; the Federals would have a very difficult time sending their
whole army into the mountains to assail the Army of Tennessee's right
without a rail line to use. While logistics was usually one of Bragg's

strong points as an army commander, in this case he paid too little heed to the problems that would logically constrain Rosecrans's options.

Bragg's assumption also meant that Forrest's command would play a critical role in detecting the Federal advance and determining if it were a feint or the real blow. To be sure, Wheeler's cavalry corps screened the Confederate left, opposite Rosecrans's bases, and their intelligence would also be vital, but Bragg expected to see the real threat materialize on Forrest's front.

Bragg still held Forrest in high regard in August 1863. Forrest, however, was dissatisfied with his current assignment and thinking of home. On August 9 he forwarded a request to leave the Army of Tennessee and return to Mississippi, where he could resume partisan warfare. He felt he could raise new troops—a division or more—and use them to harass the Federals between Memphis and Vicksburg, perhaps even as far as western Kentucky. Bragg rejected the appeal. When Forrest persisted, it was forwarded to Richmond, but Bragg added a note of his own: "It would deprive this army of one of its greatest elements of strength to remove General Forrest."[4] Richmond sided with Bragg, and for the moment the matter was tabled.

In the meantime, the Yankees were on the move. Initially, Forrest did not entirely abandon the north bank of the Tennessee to the Union army, leaving behind a sizable force under Colonel George G. Dibrell at Sparta, Tennessee. Dibrell lived in that town and raised much of the 8th Tennessee Cavalry there in 1861. Now he occupied the area in order to recruit and provide advance warning of any Federal attack. For a week, Union colonel Robert H. G. Minty's brigade skirmished and sparred with Dibrell's men, finally chasing them out of White County toward the end of the month.

This fighting presaged the opening moves in Rosecrans's offensive. Sparta needed to be cleared in order to allow Union columns to move into the Sequatchie Valley, a long narrow corridor running from the Tennessee River northeast for nearly fifty miles. The valley's eastern wall was Walden Ridge, which was the last barrier before reaching Chattanooga from the north. If the Federals controlled Walden Ridge, they could move troops up or down the Sequatchie out of sight of Bragg's scouts to appear unexpectedly almost anywhere upstream from the city. Together, the ridge and the valley were perfect for Rosecrans's intended deception.

Rosecrans, limited by the available rail lines, nevertheless intended to deceive Bragg as much as possible. The XXI Corps would open the campaign by marching southeast through Sparta into the Sequatchie Valley, then southwest toward Jasper, Tennessee. Four brigades—two mounted, two infantry—would cross Walden Ridge to both screen this movement and to deceive the Confederates into thinking that the main Federal attack would be delivered upstream. Next, Rosecrans's three corps would all cross the river between Jasper and Bridgeport and march east to threaten the Western and Atlantic Railroad. Then the Army of Tennessee, neatly outflanked, would have to retreat, hopefully to be caught and destroyed in the process.

Once again, Bragg was to be let down by his cavalry. With Dibrell driven from Sparta, Forrest essentially abandoned the north bank of the Tennessee to the Federals. Wheeler, for his part, made a greater blunder. Despite Bragg's explicit orders alerting him that "it is of vital importance that we should know the positions and movements of Rosecrans," the young cavalryman left only two regiments—five hundred men—to watch ninety miles of river.[5] The remainder of his corps retired far to the rear for a month of rest and relaxation.[6]

On August 21, to the Confederates' complete surprise, Federals from Colonel Wilder's command appeared on the north bank of the Tennessee opposite Chattanooga and proceeded to shell the town. The damage was minor, though one small steamer was sunk at the city wharf, but panic ensued. "Our pickets and scouts had given no notice of the approach of the enemy," angrily noted Confederate lieutenant general D. H. Hill, only recently assigned to Bragg's army.[7] The attack was an especially ill omen because the twenty-first, a Friday, had been declared a day of fasting and prayer by the Confederate government in response to the disasters of the summer: the surprise Yankee intrusion seemed only to further confirm that defeat was in the wind.

Rosecrans let his deception work on Bragg's nerves for a full week. Then on August 29, Union infantry began crossing the Tennessee downstream from Chattanooga. Again, the surprise was complete. The handful of horsemen Wheeler left on the river were scattered or captured within hours of the crossing. Confederate signalers on Lookout Mountain did spot the movement, but when their report reached headquarters, the Federal effort was dismissed as "a feint."[8] Belatedly, Bragg ordered Wheeler to bring his whole corps forward to reinforce the inadequate screen, but even his orders reflected his bias toward the Knoxville approach: he ordered the cavalryman to send Wharton's Division to reinforce Forrest, not to watch the downstream crossings.

Bragg was completely fooled by Rosecrans's game. On August 22 Buckner reported that the Federal advance on Knoxville had also commenced. Bragg still expected Rosecrans to stay within supporting distance of Burnside's army, But Forrest and Hill were certain that the main Federal crossing north of Chattanooga would begin at any moment. For five days, the Confederates collectively deceived themselves into thinking that the downstream crossings were a distraction. During that time, Rosecrans moved 50,000 men across the river and established himself irrevocably on the south bank. Finally, on September 2 Bragg at last grasped that the threat from the south was real and informed Richmond of that fact.[9] Yet in a sharply worded order to Wheeler, he also revealed how much he still did not know. Bragg's chief of staff, W. W. Mackall, wrote to Wheeler that afternoon: "Dear General: I am uneasy about the state of affairs. It is so vitally important that the General [Bragg] should have full and correct information. One misstep in the movement of this army would possibly be fatal. Your line of pickets now occupy on Lookout Mountain about the same advantages they possessed on the river or Sand Mountain. The passage at Caperton's Ferry [Stevenson] broke the line and a week has passed and we don't know whether or not an army has passed."[10]

In fact, an army had passed. But in yet another bad decision, more days were lost while the Confederates dithered about a risky move of their own. On September 3 Bragg discussed sending much of his army north of the river to crush those Federals busy opposite Chattanooga. He was under the impression that this force was both more significant and more vulnerable than it was. As late as 10:00 A.M. on September 4, Bragg informed Hill, "there is no doubt of the enemy's position now; one corps opposite you."[11] Based on Forrest's reports, the commander believed that the Union corps in question was Major General Thomas L. Crittenden's, numbering roughly 16,000 men.

Forrest must bear the lion's share of the blame for Bragg's misconceptions concerning Rosecrans's diversion. In reality, the four Union brigades demonstrating along the north bank of the Tennessee River numbered less than 7,000 men, a force far too nimble to be easily overcome by a surprise Confederate offensive. Forrest's responsibilities had grown by September 3, giving him substantially larger forces with which to perform his mission. On that date he was formally appointed to corps command and assigned Brigadier General John Pegram's cavalry division (from Buckner's corps) as well as his own, now led by Brigadier General Frank Armstrong.[12] Forrest, who by now should have been reporting that the force threatening Chattanooga was nothing more than a diversion, enthusiastically embraced the idea of an attack and promised Bragg that his cavalry could find sufficient fords across the Tennessee to ensure Hill's infantry a rapid crossing.[13]

This scheme was derailed by a series of increasingly disconcerting reports now filtering into Bragg's headquarters. Instead of moving directly on Chattanooga, Federal troops were apparently striking deep into North Georgia. On September 6 a report arrived confirming earlier rumors of the presence of Federals in large numbers at a place called Valley Head, in Will's Valley, just over the Alabama line forty miles southwest of Chattanooga.[14] From there the Yankees could push on over Lookout Mountain and then make for Bragg's rail connection to Atlanta. Worse yet, the news was already stale: the XX Corps had, in fact, reached Valley Head four days previously, on September 2.

With this news, Bragg understood that he would have to abandon Chattanooga immediately. Wheeler had failed him and had even refused a direct order to uncover Union strength and intentions in Will's Valley.[15] Forrest had also failed him by suggesting that a Union corps might be vulnerable opposite Chattanooga when in fact had the Confederates attempted to strike that force, they would have been chasing an illusion and placing themselves in far greater danger. Unquestionably, Bragg had been outmaneuvered, and by September 8, the Confederates evacuated the city. The next day Union troops moved in. On the face of it, Rosecrans had won another bloodless victory.

Bragg had no intention of simply retreating to the next defensible point, though. He could not afford to replicate the disaster of the loss of Middle Tennessee. Instead, he was determined to march south, concentrate all his troops at La Fayette, Georgia, and strike back. Rosecrans's various columns were widely separated, and in that separation lay an opportunity for the Confederates. Additionally, Bragg's mood was buoyed by the knowledge that reinforcements were headed to him from all over the South. In addition to Buckner's troops, two divisions of infantry were en route from Mississippi, some of whom having already arrived. Even better, another two divisions were coming from Virginia. On September 9 Lieutenant General James Longstreet and two-thirds of his famed First Corps, Army of Northern Virginia, began boarding trains for the long trip west.[16]

Rosecrans, made ebullient by his own success, now began to look far beyond Chattanooga—Atlanta might be within reach if Bragg could be kept on the run. Recalling that moment later in 1866, Brigadier General William B. Hazen sarcastically noted that Rosecrans "expected to drive Bragg into the sea."[17] Others, including Major General George Thomas, were not so sure. Thomas understood as well as Bragg that the scattered Union columns were vulnerable to piecemeal destruction and counseled caution.

The next few days saw Bragg struggle to spring the trap on at least one of those Union columns. Once again, however, he needed the cavalry to provide a clear picture of Federal moves. Forrest was assigned a dual role. His troops would cover the retreat from Chattanooga, but Forrest was also to take Dibrell's Brigade "and such other cavalry as he may deem necessary" and precede the infantry to La Fayette, there to link up with Wheeler.[18] En route Bragg, frustrated with Wheeler's balkiness, ordered Forrest even farther south to Summerville to perform the much desired reconnaissance into Will's Valley. By September 8 the Tennessean was preparing to lead nine hundred men handpicked from Dibrell's Brigade on that mission. Interestingly enough, despite his earlier protestations, once alerted to Forrest's new mission, Wheeler prepared to support the move with three hundred of his own men from Wharton's Division.[19]

Forrest might now command a corps, but it was still a very new organization and not without problems. Pegram's Division included two brigades, his own and one commanded by Colonel John S. Scott. Unfortunately, they did not get along. The previous spring Pegram had court-martialed Scott for insubordination only to see him reinstated with what amounted to a mere slap on the wrist. Thereafter the men held independent commands until Scott was again subordinated to Pegram in August. Relations between the two remained awkward. In addition, Pegram's elevation to divisional command necessitated a new brigade commander. For whatever reason, instead of choosing the ranking colonel among Pegram's regiments for the duty, Colonel Henry B. Davidson—a former staff officer of Buckner's—was tapped for the promotion. Unfortunately, Davidson was currently commanding the post at Staunton, Virginia, and it would take him several weeks to reach the army. In the meantime, Pegram chose to continue as de-facto brigade commander in addition to his new responsibilities.

In response to Bragg's September 6 order, Forrest took not only Dibrell but also Armstrong's whole division, leaving Pegram and Scott to handle rearguard duties. This proved to be a mistake. Federal infantry from Crittenden's XXI Corps, led by Wilder's Brigade, pressed Pegram heavily. In response, late on September 8 Bragg recalled Forrest. The cavalry commander reacted promptly, reporting to the general late that night while Armstrong's cavalry returned to La Fayette. The past twenty-four hours had already been exhausting for both Forrest and Armstrong's troopers, but Bragg had no time to give them an extended rest. When the general arrived at Lee and Gordon's Mill, Bragg immediately ordered him "to repair northward [and] ascertain definitely the movements of the enemy in the direction of Chattanooga."[20] Dutifully, Forrest rode east to Dalton, Georgia, while Armstrong's men rode due north to Lee and Gordon's Mill.

By sending Forrest south, Bragg blundered badly. Wheeler's cavalry should have been more than adequate to protect the move to La Fayette, and they were already in place. Nor should Bragg have tolerated Wheeler's continued insubordination concerning Will's Valley. Instead of insisting that Wheeler obey orders (or relieving him on the spot), Bragg condoned his actions by ordering Forrest's men to do the job instead. Before that could happen, however, problems on Pegram's front induced the army commander to immediately recall Forrest. This dithering committed Armstrong's men to two forced marches in as many days without accomplishing a thing.

One reason Bragg was so concerned about the threat from the north was that Crittenden's Federals were headed for Ringgold, the Army of Tennessee's railhead on the Western and Atlantic. The supplies the army needed to survive all had to arrive at Ringgold, as along with all the reinforcements now headed for northern Georgia. If Bragg hoped to defeat Rosecrans before the Federals concentrated, he would need that rail depot.

Between September 10 and 12, Forrest's corps fought an extended series of skirmishes, meeting with only mixed success. Scott's Brigade stopped a Union probe at Graysville on September 10 but could not stop Wilder's Federals from temporarily capturing Ringgold or driving the rebels as far south as Tunnel Hill on the eleventh. There, Forrest suffered yet another combat wound when he led a patrol into Union lines late that evening. One of his aides was captured, and the general was shot while riding away. Apparently, he suffered only a minor injury, but he could have very easily been killed.[21] Forrest often undertook the risks of personal reconnaissance, but now, with his increased responsibilities, his loss would have larger consequences, shattering the corps' command chain at a crucial moment in the campaign. The patrol could have been led by a captain; there was no need for the general to go himself.

In the meantime, Armstrong's men guarded the La Fayette Road. Running southeast from Chattanooga to Rossville and then turning due south to La Fayette, it was the main route the rebel army had used in evacuating Chattanooga. Bragg shifted his headquarters to La Fayette in response to information brought to him by William T. Martin of Wheeler's command: a Union force had entered McLemore's Cove, a mountain valley due west of La Fayette, and might be vulnerable to exactly the kind of piecemeal destruction Bragg envisioned.

McLemore's Cove is one of the more famous missed opportunities of the Army of Tennessee; often recounted, there is no need to do so in detail again here. Two divisions of the Union XIV Corps—11,000 men—escaped destruction by more than twice their number of Confederates due to timidity, even insubordination, on the part of the rebel commanders tasked to lead the attack. By September 12, the opportunity was gone, the Federals having realized their danger and retreated, much to Bragg's fury.

Hard on the heels of that failure, however, Bragg determined to strike at the XXI Corps, which he believed was equally scattered between Ringgold, Rossville, and Lee and Gordon's Mill. As early as September 10, Forrest tried to report this vulnerability to Bragg but missed the army commander late that night, having already departed for La Fayette.[22] Additional reports from Forrest (relayed from Pegram) still identified the Federals as badly scattered, however, and vulnerable to attack.[23] In response, Bragg ordered his army back north, directing Lieutenant General Leonidas Polk to waste no time in striking the enemy.

In fact, by the twelfth, this opportunity was also gone. Pegram's and Forrest's reports were out of date by at least twenty-four hours. By then, the XXI Corps was already concentrated at Lee and Gordon's Mill, holding a strong position on the west bank of West Chickamauga Creek. Polk was, in fact, outnumbered. Despite Bragg's repeated prodding, Polk, who had a better grasp of the situation, wisely eschewed blundering into a foolish assault. Bragg belatedly came to realize this fact when he arrived on the thirteenth, though he still felt Polk's slowness had cost the rebels yet another spectacular chance to damage a Federal column. In fact, Crittenden's men were reunited and strongly posted even before Bragg issued his first attack order. The one bright spot was that the Ringgold depot was now back in Confederate hands and much more strongly garrisoned now by some of the newly arriving units.

For a week, Bragg's men had been marching and countermarching, all to no avail. The army needed rest and resupply, and the general needed new ideas. On September 14, as most of the Army of Tennessee returned to La Fayette, Bragg contemplated his next move. The rebels had failed to capitalize on any of the opportunities handed them so far; would the next phase of the campaign be any different?

While the army rested and drew three days' rations, Bragg planned. Rosecrans's left flank was positioned at Lee and Gordon's Mill. The distance between the mill and Chattanooga was twelve miles, and only 6,000 men of three brigades from Major General Gordon Granger's Reserve Corps defended that interval. Granger's troops occupied Rossville, blocking the gap of that name, but could not effectively defend the entire twelve miles of open road. Bragg's obvious solution was to move north, interpose his army between Rosecrans and the defenses of Chattanooga, and drive the Federals south into McLemore's Cove. Additionally, with reinforcements detraining at Ringgold, rebel troops needed to make only an eight-mile march due west to reach and cut the La Fayette Road, Rosecrans's principal route into Chattanooga. Bragg initially planned to move on September 17 but chose to delay an additional day in order to allow more of Longstreet's men to arrive.[24]

Of necessity, Forrest would play a key role in this plan. His cavalrymen were already on Bragg's northern flank, screening the region between Ringgold and Lee and Gordon's Mill. Their task would be to lead the three Confederate infantry corps—21,000 men—which Bragg intended to interpose across the Federal line of retreat. The largest potential obstacle to this movement was West Chickamauga Creek, which flowed generally south to north between the two armies—its limited crossings could bottleneck the advancing rebel columns. In order to ensure a safe passage, Bragg specifically ordered Forrest to seize "Reed's Bridge, Bryam's Ford, Alexander's Bridge, and the fords next above" in anticipation of using those crossing in the next few days.[25]

Affairs did not go as smoothly as Bragg envisioned. On September 17 Granger unexpectedly sent a column from Rossville to Ringgold, their mission one of reconnaissance and harassment. Scott's Brigade, nominally picketing the latter town and its approaches, missed the movement, and the first the rebels knew of any Union presence was when Yankee artillery began lobbing shells into a confused mass of troops and teamsters at the depot.[26] They did no lasting damage and eventually withdrew in good order, but Scott's cavalry had failed badly. As a result, when the main movement began the next day, Forrest detailed Scott's entire brigade to move west along the Old Federal Road and prevent any reoccurrence, which of course subtracted these troopers from any effort to seize the crossings.

Worse yet, Forrest did not have his best troops readily at hand. Armstrong's two brigades continued to support Polk's infantry, in fact were screening Polk's left (southern) flank along the Chickamauga near Glass's Mill when Bragg issued his latest movement orders. Forrest needed Armstrong, who should have been up in time to help execute the new plan. Joe Wheeler's continued insubordination, however, prevented Armstrong from arriving.

The overall cavalry mission was clear: Wheeler's men continued to have charge of the rebel left, while Forrest's held the right. With the main body at La Fayette, this placed Wheeler still watching the approaches from Alpine. Once Bragg decided to shift the army's center of gravity northward, however, Wheeler's men should have come north as well. They did not. On September 17 Hill's Corps took over defenses near Glass's Mill, formerly in Polk's sector, as the latter's command shifted north. Armstrong also left at this time, only to be called back hastily by a near-panicky Hill, who discovered that the bridge at Glass's Mill was now unprotected and feared a Union attack. Armstrong grudgingly returned but sent messages to Wheeler to hurry forward and replace him. Wheeler, amazingly enough, declined. On September 18, when he should have been with Forrest leading Bragg's newest offensive, Armstrong was still cooling his heels on Hill's front; in frustration he finally dashed off an angry dispatch to army headquarters: "My brigade is not needed [at Glass's Mill], whilst one of Wheeler's divisions is lying one mile west of [Dr.] Anderson's [house] doing nothing."[27] Armstrong was right to be frustrated since the division he was complaining about—Wharton's command—was less than two miles away at the time this communiqué was sent. It would be another full day before Armstrong's men were relieved. Instead of having more than 7,000 men in two full divisions, Forrest was reduced to one brigade—Davidson's, still led by Pegram—and a small detachment of John Hunt Morgan's survivors with which to lead the various infantry columns: in all, less than 2,000 troopers.[28]

While Armstrong's absence was beyond his control, Forrest compounded his problems through faulty disposition of his remaining men. Bragg's plans called for a column under Brigadier General Bushrod Johnson (to be supplanted by Major General John Bell Hood once that officer arrived on the scene) to depart Ringgold and march to Reed's Bridge; Major General William H. T. Walker's Reserve Corps to move on

Alexander's Bridge; and Buckner's Corps to cross at Dalton's and Thedford's Fords. The whole advance was to begin at dawn, and each column
was supposed to be screened by Forrest's cavalry.

In keeping with the finest traditions of the Army of Tennessee, the
movement was late, confused, and poorly executed. To start with, Forrest
spent the night at Dalton, far from any of the forces intended to begin
this offensive, and did not reach Johnson's column until 11:00 A.M. on
September 18. This delay probably mattered little, for Johnson himself
had never gotten the latest set of orders from Bragg and started out on
the wrong road, following an earlier version of the plan. An aide discovered the error and rerouted the column, which then had to countermarch
several miles before even nearing Reed's Bridge late that morning. There
Johnson ran into Minty's Union cavalry, which had been alert for just
such an advance for the past three days.[29]

Walker and Buckner at least had Pegram at hand, but all three commands had to use the same road for part of their approach and thus
were delayed. Moreover, Pegram was of little use. As the infantry neared
Alexander's Bridge at noon, the cavalryman informed Walker that the
bridge was held by Yankees, though he could not say how many. Then
Pegram's men watched as one of the infantry brigades assaulted the
bridge at about 1:00 P.M., only to be repulsed by rapid fire from the
Spencer repeating rifles of John Wilder's Lightning Brigade.[30] Finally,
after several hours of fruitless combat, Walker's men moved downstream
and crossed at Bryam's Ford, eventually outflanking Wilder's stubborn
Federals. Buckner's troops faced little opposition, but since their orders
were to cross only after Walker and Johnson were firmly established on
the west bank, they accomplished almost nothing. Only two of Buckner's
six brigades even ventured across their fords by nightfall.

In the meantime, Forrest had ordered Pegram away to help at Reed's
Bridge. The timing of that order is unclear, but these men again contributed nothing to an ongoing fight: they only arrived at Reed's Bridge
late that afternoon, after the action there had concluded.[31] Johnson
forced a crossing without them in a combat that lasted several hours.
Pegram's Brigade was not involved in either affair. By nightfall, Bragg's
plans were in tatters. The infantry columns barely managed to cross the
Chickamauga, let alone cut the La Fayette Road, the intended objective.

These delays cost Bragg an entire day. Rosecrans was now alert to the
threat to his north and, more importantly, had been given time to react
to it. While Forrest was hardly solely responsible for all the problems,

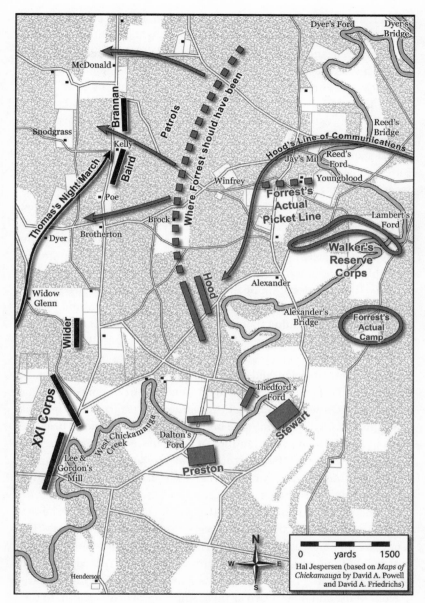

Dyer's Ford
Dyer's Bridge

McDonald

Brannan
Patrols
Where Forrest should have been
Reed's Bridge

Snodgrass

Kelly
Hood's Line of Communications
Jay's Mill
Reed's Ford

Baird
Thomas's Night March
Winfrey
Youngblood
Forrest's Actual Picket Line

Poe

Brock
Lambert's Ford

Dyer
Brotherton
Walker's Reserve Corps

Hood
Alexander

Widow Glenn

Wilder
Alexander's Bridge
Forrest's Actual Camp

XXI Corps

Thedford's Ford

West Chickamauga Creek
Dalton's Ford
Stewart

Lee & Gordon's Mill
Preston

0   yards   1500

N
W   E
S

Hal Jespersen (based on *Maps of Chickamauga* by David A. Powell and David A. Friedrichs)

Henderson

Night of September 18, 1863.

he did fail to execute the tasks he was assigned. He was personally conspicuous in the afternoon phase of the Reed's Bridge fighting, including
conducting a dramatic personal reconnaissance under fire across Reed's
Bridge, but only a handful of his men saw action on September 18.[32]

That night Forrest was responsible for picketing the army's right
flank. Johnson's column, now reinforced and commanded by Hood,
moved southwest toward Lee and Gordon's Mill, halting short of that
destination at about 9:00 P.M., when they encountered Union troops.
After a short firefight in the dark, both sides settled into an uneasy quiet.
Both the Alexander's Bridge and Reed's Bridge Roads offered any lurking
Federals access to Hood's flank and rear and were obvious candidates
for picketing. Instead, however, Forrest withdrew Pegram's men back
across Alexander's Bridge to camp on the east bank of Chickamauga
Creek, behind Hood's and Walker's columns.[33] The 1st Georgia Cavalry
did establish a picket line that night, though about four hundred yards
south of Jay's Mill, well short of Reed's Bridge.[34]

When two brigades of Union infantry ventured down the Reed's Bridge
Road at dusk, belatedly ordered to support Minty, they found only an
eerie silence. Establishing their own pickets to interdict the road, these
Yankees captured a number of Confederates belonging to Brigadier
General Matthew D. Ector's Brigade, including most of the field-hospital
staff and band (musicians did double duty as an ambulance corps) and at
least one staff officer.[35] Later that night—perhaps in response to rumors
of this capture—Pegram personally led a reconnaissance party up Reed's
Bridge Road and directly into the middle of these two Federal brigades.
Upon inquiring about the identities of these unknown commands, the
general was informed that he stood between regiments of Ohio and Illinois troops, and he quietly bluffed his way back out of trouble.[36] Pegram
then returned to his camps on the far side of Alexander's Bridge.

Colonel Scott earned no laurels that night either. After dark he took
his entire brigade south to join Forrest's command in an unauthorized
departure that once again left the main road to Ringgold completely unguarded. William Sloan of the 5th Tennessee Cavalry recorded, "we left
our position at Red House Bridge this morning as no enemy appeared
in front of us, and moved two or three miles up the river south, to Gen.
Forrest's head quarters."[37] Forrest would promptly order the colonel to
retrace his steps, but the decision reflects poorly on Scott's judgment.

It is clear that Forrest's command neglected elementary cavalry duties
on the night of the eighteenth. They established only a cursory skirmish

line that failed to cover Hood's rear, allowing Federal infantry access to the critical Reed's Bridge crossing. Where Forrest stumbled most significantly, however, was in failing to conduct any more-wide-ranging reconnaissance. The single-most-important Federal movement conducted that night went completely undetected by any rebels.

As the fighting that day drew to a close, Rosecrans was left with a clear understanding that significant rebel forces had crossed the creek below him and were now poised to strike at his left flank. In response, he decided to send George Thomas and two divisions of the XIV Corps on a night march, leapfrogging the lines of the XXI Corps at Lee and Gordon's Mill to reach the La Fayette Road near the Kelly Farm, about halfway between the mill and Rossville. These two divisions, numbering 11,000 men and six batteries of artillery, marched through the night to arrive at dawn. The rest of the corps were to follow, and when reunited, Thomas would have 20,000 men with which to hold open the way to Chattanooga. Instead of outflanking the Federals, the Confederates were themselves flanked.[38]

Thomas's redeployment radically altered the nature of the impending battle. As September 19 dawned, Bragg had no idea of what the Federals had done, but he at least was aware of what he did not know: what Federal force, if any, was looming to the northwest and who had interfered with Hood's rear echelon. Accordingly, he ordered Forrest to "move . . . down the road towards Reed's Bridge and develop the enemy, which," Forrest reported, "was promptly done."[39] Within a short time, the 1,900 men of Pegram's Brigade (now Davidson's, as that officer had arrived to assume command sometime during the morning of the nineteenth) were locked in a bloody, dismounted slugfest with 2,000 men from Union brigadier general John T. Croxton's brigade. The remaining two brigades of Brigadier General John M. Brannan's Third Division, XIV Corps were right behind Croxton. By 8:00 A.M. both sides were fully engaged, and the battle was on.

In general, accounts of Forrest's actions on the nineteenth tend to be laudatory, if somewhat fragmented. As the fight developed, the general called on brigades from Walker's Corps for support, sending them directly into action as they came up. In turn, the Federals called on their reserves, and the battle quickly escalated, with the Yankees holding the advantage. Even the arrival of Dibrell's Brigade from Armstrong's command, finally replaced by Wheeler's tardy troops, failed to redress the numerical imbalance, and the Confederates suffered severely. Colonel

Claudius C. Wilson's rebel infantry brigade achieved some initial tactical success against Croxton but was soon overmatched; Ector's regiments, when they came up, were also severely mauled. Losses in both brigades approached 50 percent.[40] Engaging two full divisions of Federal infantry, they really had little chance to prevail.

Having found the enemy, Forrest should have simply screened the Federal advance and reported the details to Bragg. Instead, he chose to precipitate a major battle with the odds stacked badly against him. His job was to gather information, not assault an enemy corps. Moreover, his unwillingness to wait and use the infantry in a coordinated fashion only made matters worse; brigades were flung into action piecemeal, against superior numbers, and lost heavily in the ensuing attacks. September 19 represents the largest force Forrest had yet commanded in combat, four brigades with a combined strength of nearly 6,000 men, but his execution was flawed.

One story, often repeated, concerns Ector's Brigade. As Ector advanced he dispatched Captain C. B. "Buck" Kilgore to find Forrest and ask the cavalryman to watch his right flank. "I'll take care of it" the general replied.[41] In due course, Dibrell's men came up and formed on the infantry's right.[42] In the meantime, Ector launched two attacks, both repulsed, against Colonel Ferdinand Van Derveer's Union brigade astride Reed's Bridge Road. During that second attack, Ector realized that his left was completely exposed, so he sent Kilgore back to find Forrest again. The aide found him at the same spot, near Captain Gustave Huwald's battery. General Ector was "uneasy about his left flank," Kilgore relayed; Forrest, never a patient man, became "furious. He turned around on me," the captain marveled, "and shouted, loud enough to be heard above the terrible din . . . , 'Tell General Ector that, by God, I am here, and will take care of his left flank as well as his right!' It is hardly necessary," concluded Kilgore, "to add that we were not outflanked on either side."[43]

This story, first published in 1908, has been related faithfully in almost every Forrest biography since. Yet those accounts fail to note that Kilgore, his memory clouded by either time or admiration for the great man, was mistaken. Ector was about to be badly mauled. Another Union infantry brigade came up immediately on his left, subjecting the rebels to a telling crossfire and routing the brigade. "[We] found [we] were flanked on the left & commenced falling back in confusion," wrote Private C. B. Carlton of the 10th Texas. "The boys were scattered pretty badly," he admitted, and when Ector ordered the brigade to march by the right flank, the confusion only increased.[44] Of the 1,199 men in Ector's ranks, 527 were killed, wounded, or missing after the morning fight.

There were larger ramifications to Forrest's combative decision as well. The fighting to the north completely derailed Bragg's attack plan, and the battle deteriorated into a confused, day-long slugging match as both sides fed troops into the action piecemeal, reacting to circumstances. Forrest's men were engaged again in the early afternoon, with Dibrell's troopers doing credible service as skirmishers alongside Major General Benjamin F. Cheatham's infantry, but neither side could claim substantial results at day's end.

On Sunday, September 20, Bragg planned to recover the initiative. He still intended to drive the Federals south, away from Chattanooga, and ordered a dawn assault. In addition, in order to simplify his command arrangements, he reorganized his army's structure. For most of its existence, the Army of Tennessee had two infantry corps. By September 1863, with all the reinforcements, Bragg had no less than five infantry and two cavalry corps, far too many for effective supervision. With James Longstreet arriving that night, however, he had the means to reduce his command burden considerably. Bragg therefore chose to reorganize the army into two wings, led by Lieutenant Generals Longstreet and Polk.

Bragg's attack plan was essentially a reiteration of the previous day: strike in the north; sweep the Federals south, away from Chattanooga; drive them back into the mountains. Because his troops were already in place on the right, Polk would initiate the attack. Longstreet would take charge of the forces on the left and strike when Polk had started driving the Federals across his front. The effort would begin at first light. Given the displeasure he already felt with Polk for his failure to attack on September 12 and 13, Bragg seems to have made his decisions about where to strike first based on necessity rather than preference, though Bragg had little choice in assigning the mission to his senior subordinate.

What followed was one of the more famous command miscues of the war. Hill's Corps, newly assigned to Polk, would lead the attack because his troops were fresh, having seen little or no combat on the nineteenth. Polk sent orders to Hill, which never arrived. Hill looked for the general's camp but never found it. Bragg awoke before dawn, expecting an assault that never materialized.[45]

Forrest was also up before dawn, sending forward cavalry probes to explore the Union positions on the north end of the field. During the night, his corps had been reunited, with the arrival of the rest of

Armstrong's Division, and now the general deployed Armstrong's men
on the army's right flank. Pegram's brigades remained separated; Scott
continued his mission at Red House Bridge, while Davidson's Brigade
served as a reserve, given their mauling of the day before. In the predawn
light the 11th Tennessee Cavalry patrolled westward, crossing the La
Fayette Road near the McDonald House. They found no formed troops,
just a scattering of demoralized Yankee stragglers.[46] Bragg's line still
overlapped Rosecrans's front.

George Thomas was aware of the problem—thinking of almost nothing else, in fact. As early as 2:00 A.M., he sent word back to Rosecrans,
alerting the army commander to this exposed flank and requesting reinforcements to shore it up.[47] Specifically, Thomas wanted Major General
James S. Negley's Second Division, XIV Corps returned to him for the
purpose. In the chaos of the fighting on the nineteenth, Negley had been
fed into the fight elsewhere and never reached Thomas; now the general
wanted to reunite his corps. Rosecrans agreed and, after a brief morning
survey, at 6:35 A.M. ordered Negley out of line to move north and extend
the Union flank. Unfortunately for Rosecrans, not only did this order
have serious repercussions later in the day but also, due to command
confusion, Negley was hours late, not even arriving in time to address
Thomas's concerns.[48]

The miscues between Hill and Polk meant that it would be mid-morning before Major General John C. Breckinridge's Division of Hill's Corps
was ready to attack. While these troops were deploying, Forrest led Hill
and Brigadier General Daniel W. Adams (of Breckinridge's Division) forward to examine the Federal positions.[49] They discovered that the Union
flank was vulnerable, defended only by a long line of skirmishers, and
that Breckinridge's troops could easily turn it. The confusion among the
rebel generals might have delayed Bragg's plan, but it had not derailed
it. At 9:30 A.M., with Armstrong's dismounted troopers on their right,
Hill's Corps attacked.

The attack succeeded brilliantly at first, routing one Union brigade,
capturing a field hospital, and wheeling south to strike into Thomas's rear
at Kelly Field. More miscues among the generals, however, meant that
no reserves came up in time to help Breckinridge exploit that success,
and by 11:00 A.M. his regiments were flung back to their starting point
by timely Yankee counterstrokes. The Federals in Kelly Field held, and
a rebel victory would have to come elsewhere.

The near-run thing on Thomas's front created ripples all down the

Union line. Negley's division had already moved north in response to earlier orders, and a little later Thomas sent a courier to another of his divisions, that of John M. Brannan, asking him to come north as well. Now it was the Yankees' turn to blunder. Brannan started to move but halted; the courier, however, rode on to Rosecrans's headquarters with a relayed request to send a force to replace Brannan's brigades. Rosecrans reacted quickly—too quickly—and dashed off an order to Brigadier General Thomas J. Wood, then in line at Brotherton Field, to move his division up and fill in Brannan's gap. There was no gap, but Wood, struck with the urgency of the order, moved anyway. Within minutes of his doing so, disaster struck.

Longstreet had spent the morning getting oriented and visiting his new divisional commanders, all the while expecting the attack to begin at any moment. Finally, he heard the sounds of Hill's assault and watched as brigade after brigade was flung into the attack. Just before 11:00 A.M. he ordered his whole force forward at once. He could not have chosen a better moment, had he but known it. Wood had just moved out, and Longstreet's main assault column was aimed directly at the newly created gap in Rosecrans's line. The result was the rout of roughly one-third of the Union army from the field. Federals rallied on Snodgrass Hill, later memorialized as Horseshoe Ridge, and held out until dark, but the Army of the Cumberland was badly defeated.

Forrest's role in the fighting on the twentieth was laudable, though secondary. His cavalry protected Bragg's right flank aggressively but could not stop Union reinforcements rushing to Thomas's aid. Granger's Reserve Corps was still defending Rossville, and at midday, when disaster struck to the south, Granger decided to go help. For a time, Forrest delayed Brigadier General James B. Steedman's division near Cloud Church, but Granger brooked no delay: "There's nothing in our front now but ragtag, bobtail cavalry," he snarled, and the Yankee infantry pushed south.[50] The cavalry harassed them with long-range artillery but could not stop them, and Steedman's men were instrumental in holding Horseshoe Ridge that afternoon. Forrest did all he could, but infantry were needed to stop Granger, and Polk's entire wing was, for the moment, out of the fight.[51]

That night the entire Union army fell back to Rossville. The rebels, battered by three days of ferocious combat, missed this movement. Despite later protestations by most of the Army of Tennessee's senior leadership that only Bragg's dereliction and pessimism prevented them from initiating a vigorous pursuit, most Confederates, their commanders included, expected to renew the contest at first light. Longstreet, later harshly critical of Bragg for this supposed oversight, declined to meet with him on the morning of the twenty-first because, as he informed the commanding general, he expected to be attacked at any moment.[52] Polk, writing to his wife on September 22, confided that it was 9:00 A.M. before he discovered that the Federals were gone.[53]

On the twenty-first Forrest was again up early. At first light his troopers were probing all along the lines looking for Yankees, with Forrest leading one such patrol personally. One of his most significant contributions to the campaign resulted from this effort. At 7:00 A.M., after a sharp fight with Minty's cavalry that cost Forrest another horse, the rebel commander reached the crest of Missionary Ridge. After climbing down from a nearby tree he used as an observation post, Forrest penned a fateful dispatch to Polk:

> Genl,
>
> We are in a mile of Rossville. Have been on the point of Missionary Ridge can see Chattanooga and everything around. The enemy's trains are leaving going around the point of Lookout Mountain.
>
> The prisoners captured report the pontoon thrown across for the purpose of retreating. I think they are evacuating as hard as they can go. They are cutting timber down to obstruct our passage.
>
> I think we ought to press forward as rapidly as possible.
>
> > N. B. Forrest
> > Brig Gen
>
> Lt Gen L Polk
> Please forward to Gen Bragg.[54]

This dispatch has served as a key piece of evidence for Bragg detractors—both contemporaries and historians—in making the case that he bungled the pursuit after winning Chickamauga. The note, which passed from Polk to Bragg and at some point on to Longstreet, seemingly should have galvanized the Army of Tennessee into action. That it did not has been laid at Bragg's feet as one of the more significant failings of his checkered military career. At first glance it would seem to be an open-and-shut case.

But Forrest was badly mistaken. What he failed to notice was the entire Union army, drawn up in good formation, deployed to block Rossville Gap to his north and to defend Lookout Valley to his west. In the night Thomas had created a new defensive line, stronger than previous ones, and was ready for another attack. Forrest likely saw supply and ambulance trains hurriedly retreating, but his dispatch omitted the most vital information of all: where the Yankee infantry was located.

At 11:30 A.M. the general sent a second dispatch, similarly worded, again urging an immediate pursuit. Again he failed to note the Federal presence at Rossville Gap, despite the fact that Davidson's Brigade had met with a sharp rebuff there that morning while trying to force a passage.[55] In fact, Forrest spent the rest of the day trying to drive off or outflank the enemy, all to no avail. Rossville Gap was Bragg's most direct access through Missionary Ridge toward Chattanooga, but it was heavily defended by entrenched Federals.

There is strong evidence that Forrest's star was waning at army headquarters by this point in the campaign. While Bragg never officially criticized the general, his dispatches were greeted dubiously on September 21. Colonel Taylor Beatty was a military judge and at army headquarters during the battle. His diary recorded the arrival of Forrest's most famous dispatch this way: "Forrest reports enemy have burned Chattanooga & fled—the truth turns out that he has never been within three miles of the place & the enemy are still there—having only burned a few houses which were in the way of the guns."[56] Clearly, Forrest was no longer one of the army's "greatest elements of strength."[57] Bragg might be right to be skeptical, but if so he failed to apply this logic equally: Wheeler's dispatches were still being taken at face value, with bombastic claims of captures in enemy troops and supplies.

For the gray cavalry, the rest of the campaign was essentially anticlimactic. On September 22 Forrest's men followed the Federals across Missionary Ridge as the Army of the Cumberland retreated into the newly strengthened earthworks that turned Chattanooga into an impregnable fort, skirmishing with rearguard elements all the way. Dibrell's men ranged as far as the foot of Lookout Mountain, finally sealing off the road at the base of that precipice on the twenty-third and effectively isolating Rosecrans inside the city. Forrest was again personally involved at the very forefront of the fight. Colonel Daniel W. Holman's 10th Tennessee Cavalry probed Union defenses on Rossville Road. About mid-morning, as Holman and his dismounted troopers were pinned down by Union fire, Forrest and his escort suddenly thundered up, the general demanding to know why the Tennesseans had stopped. Nonplussed, the colonel reported that the enemy were strongly entrenched and too numerous to charge. Forrest retorted that "there must be some mistake in that, and that he believed he could take Chattanooga with [just] his escort."[58]

Then, under the gaze of Holman's stunned troopers, the general led the escort in a reckless mounted charge right up the road. Within minutes, under a hail of Yankee fire, they came tumbling back; Forrest had lost another horse in the attempt, his second in two days.

That afternoon Forrest met Major General Lafayette McLaws, another of Longstreet's divisional commanders from Virginia, who was leading Bragg's infantry toward Chattanooga. Accounts of the encounter differ substantially. Forrest's biographers relate that the cavalryman urged an immediate attack while the Yankees were still demoralized, but McLaws declined to do so because he only had orders to picket the Union line.[59] McLaws, however, wrote that Forrest warned *him* not to attack, noting the rest of the Confederate army was still seven miles away, and McLaws would be "risking the loss of [his] command" if he did so.[60] Of course, Forrest had just rashly attempted to storm Chattanooga with nothing but his own escort company while Colonel Holman looked on in astonishment and been handily repulsed. McLaws's version of the event was likely the more accurate description.

By September 24, Bragg's infantry was coming up to complete the investment. After a day's respite on the twenty-third, Forrest's men were sent north to Harrison, Tennessee, in order to ensure that Burnside's Federals were not approaching from Knoxville to rescue Rosecrans. Bragg also intended the cavalry to slip across the Tennessee and attack what remained of the Federals' tenuous supply lines across Walden Ridge and through the Sequatchie Valley, if possible, and if there were no immediate threat from Burnside. Instead Forrest moved too far north, pressing to within thirty miles of Knoxville, and never did cross the river. His star was fully in decline now. On September 25 Bragg abruptly recalled Forrest and ordered him to send all but two of his brigades to join Wheeler, who was then preparing for the raid Bragg desired.[61] In a fit of anger, he articulated his disgust with Forrest to Brigadier General St. John Liddell when that officer visited the newly situated army headquarters on Missionary Ridge that same day. "I have not a single general officer of cavalry fit for command!" Bragg raged. "Look at Forrest! I sent him with express orders to cross the Tennessee . . . to destroy [the enemy's] provision trains . . . through Sequatchie Valley, and the man instead . . . has allowed himself to be drawn off towards Knoxville on a general *rampage*. . . . [T]he man is ignorant and does not know anything of *cooperation*. He is nothing more than a good raider!"[62]

Forrest protested the September 25 order. On the twenty-eighth Bragg insisted, and his men marched south to join Wheeler.[63] That order ended Forrest's participation in the campaign and effectively ended his service with the Army of Tennessee for more than a year. Soon afterward, Forrest took leave of the army to visit his wife at LaGrange, Georgia, 70 miles southwest of Atlanta and nearly 170 miles from Ringgold.

As denouement to Forrest's time with the army, after Chickamauga he became involved in a series of verbal clashes with Bragg, which escalated into a final confrontation between the two men that has taken on the status of legend. The first incident came on the night of September 21, when at 10:00 P.M. Forrest reported to Bragg. The cavalryman was "deeply chagrinned and depressed in view of the strange delay and inaction" that seemed to grip both Bragg and the army.[64] He conveyed his sentiments in a series of communiqués and at least one face-to-face meeting, though the various accounts of these incidents are sometimes vague and slightly contradictory. In one dispatch Forrest supposedly told Bragg that "every hour was worth a thousand men."[65] In another account he turned to a staff officer and irritably demanded, "what does he fight battles for?"[66] In yet a third Forrest demanded to know why the army had not pursued. Bragg replied that he had no supplies. "We can get all the supplies we want in Chattanooga," snapped the cavalryman.[67] All three of these versions are partisan to Forrest, and none note the presence of the intact Federal army barring the way.

The next confrontation began with a written complaint and ended verbally. It came when Forrest received the September 25 order—repeated on the twenty-eighth—attaching his men to Wheeler. He dictated a blistering reply to Bragg. Major Charles W. Anderson, the officer who took down Forrest's words, later recalled that among other things, the dispatch charged the commanding general with "duplicity and lying." Upon signing it, Forrest, grimly satisfied, said, "Bragg never got such a letter as that before from a brigadier."[68] He followed this insubordinate dispatch with a personal visit on or about September 30. Then, Bragg defused Forrest's anger by reassuring him that his men were only temporarily attached to Wheeler and his command would be restored to him when the raiders returned.[69] With that, Forrest departed on leave.

This promise was an odd one, given Bragg's growing dissatisfaction with Forrest (as expressed previously) and a false one to boot. On October 3 the general issued a new order giving Wheeler sole authority over

all cavalry in the Army of Tennessee, including Forrest.[70] He had not precisely broken his word—Forrest's command would be reinstated—but by
placing Wheeler over Forrest, Bragg had certainly shattered the latter's
understanding of how things would be. Forrest received it at LaGrange
on October 5 and immediately reacted.

The final and most famous confrontation between Forrest and Bragg
is also the hardest to substantiate. The only witness was Dr. James B.
Cowan, Forrest's chief surgeon. Cowan had been supervising the general's field hospital near Alexander's Bridge and had just finished his
work there. He notified Forrest that he was available for further orders
and was directed to join the commander at Ringgold. From there the
two men traveled to army headquarters on Missionary Ridge. Cowan's
account has Forrest storming into Bragg's headquarters, ignoring the
general's attempted courtesy, and embarking on an extensive, rage-filled
diatribe that accused Bragg of cowardice, of unceasing persecution, and
of continually robbing Forrest of commands he painstakingly recruited
and equipped from scratch. The vitriol ended with Forrest shouting:
"You have played the part of a damned scoundrel, and are a coward, and
if you were any part of a man I would slap your jaws and force you to
resent it. You may as well not issue any more orders to me, for I will not
obey them, and I will hold you personally responsible for any further
indignities you endeavor to inflict upon me. You have threatened to arrest me for not obeying your orders promptly. I dare you to do it, and I
say to you that if you ever again try to interfere with me or try and cross
my path it will be at the peril of your life."[71] According to Cowan, Bragg
was stunned into silence. Upon leaving, the doctor expected that Forrest
would be arrested immediately, but the general dismissed this thought.
Bragg would never mention this encounter.

There are a number of problems with this account, dramatic as it is.
First, there is the timing. Dr. Cowan's dramatic rendition of the incident
first appeared in 1899 in John A. Wyeth's biography of the general. Cowan
did not provide a specific date for the affair, but as presented the context
suggests it happened at the end of September, just a day or two after Forrest's angry letter responding to Bragg's orders of September 25 and 28;
the general had returned from East Tennessee but had not yet departed
on leave. In 1909 Captain John Morton was more precise: He also used
Cowan's account, unambiguously stating that the affair took place on September 30, again before Forrest's leave.[72] In their 1868 publication, Forrest's earliest biographers, Thomas Jordan and J. P. Pryor, do not men-

tion the confrontation at all. While they do describe both Forrest's letter and his meeting with Bragg at the end of September, this meeting did not end in confrontation. Instead, as noted previously, Bragg reassured Forrest that his command would be returned upon completion of Wheeler's raid. "With this understanding" Forrest applied for his ten-day leave to visit his wife. The final break did not come until the general received the October 3 order two days later, but instead of a launching personal verbal assault, Jordan and Pryor have Forrest writing a letter of resignation.[73]

Modern biographers have resolved the discrepancy by moving the confrontation to sometime after October 5. Robert Selph Henry, in his 1944 biography, surmises that the final blowup had to occur after October 5 but before Jefferson Davis arrived to visit the army on the ninth.[74] Authors writing in 1990, 1992, 1993, and 2007 all use Dr. Cowan's account, but all place the incident after October 5 without noting the timing problems.[75]

Unfortunately, advancing the date merely creates other problems. On October 5 Forrest was at LaGrange, 170 miles distant. Given the state of the Confederate rail system in 1863, returning to Ringgold was not likely to be a casual trip. It would have required a day, maybe two, to reach Bragg just to insult him. Henry times the conflict before the president's arrival on the ninth, but Jordan and Pryor note that Forrest's letter of resignation did not reach Bragg until after Davis was present. Cowan's account insists that Forrest never wrote a resignation letter because he did not want to appear to be trying to move beyond Bragg's reach if any punishment ensued. Yet the record seems clear that Davis, once advised of Forrest's intended resignation, intervened.[76]

The manner of the president's intervention further disrupts the timing. Davis wrote to Forrest, asking the cavalryman to join him in Montgomery, Alabama. The president left the army for that place on October 14, so this letter had to have been sent between October 9 and 14. If Forrest was with the army during this time, why did Davis ask to meet him in Montgomery? The request only makes sense if Forrest was already at LaGrange, southwest of Atlanta. The two men did meet, and Davis agreed to the general's request from August 1863 to transfer to northern Mississippi. He could take only a handful of men with him, though: his own escort, Morton's Battery, and McDonald's Tennessee Cavalry Battalion, 300 men total. Forrest would have authority to raise a new command in Mississippi.[77] Bragg signed off on this request on October 13 while Davis was still with the army, and doubtless at the president's urging.

With the exception of Jordan and Pryor, none of Forrest's many biographers successfully resolve the issue of timing. Only Judith Lee Hallock, in her 1991 biography of Bragg, notes the problem.[78] Jordan and Pryor, of course, never raise this issue because in their account, Forrest's verbal assault on Bragg never happened.

There are other problems as well. Bragg was not a moral or physical coward. The idea that he would simply accept such gross insubordination from Forrest defies belief, especially since he was deeply embroiled in charge and countercharge with many of his subordinates at this time. For example, he relieved General Polk, a close personal friend and confidante of President Davis, for disobedience of orders in failing to launch a timely attack on September 20. If Bragg was willing to risk open confrontation with such a senior and politically well-connected general, why would he ignore Forrest's overt insubordination? Cowan's account suggests that it was because due to fear, but that explanation makes no sense in light of the rest of Bragg's military career.

It is also important to note that Cowan is the only source for this highly charged and vitriolic confrontation and that he only first described the incident to John Wyeth in 1899, nearly forty years after the fact. He repeated it to John Harvey Mathes in 1902 and again for John Morton in 1909.[79] By then, both Bragg and Forrest were long dead. Cowan was active in veterans affairs long before Wyeth's book appeared, and in fact he was president of the Forrest Escort and Staff Reunion Association for a number of years beginning in the 1870s. Why he waited so long to present this story is a mystery. Why not sooner? Perhaps because the more survivors around, the more likely it was to be refuted or challenged. Interestingly enough, Morton alludes to just that sort of challenge in his own book: "Some discussion has arisen lately concerning General Forrest's use of such language and General Bragg's submitting to it." He goes on to add that Major M. H. Clift (probably Moses H. Clift, commissary for the 3rd Tennessee Cavalry) informed Morton that "the General [Forrest] told him the facts were about as he had heard" but offered no detailed account of his own.[80] By 1909, however, memories were growing dim and the Forrest myth was firmly established.

Forrest was a man unready for command of a cavalry corps in 1863, a year critical to Confederate fortunes. The Army of Tennessee's problems were much larger than him, of course, and started with Bragg, but Forrest did not shine in the role he was given. Too much bad intelligence was passed to army headquarters, and too often Forrest's horsemen

were caught by surprise. The general was fooled by the Union deception effort north of Chattanooga early in the campaign. In addition, he
proved unable to delegate or supervise his new subordinates effectively,
which led to a number of problems. Pegram was not a capable division
commander. Forrest was too often content to let Pegram command his
own brigade, leaving to his own devices Scott, who was manifestly not
a success in brigade command. His decision to take all of Armstrong's
Division and move personally to join Wheeler, for example, was a bad
one, leaving Pegram and Scott to mismanage covering the army's retreat
from Chattanooga on their own. On September 12 bad intelligence from
Forrest's men convinced Bragg that the XXI Corps was still scattered and
vulnerable when in reality it was concentrated in a strong position at Lee
and Gordon's Mill. Bragg blamed Polk for not attacking then, but Polk
made the right call. Scott mismanaged things again on September 17,
allowing a Federal column to surprise the rebels at Ringgold on the very
eve of Bragg's next offensive.

Minty's and Wilder's success at foiling the Confederate advance on
September 18 was again largely at Forrest's expense. Bragg expected
Walker's and Johnson's infantry columns to be properly screened by
cavalry, but Forrest failed to do so. This mistake was compounded when,
on the night of the eighteenth, Pegram's and Scott's men failed to screen
the army's flank and rear: Scott completely abandoned Red House Bridge,
and Pegram failed to detect the arrival of McCook's column or Thomas's
night march, which upset Bragg's plans.

Forrest's overheated dispatches on the twenty-first were even worse.
Certainly, they subsequently damaged Bragg's reputation beyond repair.
Forrest saw a great opportunity to attack a demoralized Federal army
as it retreated in disorder, but in fact the Army of the Cumberland was
drawn up and ready for battle at Rossville Gap by dawn on the twenty-
first. This was amply demonstrated when his own efforts at pursuit came
to an abrupt halt at Rossville early that morning.

Forrest's penchant for fighting and personal combat interfered with
his ability to effectively command a corps. Grandiose personal gestures—
at Tunnel Hill on September 11, at Reed's Bridge on the eighteenth, and
against the defenses of Chattanooga on the twenty-first—amounted to
grandstanding that exposed him to personal danger. Inspiring leadership
is one thing, and important in any army, but foolish and reckless expo-
sure is quite another. Moreover, because Forrest failed to develop either
Armstrong or Pegram as commanders, neither of those officers was likely

capable of stepping in quickly in the case of his loss. Not until 1864 would Forrest show signs of maturing into his role as a senior commander, but that was of little comfort to the Confederate cause in 1863.

ACKNOWLEDGMENTS

The author thanks the following individuals for their help with this essay, and all things Chickamauga: Sam Elliott, David Friedrichs, Evan Jones, James Ogden III, Dr. William Glenn Robertson, Ted Savas, Wiley Sword, and William Lee White.

NOTES

1. *The War of the Rebellion: A Compilation of the Official Records of the Union and Confederate Armies,* 128 vols. (Washington, D.C.: GPO, 1880–1901), ser. 1, 23(2):940 (hereafter cited as *OR;* all references to series 1 unless otherwise specified).

2. Thomas L. Connelly, *Autumn of Glory* (Baton Rouge: Louisiana State University Press, 1971), 149.

3. *OR,* 23(2):941.

4. Ibid., 509.

5. Ibid., 904.

6. Ibid., 912, 930.

7. D. H. Hill, "Chickamauga—Great Battle of the West," in Robert Underwood Johnson and Clarence Clough Buel, eds., *Battles and Leaders of the Civil War,* 4 vols. (1887; reprint, New York: Thomas Yoseloff, 1956), 3:640.

8. Col. George Brent Journal, Aug. 29, 1863, Braxton Bragg Papers, Western Reserve Historical Society, Cleveland, Ohio.

9. *OR,* 30 (4): 583–84.

10. Ibid., 584.

11. Ibid., 594.

12. Ibid., 591.

13. Ibid., 594.

14. W. T. Holt, Army of Tennessee Scout Book, Sept. 6, 1863, Museum of the Confederacy, Richmond, Va.

15. *OR,* 30(4):614–15.

16. James Longstreet, *From Manassas to Appomattox* (1904; reprint, Secausus, N.J.: Blue and Gray Press, 1984), 436.

17. William B. Hazen to Benson H. Lossing, Aug. 23, 1866, William Palmer Collection, Western Reserve Historical Society, Cleveland, Ohio.

18. *OR,* 30(4):611.

19. Ibid., 615, 627–28.

20. Thomas Jordan and J. P. Pryor, *The Campaigns of General Nathan Bedford Forrest and of Forrest's Cavalry* (1868; reprint, New York: De Capo, 1996), 306.

21. By a Confederate, *The Grayjackets: and How They Lived, Fought, and Died for Dixie* (Richmond, Va.: Jones Brothers, n.d.), 356–57. Jordan and Pryor claimed that Forrest was "little disturbed" by the injury. *Campaigns of General Nathan Bedford Forrest,* 308.

22. Jordan and Pryor, *Campaigns of General Nathan Bedford Forrest,* 308.

23. *OR,* 30(2):30.

24. William Glenn Robertson, "The Chickamauga Campaign: The Armies Collide," *Blue & Gray Magazine* 24, no. 3 (Fall 2007): 40. Robertson provides an excellent analysis of Bragg's thinking during this phase of the campaign.

25. *OR,* 30(4):657.

26. John C. Smith, *Oration at the Unveiling of the Monument Erected to the Memory of Maj. Gen. James B. Steedman* (Chicago: Knight and Leonard, 1887), 17. See also Bushrod Johnson Diary, Sept. 17, 1863, Record Group 109, National Archives, Washington D.C..

27. *OR,* 30(4):664–67. Armstrong refers to Wharton's Division. Anderson's house was only a couple of miles from Glass's Mill.

28. In July Brig. Gen. John Hunt Morgan led his division of 2,500 men on an unauthorized raid across the Ohio River, which resulted in the surrender of nearly all his men. The survivors of this raid, along with those left behind for various reasons, were combined into two ad-hoc battalions and were attached to Forrest's Corps.

29. Robert G. Minty, "Minty's Saber Brigade: The Part They Took in the Chattanooga Campaign, Part One." *National Tribune,* Feb. 25, 1892.

30. J. W. Minnich, "Unique Experiences in the Chickamauga Campaign," *Confederate Veteran* 30, no. 10 (Oct. 1922): 381.

31. J. W. Minnick [*sic*], "Reminiscences of J. W. Minnick, 6th Georgia Cavalry," *Northwest Georgia Historical and Genealogical Society Quarterly* 29, no. 3 (Summer 1997): 20.

32. William Henry Harder Reminiscences, 23rd Tennessee Infantry File, Combat Studies Institute, U.S. Army Command and General Staff College, Fort Leavenworth, Kans.

33. Curtis Green, "Sixth Georgia Cavalry at Chickamauga." *Confederate Veteran* 8 (July 1900): 324.

34. W. F. Shropshire Reminiscences, *Confederate Veteran* Papers, Perkins Manuscripts Library, Duke University, Durham, N.C.

35. Henry J. Aten, *History of the Eighty-Fifth Regiment Illinois Volunteer Infantry* (Hiawatha, Kans.: N.p., 1901), 103.

36. Gustave Huwald Letter, Oct. 7, 1866, Leroy Monicure Nutt Papers, Southern Historical Collection, University of North Carolina, Chapel Hill.

37. William E. Sloan Diary, Sept. 18, 1863, Tennessee State Library and Archives, Nashville.

38. *OR,* 30(1):55–56.

39. Ibid., 30(2):524.

40. David A. Powell, *The Maps of Chickamauga* (New York: Savas-Beatie, 2009), 56.

41. John Allen Wyeth, *The Life of Lieutenant General Nathan Bedford Forrest* (New York: Harper and Brothers, 1908), 250.

42. Letter from "osceola," "Forrest's Old Brigade in the Battle of Chickamauga," *Memphis Appeal,* Oct. 21, 1863.

43. Wyeth, *Life of Lieutenant General Nathan Bedford Forrest,* 250.

44. C. B. Carlton to D. G. Templeton, Oct. 13, 1863, J. A. Templeton Papers, Confederate Research Center, Hill College, Hillsboro, Tex.

45. For a detailed analysis of this command breakdown on September 20, see chapter 5.

46. John Berrien Lindsley, *The Military Annals of Tennessee. Confederate. First Series: Embracing a Review of Military Operations* (Nashville: J. M. Lindsley, 1886; reprint, 1 vol. in 2, Wilmington, N.C.: Broadfoot, 1995), 2:693.

47. *OR,* 30(1):251.

48. Confusion among the Union commanders was almost as bad as that found on the Confederate side of the line. Even though Rosecrans ordered Negley to move at 6:35 A.M., it would be nearly 9:00 A.M. before the division was on its way.

49. *OR,* 30(2):141.

50. J. S. Fullerton, "Reinforcing Thomas at Chickamauga," in *Battles and Leaders,* 3:666.

51. Hill's men were hors de combat after their morning attacks, and Polk was reluctant to commit the rest of his wing, most of which had suffered severely in the fighting of the nineteenth.

52. Longstreet to Bragg, Sept. 21, 1863, Headquarters and Personal Papers, Folder 10, Bragg Papers.

53. Leonidas Polk to wife, Sept. 22, 1863, Leonidas Polk Papers, University of the South, Sewanee, Tenn.

54. *OR,* 30(4):681.

55. Ibid., 675.

56. Taylor Beatty Diary, Sept. 22, 1863, Nutt Papers.

57. *OR,* 30 (4): 509. Bragg used this wording to protest against losing Forrest in August 1863, when the cavalryman first petitioned the government in Richmond to be allowed to return to Mississippi.

58. Lindsley, *Military Annals of Tennessee.* 2:694.

59. Jordan and Pryor, *Campaigns of General Nathan Bedford Forrest,* 353–54.

60. Lafayette McLaws Memoir, Cheeves Family Papers, South Carolina Historical Society, Charleston.

61. George Brent Journal, Sept. 25, 1863.

62. Nathaniel Cheairs Hughes Jr. *Liddell's Record* (1985; reprint, Baton Rouge: Louisiana State University Press, 1997), 150.

63. Judith Lee Hallock, *Braxton Bragg and Confederate Defeat, Volume II* (Tuscaloosa: University of Alabama Press, 1991), 100.

64. Jordan and Pryor, *Campaigns of General Nathan Bedford Forrest,* 352.

65. Hill, "Chickamauga," 662.

66. Robert Selph Henry, *"First with the Most" Forrest* (1944; reprint, n.p.: Konecky, 1991), 193.

67. Andrew Nelson Lytle, *Bedford Forrest and His Critter Company* (New York: Minton, Balch, 1931), 233.

68. John A. Wyeth, *That Devil Forrest: Life of General Nathan Bedford Forrest* (New York: Harper, 1959), 241–42. The exact timing of this letter is unclear. It could have been sent after the order of the twenty-fifth, necessitating Bragg's follow up order of the twenty-eighth, but most biographers place it after the latter communication.

69. Jordan and Pryor, *Campaigns of General Nathan Bedford Forrest,* 357.

70. Ibid.

71. Wyeth, *That Devil Forrest,* 242–43.

72. John Watson Morton, *The Artillery of Nathan Bedford Forrest's Cavalry, "the Wizard of the Saddle"* (Nashville, Tenn: M.E. Church, South, 1909), 130–31.

73. Jordan and Pryor, *Campaigns of General Nathan Bedford Forrest,* 356.

74. Henry, *"First with the Most,"* 200.

75. See Lonnie Maness, *An Untutored Genius: The Military Career of General Nathan Bedford Forrest* (Oxford, Miss.: Guild Bindery, 1990), 182; Brian Steel Wills, *A Battle from the Start: The Life of Nathan Bedford Forrest* (New York: HarperCollins, 1992), 144–45; Jack Hurst, *Nathan Bedford Forrest: A Biography* (New York: Random House, 1993), 139–40; and Eddy W. Davison and Daniel Foxx, *Nathan Bedford Forrest: In Search of the Enigma* (Gretna, La.: Pelican, 2007), 179.

76. Jordan and Pryor, *Campaigns of General Nathan Bedford Forrest,* 358.

77. *OR,* 31(3):646.

78. Hallock, *Braxton Bragg,* 101–102.

79. See John Harvey Mathes, *General Forrest* (New York: Appleton, 1902), 156; and Morton, *Artillery,* 130–31.

80. Morton, *Artillery,* 131.

CHAPTER 4

INCUBATOR OF INNOVATION

The Army of the Cumberland and the Spirit of Invention in 1863

DAVID A. POWELL

On June 24, 1863, the sixty thousand Union troops comprising the Army of the Cumberland marched out from their camps around Murfreesboro, Tennessee. They were moving against a familiar opponent, the Army of Tennessee, firmly entrenched behind the hills of the Highland Rim, the high ground encircling the Nashville basin. The resultant Tullahoma Campaign drew both praise and criticism. In ten days' time Major General William Starke Rosecrans outflanked and outmaneuvered his rebel opponent, forcing General Braxton Bragg into dispirited retreat and bringing Middle Tennessee under Union sway, all without a major battle or a huge effusion of blood. It was a masterpiece of planning and execution, marred only by the heavy rains that plagued much of the campaign.

Yet Bragg's Confederates escaped, living to fight another day. By this stage of the war, President Abraham Lincoln and his advisors understood that the Confederacy lived and died with its armies, and only their destruction would end the rebellion. The Army of Tennessee's survival only postponed that fight to another day. Moreover, Rosecrans's movement did not begin until the end of June. This was very late in the season for Civil War campaigning. More typically, armies opened their spring campaigns around early May at the latest. Rosecrans's procrastination had allowed Bragg's army to send reinforcements to other theaters, most notably to Mississippi, where Major General Ulysses S. Grant was investing Vicksburg. In the end, those reinforcements were unable to save the river fortress and so greatly weakened Bragg that he was unable to effectively resist the advance into Middle Tennessee, but those outcomes were not foreordained. With better handling by the generals in Mississippi, those reinforcements might well have helped defeat Grant's efforts.

Rosecrans had good reasons to wait, however. He had a complex set of problems to overcome. The Army of the Cumberland faced immense logistical and operational challenges in Tennessee of a nature not fully understood in Washington. Surmounting those obstacles would require new and innovative thinking. Of course, warfare itself was changing in the 1860s, and not all of these challenges were unique to the Army of the Cumberland. Every general and every army experienced the changing nature of war. Some commanders faced down those difficulties and prospered, others floundered. In the Army of the Cumberland, however, Rosecrans fostered a spirit of innovation unmatched in any other command. No other Federal force experienced such a flowering of so many new methods in such a short period of time. Much of the reason for this was Rosecrans himself, always open to new methods and techniques, never hidebound by traditional thinking.

The American Civil War occurred on the cusp of massive technological changes that affected almost all aspects of waging war. Weapons technology was in the middle of a profound leap forward. If the war had occurred prior to 1850, the standard infantry weapon would have been the smoothbore muzzle-loading musket, with an effective range of about seventy-five yards and a rate of fire of about three rounds a minute. This same weapon had been standard issue for soldiers for the last 150 years. Artillery followed a similar technological trajectory, with smoothbore muzzle-loaded tubes giving way to rifled cannon. At sea, iron-plating was superseding wooden walls, with steel hulls looming on the horizon.

A logistical revolution was unfolding as well. Prior to 1850, railroads covered only a small portion of the young republic. The steamboat was king, and most goods flowed on the nation's waterways. After 1850, however, iron track increasingly covered the land. By 1860, the outlines of a national rail-transport network were in place, especially in the northern states. To be sure, many problems had yet to be overcome. Most railroads ended in cities and did not connect to other lines. Differing gauges, especially in the South, made for a confusing patchwork of independent rail companies whose equipment could not easily be used on other railroads.

The growing capacity of rails to move vast quantities of troops and supplies, however, was too significant to ignore. The war would dramatically
accelerate the rise of railroads from regional to national importance as
armies increasingly relied on them for support. Improved communications accompanied this logistical revolution. The telegraph lines strung
alongside those tracks hummed with the dispatches of war. Telegraphy
revolutionized the speed with which field armies could be ordered into
action or report back to their respective war department. Messages now
took minutes or hours, not days or weeks, to reach their destinations.

When the Civil War burst forth in 1861, this modernization was well
established but hardly complete. The way forward was not obvious. Some
inventions would revolutionize warfare. Others were dead ends, or ideas
not yet capable of coming to fruition with the technology at hand. The
men charged with waging this new war all grappled with change, and
they did so with varying degrees of enthusiasm, ingenuity, and success.

In 1861 the American military establishment was a far more rudi-
mentary organization than it is today.[1] There was no formal training,
schooling, or system of professional development for officers beyond
the U.S. Military Academy at West Point. There was no central clearing-
house to disseminate lessons learned on the battlefield or recommend
doctrine. To a much greater extent than in a modern military, an army
or departmental commander's own personality set the tone for the entire command. This meant that innovation, when it happened, occurred
at the local level rather than as a matter of overall policy. Innovation
filtered up from the ranks rather than down from above, and this produced a variety of technical and technological experiments. Under the
command of generals who welcomed inventiveness, new ideas were given
root and allowed to sprout, sometimes to great success. But since there
was no armywide policy to digest, distill, and disseminate these ideas,
they often did not spread beyond their immediate command or region,
sometimes foundering if a commander was relieved or replaced. It would
take postwar contemplation to promote a broader consensus for change.
Given the relative lack of cutting-edge technology in the Confederacy,
most innovation, especially that driven by new weapons, occurred in
Northern ranks.

During the war, departmental and army commanders exercised a
great deal of autonomy within their sphere of authority. Department
commanders were especially powerful, administering not only to the
immediate needs of the field force but also holding sway over large areas

lacking civil government and controlling vital elements of the war effort, including shipping and railroads. In the spring of 1863, Major General Rosecrans headed up both the Department of the Cumberland and the field army of that name. Under his tenure, innovation flourished.

Rosecrans possessed a spark of genius. His inquisitiveness and seemingly boundless energy were ideal qualities for encouraging new ideas. He combined the qualifications of the professional soldier with a scientific bent suggestive of men like Benjamin Franklin and Thomas Edison. Rosecrans graduated from West Point in 1842, fifth in his class, and spent the next few years teaching at the academy. His classmates and colleagues considered him brilliant, and with good reason.

His inquisitiveness was not confined to things of the material world; he was also on a spiritual journey during this period. Born into a Methodist family, Rosecrans converted to Roman Catholicism in 1845 at the age of twenty-six while teaching at West Point. This was an unusual course since nineteenth-century America contained a great deal of prejudice against Catholics, yet the decision was not atypical of the man. Having made a thorough study of the question, Roman Catholicism seemed to have the best answers to his spiritual questions, and so it was the logical choice for him. Once he converted, he was fully committed to the church, and his enthusiasm for the subject was unbridled. He persuaded his younger brother Sylvester to adopt his new faith. William was so convincing that Sylvester not only converted but also became a priest and eventually a bishop.

In 1847 Rosecrans was assigned to more-practical duties. He worked on fortifications, the dredging of harbors and rivers, and various other construction projects. He proved more than capable. At Newport, Rhode Island, he so improved the dredging machinery then in use that it "proved eight times as efficient" as the previous process. A subsequent posting sent him to the Washington Navy Yard as a civil engineer for the government. While there, he worked on a diverse array of projects, ranging from railways to sawmills and large factories. Again he improved designs and invented new ways of doing things. His proudest achievement was the use of a single large engine to drive all the required machinery, a design that so impressed the navy that they made it a standard feature of future construction.[2]

Rosecrans missed the Mexican War, and thus also the chance at the brevets earned by his classmates in battle. In an army where advancement was already frustratingly slow, the lack of combat honors dimmed his prospects for promotion. Sensing better opportunities out of uniform, Rosecrans resigned his commission in 1854. No less than Secretary of War Jefferson Davis attempted to dissuade him, but his mind was set.

Now a civilian, Rosecrans pursued a variety of careers. His army training led him naturally into civil engineering and architecture. In 1856 Rosecrans took a job extracting coal from the mountains of western Virginia, which also required him to apply his skills to the construction of several dams in order to make the Kanawha River navigable so as to transport the product to market. Eventually, working with coal led him to experiment on developing a clean-burning oil for use in lamps that could replace the whale oil then in common use. These achievements secured him some patents, but while he was working on a design for an improved safety lamp, a prototype exploded in his laboratory. He was badly burned and spent the next eighteen months recuperating. Rosecrans fully recovered, but his face suffered permanent scarring.

At war's outbreak he was fully healed and initially accepted a state commission in the Ohio militia. From there he quickly rose to a brigadier generalship with the U.S. Volunteers. He served with distinction, first in western Virginia, then in Mississippi, until he replaced Major General Don Carlos Buell at the head of what soon became the Department of the Cumberland. He proved capable in both combat and in military administration.

Rosecrans's wide range of interests, abilities, and experiences made him an excellent choice for what would prove to be a difficult assignment. It also rendered him far more open to new, often unorthodox, ideas than many of his military contemporaries. He was not just mired in the minutia of things military and logistical, he also delighted in discussion of all sorts. His military family soon became accustomed to late-evening conversations of all things literary, philosophical, and scientific as well as martial.[3] Rosecrans was a man not easily swayed by other opinions. If a question interested him, he rigorously researched the issue and drew his own conclusions. He was not easily dissuaded from endorsing a new concept if he thought the idea had merit. Newspaperman Whitelaw Reid summed up his character this way: "His restless mind was constantly bent on making improvements and substituting better methods; his ingenuity left everywhere its traces in new inventions."[4] While Rosecrans commanded the Army of the Cumberland, a number of new ideas were tested, both in the realm of tactics and logistics.

Tactics and Weaponry

What came to be the basic arm of the Civil War, the muzzle-loading rifled musket, had a very short half-life as cutting-edge technology. Though the rifling increased range, muzzle loading and the continued use of the paper cartridge did nothing to improve the rate of fire. Even before the war, gunmakers were producing breechloaders in limited quantities, and inventors were working on magazine-fed arms with metallic cartridges. As the war drew to a close in the spring of 1865, most military men recognized that that the rifled musket was a dying technology, being discarded by the world's militaries as fast as they could afford to make the switch.[5]

Three significant changes in weapons technology were poised to change warfare, though all were still experimental by the war's commencement. The first was the introduction of weapons that could be loaded from the breech. If it could be perfected, this technology was both faster and safer than the standard method of the time. Muzzle-loaded weapons were difficult to load while lying down or taking advantage of cover. In the 1850s breech-loading weapons made great strides, and the army had even adopted the Sharps carbine as an official arm for cavalry in 1861.[6] The Sharps, however, still used a paper cartridge and was a single-shot weapon. Like muzzleloaders, it required a separate percussion cap with each shot.

The move to repeating, or magazine-fed, weapons would also require the development of an effective metallic cartridge. Those designs needed fixed ammunition that could be loaded and fired as a single entity. The only significant repeating weapon of the period that did not use fixed ammunition was the Colt revolving rifle, a five-shot weapon that worked exactly like the famous pistol. Paper cartridges could be loaded into each chamber of the cylinder, capped, and then fired one at a time. Once empty, reloading took some time. Many Colts saw use during the war, but they were a transitional, not a revolutionary, firearm.

Metallic cartridges (modern bullets) combined slug, powder, and igniter all in one package, and their development was greatly spurred by the war. In 1861 the Union government was besieged by inventors wishing to peddle their wares. Among the standout weapons were the Henry rifle, a sixteen-shot repeater; and the Spencer, a seven-shot repeating rifle. Both arms worked via a tubular magazine into which bullets were loaded and then fed into the firing chamber via the lever action of the trigger guard. President Lincoln personally test fired one rifle on the Washington Mall after inventor Christopher Spencer wrangled a meeting in August 1863.[7]

With the Henry and the Spencer, firepower was increased dramatically. A standard infantryman with a rifled musket was expected to fire three shots per minute. With their magazines, the Spencer could fire twenty-one shots in that time, the Henry even more. Given enough ammunition, an individual with a repeater was seven to ten times more effective than a man with a musket. Both prototypes were successful, but the Spencer proved more robust for field use.[8] More than 100,000 Spencer carbines would see service in the war, virtually all of them during the last year of the conflict.

All of this evolution in the hardware of war induced similar turmoil in what might be termed the software of war: the doctrine, drill, and tactics that transformed mobs of militia into armies of soldiers. The men who rose to command these armies saw that change all around them. Some resisted, insisting that the fundamentals remained the same despite the plethora of new weaponry offered. Others embraced the new concepts in search of the right combination of tactics and weapons that would provide unchallenged mastery of the battlefield. In the 1860s there was no single right answer, nor enough of the newest equipment to go around. The truth is that in 1861 neither side had the capacity to produce magazine-fed weapons like the Spencer or Henry rifles in sufficient numbers to equip even a few thousand men, let alone the hundreds of thousands who answered the call to arms, even assuming that such weapons were sufficiently tested and proven to be effective for use in the field. Many of the innovative arms offered up to the governments, both North and South, in fact were sadly deficient for field use and would have spelled disaster had they been adopted heedlessly. As a result, early in the war both armies drilled to older, proven tactics with muskets everyone knew would work. This was less true by early 1863, but still, advanced firearms could not be turned out in enough quantities to immediately reequip entire armies. The small arms that did make their way to the field did so only in limited quantities.

Rosecrans wanted as many of these new weapons as he could get, for he had a novel way for using them. Typically, his idea aimed to elegantly solve multiple problems at once. Rosecrans assumed command of the soon-to-be-rechristened Army of the Cumberland in late October 1862 as it was moving back from Kentucky to Nashville, following Brax-

ton Bragg's Army of Tennessee after the Battle of Perryville. Once at
Nashville, Rosecrans discovered a supply situation in peril. Confederate
raider John Hunt Morgan had blocked the Big South Railroad tunnel at
Gallatin, Tennessee, with debris and wreckage the previous August, and
Union forces in Nashville were not getting sufficient supplies through
to sustain them indefinitely. Every effort was put into clearing the tunnel, and the railroad was reopened in November. This success allowed
Rosecrans to accumulate enough supplies to essay an offensive the next
month, culminating in the Battle of Stones River. That engagement was
just barely a Union victory, but the rebels retreated twenty-five miles
to Shelbyville, Tennessee. From there, however, Confederate cavalry
constantly threatened Union supplies, and Bragg had far more mounted
men than did Rosecrans. Despite their success at Stones River, the Federals felt effectively besieged in Nashville over the next few months. All
of these factors forced Rosecrans to ponder more-reliable solutions for
defending his supply line.

On January 31, 1863, the Army of the Cumberland reported 4,549 officers and men present for duty in Brigadier General David S. Stanley's
division, the army's sole cavalry force.[9] Perhaps another 700 troopers
served as escorts or were detached on garrison duty. With an overall
field strength for the army of 70,000 men, this was a smaller percentage
of mounted troops than in most other Union departments. By way of
comparison, on February 20 Bragg's Army of Tennessee reported 12,224
mounted men present for duty.[10] Bragg might be badly outmatched in
infantry and artillery, but he possessed a 2.5-to-1 advantage in cavalry,
and more troops were on the way. By May, Confederate mounted strength
in Middle Tennessee would swell to nearly 17,000 troopers with the ac-
cession of reinforcements from Mississippi.

Rosecrans wanted more Federal horsemen to counter the rebel raiding threat. But cavalry were expensive to raise and took a long time to
train. The army in Nashville needed men now. "One rebel cavalryman,"
he informed Secretary of War Edwin Stanton, "takes on an average 3 of
our infantry to watch our communications, while our progress is made
slow and cautious. We command the forage of the country only by sending out large train guards. It is of prime necessity in every point of view
to master their cavalry."[11]

Accordingly, Rosecrans conceived of the idea of using infantry for the
job. As early as November 16, 1862, he telegraphed Washington with the
idea "to mount some infantry regiments, arm them with *revolving* rifles,

and make sharpshooters of them."[12] Then, in the wake of Stones River, he had a second brainstorm. After that fight, Rosecrans ordered each regiment to issue a "Roll of Honor" to single out men who had performed exceptionally well in the recent action. These troops would serve as an example to others, inspiring every soldier to strive for similar recognition. In addition to the tribute, the general decided that they would also serve as an elite force within the army.

Rosecrans detailed his intentions to General in Chief Henry Halleck on February 1, 1863. From this roll, each regiment would supply all the named privates, one officer, and five sergeants or corporals to form an elite battalion for each brigade. Additionally, and rashly, Rosecrans "promise[d] them the best of arms when I can get them, and will mount them for rapid field movement, like flying artillery. . . . We must create military ardor."[13] When implemented, this concept would add roughly 6,000 men in another thirty or so mobile battalions to augment Rosecrans's existing mounted arm. Further, these troops could do more than just fight enemy cavalry. The general's use of the term "sharpshooter" conveyed, in Civil War terms, the sense of elite infantry adept at tactical skirmishing as well. On the battlefield, infantry skirmishers performed many of the same functions that cavalry did on campaign. They scouted ahead of the main body, providing warning and intelligence, opposing enemy infantry, and feeling for exposed flanks. In Virginia two regiments, the 1st and 2nd U.S. Sharpshooters, had already been recruited for that purpose and had proven their worth on several battlefields. In typical fashion, Rosecrans envisioned his own elite battalions to be dual-purpose commands capable of both mounted and dismounted action.

But it was not to be. These "elite battalions" trespassed on legal boundaries that the War Department was unwilling to cross. Only Congress could authorize the creation of a host of new regular units. State governors still controlled regimental appointments of officers, which was a source of patronage and political power. Rosecrans was also treading on their toes. The Confederacy solved this problem by passing a specific law granting commanders the right to form sharpshooter battalions from handpicked men in April 1862 and would use it to great effect in the future. The Federal government never followed suit. Moreover, in Halleck's view mounted infantry were largely a waste of time, being neither fish nor fowl. In trying to be both infantry and cavalry, he believed that they would never perform well as either. In this opinion Halleck was reflecting a good deal of the Old Army's prejudice against volunteer soldiers, but he was the man in charge.

There was possibly other resistance to the idea as well. The United States was a democratic society, priding itself on equality among men. Creating a handpicked force of elites smacked of a Praetorian Guard to many politicians and soldiers alike. In the early days of the Republic, the idea of whether or not the new nation should even have a standing army of any sort was hotly debated, with some viewing that as the first step toward an inevitable military dictatorship. This sentiment was still very much alive in 1861. Union major general John C. Frémont came under harsh criticism for creating just such a self-styled "Body Guard" company in Missouri early in the war. The idea of elite troops struck many as undemocratic and anti-American. Certainly, both many civilians and old soldiers found the idea disturbing. Rosecrans's concept never moved much beyond the theoretical since it was ruled out by Halleck as soon as he heard of it.[14]

If elite battalions of mounted skirmishers were not to be, however, the idea of mounting infantry and providing them with advanced weapons was still possible. Existing regiments, even whole brigades, could be adapted for this purpose. Rosecrans returned to that concept, and while Halleck still disapproved of the idea, he grudgingly allowed it. Halleck still viewed mounted infantry as a waste of resources, but this time there were no specific legal objections, and as departmental commander, Rosecrans had enough autonomy to pursue his brainchild.

Most students of the war are familiar with the story of Colonel John T. Wilder's famous Lightning Brigade, five regiments of Illinois and Indiana troops that, in the spring of 1863, procured mounts from among the local inhabitants of Middle Tennessee. They also equipped themselves with newly purchased Spencer rifles, which initially they offered to pay for out of their own pockets, though the government ultimately footed the bill. Usually, the idea of converting Wilder's men to mounted infantry is presented as an idea conceived of by Wilder himself. Sergeant Benjamin F. Magee of the 72nd Indiana attributed the scheme to the colonel after a failed attempt to chase Confederate raider John H. Morgan in December 1862. Magee recalled that in order to keep up with Morgan's troopers, men of the 17th Indiana seized a number of mules at Bear Wallow, Kentucky, in what proved to be an ill-advised initial effort to mount an effective pursuit.[15] Then in January 1863 Wilder presented himself at headquarters and outlined his scheme. Rosecrans, as evidenced by his

November 16 communiqué, was already thinking along those same lines and approved it. He authorized two similar, lesser-known formations as well. In April 1863 he ordered the 39th Indiana to be thus organized and granted Colonel Abel D. Streight authorization to follow Wilder's lead with another entire brigade. Streight's men came to a bad end in early May, however, having been too hastily sent off on an ill-considered effort to raid the Confederate supply and industrial facilities at Rome, Georgia. This effort was doomed by a lack of horseflesh. Although Streight substituted mules where possible, he still lacked mounts for 200 of his 1,600 men on the day he commenced the raid.[16] The colonel's entire force was captured just west of Rome by Nathan Bedford Forrest. Wilder and the 39th Indiana would prove far more effective.

All but five companies of one regiment in Wilder's command were armed with Spencer rifles that spring, nearly 3,000 men in all. Wilder later described the tactics that evolved to maximize the power of these new weapons. "My Brigade . . . [was] all pretty well drilled in Hardie's [*sic*] Tactics. . . . We simply kept that manner of movement, except that we made a single line with the men at intervals of six feet." The colonel trained his men to use their fire sporadically until the enemy were "within 300 yards, when our rapid fire with aim never failed to break their charge."[17] With their magazine-fed weapons, a thin skirmish line of men proved more than a match for a standard battle line and greatly reduced Wilder's own losses as well. The 39th Indiana, though not part of his force, also acquired approximately five hundred Spencers that spring.

Impressed with the promise of overwhelming an enemy with such firepower, Rosecrans wanted multishot weapons of all types. He favored the Spencer and Henry rifles, but he also scrounged large numbers of Colt five-shot revolving rifles. A number of his cavalry units were armed with the Colts as well as the 21st Ohio Infantry. In January 1863 he harassed the War Department for more and more of these weapons until an exasperated Halleck finally exploded, via telegraph. "You already have more than your share," snapped the general in chief. "Everything has been done, and is now being done, for you that is possible by the government. . . . You cannot expect to have *all* the best arms."[18]

Despite Halleck's growing exasperation, Rosecrans's pestering did pay dividends. In addition to the substantial mobility and firepower added to the army as represented by Wilder and the 39th Indiana, the general also worked hard to greatly increase his actual cavalry force. By July 1863, the Army of the Cumberland's cavalry had grown from a division to

For being named to
Rosecrans's Roll of Honor
after Stones River, Sergeant
Gilbert Armstrong of the
58th Indiana Infantry was
awarded this Henry rifle, the
weapon he carried through
the Chickamauga Campaign.
From John J. Hight, *History
of the Fifty-Eighth Regiment
of Indiana Volunteer Infantry.*

a corps and doubled in strength, reporting nearly 11,000 officers and men present for duty.[19] They were all equipped with either single-shot breechloaders or Colt rifles. Consequently, from the summer of 1863 on, Federal forces would best their Confederate cavalry opponents in a number of instances, most notably during the Tullahoma and Chickamauga Campaigns. Moreover, there is fragmentary evidence that some advanced weapons did reach the hands of selected men in some infantry regiments and that some sort of permanent skirmisher command was established, despite the government's official prohibition of the idea. The evidence for this is fleeting and by no means definitive, but it is suggestive. One such example is documented in the regimental history of the 58th Indiana as set down by the regimental historians, Chaplin John J. Hight and former corporal Gilbert Stormont. Sergeant Gilbert Armstrong of Company E was armed with a Henry rifle after the Battle of Stones River. Armstrong carried this weapon on the field at Chickamauga until he was wounded on September 19. He then passed it to a lieutenant in his regiment, who in turn was captured on the twentieth, along with the rifle. Clearly, Armstrong was named in the *Roll of Honor* and subsequently awarded the Henry for his meritorious service. While Hight mentioned neither the *Roll* nor the elite battalions by name, his description of how Armstrong came by the rifle is exactly in line with Rosecrans's official scheme as outlined to Halleck.[20] How many more such presentations in the 58th or in other regiments went unrecorded is open to question. Even the quarterly ordnance returns maintained by the War Department are silent on the matter. The blanks used to record a regiment's weapons did not even have a line for repeating arms like the Henry or the Spencer. Armstrong's rifle and any others like it were probably privately purchased and thus not official government property.

Armstrong's record is not the only evidence for the existence of these special formations, which appeared in more than one corps of the army. The 58th Indiana served in the XXI Corps. Captain J. T. Patton of the 93rd Ohio served in the XX Corps. Sometime early in 1863, Patton was elected to command the "elite" company of the 93rd, which along with "the several regiments of the four regiments of the brigade formed a 'light battalion.' . . . We bought Henry rifles and devoted our time to special drill." But he noted, "The war department countermanded [Rosecrans's] order and we returned to our respective commands [but] the men of 'the light battalion' with their Henry rifles, did valiant service in every battle until the close of the war."[21] If Patton's 1892 recollections are accurate, this would give the 93rd Ohio approximately 30 repeaters in the ranks and the entire brigade more than 120 such weapons. At Chickamauga Patton noted that some of these men were acting as the regiment's skirmishers when they shot and killed one of Confederate lieutenant general Leonidas Polk's aides-de-camp, Lieutenant William Richmond.[22] This account is clear on several points. Not only were the Henrys purchased, but the men of the elite battalion also stayed together for some months, trained, and retained the weapons even after the battalions themselves disbanded. Patton's account further suggests that even though the battalions were gone, the 93rd Ohio at least informally maintained their light-infantry company through the end of the war.[23]

Another intriguing hint can be found in the report of Colonel Bernard Laiboldt, commander of the Second Brigade, Third Division, XX Corps. In his report of Chickamauga, Laiboldt thanked a number of officers by name for various services performed. One line is especially suggestive: "The company of sharpshooters (under Captain Ernst) did the work assigned to them faithfully."[24] Captain George Ernst was apparently an excellent officer who, in the words of the unit's modern historian, "would finish the war as one of the heroes of the regiment."[25] That one line in Laiboldt's report is all the description offered of Ernst's duties at Chickamauga. The captain's compiled service record, however, offers up slightly more detail. From June to November 1863, Ernst, who normally commanded Company E, was "absent detached cmdg [commanding] the brig[ade] sharpshooters."[26] In that same brigade, an enlisted man from the 73rd Illinois wrote home in March 1863 enthusiastic about his transfer to the new unit. "You wanted to know something about the light battalion that I am in. . . . There is to be three privates to go out of every CO in the Regt and also out of the brigade 5 corporals out of every Regt and 2 Sargents. . . . We are to be in camped near brigade head quarters [and] we are to be mounted. We are exempted from picket duty but I expect that we will make it all up in scouting."[27]

Once again, this description matches with Rosecrans's vision of elite units, though Laiboldt makes no mention of repeating weapons. Still, confirmation of the existence of a sharpshooter element, selected and detached from the various regiments in the brigade, does show that Rosecrans's plan was more than just theory. Official recognition would have been impossible, of course, but at least some commanders must have thought it worth implementing on an informal basis.

Although these hints are tantalizing, we are left with little idea of how the sharpshooters functioned in battle and if their tactics were any different than those outlined in the official manuals. The idea of skirmishers itself was not new, of course. Light-infantry units had been appearing on various army rolls for more than a hundred years in Europe, and the Napoleonic Wars saw widespread use of skirmish tactics. During the Civil War, while the main formation in combat was the two-rank line, skirmishers were usually sent out ahead of that line and deployed individually, with the men separated by up to five yards. They operated in pairs, using available cover, and were expected to use more initiative and judgment than when standing in ranks.

As noted previously, in April 1862 the Confederates passed a widely embraced law that allowed commanders to form sharpshooter battalions by drawing on handpicked men. By 1863, rebel brigades in all theaters of war adopted the idea, and so historians know a good deal more about how those units were formed, trained, officered, and used in combat. But given the paucity of advanced weapons in Confederate hands, these men were armed with the same rifled muskets employed by the line infantry and fought largely by the standard manuals.[28]

Had Rosecrans's battalions all been fully armed with repeaters, their tactics likely would have evolved much differently than called for by those manuals. Instead, they would have fought in a manner similar to that described by Wilder. Indeed, with his men six feet apart, Wilder's

usual formation was much more a skirmish line than a traditional line
of battle. His line would have a density of three men for every four yards,
while Hardee's manual called for a normal battle-line density of roughly
four men per yard. The lack of manpower, of course, was made up with
firepower. If properly armed, Rosecrans's battalions might have evolved
into more of an elite assault force than traditional skirmishers. That was
not to be, however, because while a few men in the infantry ranks might
have Henry rifles (like Sergeant Armstrong or Captain Patton's detachment), those examples seemed to be the exception rather than the rule.
Most of the Army of the Cumberland's informal sharpshooter formations
must have been conventionally armed with Springfield or Enfield rifled
muskets. Repeating arms were expensive and scarce. There can hardly
have been more than a couple hundred at most scattered through the
ranks of the army in private hands. Tracking and handling the special-
ized ammunition needed also would have been a problem.

Rapid-fire hardware was only one way to innovate, however. Other
officers were thinking of the problems presented by Civil War tactics
and how to improve upon them. One very unusual concept originated
with a German émigré officer in the Army of the Cumberland. Brigadier
General August Willich was an unusual officer by any standard. He was
a former Prussian army lieutenant who had left the king's service in the
1830s to embrace communism. He took up arms again in the revolution
of 1848 and, upon the failure of that effort, fled first to England, then
to the United States. He worked as a laborer, carpenter, and newspaper
editor. When the Civil War commenced in 1861, Willich saw it as a con-
tinuation of the same struggle against an entrenched aristocracy for
freedom and equality that he fought for in Europe. He was captured at
the Battle of Stones River but used his time in captivity profitably. Upon
his exchange and return to the Army of the Cumberland that spring, the
general started to put into practice an idea for a new kind of infantry
formation that he theorized while a prisoner of war.

Willich's idea utilized standard weapons but called for a regiment to
form in four lines instead of two. He called his new technique "Advance,
Firing." "The movement was quite simple," recounted Alexis Cope of the
15th Ohio, "being a line of battle in four ranks, each rank advancing a
few paces in front and firing, then stopping to load while the other ranks
advanced alternately, thus keeping up a steady advance and a steady fire
all the time."[29] A regiment of four hundred men, for example, would form
in four lines, one behind the other, with enough space between the men

in each line so that other troops could pass through their ranks. When the first line fired, they would immediately begin to reload, while the next line moved through them to the front and fired in turn. The third and fourth lines would follow suit, and by the time the fourth line fired, the original first line (now in the rear) would move forward to the front and fire again. The result was a methodical advance combined with a wall of fire, delivering a volley every ten or fifteen seconds while still sustaining a measured forward progress. Executed properly, "Advance, Firing" must have been devastating. The brigade used the new technique for the first time in combat during the action at Liberty Gap, Tennessee, on June 25, 1863, with significant success. At Chickamauga Willich employed it again on September 19. Entering the fight in the timber west of Winfrey Field, his brigade drove the opposing rebels for nearly a mile before being recalled.

The drill bore no resemblance to anything in any U.S. manual in use at the time. American sources attribute the concept as one purely of Willich's invention, but it is possible that the technique owed its origins to something he had learned as Prussian soldier. During the American Revolution, among the Hessian troops hired by King George III to fight the colonists were Jaegers, rifle-armed light infantry. These formations sometimes employed a four-rank street-fighting technique that seems similar to Willich's idea. How much he adapted and how much he invented, however, is an open question.

Of equal interest is who used this tactic. Willich was a brigade commander in the XX Corps. There is at least one other reference to a brigade using "Advance, Firing" at Chickamauga. The 125th Ohio, of Colonel Charles Harker's brigade in the XXI Corps, employed the technique on September 20, counterattacking the Confederates of Hood's Texas Brigade. Lieutenant Charles Clark of the 125th later recounted the action in particular detail. His description matched Cope's (of the 15th Ohio, above) in almost all particulars: "In that movement, the files doubled up, making four ranks, leaving intervals through which the rear rank passed, running rapidly forward a few paces, halting, firing and dropping to the ground to load, the next rank meantime passing still farther to the front to deliver its fire, and so on in succession."[30]

Where did the 125th Ohio learn the maneuver? There are no obvious connections between Willich and Harker, nor did the 125th ever serve under Willich. They did not fight together at Liberty Gap; the two corps were many miles apart that day. Unfortunately, Clark offered up no additional information about where the 125th acquired the technique or who trained them in mastery of it. Clearly, however, something in the culture of the Army of the Cumberland allowed innovative ideas to flourish while under Rosecrans's tenure.

Willich waxed enthusiastic about other ideas as well. For example, he wanted wagons with which to transport his brigade, thinking that the men would be both faster to reach a fight and fresher when they got there. While this idea is an intriguing precursor to the concept of modern mechanized infantry, there simply were not enough vehicles to spare for the idea to be tested. The Army of the Cumberland needed every wagon it had to haul supplies, not soldiers.

Willich was not the only officer tinkering with tactics. In the 1850s Major William J. Hardee had translated a French manual into what he titled *Rifle and Light Infantry Tactics,* which encompassed individual and regimental drill instruction. For brigade deployments and maneuvers, the standard was still Major General Winfield Scott's 1835 *Infantry Tactics*. In August 1862, however, the Union army introduced a new manual, written by Brigadier General Silas Casey. Casey's manual was intended to update and replace that of Hardee, who was by now a Confederate lieutenant general and corps commander in the Army of Tennessee, and also update Scott's volume.[31] While the modifications to individual and regimental drill were minor, brigade deployment changed substantially. Scott expected the regiments or battalions in a brigade to form a single line of battle side by side. For the first two years of the war, this is how virtually all brigades on both sides entered a fight. The U.S. Army officially adopted Casey's manual in 1862, however, and expected all units to use the new techniques.

There were two problems with Scott's deployment. First, it created too large a frontage for a brigade commander to control effectively. If all a brigade's subunits were at full strength, this line would be 1,000 yards (or more) in length. Even given the reduced sizes fielded by most Civil War regiments after any considerable time in service, a brigade front could easily stretch 300–500 yards. Second, a brigade so deployed lacked any integral reserves and proved unwieldy if forced to deal with an attack from any direction other than directly ahead. A threat to a flank was a recipe for disaster.

Casey solved both problems by mandating that brigades should enter combat in two lines of two regiments, one behind the other. This change meant that overall frontage was reduced to a more manageable 200–300 yards and that the two rear regiments could act as support for the front line. These reserve units could replace the lead regiments if needed or move more quickly to meet a threat from an unexpected quarter. While Casey's deployment was not without drawbacks (it brought to bear only half the firepower of an equally sized opponent using Scott, for example), it was in general a much more flexible formation.

Despite the fact that Casey's work became the army standard in the fall of 1862, it took time for the new tactics to gain widespread acceptance in the field. By 1863, the new system was in wide use only in one Federal department. As might be expected, of the three main Union armies in the field that year, the Army of the Cumberland was at the fore in adopting any new concept. The Army of the Tennessee used the new deployment intermittently, while the Army of the Potomac hardly used it at all. Given that Casey had himself served in the Army of the Potomac in 1862 and now was in charge of the camps of instruction outside of Washington, D.C., through which many of those Potomac troops passed, this lack of adoption by the main field army is curious. Yet it illustrates just how informal and irregular doctrinal decisions could be in the nineteenth-century military.

Four 1863 battles provide a window into the use of differing formations among the three Federal armies. In May Grant's Army of the Tennessee fought the Battle of Champion Hill as part of the campaign to capture Vicksburg. Six weeks later in early July, the Army of the Potomac engaged Robert E. Lee's Army of Northern Virginia at Gettysburg. In September the Army of the Cumberland met Braxton Bragg's Army of Tennessee at Chickamauga. Finally, that November a reinforced Union army under Grant's overall direction again fought Bragg's rebels outside Chattanooga.

At Champion Hill Grant's troops can be found using a mix of formations, suggesting only a limited adoption of the new technique. On May 16 the Union divisions of Major General John A. Logan and Brigadier General Alvin P. Hovey both employed Casey's concept as they formed for their attack. Those of Theophilus T. Gerrard and Eugene A. Carr, by contrast, formed in Scott's single line of battle.[32] Carr, Gerrard, and Hovey were all part of the XIII Corps, while Logan belonged to the XVII Corps, which suggests that the embrace of new techniques was not limited to nor advocated by any single corps command. This mixed approach can still be found six months later, when on November 25, while assaulting Missionary Ridge outside of Chattanooga, Brigadier General John M.

Corse's brigade used the double line, while Colonel John M. Loomis's four regiments used a single line.[33] Both Corse and Loomis belonged to the Fourth Division, XV Corps, suggesting that usage was not even standardized within the units of a single division.

At Gettysburg, Union brigades used single-line formations almost exclusively. When the I Corps formed their final defensive position atop Seminary Ridge on the afternoon of July 1, for example, they did so with twenty-six of their twenty-eight available regiments deployed in a single line of slightly more than a mile in length.[34] When three brigades of Brigadier General William Caldwell's First Division, II Corps went into action on July 2, each brigade also did so with all regiments abreast, two brigades forward and one in support; only the 57th New York was in a reserve position within the three brigades.[35] These deployments were far from atypical. Overwhelmingly, as Union brigades deployed for battle at Gettysburg, they formed single lines as dictated by Scott.

At Chickamauga almost every brigade in Rosecrans's army entered the fight using Casey's new "square" formation. From there they sometimes deployed into other formations, depending on circumstances. By contrast, the Confederates entered that fight in the old manner first dictated by Scott's manual. An excellent example of the two systems and how they worked can be found in examining the entry of Major General John M. Palmer's and Brigadier General Richard W. Johnson's Union divisions into the fight at noon on September 19, opposing Major General Benjamin F. Cheatham's Confederate division. Johnson's command, of the XX Corps, and Palmer's, of the XXI Corps, went into action side by side that day, fighting in Brock and Winfrey Fields. Both commands initially deployed exactly alike, two brigades abreast and one in reserve, each with two regiments up and two in support.

Cheatham's line formed with three brigades in front, each in a single line of regiments, and extended almost a mile in length. Two brigades, also formed singly, were in support. As each side advanced, the advantages of the new formation became apparent. Each Federal division commander, centered within his compact divisional front, was never more than a couple of hundred yards from his key subordinates. This was a decided benefit in terms of reaction time, as Palmer's men soon discovered. When a courier from Rosecrans brought word that Palmer should watch his right flank, the general was able to shift his brigades into an echeloned (staggered) formation for better flank protection, all while on the move. Both Palmer and Johnson maintained tight forma-

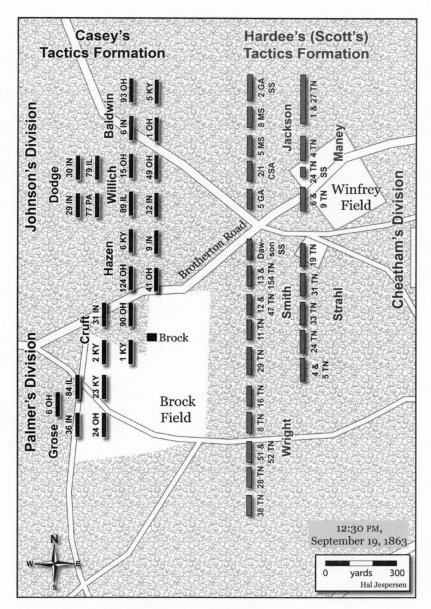

Casey's Tactics Formation

Hardee's (Scott's) Tactics Formation

Johnson's Division

Baldwin
93 OH | 5 KY
6 IN | 1 OH

Dodge
29 IN | 30 IN
77 PA | 79 IL

Willich
15 OH | 49 OH
89 IL | 32 IL

Hazen
6 KY | 9 IN
124 OH | 41 OH

Cruft
31 IN
90 OH
2 KY | 1 KY

Palmer's Division

Grose
6 OH | 84 IL
36 IN | 23 KY
24 OH

■ Brock

Brock Field

Jackson
2 GA | SS
8 MS
2/1 | CSA
5 GA

1 & 27 TN
4 TN
24 TN | SS
6 & 9 TN

Maney

Winfrey Field

Brotherton Road

Smith
13 & | Daw-
154 TN | son SS
12 & | 47 TN
33 TN | 31 TN | 19 TN
24 TN
4 & | 5 TN

19 TN

Strahl

Cheatham's Division

16 TN
8 TN
51 & | 52 TN
28 TN
38 TN

Wright

12:30 PM,
September 19, 1863

N
W   E
S

0   yards   300

Hal Jespersen

Casey's Tactics Versus Hardee's Tactics at Chickamauga.

tions as they advanced, and when they found the enemy, they entered the fight almost simultaneously.

Cheatham's men had harder going. His long line attenuated further as his brigadiers struggled to control their brigade frontages. They soon lost control of their formations. Gaps opened in the line between and sometimes in the middle of each brigade. Instead of striking the Union forces in a compact mass, Cheatham's brigades entered the fight singly— in some cases regiment by regiment—negating any theoretical advantage of having all of a brigade's firepower in the front line.

Replacing those engaged units as their ammunition was exhausted was also a much simpler process for the Yankees. Union brigadiers could simply swap front and rear regiments, allowing the relieved front line to replenish ammunition and take a breather as needed. Cheatham had to replace whole brigades or risk opening huge gaps in his front. This took much more time, and several times Confederate infantrymen found themselves out of bullets, enduring Union fire with no way to return it, while awaiting replacement. All in all, the firefight in Brock Field that afternoon was clear proof that the new formation was of real value in combat.

The remarkable consistency found in the Army of the Cumberland's deployments is a tribute to the degree to which Rosecrans not only embraced new ideas but also insisted they be properly implemented. He enthusiastically adopted Casey's manual once it was officially anointed by the War Department. It is also worth noting, however, that Rosecrans did not stop tinkering with new tactical ideas once Casey was the standard; he let Willich conduct his experiments, pushed for his own tactical innovation in the form of the elite battalions, and authorized Wilder's improvements in mounted infantry.

Command and Logistics

Rosecrans's influence in the tactical realm is fascinating, but the long-term effect was minor. His departure in the wake of defeat at Chicka-mauga happened before some of the most important changes had fully blossomed, and as a result they remain only footnotes to history. The general's influence on the logistics of the war in the western theater proved far more lasting. In fact, the framework of William T. Sherman's drive to capture Atlanta in 1864 was laid by Rosecrans and would not have been possible without the careful preparations he fostered. The single largest component of Sherman's forces in that campaign was the Army of the Cumberland, and with it came all of the supply-and-support structure Rosecrans created.

Rosecrans commanded both the Army of the Cumberland and the department of the same name. As such, his priorities between field army and department sometimes conflicted. The former required a constant flow of supplies and sufficient manpower to mass against the enemy, while the latter was also responsible for securing huge tracts of once-rebellious territory, administering military justice in the wake of a collapsed civil government, and protecting Unionist civilians. To manage all these diverse responsibilities, Rosecrans developed a sophisticated staff system, one far more involved than what had been anticipated early in the war. He was not the only Union commander to serve in this dual capacity, but he was the most forward looking in developing the administrative structure needed to run such complex operations.[36] Exploring the full scope of the Department of the Cumberland's wide-ranging and evolving staff organization is beyond the scope of this study. In two critical areas, however, Rosecrans's innovative approach to problem solving made lasting contributions to the Union war effort.

Two factors dictated Rosecrans's priorities as he contemplated the tasks expected of him upon assuming his new command in November 1862. The first—and most important—was supply. As already alluded to, the Federal hold on Nashville that winter was rendered tenuous by the evidenced fragility of the rail link back to Louisville, through which virtually all of his army's needs flowed. Rosecrans had to have a secure and steady flow of supplies even if this line were interrupted for a time. Moreover, given the distance involved (which only increased with every step southward), guarding every mile of track, every bridge, and every tunnel was a massive task. It was simply not possible to guarantee that the rail line would remain free of enemy raiders. Instead, Rosecrans intended to accumulate massive supply dumps at forward depots, from which the army could live and function even if the track behind was broken for any length of time. Thus, the army needed more than just a day-to-day flow of materiel when the line was working, surpluses had to be accumulated in the forward dumps to cover the expected interruptions. Additionally, any breaks in rail lines had to be repaired and service restored as quickly as possible lest forward depots become exhausted and the army was once again threatened with retreat or starvation.

The army's 70,000 men and all their attendant animals could consume vast quantities of supplies on a daily basis. In forage for the horses and mules alone, requirements were approximately 300,000 pounds per day. An average soldier's daily ration in 1863 weighed about 4 pounds (an increase of 0.75 pound from the previous year), for another daily need of 280,000 pounds. In addition to more than 500,000 pounds of consumables per day, the army also needed to haul thousands of artillery rounds and millions of rifle cartridges for the army's fighting needs.[37]

The second factor was one of tactical mobility. While strategically the Federal army in Middle Tennessee was tied to a single lifeline (the railroad), Rosecrans favored a wide-ranging campaign of feint, deception, and maneuver. A single-minded advance from Nashville to Chattanooga simply following the path of the rails would force the Federals into a series of bloody and possibly disastrous frontal attacks on battlefields of Bragg's choosing. Instead, Rosecrans preferred to outflank his opponent and, if possible, fight the resultant battles on his terms. Doing so, however, would require two things: a thorough knowledge of the country ahead and the flexibility to cross the myriad of creeks, streams, rivers (both major and minor), and mountains that comprised the rugged terrain of southeast Tennessee, northeast Alabama, and northwest Georgia.

For all of these missions, Rosecrans turned to his engineers. In the antebellum army, engineers were the service's aristocracy of military professionals. Only the top graduates of West Point were allowed to select the engineering branch. This winnowing process ensured quality but limited the service's numbers. Moreover, the engineering branch was comprised almost entirely of officers. The peacetime army included only one company of enlisted men to supply skilled labor.

The war created a huge demand for engineering troops of all kinds, far outstripping the available force. Yet the government and the army only authorized an additional three companies of engineers at the war's outset. Historian Mark Hoffman has noted that "as late as January 1865, the Corps of Engineers numbered fewer than six hundred enlisted men . . . and eighty-six officers."[38] As a result, volunteers had to fill the void. A number of state regiments of actual engineering troops were recruited, most notably the 1st Michigan, as well as no less than four New York units. Both sides would soon also make use of thousands of blacks, either recruited as "contrabands" or impressed labor, but there remained a need for a large force of skilled manpower. Rosecrans's vast need for such troops was further complicated by the fact that three of the four

Regular Army engineering companies served in the eastern theater as a battalion within the Army of the Potomac. So too were most of the volunteer engineering regiments; only the 1st Michigan Engineers and Mechanics was stationed in the department when Rosecrans assumed command.

Within days of taking up his new duties, however, Rosecrans moved to augment these meager engineering assets. On November 3, 1862, he ordered that twenty men from each regiment, "half laborers and half mechanics," be selected for a permanent detail. Each detachment should be commanded by "the most intelligent and energetic lieutenant" with a knowledge of civil engineering, all grouped together in a new organization known as the Pioneer Brigade.[39] A prototype for this organization might have been a similar order issued by then-Colonel Willich in 1861 that created a small pioneer corps for his regiment, the 32nd Indiana Infantry. Clearly, Willich was not interested in tactical innovation alone. This force of some forty men was commanded by Lieutenant Joseph Peitzuch, who had served as a military engineer in Bavaria. One interesting feature of Willich's scheme was the wagons he intended to employ. Union veteran William Sumner Dodge recalled that their "bodies were built much like those of ordinary wagons, [but also] answered the purpose of pontoons, and with them a small stream could be easily and rapidly bridged."[40] Peitzuch's pioneer platoon, despite its small size, garnered a lot of attention. This idea was soon copied by Willich's divisional commander, Major General Alexander McCook, who formed a similar organization in his command that fall. Unfortunately, the idea died a-borning. A jurisdictional squabble concerning efforts to bridge the Green River at Munfordville, Kentucky, erupted between McCook's pioneers and the 1st Michigan Engineers in late 1861, which resulted in the pioneers being disbanded.[41] The then army commander, Major General Don Carlos Buell, unlike Rosecrans, did not tinker in experimentation. But under Rosecrans, this idea was born anew. His November order netted the Army of the Cumberland roughly 3,000 additional skilled laborers and would prove of great value in the army's subsequent campaigns. Their commander was a brilliant young West Pointer cast much in the mold of Rosecrans himself. Brigadier General James St. Clair Morton matriculated at the University of Pennsylvania at the age of fourteen and subsequently graduated from West Point in 1851, aged twenty-two and second in his class. Ranking into the engineers, Morton worked on seacoast defenses in New York, Charleston, and Savannah before the war. By 1862 he labored as Buell's chief engineer; Rosecrans retained his services.

The creation of the corps was not without renewed controversy. Once the regimental and brigade commanders in the army realized that the loss of so many of their best men was permanent, they protested vehemently. Brigadier General William B. Hazen felt that he had been tricked by the new army commander. He was under the impression that the pioneers would serve most of the time with their brigades and only rarely with the new command. According to Hazen, removing the men from their regiments for long periods of time was both bad for discipline and wasteful. He believed that more could be done with the men kept close at hand.[42]

While the pioneers served well in both their stated function and as infantry in the fighting line at Stones River, some of Hazen's complaints were borne out in the subsequent Tullahoma Campaign. General McCook, now a corps commander, discovered the pioneers ahead of his XX Corps at one point moving too slowly and blocking the roads, which earned Morton a blistering rebuke from Rosecrans. Still, the organization persisted. Discipline was tightened. The pioneers provided invaluable service in the campaign for Chattanooga. In addition to repairing bridges, corduroying roads, and bridging the myriad of rivers, they created the entrenched forward depot at Murfreesboro, christened "Fortress Rosecrans" in honor of their chief, the largest earthen bastion constructed during the entire war. The pioneers also built the sheds, warehouses, and other facilities that become the major supply depots at Bridgeport and in Chattanooga itself once that city fell into Union hands.

The pioneers' contribution to the Army of the Cumberland's campaigns was immense. Fortress Rosecrans proved an essential part the Union answer to the problems caused by Confederate raiders in 1862 by becoming the immense forward depot Rosecrans envisioned. The site embraced 225 acres, could hold enough rations for 100,000 men for six months, and was estimated to be able to withstand an attack from up to 60,000 rebels. It eventually held a convalescent hospital and 50-acre vegetable garden as well as the warehouses for the army's hoarded supplies. Constructed between January and June 1863, it foreshadowed similar entrenchments at Bridgeport and Stevenson constructed that August as well as the fortified camp that Chattanooga eventually became prior to the 1864 drive toward Atlanta.[43]

After Tullahoma in July 1863, many of the supplies stockpiled in Fortress Rosecrans were redeployed to Bridgeport in order to shift the reserve closer to Chattanooga. All of this took time, especially over the relatively rickety rails of the Nashville and Chattanooga Railroad, which did not have the benefit of Federal expertise to help maintain the route until mid-July 1863. By August 20, however, several weeks' worth of re-serve rations were on hand, allowing Rosecrans to safely undertake the next stage of his campaign and initiate his march toward Chattanooga.

Authorities in Washington, D.C., often failed to appreciate the unique difficulties faced by the Army of the Cumberland. Not until Quartermas-ter General Montgomery C. Meigs traveled to Chattanooga in the wake of Chickamauga to examine the situation firsthand did the War Department gain a full understanding of those challenges. On September 27, 1863, Meigs telegraphed a description of affairs to Secretary of War Stanton. "The difficulties of transportation of supplies are immense," he wired, adding details of railroads, wagons, bridges, and steamboats. His lengthy cable concluded with the following: "Of the rugged nature of this region, I had no conception when I left Washington. I never traveled on such roads before."[44]

One final example of the type of careful planning that hallmarked Rosecrans's preparations for a campaign bears closer examination. The Tennessee River was the most significant natural obstacle facing the Army of the Cumberland. If the army intended to advance beyond Chattanooga, the Nashville and Chattanooga railway would have to be extended to that city before any new campaign could begin. Two major bridges would have to be rebuilt in order to do this. The first carried the rails across the Tennessee proper at Bridgeport; the other spanned a narrow canyon at Running Water Creek, which cut through Raccoon Mountain between Bridgeport and Chattanooga. Both structures were destroyed by the Confederates as they fell back from Middle Tennessee.

As departmental commander, Rosecrans contracted with firms in Cincinnati and Chicago to rebuild the two bridges, choosing from among the most prestigious and experienced railroad builders in the business.[45] While those bridges were under construction, the general also planned for an interim solution to establishing a new base in Chattanooga by using steamboats. The only problem with that plan was the fact that the Tennessee River was not navigable for its entire length. Muscle Shoals, in Alabama, precluded simply sailing the needed vessels upriver all the way from the Ohio. Instead, Rosecrans intended to build five small steamers at Bridgeport, hauling the necessary engines and other hardware over the rails.

Union army assistant quartermaster William G. Le Duc later described the first of these boats, the *Chattanooga*. "By mounting an engine, boiler, and stern-wheel on a flat-bottomed scow," he noted, serviceable shallow-draft boats could be "used in carrying and towing up supplies until the completion of the railroad."[46] The 1st Michigan Engineers and Mechanics furnished much of the rough labor. An expert boat builder named Turner was brought in from Lake Erie to supervise the impromptu shipwrights. In time this degree of foresight would pay tremendous dividends in breaking the Confederate stranglehold on the Union army after its defeat at Chickamauga. With the overland routes so poor and mountainous, the Federals were slowly starving in place until the river could be reopened and these vessels began hauling supplies upriver to Brown's Ferry.

Eventually, the steamboat fleet far exceeded even Rosecrans's expectations. The "cracker line" (as the impromptu supply line was christened by hungry troops after it was established at the end of October 1863) included a dozen boats built at Bridgeport. The *Chattanooga* and the *Chickamauga* were the first two launched, to be joined over the next year by the *Atlanta,* the *Bridgeport,* the *General Sherman,* the *General Thomas,* the *Kingston,* the *Lookout,* the *Missionary,* the *Resaca,* the *Stone River,* and the *Wauhatchie.* Another five boats were raised and repaired from vessels sunk at the Chattanooga docks: the *Dunbar,* the *James Glover,* the *Holston,* the *Tennessee,* and the *Paint Rock.* All of these boats would play an important role in supporting Union operations along the upper Tennessee River through the end of the war.[47]

In addition to the above-named vessels, the engineers embarked on boat building of a more informal kind. They constructed dozens of barges and pontoons, including the square-prowed craft that the Federals used to capture Brown's Ferry at the end of October. Since there was not enough cut lumber to be had in Chattanooga, they had to turn their hand to running sawmills, eventually turning out thousands of board feet of timber for use in trestles and buildings as well as nautical needs.

Equally as important as supplies or engineering capacity was knowledge of the country. In his campaigns Rosecrans favored wide envelopments, turning movements designed to outflank and discomfit the enemy via maneuver rather than drive him from position after position with head-on assaults. In doing so, the general by necessity scattered his army, moving in multiple columns across a wide front. Such methods were faster than attempting to move the entire army along a single axis of advance. These tactics also had the benefit of confusing his Confederate opposition as to which column would prove to be the main blow. In the days before instant communication, of course, these methods also entailed great risk. Dividing one's forces gave even a badly outnumbered enemy the opportunity to defeat any single column isolated from the others. In such a case, faulty maps could prove fatal. If the advancing army needed to concentrate rapidly in order to meet a threat, then wrong turns, unexpected terrain, or poorly estimated distances could spell disaster.

Knowledge of the terrain ahead was key. If the marching distance between two points was assumed to be fifteen miles and instead turned out to be twenty-five, the troops traversing that route could arrive either a day later than expected or too exhausted and straggled out to fight. A house or named location that turned out not to exist or was incorrectly labeled could send a column marching fruitlessly in the wrong direction. To use one famous example, the Confederate army was much plagued by bad maps during the summer of 1862, when defending their own capitol at Richmond. An "old Cold Harbor" and a "new Cold Harbor," coupled with an overly taciturn Stonewall Jackson, led a local guide to direct nearly 30,000 Confederate troops to the wrong part of the battlefield at Gaines's Mill on June 27, 1862. Just a few days later, Major General John Magruder experienced similar frustration and misdirection because two roads had the same name. Magruder had no idea that there were two "New Market Roads" and inadvertently took the wrong route. If the Confederates had so much trouble with confusing maps just a few miles outside their own capital city, how much trouble might a Federal army have in obtaining information about Middle Tennessee or North Georgia?

To solve this problem, Rosecrans assembled a topographical-engineering department unequalled in any other Union field army. If engineers were the Old Army's elite, the Topographical Engineers were the elite of the elite. Only the top West Point graduates were assigned to that task. In the prewar army the department was an exceedingly small organization, with entry restricted to only a handful of men each year. The force shrunk again with the outbreak of war. In addition to those men who resigned to join the budding Confederacy, many of these exceptional graduates, considered rising stars by their peers, rose to high commands at the outbreak of war.

Despite this lack of available professionals, Rosecrans again found plenty of supplemental civilian talent to draw from in the form of skilled volunteer officers. The two men who ultimately ran the general's mapping effort were a case in point. Both young and full of talent, Captains

William E. Merrill and William C. Margedant soon gained their commander's esteem. Merrill graduated from West Point in 1859, a class-
mate of Confederate cavalryman Joe Wheeler. Margedant was a German
immigrant, a machinist who arrived in America in 1854. Together they
married the professional mapping skills Rosecrans required with a spirit
of innovation and creativity that provided the Army of the Cumberland
with a topographic department unmatched in Federal service. Merrill
and Margedant formed the nucleus of this force, serving on Rosecrans's
staff, but they were far from the only members.

In 1887 Margedant discussed the nature of the Army of the Cumberland's topological-engineering department in considerable detail. He and
Merrill served as the army's central mapping detachment at Rosecrans's
headquarters, preparing maps that were disseminated to the various
subcommands. This marked only the beginning of the process, however.
"We had representative engineers and surveyors with brigades, divisions,
and army corps and even with regiments and outposts. No scouting or
reconnoitering party went out without its engineer."[48] These men were
the field researchers and kept careful notes of all important features.
Road mileage was recorded between all significant points. Villages, rural
post offices, and even prominent individual dwellings were among the
details recorded. Hills, mountains, passes, and other geological features
figured prominently, with rivers being especially important. Bridges and
fords, as well as their conditions and quality, were all among the data
gathered and appended to the existing base maps.

These amended maps then flowed back up the chain of command.
"Additions and corrections to our information maps had to be sent daily
to . . . headquarters," Margedant continued, where "we corrected, en-
larged, and combined our maps" with these field observations. Even
more intelligence was gathered at army headquarters from "prisoners,
scouts, and our own personal reconnoitering," which further enhanced
the new maps.[49]

All this effort would be of limited value, however, if there were no
quick way to reverse the process and send revised maps back down
the chain of command. Merrill and Margedant had an answer for that
problem too. "The revised maps were then printed at night or in a special printing wagon . . . and distributed . . . through . . . the army." With
new maps in hand, further new data or corrections could be appended
by the field engineers, and the process would repeat again. "Engineers

and commanders . . . were thus constantly kept advised and ordered to make additions and corrections at once." The process was labor intensive. The detachment "often employed as high as thirty draftsmen; we had a large and full equipment of photographic apparatuses, among them solar cameras to enlarge views of rebel fortifications. We [also] had two lithographic presses," Margedant continued.[50]

Among the most ingenious processes was one Margedant claimed to have invented himself. Solar cameras, also known as solar printing, was a process by which, through the use of chemicals and treated paper, drawings could be reproduced simply by exposing them to sunlight for a few minutes to create a "reverse image," white lines and lettering on a black background. A large number of such copies could be made quickly. In the field the topographical engineers could modify these "black maps" directly by drawing on them with potassium, which would bleach the black paper into new white lines. It was, in effect, an early form of blueprinting.[51]

The whole system was a highly efficient means of passing information both up and down the chain of command and contributed immeasurably to the success of campaigns like Tullahoma and the early stages of the advance on Chattanooga. Of course, much depended on the skill and accuracy of the data collectors, those topographical engineers serving on staffs at brigade and division. These men did not need to be military-trained engineers. Those with civil engineering or surveying experience, or other intelligent officers or enlisted men with drawing skills and a quick eye for terrain, proved adept for the task. By far the best-known example was Lieutenant Ambrose Bierce, who served on the brigade staff of General Hazen. Bierce eventually became famous for his writing rather than his engineering skills and would later become a famous journalist and fiction author. But he also possessed the expertise necessary to make for a very capable field engineer. With guidance from his superiors, the young lieutenant's talents could be fully utilized by the trained, professional military engineers at army headquarters.[52]

"The organization of a topological department," Margedant concluded, reminiscing to Rosecrans in 1887, "was not specified in the army regulations. It was a creation of our own, brought to life by your [Rosecrans's] orders and directions, and inspired by your personal influence." Moreover, he continued, "there was no material change in the department when you [Rosecrans] left; we kept onward following the spirit of the founder."[53]

Taken in total, it is striking to see how much innovation flourished under William Starke Rosecrans's eleven-month tenure as commander of the Army of the Cumberland. While by no means did every idea germinate with him alone, he nevertheless seized upon good ideas when he saw them, extrapolated where necessary, and embraced often unconventional and resourceful thinking in others. Not every one of the innovations Rosecrans fostered or encouraged survived to the end of the war, but many did. His logistical and topographical concepts proved the most lasting, producing triumphs both under his command and serving as the foundation of later Army of the Cumberland victories won in 1864, well after he had been relieved. His tactical ideas met with less permanence, though they were highly effective. Had Rosecrans been in command of the Army of the Cumberland in the latter half of the war, when many more modern arms found their way into the Union ranks, those ideas might have taken deeper root. Even tactically creative solutions such as Willich's "Advance, Firing" technique might have garnered much wider interest.

Of course, General Rosecrans did not remain in command; a series of costly missteps at the Battle of Chickamauga led to his departure. Historians will continue to debate whose fault those blunders were and whether or not Rosecrans was unjustly relieved. What is clear is that Major General George Thomas was more of a traditionalist than the man he replaced and discontinued some of the more interesting techniques then budding in the ranks of the Army of the Cumberland. Among them was Willich's concept. Perhaps to the detriment of future operations, "Advance, Firing" was destined to spread no further. Shortly after taking command, Thomas ordered Willich's men (and presumably any others using it) to return to the traditional drill manuals. He also favored converting the mounted infantry into conventional cavalry units, much to the dismay of Wilder's troops.

Thomas was no fool, however, and certainly understood the benefits the army derived from the logistics net and staff departments Rosecrans had built. He retained the mapmakers as well as the pioneers, eventually converting the latter to volunteer engineer regiments. Sherman made extensive use of the Army of the Cumberland's topographic department throughout that summer and fall of fighting in 1864. His entire advance toward Atlanta that year would not have been possible without the immense logistical framework Rosecrans had conceived and initiated at Chattanooga, greatly expanded upon by Thomas in the fall of 1863, and Sherman admitted as much. The Army of the Cumberland "was much the largest of three [I commanded], was best provided for, and contained the best corps of engineers, railroad managers, and repair parties, as well as the best body of spies and provost-marshals." Accordingly, noted Sherman, "on [Thomas] we were therefore compelled in great measure to rely for those most useful branches of service."[54] All of these elements would contribute significantly to the final victories in the last full year of the war.

ACKNOWLEDGMENTS

The author would like to thank Dr. William Glenn Robertson and National Park Service historian James Ogden III for the help and encouragement they have provided over the years.

NOTES

1. For a discussion of the expansion of the curriculum at West Point in the 1850s, see Wayne Wei-Siang Tshieh, *West Pointers in the Civil War: The Old Army in War and Peace* (Chapel Hill: University of North Carolina Press, 2009), 88–89.

2. William M. Lamars, *The Edge of Glory: A Biography of General William S. Rosecrans, U.S.A.* (New York: Harcourt, Brace, & World, 1961), 16.

3. Glenn Tucker, *Chickamauga* (1961; reprint, Dayton, Ohio: Morningside, 1981), 40–41.

4. Whitelaw Reid, *Ohio in the War: Her Statesmen, Her Generals, Her Soldiers, Volume 1* (Cincinnati: Moore, Wilstach, and Baldwin, 1868), 313.

5. The nature and influence of the rifled musket on the Civil War has been much debated and need not be detailed again here. For three interesting and evolving views on the influence of the rifle, see Paddy Griffith, *Battle Tactics of the Civil War* (New Haven, Conn.: Yale University Press, 1987); Brent Nosworthy, *The Bloody Crucible of Courage* (New York: Carroll and Graf, 2003); and Earl J. Hess, *The Rifle Musket in Civil War Combat* (Lawrence: University Press of Kansas, 2008).

6. Joseph G. Bilby, *Civil War Firearms* (Conshohocken, Pa.: Combined Books, 1996), 130.

7. John Walter, *The Rifle Story* (London: Greenhill, 2006), 69. Lincoln did not personally intervene and order the War Department to buy Spencer's rifles, as has sometimes been alleged. Spencer already had an army contract for a number of weapons and was about to sign a much larger deal for a carbine version for the cavalry, but the added publicity certainly did not hurt.

8. Though several thousand Henry rifles were used during the war, the Henry would go on to greater fame as the Winchester, after the Winchester Arms Company of New Haven, Connecticut, put an improved version on sale in 1866.

9. U.S. War Department, *The War of the Rebellion: A Compilation of the Official Records of the Union and Confederate Armies,* 128 vols. (Washington, D.C.: GPO, 1880–1901), ser. 1 (hereinafter cited as *OR;* all citations to series 1 unless otherwise specified), 23(2):29.

10. Ibid., 643.

11. Ibid., 34.

12. Ibid., 20(2):58–59.

13. Ibid., 51.

14. As will be seen, there is some fleeting evidence that at least some "elite battalions" were formed, if only for a short time.

15. Benjamin F. MaGee, *History of the 72nd Volunteer Infantry of the Mounted Lightning Brigade* (Lafayette, Ind.: S. Vater, 1882), 89.

16. Robert L. Willett, *The Lightning Mule Brigade, Abel Streight's 1863 Raid into Alabama* (Carmel, Ind.: Guild, 1999), 72.

17. See George H. Morgan, "Cavalry in the Eastern Theater, 1862" (class thesis, U.S. Army War College, 1913).

18. *OR,* 23(2):51.

19. Ibid., 574.

20. John J. Hight and Gilbert R. Stormont, *History of the Fifty-Eighth Regiment of Indiana Volunteer Infantry, Its Organization, Campaigns, and Battles from 1861 to 1865* (Princeton, Ind., 1895), 185, 187, 192, 337, 368.

21. J. T. Patton, *Personal Recollections of Four Years in Dixie: A Paper Read before the Commandary of the State of Michigan Military Order of the Loyal Legion of the United States* (Detroit: Winn & Hammond, 1892), 10.

22. Ibid., 15.

23. A letter published in the *Dayton Weekly Journal* on May 15, 1863, notes that the elites were only disbanded at the end of April.

24. *OR,* 30(1):590.

25. Donald Allendorf, *Long Road to Liberty* (Kent, Ohio: Kent State University Press, 2006), 106.

26. See 15th Missouri Volunteer Infantry, Compiled Service Records, microfilm M405, National Archives, roll 499.

27. Unknown private's letter, 73rd Illinois, Mar. 23, 1863, copy in author's collection.

28. One exception to this rule would be the small number of Whitworth and Kerr rifles that allowed some Confederates to form what the modern military would call sniper teams. For a good look at these Confederate sharpshooter battalions, see Fred L. Ray, *Shock Troops of the Confederacy* (Asheville, N.C.: CFS, 2006).

29. Alexis Cope, *The Fifteenth Ohio Volunteers and Its Campaigns* (Columbus, Ohio: A. Cope, 1916), 279.

30. Charles T. Clark, *Opdyke Tigers: 125th O.V.I., History of the Regiment and of the Campaigns and Battles of the Army of the Cumberland* (Columbus Ohio: Spahr and Glenn, 1895), 107. This tactic does not exist in any U.S. manuals of the time. It was either invented by General Willich or copied by him from a European, perhaps Prussian, manual. Only Willich's brigade used the tactic, however, and there is no obvious connection explaining how any of Harker's men came to learn it.

31. Hardee commanded a Confederate corps against Rosecrans and the Army of the Cumberland at the Battle of Stones River but was absent for Chickamauga, having been transferred to Mississippi in the early fall of 1863.

32. Timothy B. Smith, *Champion Hill: Decisive Battle for Vicksburg* (El Dorado Hills, Calif.: Savas-Beatie, 2004), 183, 312.

33. Peter Cozzens, *The Shipwreck of Their Hopes* (Urbana: University of Illinois Press, 1994), 207, 213, 226, 228.

34. For the composition of this line, see Bradley M. Gottfried, *Maps of Gettysburg* (El Dorado Hills, Calif.: Savas-Beatie, 2007), 85, 93, 109.

35. Ibid., 171.

36. See Robert J. Dalessandro, *Major General William S. Rosecrans and the Transformation of the Staff of the Army of the Cumberland: A Case Study,* (Strategy Research Project, U.S. Army War College, Carlisle Barracks, Pa., 2002), online version at http://www.dtic.mil/cgi-bin/GetTRDoc?Location=U2&doc=GetTRDoc.pdf&AD=ADA404422. Dalessandro argues that Rosecrans's staff evolved into the most complex of the war and proved to be a critical asset in winning the conflict, for Sherman relied on this same administrative structure to sustain his advance in 1864.

37. See Arthur L. Wagner, *Organization and Tactics* (Kansas City, Mo.: Hudson-Kimberly, 1891), 25–26, 499. Each mule required nine pounds of forage per day, each horse twelve pounds per day. The Army of the Cumberland contained approximately 30,000 horses and mules.

38. Mark Hoffman, *"My Brave Mechanics": The First Michigan Engineers and Their Civil War* (Detroit: Wayne State University Press, 2007), 1.

39. *OR,* 20(2):6.

40. William Sumner Dodge, *History of the Old Second Division* (Chicago: Church and Goodman, 1864), 90.

41. Hoffman, *"My Brave Mechanics,"* 42–43, 345n21; Dodge, *History of the Old Second Division,* 133.

42. A detailed examination of Hazen's objections to the practice can be found in William B. Hazen, *A Narrative of Military Service* (Boston: Ticknor, 1885), 405–409.

43. Today a local park at Stevenson, Alabama, preserves and commemorates Fort Harker, a Union earthwork established in the summer of 1862.

44. *OR,* 30(1):890–91.

45. William S. Rosecrans, "The Campaign for Chattanooga," *Century Magazine* 34, no. 1 (May 1887): 132.

46. William G. Le Duc, "The Little Steamboat that Opened the 'Cracker Line,'" *Battles and Leaders,* 3:676.

47. Charles Dana Gibson, with E. Kay Gibson, *The Army's Navy Series Volume II: Assault and Logistics, Union Army Coastal and River Operations, 1861–1866* (Camden, Maine: Ensign, 1995), 380.

48. William C. Margedant to Rosecrans, Sept. 21, 1887, William Starke Rosecrans Papers, Charles E. Young Research Library, University of California, Los Angeles.

49. Ibid.

50. Ibid.

51. The invention of blueprinting is usually attributed to a French chemist, Alphonse Poitevin, in 1861. Margedant's claim to have invented the "black map" process cannot be substantiated, and it may be that he meant only that he was the first to adapt the idea to field use and to use a potassium solution for corrections.

52. For the most extensive look at Ambrose Bierce's Chickamauga experience, see chapter 9.

53. Margedant to Rosecrans, Sept. 21, 1887, Rosecrans Papers.

54. William T. Sherman, *Memoirs of General W. T. Sherman* (1875; reprint, New York: Library of America, 1990, 2 vols. published as one), 466.

CHAPTER 5

A TALE OF TWO ORDERS

Chickamauga, September 20, 1863

WILLIAM GLENN ROBERTSON

Of all the events that comprise the Battle of Chickamauga, arguably the most critical are two that occurred between 11:30 P.M. on September 19 and 11:30 A.M. the following day. The first event of note is the four-hour delay in beginning the Confederate attack at first light on September 20 as General Braxton Bragg intended. The second is the opening of the gap in the Federal line around 11:00 A.M. on the same day, a gap that facilitated the disintegration of the right wing of the Army of the Cumberland and resulted in its defeat. The significance of these events has long been recognized, and a considerable body of analysis has been erected upon the surprisingly scant facts that form the traditional narrative of both cases. Analysis of each event has followed a generally similar pattern. First, there must be a favored outcome. Second, there must be an individual who, either by action or inaction, prevents the favored outcome from occurring. The fault may be willful or inadvertent, malicious or incompetent, but it must be pinned upon one individual if possible. Finally, the result must be extremely serious or catastrophic to the individual's own side. In other words, the simpler the story, the more dramatic the tale, the better the narrative becomes, and the longer it lives to be repeated over the years. Yet complex affairs, such as battles involving more than 100,000 combatants, seldom can be analyzed in such simple fashion without doing violence to the truth and unfairly besmirching the reputations of commanders. In both cases to be described below, the traditional story arc has been one of simplification and single-minded blame heaped upon two individuals. A closer look at these events, utilizing recent scholarship, shows that the traditional account is overly simplified at best and completely wrong at worst. It is indeed time for the record to be corrected.

Before the two critical events are reexamined in detail, it may be useful to summarize the traditional version of each. In regard to the delayed Confederate attack on the morning of September 20, the villain is Lieutenant General Leonidas Polk, commander of the Right Wing of the Army of Tennessee. In a meeting at army headquarters during the evening of September 19, Polk received instructions from General Bragg to begin the next morning's attack at "day-dawn." As a control measure, all other Confederate units were to follow Polk's lead, with each unit stepping off when the unit on its right advanced. Thus his role was critical to beginning the attack plan Bragg had conceived. Polk, however, was remiss in not notifying all of his subordinates, most notably Lieutenant General D. H. Hill, whose troops formed Polk's right. When morning came without Confederate movement, the wing commander was slow to react and ultimately acquiesced in Hill's decision to take an additional four hours to prepare. Those four hours of daylight were a gift to Polk's opponents, who improved their defenses so well that his tardy attack was doomed to utter and bloody failure. On the Federal side of the lines, the malfeasance belonged to Brigadier General Thomas Wood, commanding the First Division, XXI Corps. Ordered to replace another division in the line of battle in midmorning on September 20, Wood was so slow to execute his orders that he was reprimanded publicly by Major General William S. Rosecrans, commander of the Army of the Cumberland. Smarting under the rebuke, Wood acted impulsively ninety minutes later when he received a poorly worded order to leave the line and support another division. Rather than seek clarification or arrange a replacement, Wood perversely withdrew his division without coordination with other commanders, thereby opening a wide gap in the Federal line. Confederate divisions under Lieutenant General James Longstreet, commanding the Left Wing, promptly exploited the opening, causing the rout of much of the Federal army and the loss of the Battle of Chickamauga. In some variants of the story, several staff officers share the blame with Wood, but he is the primary villain. In both of these cases, the traditional view assumes either incompetence or gross malfeasance. The facts, however, are not quite so simple, and the blame is far less easy to apportion.[1]

Polk's Undelivered Order

By the time the confused fighting of September 19 ebbed to a close, Braxton Bragg found himself faced with an entirely new situation. He had planned a flank attack that morning that would sweep down upon the Federal left, which he believed to be at Lee and Gordon's Mill. Unknown to him, the movement of the XIV Corps several miles north of the mill during the evening had entirely rearranged the dispositions of the Army of the Cumberland. When elements of both armies met on the morning of the nineteenth, the encounter came not at Lee and Gordon's Mill but in Bragg's rear. Forced to improvise, Bragg spent the day funneling divisions northward to stabilize the situation and regain control of the initiative. When darkness fell upon the blasted woods and trampled fields just east of the north–south La Fayette Road, the situation had indeed stabilized to Bragg's satisfaction. He had several major formations that had not yet been committed to the fight, and General Longstreet was momentarily expected to arrive from the Confederate railhead at Catoosa Station with additional units. Thus, Bragg remained confident enough to plan for a resumption of the offensive on the morrow. Still, with so many corps commanders operating in the tangled forest, command and control had been difficult to maintain. The five infantry corps commanders (Lieutenant Generals Polk and Hill, and Major Generals William H. T. Walker, Simon Buckner, and John Hood) had not worked especially well together, and if Longstreet arrived before dawn, he would complicate matters even further. Bragg's primary subordinates were all highly individualistic and very hard to control on a field where the army commander's visibility was limited. Thus, Bragg resolved to simplify his command structure for the twentieth by dividing the army's infantry formations into two wings. As the senior lieutenant generals, Polk and Longstreet (if he arrived in time) would command the halves of the army, Polk taking the Right Wing, Longstreet the Left Wing.[2]

Bragg envisioned that Polk, with the corps of Hill and Walker plus Major General Frank Cheatham's division of Polk's own corps, would initiate the attack on the morning of the twentieth. If successful, he would turn the Federal left, pulverize it, and drive the enemy southward, away from Chattanooga. As the Right Wing advanced, Longstreet's Left Wing would join the action, and the Federals would ultimately be driven into the mountainous terrain to the south. There, Rosecrans's army would

be either destroyed or starved into surrender. Yet all depended upon
Polk's Wing initiating the battle, which was to occur at first light. With
a line of battle more than two miles long, a control measure was needed
to ensure unity of action. The firing of a signal gun was deemed too easy
to misinterpret and was at the mercy of a random Federal shot inadvertently triggering the attack. Thus, Bragg decided simply that whenever
a commander saw the unit on his right advance, he should immediately
join the charge. The right-hand brigade of the right-hand division of the
right-hand corps in Polk's Wing would therefore control the timing of
the attack. If that brigade stepped off at "day-dawn," units would engage
sequentially in a ripple effect until the entire Army of Tennessee was
in action. The opening of the attack would therefore be entirely in the
hands of Leonidas Polk and his Right Wing. To ensure that the general
understood his role, Bragg called him to army headquarters at Thedford's
Ford for a face-to-face discussion.[3]

Accompanied by aides Henry Yeatman and William Richmond, Polk
arrived around 9:00 P.M. and immediately entered into conference with
the army commander. Bragg described the wing arrangement, noting
that Lieutenant General Hill would now be under Polk, his rank notwithstanding. Although he had been nominated to the rank of lieutenant
general, Hill had not yet been confirmed by the Confederate Congress,
making his rank provisional only. Next Bragg explained the scheme of
maneuver for the following morning and the role of the Right Wing in
initiating the battle. From all appearances, Polk understood both the
realignment of forces into wings and the plan to be followed at daybreak.
While at headquarters, Polk met Major Generals Hood, Buckner, and
John Breckinridge, but he did not tarry long. After exchanging a few
pleasantries with Hood and Buckner, he and his two aides departed for
Polk's headquarters near Alexander's Bridge on Chickamauga Creek.
Breckinridge, whose division belonged to Hill's Corps and thus was part
of Polk's Wing, accompanied the small party with members of his own
staff. Having begun the day far to the south, Breckinridge's Division was
even then marching through the night east of the creek en route to a junction with the remainder of the corps. Polk, Breckinridge, and the aides,
however, were on the west side of the creek traveling a path through the
forest known today as the Viniard–Alexander Road. Somewhere along
the way, the party encountered Lieutenant Colonel Archer Anderson,
Hill's assistant adjutant general, accompanied by a junior staff officer,
probably Lieutenant R. H. Morrison. Anderson was seeking Hill, without

success, and thought he might be at Bragg's headquarters. Halting in the smoky woods, Polk and Anderson began a conversation about the next day's events.[4]

The colloquy between Polk and Anderson would later become the subject of controversy. According to the general, he informed the officer of three key things: first, that Hill's Corps was now part of Polk's Wing; second, that he desired to see Hill at his own headquarters as soon as possible; and third, that the attack would commence on the army's right at daybreak. Further, Polk told him that he wanted Breckinridge's Division to form in support of Hill's other division, Major General Patrick Cleburne's. When Anderson stated that Hill preferred Breckinridge to be on Cleburne's right, Polk acquiesced, permitting the general to post his corps as he chose. According to Anderson, he received the information on the new command relationships and the fact that Polk wanted to see Hill that night. He was adamant, however, that he was never told that the attack was to begin at daybreak. Later, when everyone involved in the affair tried to recall what had been said, positions of the principals hardened into the competing versions recounted above. A private letter from Henry Yeatman written less than three weeks after the event, however, indicates that Polk himself was not sure of exactly what he had told Anderson. Whatever was said, Breckinridge was a witness, and he later claimed not to have heard anything about a daybreak attack. Unfortunately, Yeatman did not hear the conversation, being at the rear of Polk's group talking to one of Breckinridge's staff. Lieutenant Richmond was nearer Polk and Anderson but did not record his recollections before he was killed the next day. Major A. C. Avery, Hill's assistant inspector general and who arrived during the Polk-Anderson discussion, later supported Anderson's version of events. Finally, all agreed that Polk stated that fires would be built at Alexander's Bridge, with sentries standing ready to convey Hill to his headquarters. Believing that he had done everything necessary to ensure that Hill knew what to do, Polk and his party continued their ride through the dark woodland to the wing commander's headquarters bivouac, while Anderson continued his search for Hill. At some point along the way, Polk's party encountered James Longstreet, who was riding to Thedford's Ford to find Bragg. After an exchange of pleasantries, both parties went their separate ways.[5]

Like so many other facts in this episode, the exact location of Polk's headquarters at Alexander's Bridge on the night of September 19 is in dispute. According to Captain Walter Morris, who established it during the afternoon, the camp was approximately fifty yards from the bridge on the east side of Chickamauga Creek. Morris offered this information to the general's son long after the war, when William Polk was preparing a biography of his father. Contemporaneous testimony, however, does not support this location. According to a deposition taken ten days after the battle, Private Lucien Charvet of the Orleans Light Horse, Polk's guard, testified that the headquarters site was "about one-half or three-quarters of a mile" from the bridge and one hundred yards from the main road down a side path. Charvet's statement was sworn before Andrew Ewing, presiding judge of the military court of Polk's Corps, and must be given considerable weight because the private was under oath and the events were both dramatic and recent. Both he and another private of the Orleans Light Horse, John Perkins, also testified that they served as guides directing all who sought Polk's headquarters on the night of the nineteenth. Perkins guarded the bridge itself, maintaining a fire there until 2:00 A.M., when he stoked it and retired for the night. Charvet, meanwhile, took position at the fork of the road leading to Polk's camp after being relieved from duty at the bridge at 9:30 P.M.[6]

Polk, Breckinridge, and their aides arrived at the camp, wherever located, around 11:00 P.M. There, Polk informed Lieutenant Colonel Thomas Jack, his assistant adjutant general, of what had transpired at Bragg's headquarters and directed him to prepare the orders for the next morning's attack. According to Jack's postbattle deposition, he drafted orders for Generals Hill and Cheatham to initiate the army's attack at daylight, holding Walker's Reserve Corps in its namesake capacity during the early phase of the operation. Jack then woke Captain Leeds Greenleaf, commanding the Orleans Light Horse, and asked him to provide couriers to carry the orders through the smoky woods to their addressees. All of the orders were sealed in envelopes; return of the opened and empty envelopes would signify delivery. Private John Fisher, the courier sent to find Hill, was told to seek him at Thedford's Ford, where Lieutenant Colonel Anderson had told Polk that Hill's headquarters would be located that evening. Fisher and the courier assigned to deliver Cheatham's orders departed quickly, but before the courier to Walker could leave, Walker himself appeared, having been brought to Polk's headquarters by the bridge guard, Private Perkins. After receiving his orders directly from Lieutenant Colonel Jack, Walker returned to his command. While Jack arranged the transmission of the orders, Polk and Breckinridge shared a brief supper, discussed the placement of Breckinridge's Division on the right of the line, and then slept for a few hours. Breckinridge left orders to be awakened at 2:30 A.M. so that he could rejoin his division before dawn. Meanwhile, his men bivouacked in a large field on the west side of Chickamauga Creek near Alexander's Bridge.[7]

While Private Fisher rode through the night fruitlessly searching for Hill, the general himself was also on the move. During the day, as his corps moved piecemeal northward to the battlefield, Hill had accompanied Cleburne's Division. That unit had gone into action around sunset on the north end of the battlefield and had not concluded its successful advance around the Winfrey Field until approximately 9:00 P.M. Having only one division to supervise because Breckinridge had not yet reached the field, Hill had then spent considerable time discussing the action with Cleburne and each of his three brigade commanders. Around 10:00 P.M. he started toward Thedford's Ford to receive orders from Bragg for the next day's fighting. Accompanying Hill were Captain Thaddeus Coleman, engineer, and Lieutenant James Reid, aide-de-camp. Their exact route to Thedford's is unknown, but it appears that they traveled from the Winfrey Field to Alexander's Bridge, where they crossed to the east bank of the Chickamauga. From the bridge, Hill's party passed up the Chickamauga valley in search of the ford. Along the way they met soldiers who told them that Breckinridge's Division was nearing Alexander's Bridge. On receipt of that news, Hill ordered Lieutenant Reid to find Breckinridge and escort him and his command to the right side of the corps's line. Reid obediently retraced his steps to Alexander's Bridge, where he eventually found Breckinridge at Polk's headquarters. When told that Hill wanted the Kentuckian's division to move up to the line of battle, Breckinridge responded that Polk had permitted him to rest his men briefly but that they would move before dawn. Reid then rode to Thedford's Ford to report to Hill.[8]

After dispatching Reid to find Breckinridge, Hill and Coleman continued southward on the east side of Chickamauga Creek. The passage of a cold front had caused the temperature to plummet, making the ride extremely unpleasant. Farther along, a dense fog developed in the valley and added its obscuring effects to the large amount of smoke hanging in the thick woods. Somehow Hill and Coleman missed Thedford's Ford and, unaware of that fact, continued upstream. Eventually, they found a crossing of the creek at Dalton's Ford, half a mile from Thedford's by water but approximately a mile by road. Now amid thousands of troops resting in the woods on the west bank, they easily gained directions to Thedford's

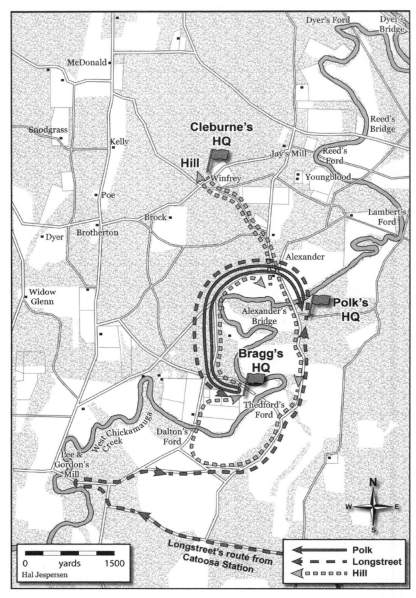

Movements of the Confederate High Command, Night of September 19, 1863.

Ford and went in search of Bragg's headquarters. Before finding Bragg, though, they encountered Archer Anderson and his party. Anderson quickly informed the general that he now reported to Polk, making it unnecessary for Hill to seek Bragg any longer. Probably disgusted at this news, certainly weary from a long day and night in the saddle, and possibly in pain from his chronic spinal problem, Hill elected to bivouac in the woods for several hours before returning to Alexander's Bridge. The time was near midnight, not long after Polk's orders were dispatched and while Longstreet was conferring with Bragg somewhere nearby. Sometime later, Lieutenant Reid arrived and was instructed by Hill to depart at 2:00 A.M. to guide Breckinridge's Division to the northern end of the line of battle. Hill, Anderson, Coleman, and the remaining staff officers then resumed their uncomfortable bivouac in the foggy woods. Meanwhile, Private Fisher, carrying Hill's instructions, continued his search for the corps commander.[9]

Back at Polk's headquarters, the fog thickened and the babble of noise quieted as those who could rest snuggled into their blankets. Polk, Breckinridge, and Lieutenant Colonel Jack all went to bed. Sometime after 1:00 A.M., the courier carrying the attack order to Frank Cheatham returned with the unsealed envelope, having accomplished his task. Before Jack went off duty, he instructed a clerk named McReady not to disturb either him or Polk during the remainder of the night. Around 2:00 A.M. Private Perkins, the sentry at Alexander's Bridge, stoked the beacon fire and retired for the night. He had been ordered to maintain his post until 1:00 A.M., but in view of Hill's non-arrival, he had conscientiously remained an additional hour. Around 2:30 A.M., Breckinridge awakened and soon departed with his division for the northern end of the battlefield. They were guided by Lieutenant Colonel T. F. Sevier, Polk's inspector general, and by Lieutenant Reid, who had ridden from Thedford's Ford to Alexander's Bridge in accord with Hill's directive. Around 3:00 A.M. Hill awakened at Thedford's, gathered his party, and headed for Alexander's Bridge. Reaching a point several hundred yards from the span, the general sent Captain Coleman to the stream in search of the sentries and signal fires Anderson had been told to expect. By this time, the fog in the creek valley had become extremely dense, and even though the road to the bridge passed through open fields, Coleman could see nothing. Finding neither sentries nor fires, he returned to Hill and reported that Polk's headquarters was nowhere to be found. Frustrated and disgusted, the general instructed Lieutenant R. H. Morrison, an aide-de-camp, to continue searching for the wing commander and tell him that Hill could be found with his troops if Polk still wanted to see him. Not long after the corps commander departed, Private Fisher returned to Polk's headquarters still carrying the sealed envelope with Hill's attack orders. He found only Jack's clerk on duty, and McReady repeated his instructions to awaken no one. Without further guidance, Fisher elected to return to the nearby camp of the Orleans Light Horse and warm himself at a convenient fire.[10]

Sunrise on September 20 came at 5:47 A.M., but morning twilight began at least thirty minutes earlier. The fog and pall of smoke notwithstanding, General Bragg expected the battle to be resumed as soon as there was enough light to facilitate an advance. On the north end of the army's line of battle, the three brigades of Breckinridge's Division were just coming into line on the right of Cleburne's Division. As they did so, Hill joined his division commanders around a campfire in the woods west of the Winfrey Field. At his headquarters east of Chickamauga Creek, Polk arose early. He quickly discovered that Private Fisher had not found Hill and instantly realized that the man who was to initiate the "day-dawn" attack had not received instructions to do so. Springing into action, Polk ordered Lieutenant Colonel Jack to write new attack orders addressed directly to Major Generals Breckinridge and Cleburne. Timed at 5:30 A.M., the new orders instructed the two division commanders to strike the enemy as soon as they were in position, without reference to the corps commander. This time the orders were entrusted not to a private but to Captain Frank Wheless, an assistant inspector general on Polk's staff. Jack explained the situation to Wheless while Polk enjoined the captain to hurry. Wheless spurred his horse and dashed toward Alexander's Bridge, shrouded in thick fog. As he crossed the bridge, he caught a glimpse of the sun rising and, keeping it on his right, found his way to Cheatham's headquarters. Quickly giving Cheatham his copy of the new orders, Wheless rode forward to the line, then turned north and entered the sector of Hill's Corps. Coming upon Archer Anderson and one of Breckinridge's aides, he sought assistance in locating Hill's division commanders. Anderson obliged, and the courier continued his journey.[11]

Reaching a campfire in the forest just west of the Winfrey Field, Wheless discovered Hill, Breckinridge, and Cleburne drinking coffee and warming themselves. When the captain dismounted, Hill put forward his hand to receive the orders, but the staff officer officiously declined, saying that the orders were for the two division commanders only. Breckinridge and Cleburne quickly passed the orders to their corps commander, however, and a discussion ensued regarding the feasibility of implementing the attack order at once. Cleburne noted that the men were just then beginning to receive rations, having not been fed for more than a day, and he proposed to wait for the food to be distributed and consumed. Hill readily agreed, to Wheless's dismay, then asked the staff officer if he would take a note to Polk in response. The captain offered to take a verbal message to the wing commander, but Hill preferred to put his thoughts in writing. Again to Wheless's chagrin, the general spent ten to fifteen minutes writing the note on a small piece of paper, all the while chatting amiably with Breckinridge and Cleburne. Wheless was about to interrupt Hill when the corps commander completed his response and offered it for transmission to Polk. The note detailed the question of rations and indicated that Cheatham's Division, to Hill's left, was seriously misaligned with the corps, a situation that could be rectified while Hill's men ate breakfast. As he rode rapidly toward Alexander's Bridge, Wheless encountered Captain Minnick Williams, also of Polk's staff, who was riding with duplicate orders to the division commanders. Wheless assured Williams that his mission was now superfluous but that Williams should ride to Cheatham and tell him that it would be several hours before Hill was ready to initiate the attack. As Williams departed, Wheless continued his ride toward Alexander's Bridge. A few hundred yards down the trail he met Polk on the way to the front with his staff and escort.[12]

Contrary to the story that would later be repeated in numerous accounts of the battle, Polk had been busy since first light. After dispatching Wheless and later Williams with the new orders, the general had begun to gather his staff and escort in preparation for riding to the line of battle. Before he was able to depart, Major Pollock Lee of Bragg's staff appeared. Lee had been sent to learn the cause of the delay in starting the "day-dawn" attack. Polk explained that Hill had not received the attack order during the night and that he was in the process of rectifying the matter. Lee departed to return to Bragg while Polk and his entourage headed for the line of battle. In one of the strangest episodes of the entire affair, Lee would later report to Bragg that he had found Polk sitting on the porch of a house, reading a newspaper, waiting for his breakfast. Bragg believed the story to be factual rather than the hyperbole it obviously must have been, and repeated it in two private letters to his wife shortly after the battle. Much later, members of Polk's staff would challenge Lee to a duel over the matter, but he demurred. All that, however, was in the future, and Polk now concentrated on going to the front. As the party crossed Alexander's Bridge, some members of the Orleans Light Horse spotted Private Fisher with other soldiers gathered at a fire. While his comrades made sport of him, Fisher reported his adventures of the previous night to the general, who chose not to punish the courier for his failure to find Hill.[13]

As Polk and his retinue rode northward, they first encountered Captain Wheless, returning from Hill's Corps. The meeting occurred roughly at the intersection of the modern Jay's Mill Road and the Alexander's Bridge Road. Polk asked him to read Hill's note, and the captain did so, adding that he believed Hill's estimate of an hour's delay was wildly optimistic. When Polk asked the reason for such pessimism, Wheless described the general's casual demeanor upon receipt of the order. Momentarily seeing the need to exert his will on the situation, Polk dashed off a note to Bragg, explaining Hill's delay. He then instructed Wheless to establish wing headquarters nearby, while Polk himself continued forward toward Cheatham's Division. En route he met Captain Williams, returning from Cheatham's command, and the staff officer quickly led Polk to the wing's left-most division. The time was now at least 7:00 A.M., ninety minutes after the attack should have begun. Leaving Cheatham after a few words, Polk rode northward until he reached Hill's position. Both Major W. C. Duxbury and Captain Henry Semple of Hill's staff noted that Polk arrived at 7:25 A.M. By this time his ardor had cooled, and he simply asked Cleburne if he had received the order to attack. Cleburne replied affirmatively but stated that Hill had ordered the men to be fed before moving. Polk apparently made no mention of the original "day-dawn" attack order, and when Hill commented on the misalignment of Cheatham's command on his left, he seemingly acquiesced in whatever delay the corps commander felt necessary. Long after the battle, Polk partisans asserted that Polk was firm in both words and tone, but all actual participants in the discussion indicated that he accepted Hill's arguments with quiet resignation.[14]

While Polk and Hill talked, Captain Wheless was in the process of establishing a forward-headquarters location for the wing commander. Approximately fifteen minutes after Polk left Wheless, General Bragg arrived and, with considerable impatience, asked for Polk's location. The captain reported that Polk had gone to the front momentarily and that the commander could find Polk sooner by going to the line of battle himself. Still angry that Hill had appeared so cavalier in his response to Polk's explicit orders, Wheless volunteered an account of the morning's activities to Bragg. Focusing upon Hill's casual attitude and his reasons for delaying the attack, he compared the general's behavior to Polk's efforts to expedite the Confederate assault. When Bragg mildly defended Hill, Wheless refused to be mollified and continued to denigrate both Hill's attitude and his performance to date. Ending the conversation, Bragg rode to find Polk. He did not locate the wing commander but did come upon Hill. Surprisingly, given all the conversation about attacking at once, Hill later claimed that Bragg was the first to inform him that the attack was supposed to begin at dawn. However that may have been, Hill now explained that he had additional things to do before any attack could commence. Most notably, there had been no reconnaissance of the Federal position up to that time nor had he coordinated for cavalry under Brigadier General Nathan Bedford Forrest to cover his right flank. By now resigned to an extended delay before his battle plan could be implemented, Bragg deferred to Hill's request for additional time. Like Polk before him, he placed the timing of the critical attack securely in the hands of D. H. Hill, a man who appeared to be in no hurry to act.[15]

It was approximately 9:30 A.M. when Hill was finally satisfied that the troops had been fed, the lines rectified, the reconnaissance done, and cavalry protection for his flank arranged. At that moment Brigadier General Daniel Adams's brigade, Breckinridge's right-most unit, initiated the attack Bragg had long awaited. The four hours of daylight granted to soldiers of Major General George Thomas's XIV Corps had been used to improve makeshift breastworks of logs and rocks erected during the night. Indeed, Cleburne had noted hearing Federal axes at work before dawn during Wheless's visit to Hill, and yet another three hours passed before Hill ordered the advance. In addition, Major General William Rosecrans, commander of the Army of the Cumberland, had begun to send reinforcements to Thomas's threatened left flank. By 9:30 A.M., one brigade of Major General James Negley's division had arrived to extend the Union line, a second was on the way, and the third was preparing to follow the others. It is impossible to state with certainty how Hill's two divisions might have fared against Thomas's troops if they had attacked out of the fog at 5:30 A.M., but it is clear that his task now was much more difficult because of the Federals' improvised fortifications and the extension of their line. How many of Hill's men died with full stomachs who might have lived had they not delayed to eat breakfast? Afterward, both Polk and Hill lost their commands and the latter his reputation, but the real loss from the Confederate perspective was the number of good infantrymen whose lives were snuffed out in front of Thomas's breastworks without success. Also postbattle, all of the senior commanders gathered facts to bolster their respective cases, with Hill deposing his staff and Polk taking testimony from both officers and privates. Eventually, the complex web of facts thus generated was forgotten, to be replaced by a simpler, more satisfying tale of singular incompetence by Leonidas Polk, and Pollock Lee's version of events has persisted over the years.[16]

The Order to Wood

Just as it had on the Confederate side, nightfall of September 19 offered an opportunity for the leaders of the Army of the Cumberland to reflect on the day's events and their prospects for the next day. Major General Rosecrans followed his usual practice and gathered his three primary infantry corps commanders and several staff officers for a conference to decide what the army would do next. During the afternoon of the nineteenth, Rosecrans had made his headquarters at the modest cabin of Eliza Glenn, a young widow with two small children, on what had become the southern end of the Federal line of battle. The Glenn family had left in search of safer quarters by the time the generals convened. Present were Rosecrans; Major General Thomas, commanding the XIV Corps; Major General Alexander McCook, commanding the XX Corps; Major General Thomas Crittenden, commanding the XXI Corps; several division commanders; and assorted staff officers. Absent were Major General Gordon Granger, located four miles north of the battlefield at Rossville with three Reserve Corps brigades, and Brigadier General Robert Mitchell, Cavalry Corps commander, south of the battlefield at Crawfish Springs. Because a telegraph line had been strung from the Widow Glenn's cabin to Rossville, Granger was able to receive quickly any orders generated at the conference. The meeting, as was Rosecrans's habit, lasted many hours and did not conclude until well after midnight. After weighing the available options, Rosecrans decided that the army was in no condition to attack but should not retreat without standing on the defensive at least another day. Thomas's corps, strengthened by a division each from McCook and Crittenden, would hold the army's left, protecting retreat routes to Chattanooga. McCook's remaining divisions would prolong the line southward, while Crittenden's two divisions would be held in reserve. Granger would stand ready to assist Thomas if necessary, and Mitchell would protect the army's hospitals south of the battlefield. With the plan decided, the generals returned to their respective bivouacs.[17]

Although he was exhausted from three weeks of campaigning over mountainous terrain and the stress of managing a large field army in the presence of a dangerous enemy, Rosecrans continued to drive himself unmercifully. After little if any sleep, he rose around sunrise on September 20 and prepared to direct his army's resolute defense of the ground occupied on the previous day. Private John Ely, whose regiment lay near the Widow Glenn cabin, saw the army commander leave the building and commented that Rosecrans "wore a heavy expression of care but he has a noble self relying look and if there is a General in our Armies that can win a victory here Rossie is the one." With his chief of staff, Brigadier General James Garfield, and other staff officers, Rosecrans rode to inspect his line of battle from south to north. Beginning with McCook's corps, he directed that Brigadier General Jefferson Davis's division close a yawning gap between Major General Philip Sheridan's division on the south and Major General James Negley's division on the north. Negley commanded George Thomas's Second Division but had been separated from his parent corps two days earlier during the march northward. He thus occupied the northern portion of McCook's sector of the line. Beyond Negley's division, everything belonged to George Thomas. In order, south to north, Thomas's units were the divisions of Brigadier General John Brannan, Major General Joseph Reynolds, Major General John Palmer, Brigadier General Richard Johnson, and Brigadier General Absalom Baird. The XIV Corps line, which crossed to the east side of the north–south La Fayette Road in Reynolds's area, ended short of a critical road leading west through McFarland's Gap toward Chattanooga. Thomas learned of this deficiency only when he returned from the conference at the Widow Glenn's around 2:00 A.M.[18]

After slightly repositioning Crittenden's two XXI Corps divisions, Rosecrans and his retinue continued trooping the line of battle, giving special attention to Thomas's defensive arrangements. Before he found Thomas at the modest log cabin of John McDonald, several hundred yards northwest of the end of his line, the corps commander had already initiated a request that Negley's division be returned to his control. If Negley could be spared from McCook's sector, he could extend the XIV Corps line to cover the McFarland's Gap road to Chattanooga. Upon Rosecrans's arrival at the McDonald House, Thomas renewed this request. Seeing the necessity of extending the army's left and knowing that McCook could fill Negley's position in the line by sliding his own divisions northward, Rosecrans agreed that Thomas could have the division as soon as it could be relieved from its original position. At 6:30 A.M. General Garfield dispatched a message to Negley from the McDonald House calling him forward to rejoin Thomas as soon as he was relieved. Five minutes later Garfield sent a similar note to McCook, informing the corps commander of Negley's new orders and directing McCook to close the gap in the line created by the division's departure. Satisfied that he had done all he could to prepare for the Confederate attack that appeared to be imminent but surprisingly had not yet occurred, Rosecrans and his staff left Thomas and rode southward, again surveying the line of battle.[19]

When the commander reached Negley's position, he was chagrinned to find that the division had not yet been relieved by troops from Mc-Cook's corps. Negley had only two brigades, those of Colonels Timothy Stanley and William Sirwell, in the line of battle, with Brigadier General John Beatty's brigade several hundred yards in the rear as a reserve. Rosecrans authorized Negley to keep Stanley's and Sirwell's commands in line until relieved by other units but permitted him to send Beatty's brigade immediately to Thomas's relief. The time was now approximately 8:00 A.M., and the expected Confederate attack still had not materialized, although skirmishers were becoming active on Negley's front. Unhappy that McCook had not relieved the division in a timely fashion, the impatient Rosecrans instantly decided to take a division from Crittenden's corps to execute the task. Obediently, staff officers carried orders for Crittenden to send a division to relieve Negley's remaining two brigades while also notifying McCook that the mission was no longer his. Again believing that he had solved the problem, Rosecrans continued his ride southward to see McCook. The details of the conversation between the two officers have not been found, but Rosecrans in his after-action report stated that he found the defensive arrangements of the XX Corps to be unsatisfactory, even after his earlier instructions. In closing, the general strongly admonished McCook to keep his troops tightly closed upon the units to his north, no matter what the difficulty. At the end of what must have been an unpleasant colloquy, Rosecrans once more resumed his morning ride, this time again turning northward. When he reached Negley's position a final time, he discovered the remaining two brigades still in the line, although Beatty's brigade had already departed to join Thomas. Frustrated that his seemingly clear instructions had not yet been obeyed, even in the face of imminent Confederate threat to the northern end of the army's line, Rosecrans finally noticed Brigadier General Thomas Wood's division from Crittenden's corps approaching from the west.[20]

Riding to Wood, who was leading his division forward, Rosecrans sternly inquired about the apparent delay in the unit's movements. At this point, historical accounts of the conversation diverge in major ways. According to one published in 1882 by Henry Cist, Rosecrans in very forceful language berated Wood publicly for his tardiness and directed him to relieve Negley's two brigades immediately. Smarting under the stinging rebuke, Wood finally occupied the assigned sector, permitting Stanley's and Sirwell's brigades to depart northward. Incorporated in the Army of the Cumberland volume in publisher Charles Scribner's Sons' prestigious Campaigns of the Civil War series, this story made quite a stir. Cist, however, was not an actual witness to the altercation between Rosecrans and Wood. In September 1863 he was a lieutenant recently added to the staff of the Army of the Cumberland and on duty with the army's rear echelon in Chattanooga. By the end of the war, he had gained the brevet rank of brigadier general and postwar was a prominent attorney and strong Rosecrans partisan. Although Cist's information was secondhand at best, few questioned the accuracy of his account. In 1936 another writer, Edwin V. Westrate, added dramatic dialogue to Cist's version of events: "What is the meaning of this, sir? You have disobeyed my specific orders. By your damnable negligence you are endangering the safety of the entire army, and, by God, I will not tolerate it. Move your division at once, as I have instructed, or the consequences will not be pleasant for yourself." Thereafter, although Westrate's quote lacked any documentation whatsoever, other writers repeated his words, and the story of the army commander berating a recalcitrant subordinate continued to grow. Had nothing else transpired between Rosecrans and Wood that morning, this event, even if true, would hardly have merited a footnote. As it happened, however, there would be another interaction between the two, and the altercation would be used as the catalyst for otherwise seemingly inexplicable actions by Wood that had enormous consequences for the outcome of the battle.[21]

While Cist's account of the altercation carried the day in the public

prints, an alternate version offered by an actual participant gained little
or no traction as published accounts of the Battle of Chickamauga grew
over the years. Responding to Cist's charges, Wood penned a sharp re-
joinder in the *New York Times* of November 19, 1882. According to Wood,
he and Rosecrans did meet, and the army commander asked "without
heat of language or manner" why he had not replaced Negley's troops
earlier. Wood responded that he had put his division in motion as soon as
he received the order from his corps commander. Rosecrans then ended
the conversation by telling him to hurry forward as rapidly as possible.
According to Wood, there was no harsh language, no embarrassing
public confrontation, and nothing beyond a sense of urgency that Negley
be relieved quickly. He stated, "I certainly did not feel that I had been
censured by Gen. Rosecrans." Wood buttressed his account by quoting a
letter from Captain Marcus P. Bestow, an assistant adjutant general on
his staff and a witness to the discussion, in which Bestow corroborated
the general's story in every respect. In Bestow's telling, Rosecrans was
indeed agitated, though toward an unnamed corps commander instead
of Wood. Whether or not Wood was reprimanded, and the best testimony
is that he was not, he quickly replaced Negley's two brigades in the line of
battle. Having left Brigadier General George Wagner's brigade to garrison
Chattanooga, Wood had only two brigades of his own. Those two units,
commanded by Colonels George Buell and Charles Harker, had both
lost heavily on the previous day. To remedy that defect, Wood had been
given Colonel Sidney Barnes's brigade from Brigadier General Horatio
Van Cleve's XXI Corps division. By 9:30 A.M., Wood had accomplished
the relief, and Negley's troops passed out of sight to the north.[22]

Upon entering the line, Wood placed Barnes's attached brigade on his
left, Harker's brigade in the center, and Buell's brigade on the division
right. The position surveyed the farm of George Brotherton from the
woods bordering the farm's western edge. Eastward, the cleared fields
ranged slightly upward, culminating on a low ridge that rose above the
La Fayette Road. Near the road stood Brotherton's log cabin and outbuild-
ings. The left of Barnes's brigade connected with Colonel John Connell's
brigade of Brannan's XIV Corps division. On the right, Buell's troops connected somewhat more loosely with Brigadier General William Carlin's
brigade of Davis's XX Corps division. The frontage of the position was
approximately 650 yards. Each brigade commander formed his command
in two lines, with two regiments in the front line and two in reserve. For
some time, there was little activity from the Confederates known to be

lurking in the woods beyond the La Fayette Road, although skirmishers from both sides were active. Negley's men had previously gathered limbs, fence rails, and rocks to form makeshift breastworks just inside the tree line, and Wood's troops used them to shield themselves from the random shots. Suddenly, to Buell's dismay, Colonel Frederick Bartleson's 100th Illinois Infantry Regiment, on the left of the brigade line, dashed to the front in an effort to clear the Brotherton buildings of Confederate skirmishers. The aggressive Bartleson not only pushed through the Brotherton property but also into the woods beyond the La Fayette Road. There, he encountered far more Confederates than he could handle and ordered a hasty withdrawal. Amid the precipitate retreat, Bartleson was wounded and left at the Brotherton cabin. The regiment finally rallied in its original position, though without its colonel and several soldiers. There was no Confederate pursuit, and relative quiet again descended on the Brotherton Farm. To the north, however, the sounds of battle were swelling to a crescendo.[23]

The heavy fighting that had enveloped the left flank and front of Thomas's position after 9:30 A.M. was the result of D. H. Hill's long-delayed attack at the north end of the battlefield. Beginning his advance at that hour, Breckinridge was at last able to turn the Federal flank with two of his three brigades. Facing those brigades to the south, he then drove down the La Fayette Road toward the rear of Thomas's position, brushing aside the first of Negley's brigades to reach the scene. Although Breckinridge would ultimately be halted and driven back by the fortuitous arrival of Negley's second brigade and a brigade of Brannan's division, Thomas was unsure of a favorable outcome and sought additional assistance. Calling Captain Sanford Kellogg to his side, the general ordered him to ride southward in a desperate effort to find troops to reinforce his crumbling left flank. At this point the story again becomes clouded with varying accounts of Kellogg's mission. In the traditional version, repeated for many years, Kellogg was sent directly to Rosecrans with the request for aid. According to that version, as he made his way to the army's field headquarters, now located on a knoll west of South Dyer Field, Kellogg somehow missed seeing Brannan's division in line between those of Reynolds and Wood. Upon reaching Rosecrans, Kellogg breathlessly repeated Thomas's call for assistance and reported that there was a large gap in the Federal line of battle where Brannan's division should have been. Kellogg's information thus caused Rosecrans to issue orders to Wood to close the apparent gap before the Confederates exploited it. This is essentially the story that Cist first told in 1882, although he confused Kellogg with Lieutenant Colonel Alexander Von Schrader, captured on the previous day. Because Kellogg was an inexperienced twenty-one-year-old nephew of Thomas's wife and was participating in his first battle, there were plausible reasons for accepting it.[24]

Just as in the earlier Rosecrans-Wood confrontation, an alternate version of the Kellogg ride is available but rarely cited. Major General Reynolds, commanding the Fourth Division, XIV Corps, was in line between Palmer's division on his left and Brannan's division on his right. According to a statement Reynolds provided to the Chickamauga Park Commission in 1895, he was approached in midmorning by Brannan and Captain Kellogg. The staff officer had been sent by Thomas to Brannan with an order for his division to move north to support the left flank, then in process of being turned. Apparently, Thomas believed that Brannan's three brigades were in reserve behind the line of battle. In fact, during the night of the nineteenth, two of these brigades had been placed in the front line between Reynolds and Negley, while the third remained in reserve. Brannan had started that reserve brigade, Colonel Ferdinand Van Derveer's, to Thomas's aid, but he was reluctant to take the brigades of Colonels John Connell and John Croxton from the line without further approval from someone. During the campaign of maneuver prior to the battle, the relatively inexperienced Brannan had been placed under the protective wing of Reynolds, so it was only natural to seek that officer's advice before acting on an order that would leave Reynolds's right flank unprotected. Thus, Brannan brought Kellogg with him as he consulted the general on the proper course of action. Reynolds agreed that Brannan should march to join Thomas, but he also recognized that such a move would endanger his own division. Therefore, he counseled the general to execute Thomas's order but also instructed Kellogg to tell Rosecrans that Brannan's departure would create an opening in the general line of battle. The captain thus rode in search of the army commander while Brannan prepared to leave the line. Although penned more than thirty years after the events it described, Reynolds's account is consistent with what actually happened and does not require impugning either Kellogg's courage or his intelligence. Unfortunately, Brannan remained in place after Kellogg's departure, probably fixed by the premature attack of part of Longstreet's forces.[25]

Captain Kellogg now hastened to army headquarters on the slight knoll on the west side of South Dyer Field. Upon arrival he found Rose-

crans, Crittenden, Garfield, numerous staff officers, and Assistant Secretary of War Charles Dana. Behind the knoll lounged Colonel William
Palmer's 15th Pennsylvania Cavalry Regiment, Rosecrans's headquarters
guard, and not far behind them stood a group of ammunition wagons
and several Confederate artillery pieces captured on the previous day.
Just to the north were the two remaining brigades of Van Cleve's division.
Nearby, signal personnel were attempting to activate a field-telegraph
line to Rossville. All in all, the scene was a busy one even though few
Federal units and no Confederate troops were in view. Exhausted as he
was from many sleepless nights, Rosecrans still maintained his com-
posure. As far as he was concerned, his army was holding its own. Mc-
Cook's alignment had been a problem earlier, but corrective action had
been taken, and the battle now developing seemed to be concentrated
in Thomas's sector. Rosecrans trusted Thomas implicitly, having promised the XIV Corps commander all necessary support as early as the
previous night's conference. Thus, when Kellogg arrived with the news
that Thomas had ordered Brannan's division to move north and that
Reynolds believed this action would uncover his right flank, Rosecrans
immediately sprang into action. Because Chief of Staff Garfield was
momentarily writing an order to Crittenden, Rosecrans turned to his
senior aide-de-camp, Major Frank Bond. He dictated to Bond the following order to Wood: "The general commanding directs that you close
up on Reynolds as fast as possible, and support him." Marked "Gallop"
to signify the urgency of the situation, the message was then handed to
Lieutenant Colonel Lyne Starling, Crittenden's chief of staff, for delivery
to Wood. The time was 10:45 A.M.[26]

Rosecrans's order to Wood, later dramatically characterized as the
"fatal order of the day," has been controversial since its inception. On
its face, it called for two separate actions, each mutually exclusive. To
"close up on" meant that Wood was to slide northward until he touched
Reynolds's right flank; to "support" meant that Wood was to move behind Reynolds's division. The only unambiguous directive in the order
was to execute it quickly. Confusion over its meaning was inadvertently
highlighted during a court of inquiry convened in early 1864 to assess the
performance of corps commander Thomas Crittenden at Chickamauga.
On February 9 Lyne Starling testified under oath that he himself was
unsure of the order's meaning and queried Garfield about it. Now free,
Garfield explained verbally that the order was written because Brannan
was leaving the line. In 1880, when Garfield was running for president,

his partisans delightedly distanced him from the message written by
Bond, but Starling's sworn testimony before the Crittenden Court makes
it clear that Garfield was well aware of the order's contents. Nor was
Crittenden himself ignorant of these events because Starling also testified that he received the order in that general's presence. Armed with
Garfield's explanation, Starling galloped across South Dyer Field and into
the trees on its eastern side in search of Wood. After a ride of some 750
yards, he found the general behind his line of battle. At this point, the
traditional story holds that Wood instantly decided to obey the order,
although he knew that Brannan's division remained in place to his north.
Cist quoted an unnamed orderly as saying that Wood stated that he "was
glad the order was in writing, as it was a good thing to have for future
reference." Postbattle army gossip reported that he said: "Gentlemen, I
hold the fatal order of the day in my hand and would not part with it
for $5,000." Either way, Cist's anonymous orderly recalled that Wood
carefully folded the order and placed it in a notebook he carried. The
clear implication was that the general knew full well that execution of
the order would be disastrous to the army. Nevertheless, in a fit of pique
resulting from his earlier altercation with Rosecrans, he chose to move
out smartly without questioning the order or seeking clarification.[27]

When Cist's story reached print, Wood responded vigorously through
the *New York Times,* as mentioned previously. Having denied he was
acting upon hurt feelings, he described what happened when Starling
arrived with the order. Wood explained to Starling that Brannan was
not out of line but remained between his division and that of Reynolds. Nevertheless, the order was peremptory, even though Starling
said that if Brannan had not left the line, the order had no meaning.
Agitated because he knew the order was ambiguous and the situation was
grave, Wood was relieved to find Major General McCook approaching.
He handed the order to the corps commander, who perused it carefully,
then opined that the order must be obeyed. In McCook's opinion, neither
he nor Wood could know the exact circumstances facing Rosecrans at
that moment, and that even then similar orders might be en route to
McCook himself. Although Wood belonged to the XXI Corps, McCook
commanded the sector in which Wood found himself, and McCook's
rank made him the superior officer. Further, McCook promised to fill
the gap in the line with troops from Davis's division to the south. Perhaps unaware that that unit then consisted of only two small brigades,
Wood was relieved that his position would not be left uncovered when

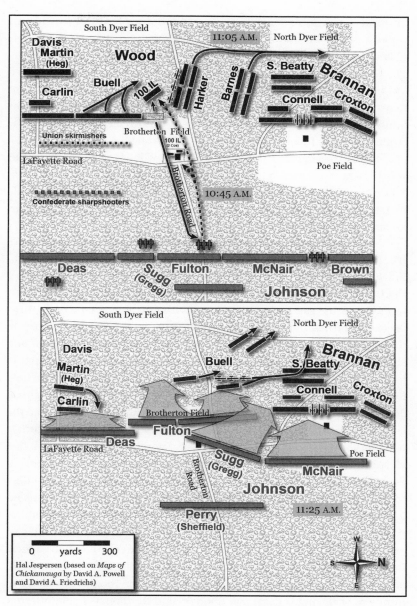

Confederate Breakthrough Assault, September 20, 1863.

he departed in haste. Thus, he decided to withdraw his three brigades as
rapidly as possible and march behind Brannan's position toward Reynolds's location. McCook then departed to see to his own arrangements.
The time was around 11:00 A.M. Wood's 1882 testimony is corroborated
by Captain Marcus P. Bestow, Lieutenant Thomas Ehlers, and Lieutenant
George Shaffer, all members of his staff, as well as by Adjutant Brewer
Smith of the 65th Ohio Infantry Regiment. It is further corroborated by
Captain William Richards of McCook's staff. While the testimony of these
witnesses varies in minor detail, all state that Wood questioned the order,
was reluctant to move, and did so only when McCook assured him that
XX Corps units would cover the gap. As for the alleged statements made
by Cist's anonymous "orderly," Wood declared them to be "a clean-cut
lie out of the whole cloth."[28]

Wood's departure from the line occurred so quickly that skirmishers
from some of his regiments remained behind. As the brigades began to
move, three Confederate divisions began their advance straight toward
the Brotherton Farm. Numbering approximately 10,000 troops, these
units struck the gap in the Federal line with great force. Of Wood's three
brigades, Barnes and Harker successfully made the transition from line
to column and escaped cleanly, but Buell's regiments were caught and
shattered by the Confederate advance. Similarly, Colonel John Martin's
brigade of Davis's division was crushed as it attempted to plug the hole
left by Wood's departure. As Confederate brigadier general Bushrod
Johnson's division rushed through the opening, Rosecrans witnessed the
collapse from the west side of the South Dyer Field. He had kept things
together for three long grueling weeks, and now, with one misstep, it had
all come undone. To his credit, he hurried southward to rally elements of
Sheridan's division, but his efforts and those of his staff proved ineffectual. Soon the entire right side of the Army of the Cumberland crumbled
and headed west in piecemeal fashion. Carried along with the flood of
retreating soldiers were Rosecrans, McCook, Crittenden, and a host of
other officers. The generals did not halt until they entered Chattanooga.
Eventually, General Longstreet failed to maintain his troops' momentum,
and the gray tide halted just long enough for George Thomas to rally large
numbers of fleeing Federals on Snodgrass Hill. Thomas held both that
position and an enclave around Kelly Field until nightfall, then orchestrated a successful withdrawal. Although the Army of the Cumberland
was saved and Chattanooga remained in Federal hands, the Battle of
Chickamauga was lost, and Rosecrans, McCook, and Crittenden all for-

feited their commands. Perhaps the outcome of the battle might have ultimately been the same had Rosecrans not dictated the "fatal order" to Major Bond or Wood not accepted McCook's advice to leave the line of battle
in haste. Still, it is unlikely that three-fourths of the army's senior leadership would have been so discredited under any other scenario. Rosecrans's seventeen-word message to Wood was indeed the "fatal order."[29]

The story of these two orders—one delivered late, the other delivered too
quickly—is instructive in several ways. First, a minute examination of
the two situations reinforces the well-known but often forgotten truism
that wars are fought by fallible human beings. Most soldiers, including
the officers of highest rank, strive to do the best they can in a tragic and
chaotic situation. It is exceedingly rare to find an example of a senior
leader who knowingly and willingly acts to cause loss and defeat to his
command. Neither Leonidas Polk nor Thomas Wood began that terrible
day of September 20, 1863, intending to harm their army's chances for
victory, yet that is the way they are portrayed in the traditional accounts
of the Battle of Chickamauga. As soon as he discovered that his attack
order to D. H. Hill had miscarried, Polk tried mightily to rectify the situation. His fault was not indifference to the loss of precious hours but a
failure to impose his will sufficiently upon Hill after meeting the latter
face to face. Similarly, Wood did not knowingly endanger the Army of
the Cumberland in a fit of pique over a supposed slight that occurred
two hours earlier. Nor did he act without authorization from Alexander
McCook, who really believed that he could cover the gap in the line. Braxton Bragg was not trying to slight Hill when he reorganized the Army of
Tennessee prior to the day's fight; he was simply trying to maximize his
army's chances for victory by simplifying his chain of command. William
Rosecrans was not so insensitive as to upbraid a subordinate engaged
in a critical mission and, exhausted as he was, acted upon Captain Kellogg's information in good faith. Indeed, there is no reason to believe
that any of the senior participants acted in other than good faith. It is
dangerous for historians to ascribe simplistic motives to individuals or
to cavalierly assign blame for failures without either knowing all the
facts or understanding the role that personality and human factors like
fatigue play in major decisions. While both mendacity and gross incompetence occasionally can be found in the study of men in battle, it is far

more instructive to seek the causes of events among the more-mundane factors of human existence common to us all.

A second point worth noting is that military historians should look as closely at staff officers and staff procedures as at commanders. The mostly younger men who served both armies' senior leaders were subject to the same human factors of courage, fear, and fatigue, among others, that afflicted their superiors. Frequently, the orders they carried were verbal and thus subject to being garbled in transmission, often in the most subtle ways. They too could become momentarily lost in a fog- and smoke-shrouded woods as their horses picked their way amid the dead and the dying. More often than not, they were partisans for their commanders and denigrated subordinate leaders and staffs who failed to credit the brilliance of their chiefs. Witness the performance of Frank Wheless in his interaction with General Hill. When the situation required it, they provided advice, offered a sympathetic ear, relieved stress, and provided creature comforts for those who bore the burden of command. Whether it was Archer Anderson, who influenced both Polk and Hill in critical ways on the night of September 19, or Lyne Starling, who wisely questioned an order before transmitting it to Wood, the many staff officers who played major roles in these two episodes are worthy of study. Similarly, the staff protocols developed in both armies can also be investigated with profit. Polk's headquarters was clearly not a twenty-four-hour operation, and for that lapse Thomas Jack should be held accountable. The informality of Rosecrans's headquarters in which staff officers were considered interchangeable was a distinguishing characteristic of his army's operations. Garfield wrote most of the orders on the field of Chickamauga but not all of them by any means. Frank Bond just happened to be available when Rosecrans needed to dictate an order, and thus he entered the historical record in a disastrous way. Would Garfield have been more precise in language than Bond, or would he have simply written what a frazzled army commander dictated? The question is unanswerable, but the staff procedures in effect made it possible for Bond to be in that predicament and Garfield seventeen years later to have plausible deniability.

Finally, this story of two orders is a cautionary tale for military historians in yet another way. The traditional account of these two episodes at Chickamauga is demonstrably wrong in many particulars, yet it has survived for well over a century of historical writing. Traced back to the earliest sources, this account seems to have been built originally upon partisanship, army gossip, and a simplistic view of causation. Rather than being questioned by subsequent authors, the original story has been repeated as truth ever since. Most likely, this situation has prevailed for two primary reasons. First, in both the Polk and Wood episodes, the tale was plausible because it built upon known characteristics of the primary individuals involved—in Polk's case, a courtly, time-insensitive manner, and in Wood's case, a profane irascibility. Second, rather than search ever more diligently for obscure sources that might force an author to abandon a dramatic story, the easier path was to simply repeat and, in the case of Edwin V. Westrate, embellish the original storyline. As the years passed, the traditional account gradually became fixed in place. When military historians assess the performance of generals on the field of battle, simple justice requires that they make the best possible effort to determine the truth of complex events and render that complexity as faithfully as they can. Otherwise, the result is no better or more instructive than historical fiction. As an old-time humorist once put it, "It's not what folks don't know that hurts them, it's what they know that ain't so." This tale of two orders on the second day at Chickamauga is an excellent example of this phenomenon. How many other critical episodes in American Civil War military history are simply the traditional story endlessly repeated, unexamined by modern historical detective work? In this sesquicentennial season, there is yet much work to be done.

ACKNOWLEDGMENTS

This essay owes a great debt of gratitude to many people, beginning with my grandmother, Emily Pope Wright, who first introduced me to the battlefield of Chickamauga in the summer of 1954 and who climbed to the top of Wilder Tower on Widow Glenn's Hill with me when no one else would. Next, I would like to thank the late General Donn A. Starry, who had the vision to see that timeless and universal truths about battle could still be gained on Civil War battlefields and who directed that the U.S. Army Command and General Staff College reinstitute the particular type of battle analysis known as the "Staff Ride" in 1981. That concept had sprung from the fertile brain of Major Arthur Wagner at Fort Leavenworth, Kansas, in 1895; had been first instituted by Major Eben Swift in 1906; and had languished since 1910. Colonel William A. Stofft, director of the Combat Studies Institute, gave me the opportunity to create the modern Staff Ride, with the assistance of Lieutenant Colonel Karl Farris, beginning in 1983, and the venue became Chickamauga for the next twenty-five years. At Chickamauga itself, the late Park Historian Edward Tinney, who loved the battlefield and knew it better than anyone alive, was my first mentor on the site, and Chief Ranger John Cissell literally opened many gates for me to explore. Of the thousands of officers who have walked with me at Chickamauga over the years, Major Peter Kafkalas is most relevant to this essay. Kafkalas did not have the proof in 1985, but he voiced his doubts about the traditional Wood narrative in a way I never forgot. The proof came later, through the collective efforts of publisher Robert Younger, Congressman Charles Whalen, and attorney Steven Wood to place certain illuminating documents in my hands. Similarly, archivist Ray Barker found for me the Henry Yeatman letter at the William L. Clements Library of the University of Michigan, thereby adding a hitherto unknown dimension to the Leonidas Polk story. I stand on the shoulders of these individuals, and I salute them all.

NOTES

1. For the traditional story arc of these two episodes, see the following as a sampling: Henry M. Cist, *The Army of the Cumberland* (New York: Charles Scribner's Sons, 1882), 199–203, 220–23; Glenn Tucker, *Chickamauga: Bloody Battle in the West* (1961; reprint, Dayton, Ohio: Morningside, 1972), 221–31, 205–207, 250–59; William M. Lamers, *The Edge of Glory: A Biography of General William S. Rosecrans, U.S.A.* (New York: Harcourt, Brace, & World, 1961), 341–45; Hal Bridges, *Lee's Maverick General: Daniel Harvey Hill* (New York: McGraw-Hill, 1961), 206–16; Thomas Lawrence Connelly, *Autumn of Glory: The Army of Tennessee, 1862–1865* (Baton Rouge: Louisiana State University Press, 1971), 208–21; Peter Cozzens, *This Terrible Sound: The Battle of Chickamauga* (Urbana: University of Illinois Press, 1992), 299–304, 310–14, 357–67; Steven E. Woodworth, *Six Armies in Tennessee: The Chickamauga and Chattanooga Campaigns* (Lincoln: University of Nebraska Press, 1998), 103–105, 113–16; and Larry J. Daniel, *Days of Glory: The Army of the Cumberland, 1861–1865* (Baton Rouge: Louisiana State University Press, 2004), 323–29.

2. U.S. War Department, *The War of the Rebellion: A Compilation of the Official Records of the Union and Confederate Armies,* 128 vols. (Washington, D.C.: GPO, 1880–1901), ser. 1, 30(2):32–33 (hereinafter cited as *OR;* all citations to series 1 unless otherwise specified).

3. Ibid., 33.

4. Henry C. Yeatman to "Dear Ham," Oct. 7, 1863, William L. Clements Library, University of Michigan, Ann Arbor; *OR,* 30(2):198, 203; Leonidas Polk to D. H. Hill, Sept. 30, 1863; and Leonidas Polk to George W. Brent, Sept. 28, 1863, both in D. H. Hill Papers, Library of Virginia, Richmond (hereinafter cited as Hill Papers, LV; and Archer Anderson statement, n.d.; and A. C. Avery statement, n.d., both in D. H. Hill Papers, North Carolina Department of Archives and History, Raleigh (hereinafter cited as Hill Papers, NCDAH). According to Avery, who arrived in the middle of the conversation, the additional staff officer was Lt. James Reid. Reid, however, was with Hill at this time, not Anderson. Morrison, an aide-

de-camp who was with Hill later in the evening, was a more likely candidate, though not the only possibility.

5. Henry C. Yeatman to "Dear Ham," Oct. 7, 1863; Leonidas Polk to D. H. Hill, Sept. 30, 1863; Leonidas Polk to George W. Brent, Sept. 28, 1863; *OR,* 30(2):140; Archer Anderson statement, n.d.; A. C. Avery statement, n.d.; John C. Breckinridge to D. H. Hill, Oct. 16, 1863, Hill Papers, NCDAH; Frank A. Burr, "Chickamauga," *Cincinnati Enquirer,* Apr. 1, 1883.

6. Walter Morris to William Polk, n.d., Leonidas Polk Papers, University of the South, Sewanee, Tenn. (hereinafter cited as Polk Papers, UOTS); *OR,* 30(2):58–60.

7. Leonidas Polk to George W. Brent, Sept. 28, 1863; *OR,* 30(2):48, 52, 57–58, 60, 198; Leeds Greenleaf to W. E. Huger, Oct. 11, 1863, Polk Papers, UOTS; Henry C. Yeatman to "Dear Ham," Oct. 7, 1863; W. D. Gale to Winchester Hall, Dec. 23, 1872, copy in Chickamauga and Chattanooga National Military Park, Ft. Oglethorpe, Ga. (hereinafter cited as CCNMP); William M. Polk, *Leonidas Polk, Bishop and General,* 2 vols. (New York: Longmans, Green, 1894), 2:244.

8. *OR,* 30(2):64, 140; Thaddeus Coleman statement, Oct. 13, 1863; and James A. Reid statement, n.d., both in Hill Papers, NCDAH. In some accounts, Hill placed his departure from the line at 11:00 P.M., but that time is contradicted by other statements of the general and the testimony of his companion Lieutenant Reid. Had 11:00 P.M. been the departure time, Hill would have more than likely encountered either Polk or his bridge guards, and he did not.

9. Thaddeus Coleman statement, Oct. 13, 1863; James A. Reid statement, n.d.; *OR,* 30(2):57–58, 64, 140. For Hill's spinal difficulties, see Jack D. Welsh, *Medical Histories of Confederate Generals* (Kent, Ohio: Kent State University Press, 1995), 100–101.

10. W. D. Gale to Winchester Hall, Dec. 23, 1872; Y. R. LeMonnier, "Lieut. Gen'l Leonidas Polk at Battle of Chickamauga," Louisiana Historical Association Collection, Tulane University, New Orleans; *OR,* 30(2):58, 60, 140–141, 198; John C. Breckinridge to D. H. Hill, Oct. 16, 1863; James A. Reid statement, n.d.; Anderson-Coleman-West statement, Oct. 13, 1863, Hill Papers, NCDAH; Leeds Greenleaf to W. E. Huger, Oct. 11, 1863; Henry C. Yeatman to "Dear Ham," Oct. 7, 1863.

11. Polk, *Leonidas Polk,* 2:249–50n; *OR,* 30(2):52, 58, 61, 198, 203; Leonidas Polk to George W. Brent, Sept. 28, 1863; John F. Wheless to W. D. Gale, Oct. 8, 1867, Leonidas Polk Papers, University of North Carolina, Chapel Hill, microfilm.

12. *OR,* 30(2):60–61, 141; John F. Wheless to W. D. Gale, Oct. 8, 1867; Henry C. Yeatman to "Dear Ham," Oct. 7, 1863. Although Hill later claimed that this meeting with Wheless occurred at 7:25 A.M., it must have been approximately one hour earlier, given the testimony of other witnesses and subsequent events.

13. Leeds Greenleaf to W. E. Huger, Oct. 11, 1863; *OR,* 30(2):47, 63; F. H. McNairy to W. M. Polk, Sept. 18, 1885; and James H. Polk to W. M. Polk, Aug. 23, 1918, both in Leonidas Polk Papers, University of North Carolina, Chapel Hill, microfilm; Leonidas Polk to George W. Brent, Sept. 28, 1863; Polk, *Leonidas Polk,* 2:251–52n; Braxton Bragg to his wife, Sept. 22, 1863, Braxton Bragg Papers, Library of Congress, Washington, D.C.; Braxton Bragg to his wife, Sept. 27, 1863, *Chattanooga Times,* Oct. 25, 1921, clipping in Hamilton County Bicentennial Library, Chattanooga; LeMonnier, "Lieut. Gen'l Leonidas Polk at Battle of Chickamauga."

14. *OR,* 30(2):53, 60–62; John F. Wheless to W. D. Gale, Oct. 8, 1867; W. C. Duxbury statement, Nov. 6, 1863, Hill Papers, LV; H. C. Semple to D. H. Hill, Oct. 13, 1863, Hill Papers, NCDAH; LeMonnier, "Lieut. Gen'l Leonidas Polk at Battle of Chickamauga."

15. *OR,* 30(2):62, 141; John F. Wheless to W. D. Gale, Oct. 8, 1867.

16. *OR,* 30(2):55, 62, 141, 149, 198, 30(1):329.

17. Ibid., 30(1):56–57, 69, 137, 854; William R. Plum, *The Military Telegraph during the Civil War in the United States,* 2 vols. (Chicago: Jansen, McClurg, 1882), 2:67; James Alfred Sartain, *History of Walker County Georgia* (Dalton, Ga.: A. J. Showalter, 1932), 109; W. C. Margedant, quoted in L. W. Mulhane, *Memorial of Major-General William Stark Rosecrans* (Columbus, Ohio: Columbian Printing, 1898), 68–69.

18. John Ely Diary, Sept. 20, 1863, copy at CCNMP; *OR,* 30(1):58, 126, 250–51, 328–29.

19. *OR,* 30(1):58, 69–70, 251, 137–38.

20. Ibid., 58, 329–30, 489, 609. Perhaps not surprisingly, McCook makes no reference to this episode in his after-action report.

21. Cist, *Army of the Cumberland,* 219–20; Henry M. Cist to his mother, Sept. 20, 1863, Cist Family Papers, Box 8, Cincinnati Historical Society, Cincinnati, Ohio; *New York Times,* Dec. 18, 1902; Edwin V. Westrate, *Those Fatal Generals* (New York: Knight Publications, 1936), 222–23.

22. Thomas J. Wood, "The Gaps at Chickamauga," *New York Times,* Nov. 19, 1882; *OR,* 30(1):329, 629, 634.

23. *OR,* 30(1):634, 646, 655–56, 659–60, 694, 840.

24. Ibid., 58–59, 251, 256; Cist, *Army of the Cumberland,* 205–206; *Washington Post,* Feb. 8, 1904; Francis F. McKinney, *Education in Violence: The Life of George H. Thomas and the History of the Army of the Cumberland* (Detroit: Wayne State University Press, 1961), 492n25.

25. Maj. Gen. Joseph J. Reynolds, "An Incident of the Second Day at Chickamauga," Eyewitness Accounts Folder, CCNMP; *OR,* 30(3):411, 30(2):288, 363–64.

26. *OR,* 30(1):59, 71, 635, 646, 983; Plum, *Military Telegraph,* 2:67; *OR,* 30(2):459, 475; Charles H. Kirk, ed., *History of the Fifteenth Pennsylvania Volunteer Cavalry* (Philadelphia, 1906), 235. Henry Cist denigrates Bond's professionalism, but Bond had been with Rosecrans since before Stones River, and there is no reason to believe he did more than simply reflect the words of the army commander. Cist, *Army of the Cumberland,* 220; William H. Powell, *Officers of the Army and Navy (Volunteer) Who Served in the Civil War* (Philadelphia: L. R. Hamersly, 1893), 52.

27. Alexander D. Bache to William S. Rosecrans, Jan. 12, 1864, William Starke Rosecrans Papers, Box 9, Folder 57, Charles E. Young Research Library, University of California, Los Angeles; *OR,* 30(1):983; Cist, *Army of the Cumberland,* 220–23. A saltier version of Wood's alleged remarks upon receiving the order, reflecting strong anti–Roman Catholic sentiment, has been circulating for many years in National Park Service circles, but to date it is without substantive documentary foundation. For one possible source, see Charles and Barbara Whalen, *The Fighting McCooks* (Bethesda, Md.: Westmoreland, 2006), 228.

28. Wood, "Gaps at Chickamauga"; *OR,* 30(1):983–84; John K. Shellenberger to Thomas J. Wood, Nov. 1890; George K. Shaffer to Thomas J. Wood, Oct. 29, 1883; George K. Shaffer to George H. Wood, Jan. 20, 1905; and Brewer Smith to George H. Wood, Jan. 4, 1909, all in personal collection of Stephen Wood, Washington, D.C.; William J. Richards, "Rosecrans and the Chickamauga Campaign," in *War Papers Read before the Indiana Commandery, Military Order of the Loyal Legion of the United States* (Indianapolis, 1898), 475n.

29. *OR,* 30(1):59–60, 252–54, 491, 530, 612, 656, 694, 840.

CHAPTER 6

WAR AND POLITICS

Jefferson Davis Visits the Army of Tennessee

CRAIG L. SYMONDS

On October 9, 1863, President Jefferson Davis arrived at General Braxton Bragg's headquarters on Missionary Ridge overlooking Chattanooga. He was accompanied by Lieutenant General James Longstreet and Major General John C. Breckinridge, who had met him in Atlanta at his request and ridden up with him on the Western and Atlantic Railroad. Davis's arrival was not unexpected. In fact, he had considered making the trip for more than a month because of serious command problems within Bragg's army; letters had been landing on his desk for months complaining of the general's ham-fisted and self-destructive command style. In early September Davis had sent his young aide Preston Johnston, son of the martyred general Albert Sidney Johnston, out to the Army of Tennessee to assess the situation, and Johnston had reported that things were so chaotic that Davis should come himself. The president was preparing to do so but postponed his trip when news of the Confederate victory at Chickamauga allowed him to hope that success would quiet things down. To find out, he sent another aide, James Chesnut, who reported that if anything, the victory at Chickamauga had only exacerbated the problems, writing Davis, "Your immediate presence in this army is urgently demanded." And so the Confederate president had come west personally in the hope of quelling the unrest in the army's high command.[1]

Command difficulties had been endemic in the Confederacy's western armies almost from the beginning. For most of the summer, the western theater had been under the putative command of General Joseph E. Johnston (never one of Davis's favorites), who had struggled with a command arrangement that he disliked and, indeed, barely understood.

As Davis envisioned it, Johnston would exercise authority over both of the Confederate field armies that operated within his theater—the Army of Mississippi, under Lieutenant General John C. Pemberton, and the Army of Tennessee, under Bragg—and coordinate their movements. But for an old soldier like Johnston, this was an ambiguous, confusing, and even nonsensical assignment. In his view it was a general's job to *command,* and in this new assignment, he did not command anything directly except whenever he was physically present with one army or the other, in which case he was expected to exercise authority over that army. It struck Johnston as both indecorous and disruptive for him, as an outsider who lacked detailed knowledge of either army's day-to-day circumstances, to displace an army commander whenever he happened to be present. Unwilling to do that, Johnston had barely exercised any command authority at all.[2]

By the late summer of 1863, Johnston was gone. His inability (or, some said, unwillingness) to succor Pemberton's besieged army inside Vicksburg marked the end of a command experiment that had never really worked, and the surrender of the Army of Mississippi on July 4 meant that there were no longer two field armies for Johnston (or anyone else) to coordinate anyway. After that, the Confederacy's fortunes in the West depended almost entirely on the success or failure of the Army of Tennessee under Bragg.

Of course, Bragg came with significant baggage of his own. Unlike Johnston, he got along well with the Confederate president, but whereas Johnston was and remained popular with the officers and men, Bragg was roundly disliked, even despised, within the army. He had never been what anyone would call a "people person" in any case, and by the fall of 1863, his dyspeptic and acerbic demeanor had offended almost every one of his generals at one time or another. Many of them, remembering past slights or criticisms, became wary. Aware that the literal-minded Bragg was likely to hold them strictly accountable for their responses to his orders, they got into the habit of carefully parsing the language of his orders to ensure that they were not being set up. Worse, in an ominous development, some of the senior officers in the army had begun to gossip about Bragg's shortcomings with one another, which came perilously close to conspiracy. As early as midsummer, one of them (Lieutenant General William J. Hardee) wrote to another (Lieutenant General Leonidas Polk): "I think we ought to counsel together."[3]

The victory at Chickamauga was bracing, to be sure, but it fell far short of the kind of decisive triumph Bragg had imagined, and its disappointing strategic harvest did nothing to soothe the antagonism between the army commander and his subordinates. The disappointments resulted from a number of factors. Bragg had been forced to reorganize the army on the virtual eve of battle, an adjustment made necessary by the arrival of welcome reinforcements from Virginia under Lieutenant General James Longstreet. Then too, the sheer size of the battlefield and the confusing terrain meant that Bragg's orders were often delayed when couriers got lost in the thick woods or failed to find units that were not where headquarters presumed them to be. In addition to those factors, Bragg could not adjust to the fact that the battle did not progress according to his preconceived vision of how it would unfold. When his planned attack on the morning of September 20 was both late and disjointed, instead of attributing it to the friction of war, he sought to identify those responsible: the generals who (as he saw it) had failed to do their full duty and thereby contributed to both the collapse of his plan and the eventual escape of the Federal army. In a word, Bragg sought scapegoats.[4]

The ensuing siege of Chattanooga gave him plenty of time to pursue them. After the Federal retreat from the battlefield at Chickamauga, Bragg approached Chattanooga expecting to find the enemy hurriedly evacuating. Instead, he found the Yankees fortifying the city, demonstrating an apparent determination to stay. He did not feel strong enough to force his way in, and the Federals were too weak to fight their way out, so—almost by default—the campaign lapsed into a kind of siege, with the Union army occupying the city and the rebels bivouacked on the high ground that surrounded it to the west, south, and east—though not to the north.

Conditions on both sides were Spartan. Cut off from supplies by all routes except the narrow and unreliable mountain trails north of the city, the Federals in Chattanooga survived mostly on hardtack and water. The rebel supply system was not much better, and Southern soldiers too got by on slim rations that consisted of a small "pone" of corn and a cup of corn coffee twice a day. Nor did the weather cooperate. The rain fell impartially on both armies, but at least the Federals in the city had decent accommodations—some slept with a roof over their heads. By contrast, the Confederates on the surrounding hills had to bivouac in the open; many of them lacked tents and had to sleep on the exposed rocky slopes, with only a groundcloth under them and perhaps a thin blanket over them. In the low ground between the hills it was worse. There, the mud from the nearly constant rain was so deep that one unit posted a sign reading "Mule Under Here" to show the spot where one of the army's draft animals had purportedly disappeared into the bottomless muck. Such conditions did little to sustain morale, and while the soldiers tried to make the best of their difficult circumstances, Bragg and the other generals engaged in an alarming and bitter bout of finger pointing and posturing.[5] Bragg made the first move by suspending Major General Thomas Hindman from his command for having failed to be sufficiently aggressive in a prebattle skirmish in McLemore's Cove on September 11. Then he penned a formal letter to Polk to demand an explanation for his late attack at Chickamauga on September 20. The two generals had a history. Following the Battle of Perryville in Kentucky more than a year before, Bragg had publicly and formally criticized Polk for failing to obey orders. Now, he was convinced that at Chickamauga, Polk's tardiness and inattention had once again cost him a complete victory.

In receipt of Bragg's note, and sensitive to the probability that it was merely the opening salvo of an eventual court-martial, Polk did not reply at once. An impatient Bragg prodded him with a second note the next day in which he demanded an immediate response. But it was a full week later before Polk offered a terse explanation that laid much of the blame for his late start on September 20 on Lieutenant General Daniel Harvey Hill. Bragg immediately declared his response "unsatisfactory" and relieved Polk of his command, though he also added Hill's name to his list of culprits, relieving him of his command as well.[6]

Bragg's preemptive strike put Jefferson Davis in an awkward position—especially the relief of Polk. Davis was friendly with both men—indeed, he may have been the only person in the Confederacy who was—and when he learned that Bragg had summarily dismissed Polk, a lieutenant general, he wired the army commander from Richmond to tell him that he could not do so without a court-martial. Very likely he hoped this would encourage Bragg to rescind his order. Instead, Bragg ordered Polk's arrest.

Davis tried again. "I can well appreciate the disapproval resulting from the delays and disobedience of order to which you refer," he wrote to Bragg on October 3, but surely the cause must come first. "When I sent you a dispatch recommending that Lieutenant-General Polk should not be placed in arrest, it was with a view of avoiding a controversy which could not heal the injury sustained, but which I feared would entail further evil." If Polk had behaved badly at Chickamauga—and Davis did not dispute that he had—it was surely not from "any intention to disobey your orders" but simply from confusion or uncertainty. There were errors in every battle, he noted. An effort to pin those mistakes on particular individuals was likely to depress morale and harm the cause for which they fought. To press the case against Polk now, Davis wrote, "diminishes the credit due, impairs the public confidence, undermines the morale of the army, and works evil to the cause for which brave men have died." Even if the general had disobeyed orders, and even if his failures were deliberate, it would only hurt the cause to prosecute him now. "I frequently pray that you may judge correctly, as I am well assured you will act purely for the public welfare."[7]

Davis's plea fell on deaf ears. Bragg was determined that Polk must be held accountable and, moreover, that he must be forced to acknowledge his guilt publicly. For his part, Polk was equally eager for a court-martial so that he could reveal not only his own innocence but also Bragg's manifest failures as an army commander. Meanwhile, Davis prepared to come west personally to see what he could do to prevent a complete breakdown of the army's high command.

Amid all of this was the central yet ambiguous—even enigmatic— figure of James Longstreet. Old Pete, as he was known, was new to the Army of Tennessee, having arrived with two divisions from General Robert E. Lee's Army of Northern Virginia only hours before the Battle of Chickamauga. In that fight his troops had executed the crucial break- through, and he could claim with some justification that his command had won the day. Even without that, however, Longstreet constituted a threat to Bragg's authority by his very presence with the western army. He may have come west in the first place in the expectation that he would inherit an independent command—something that was unlikely ever to happen in the eastern theater. His triumph at Chickamauga did little to quell either his ambition or his expectations. It was natural that Bragg's many enemies in the army would look to Longstreet as a likely ally and a potential savior. Moreover, even in the short time he had been there, Longstreet could hardly help contrasting Bragg's dour and confrontational style of command in the Army of Tennessee with the paternal and solicitous character of Lee's command style in the Army of Northern Virginia. Even without the element of personal ambition, Longstreet came to believe that Confederate success in the West depended on having someone other than Braxton Bragg in command of the Army of Tennessee. He even suggested that Lee himself should come west to take command, though he must have been aware that Lee was unlikely to embrace such a suggestion and that Davis was unlikely to approve it.[8]

At some point a number of Bragg's generals began to discuss how they could rid themselves of their despised commander. This was, of course, a delicate issue, and as a result, their conversations sheltered behind a solicitous concern for Bragg's poor health. There was justification for such concern. Bragg's appalling health, which included frequent migraine headaches, an unsteady stomach, a nervous condition that manifested itself in frequent outbreaks of boils, and crippling rheumatism, got even worse when he bore the burden of command. During the summer, he had suffered a physical breakdown so debilitating that he felt compelled to surrender his command briefly to Joe Johnston. His health had improved somewhat since then, but the burden of maintaining a siege of Chattanooga while conducting a war with his own subordinates was wearing on him, and it showed. Yet it was (and is) evident that at least some, and probably most, of those who participated in these conversations understood that Bragg's health was mostly a pretext and that the real concern was the health of the army rather than its commander. By the end of the month, a number of these generals had concluded that they should express their concerns about Bragg—that is, about his health—in a petition to the president.[9]

Major General Simon Bolivar Buckner may have been the first to propose it, for circumstantial evidence suggests that it originated in his headquarters, and his was the first signature attached to it. He may, in fact, have written all or part of it. It was worded carefully to avoid any personal criticism of Bragg and urged Davis to relieve the general from command solely for the sake of his health. Even with that fig leaf, however, the circulation of such a petition constituted a conspiracy at best, a mutiny at worst. Nevertheless, a dozen officers signed it, including eleven generals: two lieutenant generals, two major generals, seven brigadiers, and one colonel who commanded a brigade. After Buckner, all three of Buckner's division commanders (William Preston, Archibald Gracie, and John C. Brown) added their names to the petition. Apparently, the document then went to D. H. Hill's headquarters, for Hill was the next to sign. The petition apparently sat there for several days. Hill invited Breckinridge to sign, but the Kentuckian demurred, though two of his three brigade commanders did sign. Major General Patrick Cleburne signed, as did Lucius Polk, one of Cleburne's brigade commanders and Leonidas Polk's nephew. Then someone carried the document over to Longstreet's headquarters. There, both Longstreet and Bushrod Johnson signed it. Even before this remarkable document found its way to Richmond, Davis was already on his way to Georgia to suppress what began to look like an incipient mutiny.[10]

The president had a lot of time to consider possible outcomes as he rode the train southwest to Atlanta. He had no good options. It was unthinkable that he should give in to the petitioners and sack a commanding general upon the protestations of his subordinates. He could, of course, use the excuse of Bragg's poor health as a justification, but everyone in the army would know what had happened, and it would set a terrible precedent. In addition, he felt an instinctive sympathy for Bragg, besieged as he was by complainers and critics, since Davis also often felt besieged by detractors in the government and in the press. And finally, there was the problem that if Bragg were to go, someone would have to take his place. There was Longstreet, of course, but it would be particularly disruptive to reward one of the chief conspirators with the prize he sought. The only other candidates were Joe Johnston and P. G. T. Beauregard, both of whom Davis believed would be far worse than the incumbent. Even before he left Richmond, therefore, the president had implied to Secretary of War James Seddon that it would be impossible to remove Bragg because there was no one to put in his place.[11]

But if he sustained Bragg, what was to be done with the complainants? If Bragg stayed, did his detractors have to go? And if so, how many of them? Potentially, it was a long list, starting with the twelve men who had signed the petition. Sending them all off to other responsibilities would strip the army of many of its experienced and beloved senior commanders. The army might not recover from such a blow. The best outcome, surely, was to see if he could broker some kind of accommodation. Could the dissatisfied generals be persuaded to tolerate Bragg for the good of the cause; could Bragg be persuaded to reconsider his determination to purge the army of his enemies?

Whatever thoughts raced through Davis's mind as he headed west, he had already committed a grievous error by inviting John C. Pemberton to come with him. Very likely he invited Pemberton to accompany him because he thought that if he could not talk Bragg into retaining Polk, that Pemberton—also a lieutenant general—could replace him. If so, it was a terrible miscalculation. Pemberton bore the incubus of having

surrendered the Confederate citadel at Vicksburg in July, and some in
the South remained suspicious of his Pennsylvania origins—he had been
born in Philadelphia, and two of his brothers fought in the Union army.
Davis himself blamed Joe Johnston and not Pemberton for the loss of
Vicksburg, and he dismissed outright the mean-spirited rumors of Pemberton's lack of loyalty. Alas, the general had other baggage. He shared
with Bragg a cool demeanor that did not attract the kind of enthusiastic
loyalty that binds an army to its commander. Arriving in the West with
Pemberton in tow did nothing to assure the unhappy generals in the
Army of Tennessee that Davis was in touch with the mood of the army.

Arriving in Atlanta on October 8, Davis was greeted by Georgia's
governor, Joseph Brown, and he offered a brief morale-boosting speech
from the back of his train, praising the service of Georgia soldiers in
the war. Afterward he telegraphed both Longstreet and Breckinridge
asking them to come down to meet him so he could talk with them during the train ride north the next morning. First, however, he met with
a self-righteously indignant Leonidas Polk, who vigorously defended
his actions at Chickamauga and characterized Bragg's persecution of
him as a symptom of the army commander's incompetence and mental
instability. No record of their conversation survives, but two days later
Polk revealed his mood in a letter to his daughter. Bragg, he wrote, was
"a poor feeble . . . irresolute man of violent passion . . . without elevation
of character and capable of petty evasions to cover his incapacity and
blunders." Very likely, Polk expressed similar thoughts, perhaps even
similar language, in talking to Davis. In the hope of assuaging his friend,
Davis conceded that Bragg's charges against him were no doubt unjusti-
fied, but he pleaded with him to accept a transfer to a new command for
the sake of harmony. Polk would not hear of it. Though he expressed a
determination never to serve again under Bragg, he had no intention of
quietly stepping aside. He *wanted* a court-martial, even demanded it,
in order to expunge the tarnish of Bragg's baseless charges. After this
conversation, Davis almost certainly concluded that an accommodation
between the generals was unlikely.[12]

The next morning, October 9, Longstreet and Breckinridge reported as
requested, and Davis talked with them on the ride northward. He solic-
ited their views about the source of the problems in the army and about
how these might be resolved. Breckinridge, who had declined to sign
the petition against Bragg, was guarded in his comments; perhaps his
experience as James Buchanan's vice president had made him politically

cautious. Longstreet was less circumspect. Like Polk, he laid the army's problems at the feet of its commander, who, according to Longstreet, had been an inactive, indeed virtually absent, presence on the battlefield at Chickamauga. Davis listened carefully, but nothing he heard convinced him that the best solution was a change in army command.[13]

Arriving at last at Bragg's headquarters on Missionary Ridge, Davis and the man who was the target of all the abuse conferred privately at some length. One can only imagine the feelings of the army's generals as that conversation took place behind closed doors. Once again, there is no record of what was said, but according to tradition, Bragg offered to resign and Davis rejected the offer. Almost certainly, the president asked him to explain the army's difficulties, and Bragg very likely fingered Polk, Hindman, Hill, and perhaps Buckner as the principal troublemakers. Davis had already decided that he was going to sustain his western army's commander. It now became clear that to do that, he would have to sacrifice or at least transfer some of the men that Bragg identified as intransigents. The question was how many of them would have to go before order could be restored, and how to do it.

With hindsight, it is evident that the best course of action would have been for Davis to emerge from his meeting with Bragg to announce an uncompromising endorsement of the general. Then the president could have met separately with the several incorrigibles within the high command to assess their level of anger/disappointment/chagrin and determine on a course of action for each of them. Instead of that, however, Davis did what may have been the most destructive thing of all: without revealing that he intended to support Bragg, he invited the corps and division commanders to join the meeting. This encouraged the generals to believe that they had been summoned to discuss the merits and shortcomings of their commander. As Davis's biographer William C. Davis has put it, "the generals believed that the subject of Bragg's tenure was still an open question." It was more than a little awkward that the general himself remained in the room, and the result was a curious, unprofessional, and even surreal conversation.[14]

In his memoir (which is not always trustworthy), Longstreet claimed that Davis began the meeting by inviting Bragg's subordinates to present "their opinion of their commanding officer," turning first to Longstreet for an assessment. It seems odd that Davis should make such a request since he had already heard Longstreet's views on the subject during the train ride that morning. Perhaps he sought to find out if Old Pete was willing to make the same arguments in front of his commanding officer. Perhaps Davis's request was a more general one, in which he invited the corps and division commanders to suggest plans for the army's future operations, which Longstreet mistakenly interpreted as an invitation to criticize the commanding general. In any case, Longstreet asserted that any future operations were unlikely to be successful with the army's present commander. Longstreet later claimed that he had tried to deflect the question but that Davis had insisted on a direct response. However it happened, Longstreet did repeat his criticisms of Bragg, concluding (as he put it later), "our commander could be of greater service elsewhere than at the head of the Army of Tennessee." With the ice broken, both Buckner and Cheatham offered similar views. It was D. H. Hill, however, who was the most vociferous. Hill was famous for his temper, and it got the better of him this time as he offered a diatribe so abusive and unprofessional that the president took offense and cut him off.[15]

None of this should have caught Davis by surprise. Perhaps he had counted on Bragg's presence to inhibit any direct criticism. Perhaps he and Bragg had decided to give the detractors an opportunity to hang themselves. In any case, after listening to his generals, Davis thanked them and dismissed them, but he did not announce a decision, though almost immediately rumors began to circulate that Bragg was perhaps not going to be relieved after all.

The next day, October 10, Davis met individually with several of the complaining generals, something he probably ought to have done first. The most important conversation was with Longstreet, and it was a long one—Longstreet later described it as lasting "all day." By now, Old Pete very likely regretted his behavior in the meeting the day before. Perhaps recognizing that the wind had shifted, he offered to resign, not just from the Army of Tennessee but from Confederate service altogether. Davis dismissed that notion out of hand, but Longstreet persisted, suggesting that perhaps he should be transferred to the Trans-Mississippi West, where after a decent interval, he could resign from the army without attracting public attention. Davis may have suspected that the general was merely grandstanding, but soon it did not matter, for when Longstreet suggested that Joseph Johnston, whom Davis despised, might be brought back to resume his theater command in the West, the president finally showed some emotion, expostulating at length about political generals and disloyal factions that undermined the Confederate cause.[16]

Davis also met with Buckner, the probable author of the removal petition, who was still hoping that he could convince him to let Bragg go. The president and Buckner rode together along the crest of Missionary Ridge in animated conversation. Again Davis listened without committing himself, though very likely he had already made his decision. This gambit—allowing Bragg's critics to continue to condemn him even though Davis had very likely already decided to sustain him—was either cruel, foolish, or both. Historian Thomas Connelly suggests that Davis engaged in these conversations "more for show than earnestness," which if true made this behavior even more questionable. By openly attacking their commanding officer in front of the president, the critics were burning their bridges, and unless Davis was willing to jettison them entirely, he should never have let them do it, much less encouraged it.[17]

Not until October 12 did the president announce his decision. In a public statement he declared that Bragg was "worthy of all confidence" despite the "shafts of malice" that had been hurled against him. So Bragg would remain in command, but at what cost? Sustaining the general required Davis to confirm Bragg's dismissal of both Polk and Hill. Moreover, the president denied both men their day in court by refusing their requests for courts-martial. Disappointed that the army was obviously unwilling to accept Pemberton as a replacement for either man, Davis named Lieutenant General William J. Hardee as Polk's replacement. Davis hoped that by returning to the Army of Tennessee, Hardee, who had written the Old Army's tactics manual, could bring a sense of quiet professionalism to the command. "I rely greatly upon you," he wrote to Hardee, "for the restoration of a proper feeling" in the army—in other words, to restore a professional demeanor. For his part, Bragg was probably unhappy with Hardee's appointment, for he had previously clashed with that general as well. As for Longstreet, Davis suggested that Old Pete and his command could be sent off to drive Major General Ambrose Burnside's Union army out of Knoxville. It would be an independent command after all, and the recapture of that city would regain East Tennessee for the Confederacy.[18]

This was as far as Davis would, or could, go. If Bragg was still unhappy that other recalcitrant generals remained with his army, Davis told him, in effect, to deal with it. "I prefer to postpone the consideration of any further removal of general officers from their commands," he wrote to Bragg in late October after he had returned to Richmond, and he urged the commander not to let his "personal antipathies" get in the way of his duty. With that, he left the issue in Bragg's hands. I "must leave it to you to combat the difficulties arising from the disappointment or the discontent of officers by such gentle means as may turn them aside." "Gentle" was not a word anyone else used to describe Braxton Bragg's command style, but for once, the general was contrite: "I shall faithfully endeavor to discharge the difficult and responsible trust with forbearance but firmness," he wrote.[19]

The episode did not end the bickering. Bragg continued to complain about Longstreet, and Longstreet continued to correspond with others, including Buckner, about Bragg, whose tenure was coming to an end in any case. On November 25, Union soldiers surged up over Missionary Ridge, and the poorly supplied and poorly led soldiers of the Army of Tennessee—almost forgotten amid their generals' quarreling—broke and ran. For a few days, Bragg thought he could redeem both the defeat and his command. He reported to Davis that the Federals had won "by sheer force of numbers," as if that explained and excused the ignominious defeat. He declared defiantly, "we can redeem the past," and he suggested that all the forces of the Confederacy should be concentrated for a counterattack. In a sentence that could have been written by Beauregard at his most fanciful, Bragg outlined his plan: "Let us concentrate all our available men, unite them with this gallant little army . . . , and with our greatest and best leader at the head, yourself if practicable, march the whole upon the enemy and crush him," adding, "I trust that I may be allowed to participate."[20]

He would not. Belatedly accepting the inevitable, Bragg saw that his tenure of command had run its unhappy course, and he tendered his resignation. Hardee temporarily took his place, and on December 16, Jefferson Davis swallowed a bitter pill by appointing Joe Johnston to command the Army of Tennessee.

ACKNOWLEDGMENTS

Many individuals have helped sharpen my understanding of Jefferson Davis, his burdens, and his political environment. In particular, I am indebted to the works of William C. "Jack" Davis, Bill Cooper, and Steven Woodworth. I have also benefited from verbal jousting with Richard McMurry over the years about Davis's (and Joe Johnston's) various foibles. All of my work benefits from the keen editorial eye of my wife, Marylou Symonds.

NOTES

1. William C. Davis, *Jefferson Davis: The Man and His Hour* (New York: HarperCollins, 1991), 517–19; Chesnut to Davis, Oct. 5, 1863, U.S. War Department, *The War of the Rebellion: A Compilation of the Official Records of the Union and Confederate Armies,* 128 vols. (Washington, D.C.: GPO, 1880–1901), ser. 1, 52(2):38 (hereinafter cited as *OR;* all citations to series 1 unless otherwise specified).

2. Craig L. Symonds, *Joseph E. Johnston: A Civil War Biography* (New York: W. W. Norton, 1992), 187–203.

3. Judith Lee Hallock, *Braxton Bragg and Confederate Defeat, Volume II* (Tuscaloosa: University of Alabama Press, 1991). Hardee is quoted in Joseph H. Parks, *General Leonidas Polk, C.S.A.: The Fighting Bishop* (Baton Rouge: Louisiana State University Press, 1960), 315. See also Steven E. Woodworth, *No Band of Brothers: Problems of the Rebel High Command* (Columbia: University of Missouri Press, 1999), 70–80.

4. Peter Cozzens, *This Terrible Sound: The Battle of Chickamauga* (Urbana: University of Illinois Press, 1996); Craig L. Symonds, *Stonewall of the West: Patrick Cleburne and the Civil War* (Lawrence: University Press of Kansas, 1997), 147–51.

5. Philip D. Stephenson, *The Civil War Memoir of Philip Dangerfield Stephenson, D.D.,* ed. Nathaniel C. Hughes Jr. (Conway: University of Central Arkansas Press, 1995), 135; Jim Turner, "Co. G. 6th Texas Infantry, CSA, from 1861 to 1865," *Texana* 12 (1974): 165; Peter Cozzens, *The Shipwreck of Their Hopes: The Battles for Chattanooga* (Urbana: University of Illinois Press, 1994), 119–20; Wiley Sword, *Mountains Touched with Fire: Chattanooga Besieged, 1863* (New York: St. Martin's, 1995), 105–11.

6. Thomas L. Connelly, *Autumn of Glory: The Army of Tennessee, 1862–1865* (Baton Rouge: Louisiana State University Press, 1971), 235–36; Hallock, *Braxton Bragg,* 90.

7. Davis to Bragg, Oct. 3, 1863, *OR* 52(2):535.

8. Longstreet to Seddon, Sept. 26, 1863; and Lee to Longstreet, Oct. 26, 1863, both in ibid., 549. Longstreet's critics assert that his suggestion was a kind of stalking horse intended to advance his own appointment to command.

9. On Bragg's health, see Hallock, *Braxton Bragg,* 4–5.

10. For a discussion of the possible authorship of the petition, see Connelly, *Autumn of Glory,* 239.

11. Davis, *Jefferson Davis,* 519.

12. Polk to "My dear daughter," Oct. 10, 1863, quoted in Hallock, *Braxton Bragg,* 92.

13. Davis, *Jefferson Davis,* 519.

14. Ibid.

15. James Longstreet, *From Manassas to Appomattox* (Philadelphia: J. B. Lippincott, 1896), 465–66; Davis, *Jefferson Davis,* 521–22.

16. Longstreet, *From Manassas to Appomattox,* 466–67; Davis, *Jefferson Davis,* 520.

17. Connelly, *Autumn of Glory,* 246.

18. Davis to Bragg, Oct. 29, 1863, *OR,* 52(2):554; Connelly, *Autumn of Glory,* 245; William J. Cooper Jr., *Jefferson Davis, American* (New York: Alfred A. Knopf, 2000), 465–67.

19. Davis to Bragg, Oct. 29, 1863; and Bragg to Davis, Oct. 31, 1863, both in *OR,* 52(2):555, 557.

20. See, for example, Longstreet to Buckner, Nov. 5, 1863, ibid., 559–60. Bragg's fanciful proposal is in Bragg to Davis, Dec. 2, 1863, ibid., 568.

CHAPTER 7

A "MALIGNANT VINDICTIVENESS"

The Two-Decade Rivalry between
Ulysses S. Grant and William S. Rosecrans

EVAN C. JONES

By the autumn of 1863, much of the Federal high command in the Civil War's western theater had fractured into a team of rivals. Among the fluid alliances between brother officers could be found no more volatile a rapport than that which existed between Major Generals Ulysses S. Grant and William S. Rosecrans. These two men, each in separate turns, dominated the Union's five-month struggle to secure Chattanooga in 1863. Yet before either man arrived at that city, they had already become, in the words of historian Wiley Sword, "the two great rival Union generals in the West."[1] Not surprisingly, the Chattanooga theater was, quite simply, not big enough for the two men, who at the time towered far above other Union war heroes. When posed with the opportunity to be rid of his rival, Grant seized it, ordering Rosecrans relieved from command over the Army of the Cumberland on October 19, 1863. This decision, however, proved one that would stalk Grant for the rest of his life, following him all the way to his deathbed almost twenty-two years later.

Nearly fifteen years after the Chattanooga Campaign, while traveling in Germany in the summer of 1878, Grant sat for a candid interview with a correspondent from the *New York Herald*. The *Herald* had long been a newspaper loyal to Grant and one in which he could broadcast his message.[2] Now, removed from the war by time and distance, old scores continued to fester. "There were a few men when the war broke out to whom we who had been in the army looked for success and high rank—among them . . . Rosecrans," he confessed. "Rosecrans was a great disappointment to us all—to me especially."[3] This interview proved one

Major Generals Ulysses S. Grant (left) and William S. Rosecrans (right).
Their friendship, turned rivalry, turned enmity was a faceoff that ultimately cost
Rosecrans his military career. Library of Congress (left), National Archives (right).

of many occasions in which Grant slapped down his onetime friend in a
seemingly conscious effort to subordinate Rosecrans's place in American
history. Today it seems Grant's interpretation lives on, for in the minds
of many if not most Civil War historians, Rosecrans is dismissed as a
disappointment to the Union war effort, a vanquished army commander
routed from the battlefield at Chickamauga only to prove himself inept
under the strain of the Chattanooga siege. Posterity has chiseled Rosecrans's military epitaph with words from President Lincoln, who after
Chickamauga regarded him as acting "confused and stunned like a duck
hit on the head."[4] Nothing could have been further from the truth.

Much of what both Lincoln and posterity have come to think about
William Starke Roescrans has been filtered through the general's detractors, in wartime dispatches, newspapers, and postwar memoirs. At the
center of everything lies the murky Grant-Rosecrans relationship. To
understand this rivalry and its influence on the Chattanooga Campaign,
one must examine the anatomy of the traditionally obscured battle of
Iuka, Mississippi, and the brief period when the two men served side by
side during the autumn of 1862. The story of how these friends became

fierce rivals and ultimately bitter enemies reveals, in microcosm, a hazardous instability within the Federal high command during the American
Civil War.

———∞∞∞———

For men who later wielded their differences against one another, Grant
and Rosecrans had much in common. Both were native Ohioans and by
the time of the siege at Chattanooga had known each other for twenty-
four years, having met as underclassmen at the U.S. Military Academy
at West Point in 1839. There, late on a summer evening, Rosecrans, the
cadet officer of the day, found Grant, a first year "plebe," standing guard
over a water pump. Recognizing his naive colleague as the victim of a
prank, Rosecrans ordered him to stand down and retire to bed. Their
friendship thus began with an expression of charitable kindness. Among
the academy's best students, "Old Rosey" (as Rosecrans was already
known) graduated fifth in the class of 1842, standing as the first west-
erner ever to rank into the army's elite Corps of Engineers. Trailing him
by a year, Grant excelled only in horsemanship, graduating twenty-first
in the class of 1843. Across this divide of academic achievement, their
paths parted. In 1845 Rosecrans returned to West Point as an instructor
of engineering, serving as colleague to the legendary professor Dennis
Hart Mahan. Grant, in contrast, met with a series of mediocre assignments at backwater frontier outposts, a career highlighted only by distinguished battlefield gallantry during the Mexican War, which twice won
him brevet promotions. Rosecrans, like so many engineers as decreed
by the War Department, was retained at home, having to sit out the war
with Mexico. Then in 1854, both men resigned their commissions and
left military service.[5]

After the secession crisis brought war in 1861, both Grant and Rosecrans marshaled themselves from civilian life and rejoined the army,
where nearly identical experiences played out. Both began the war seeking to serve directly under Major General George B. McClellan, though
only Rosecrans would get the job. Both helped raise volunteer units,
Grant in Illinois, Rosecrans in Ohio. Both reentered army service as
staff officers, Grant in the office of the adjutant general of Illinois, Rosecrans as aide-de-camp to McClellan at a troop-training grounds. Almost
simultaneously, both were promoted to brigadier general of volunteers,
with Rosecrans's commission dating to May 16 and Grant's to May 17,

1861.[6] Both served subordinate under commanders who claimed the lion's share of glory for their accomplishments. Rosecrans watched with envy as McClellan propelled himself to national renown when appointed founding commander of the Army of the Potomac on the coattails of their successful July 1861 dual assault on Rich Mountain in the Alleghenies of western Virginia. Across the mountains, in the western theater, Grant begrudgingly observed Major General Henry W. Halleck behave similarly during their advance into Tennessee. Though he did not actually serve at the battlefront, Halleck was credited as being the strategic architect of the capture of Forts Henry and Donelson in February 1862, a move that helped secure him promotion to theater commander. Then in July, Halleck was allowed to take his self-polished laurels to a desk at the War Department in Washington, D.C., having been proffered another promotion, this time to serve as general in chief of all U.S. armies.

It is during this time that the two men also met with disparaging aspersion. Among the overwhelmingly Protestant officer corps in the army, the air had long been redolent with misgivings and mistrust for the Holy Roman Catholic Church, and Rosecrans could not have been more outspoken regarding his devotion to the Vatican and Pope Pius IX. One colleague described him as "a Jesuit of the highest style of Roman piety."[7] A rosary always at hand, Rosecrans became one of but two Catholic generals to serve in the Union army during the Civil War, the other being Brigadier General Thomas Meagher, commander of the celebrity-bound Irish Brigade within the Army of the Potomac.[8] Rosecrans too, like the vast majority of Catholic Americans, was a member of the Democratic Party, an affiliation that precariously placed him in the crosshairs of some within the Lincoln administration.[9] This was at a time when Catholic Democrats were broadly characterized as Confederate sympathizing "Copperheads," a name gleaned from the venomous southern viper and reserved for the most seditious critics of President Lincoln. Yet Rosecrans, a "War Democrat," supported the Lincoln administration, both in its policy and its prosecution of the war. Despite this, Rosecrans hailed from Cincinnati, a hotbed of Copperhead activity, undertaken by Catholic Democrats who went so far as to instigate the first race riot of the war in July 1862 in protest of Lincoln policies toward black free labor in the North. The city too was home to the prominent anti-Lincoln, antiwar newspaper, the *Cincinnati Enquirer,* whose editor, James Faran, was an Irish-Catholic Democrat. Yet even within print culture, the Rosecrans family defended the president. The general's brother, Catholic bishop Sylvester Rosecrans, helped wage an antidissent campaign within the *Catholic Telegraph* of Cincinnati. The general himself wrote a public letter to the Ohio legislature wherein he exhorted: "I am amazed that any one could think of 'peace on any terms.' He who entertains the sentiment is fit only to be a slave; he who utters it at this time is, moreover, a traitor to his country, who deserves the scorn and contempt of all honorable men."[10] Despite this confirmed and unwavering allegiance to national war policy, General Rosecrans's religious beliefs, political leanings, and even his hometown helped sustain an air of mistrust that lingered about him in the army. At a time when Secretary of War Edwin M. Stanton sought to flush out Copperheads by personally ordering a number of Catholic Democrats jailed for months on end without evidence of wrongdoing, Rosecrans seemed a less than ideal colleague to work with the War Department.[11]

Meanwhile, Grant had far more ferocious detractors to face down. Rumors of drunkenness had trailed him since his service in the antebellum army, and in April 1862 they returned to sweep through the ranks of his new command as well as the Northern press with renewed fervor. When Grant's encamped force at Shiloh, Tennessee, initially scattered in the face of a Confederate surprise attack, some critics charged that the Ohioan's unpreparedness resulted from drunkenness on the eve of the battle. Lamentably for Grant, various rumors originated with his immediate superior, Henry Halleck, who temporarily subordinated him to an ineffective command.[12] Despite ultimate battlefield success at Shiloh, the true story of a successful Union standoff became trumped by erroneous newsprint of both an incompetent and a drunk at the helm of western Federal fortunes. Grant detested the rumors and reassured his wife that he was "as sober as a deacon no matter what is said to the contrary."[13] To protect their own reputations during the post-Shiloh fallout, two of Grant's three division commanders, Major Generals Lew Wallace and John McClernand, kept silent and did not rebuke the criticism directed against him.[14] During this time, Grant had but one guardian in the army.[15] To his wife he confided, "In Gen. Sherman the country has an able and gallant defender and your husband a true friend."[16] But another friend was on his way.

And so it was in the shadow of controversy surrounding Shiloh that on May 23, 1862, Rosecrans stepped off a steamboat at Pittsburg Landing, Tennessee, to join Grant's gathering Department of Mississippi and the campaign against the Confederate rail hub at Corinth, Mississippi.[17]

When John Rawlins, Grant's adjutant general, saw Rosecrans that day, he was "not surprised" that the two generals greeted each other so cordially. "How are you Grant, how are you Rosey," they exchanged. During this time, Grant spoke of Rosecrans as a "warm personal friend [and] one of the ablest and purest of men, both in motive and action." At the time, Grant regarded his old West Point acquaintance as one of a select few officers in whom he could confide. When Major General John Pope was selected over Grant that spring to the command of the Army of Virginia, Rawlins heard Grant state that he would, "willingly serve under" but two junior officers in his department—William Tecumseh Sherman or William Starke Rosecrans.[18]

After joining Grant's department, Brigadier General Rosecrans found that Grant placed greater confidence and trust in him than most of the department's six major generals, who outranked the newly arrived Ohioan. Within weeks Rosecrans was promoted to command over the Army of the Mississippi. "General Grant, who is an honest man, relies on me and gives me all the troops of this army while three Major Generals [here] have less . . . than I have," he boasted. Despite Grant's endowed confidence, Rosecrans grew envious for promotion. His jealousy quickly turned to resentment against brother officers after observing rowdiness among some of the department's various headquarters staffs. To his wife, Rosecrans assessed himself as "being the only officer who has not been promoted who having had a responsible position here behaved himself well in it."[19] While Grant was wrongfully accused of inebriation at Shiloh, a clear culture of drinking did exist within his department, and it threatened to hinder the cohesiveness of operations. A friend warned Rosecrans that Brigadier General Charles Hamilton's "staff officers," for example, "did not include two men of any ability whatever, and were rarely free from the influence of liquor."[20] Rosecrans detested drunkenness and did not tolerate it within his own staff (the following year he took on an aide-de-camp, Colonel Joseph C. McKibbin, who, after Chickamauga, he "sent away for drunkenness").[21] Historian Edward G. Longacre has written that during this time, Rawlins confided in a colleague that "Grant's overindulgence" in alcohol was a reality and that it "was largely the result of his fraternizing with irresponsible staff officers who deserved to be dismissed from their posts."[22] One Illinois major complained of the general's staff to Representative Elihu Washburne, writing, "I doubt whether either of them have gone to bed sober for a week."[23] Among the drunks named was a young colonel, Clark Lagow.

In time his unruly conduct, as well as that of another obscure colonel, Theophilus Dickey, would directly and adversely influence the Grant-Rosecrans friendship.

Yet if Rosecrans felt out of place in the department, he knew that he had Grant to depend upon. In a moment when it seemed Rosecrans might lose his army command to one of the theater's major generals, Grant stepped up to protect his friend and lobby on his behalf for promotion. "I am anxious to keep the whole of the Army of the Mississippi together, and under the command of Brig. Gen. Rosecrans," he wired the War Department. "Having so many Maj. Generals to provide commands for, this may be difficult. I regret that Gen. Rosecrans has not got rank equal to his merit."[24]

Then on September 13, 1862, a Federal supply outpost at the railside village of Iuka, twenty-five miles southeast of Corinth, fell into the hands of Major General Sterling Price and 12,000 rebels. In striking back, Grant seized upon a rare opportunity to surround and capture this isolated Confederate army. The plan called for a daring strategy. Two independent Federal columns would converge on Iuka from opposite directions, cutting all escape routes. Between the jaws of this pincer movement, Grant surmised, Price's outnumbered command would have no option but to surrender. Major General Edward O. C. Ord was delegated to strike first, from the north and west, down the Burnsville Road with about 6,500 troops. With the Confederates drawn north of Iuka to defend against Ord, Rosecrans, with a force of 9,000 men, would strike second, seizing the road network south of town, cutting both the Jacinto and Fulton Roads, and thus preventing a rebel retreat. The successful coordination of such an intricate assault called for a flawlessly executed timetable.[25]

By the morning of September 18, both divergent columns were traveling their separate routes, closing on the ill-prepared and unsuspecting Confederates at Iuka. Down the Memphis and Charleston Railroad, Ord's three divisions steamed for the Burnsville depot, where they detrained to march the remaining twelve miles to Iuka. To the south, without benefit of a rail line, Rosecrans's blue columns—two divisions, four brigades in all—slogged muddily along a winding, confusing route of some thirty-four miles across swollen bayous and poor country roads. Grant, meanwhile, made headquarters at Burnsville, where he maintained an easy contact with Ord's column via the Burnsville Road. Rosecrans, however, was separated from him by miles of ravines, swamps, and tangled forest, described by one courier as being "impassable for a man on horseback." Innovatively, the two commanders maintained a limited contact, sending messages along a line of cavalry vedettes that extended across this Mississippi backcountry. The twisting and confusing route, however, significantly delayed communication and jeopardized the plan's success.

During this complicated offensive, Grant's mind was elsewhere. Still preoccupied with curbing the public outcry against him, he scorned his own father for submitting a cache of his private comments to the *Cincinnati Commercial* newspaper. Grant snarled:

> I would write you many particulars but you are so imprudent that I dare not trust you with them; and while on this subject let me say a word [further]. I have not an enemy in the world who has done me so much injury as you in your efforts in my defence [*sic*]. I require no defenders and for my sake let me alone. I have heard various sources and persons who have returned to this Army [saying that] you are constantly denouncing other General officers and the inference with people naturally is that you get your impressions [from] me.
>
> Do nothing to correct what you have already done but for the future keep quiet on this subject.[26]

Distracted from the operation at hand, Grant's contact with Rosecrans's distant column became less frequent.

On the critical day of September 18, a vacuum of leadership at Grant's headquarters endangered the success of the operation and the safety of his army. A prearranged timetable called for Ord and Rosecrans to be assembled at jumping-off points around Iuka that evening and launch their attacks the following morning. To the south, however, Rosecrans had run into trouble. A local guide, either by accident or in an effort to hinder the progress of the Union advance, led Rosecrans's lead division off course. By nightfall, that column had made it only as far as Jacinto Courthouse and was still fourteen miles southeast of Iuka.

Going into camp for the night, Rosecrans sent word back to Grant, notifying him of the delay but promising that he would renew his march at 4:30 A.M. and attack Iuka that afternoon, October 19. Sometime after midnight Grant received the news, "very much disappointed." He later admitted that he "did not believe [Rosecrans's plan] possible because of the distance and the condition of the roads."[27] To adjust for this forecasted failure, Grant changed the overall battle plan. With a dispatch written and signed on his behalf in the handwriting of a staff officer,

Colonel Clark Lagow, Grant alerted Ord: "You will see that [Rosecrans] is behind where we expected him. Do not be to [*sic*] rapid with your advance this morning unless it should be found the enemy are evacuating."[28] Amazingly, Grant never notified Rosecrans of this change of plan, and the confusing order resulted in Ord halting his advance entirely. In his *Personal Memoirs* decades later, Grant defended that he "ordered [Ord] to be in readiness to attack the moment he heard the sound of guns to the south or south-east."[29] In an after-action report, he insisted that "of this change General Rosecrans was promptly informed by dispatch."[30] To this day, however, no such communiqué, either to Ord or Rosecrans, has ever been found.[31]

In the predawn darkness of September 19, Rosecrans's columns assembled to begin the final push to Iuka. Shortly after noon, the general halted briefly for a meal and final strategy session at Barnett's Crossroads, six miles south of Iuka. As his Federal infantry filed through the road junction to turn north up the Jacinto Road, Rosecrans and his staff stepped into a farmhouse to reexamine their plan of attack. Moments later, at approximately 12:30 P.M., Grant's two staff officers, Colonels Dickey and Lagow, arrived from Burnsville and joined the conference. There at the obscure crossroads in the Mississippi hinterland, Rosecrans convened what, in retrospect, must have proven to be one of the most bizarre meetings of his life, one that altered Union fortunes at Iuka and forever changed his relationship with Grant. In the presence of Dickey and Lagow, the general altered his own attack plan. The original plan, agreed to by Grant, called for Rosecrans to split his force at Barnett's Crossroads, sending two brigades farther east to Cartersville to seize the Fulton Road, a certain Confederate escape route. Instead, he would hurl his entire command north up the Jacinto Road toward Iuka. Then, arriving at the east–west Bay Springs crossroad one mile south of town, Rosecrans could shift half his force to the east, cutting the Mill Road and Fulton Road, thereby closing the Confederate escape routes.

The plan hinged on Ord beginning his attack that very afternoon. With the Confederate strength drawn north of Iuka to face him, the Bay Springs Road and thus the Fulton Road would be lightly defended, if at all. This new, more cautious plan would prevent Rosecrans from dangerously dividing his force by several miles. If split, each wing would be beyond the other's support, separated by dense forest and marshy swampland. He had no reason to think that Ord would delay the attack from the north, and Grant's two staff officers gave him none.

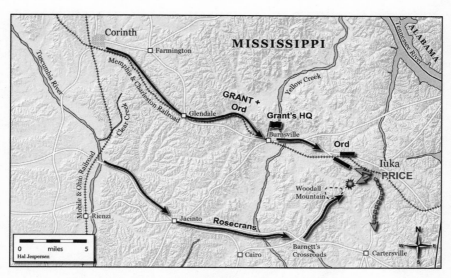

The Grant-Rosecrans Pincer Movement at Iuka, Mississippi.

At the conference table, Lagow and Dickey held their tongues. Lagow had personally written out and delivered Grant's dispatch to Ord, ordering him to halt his advance and attack Iuka only after Rosecrans's assaults had begun. The two colonels, now the only men on the entire campaign with full knowledge of both pincer commanders having altered their attack plans, said nothing to enlighten Rosecrans. With an odd mixture of obsequiousness and evasiveness, the colonels entered into a dialog asking the general if he *actually intended* to attack Iuka that afternoon. "Yes, of course," Rosecrans replied, "that is the understanding of my movement. . . . We ought to hear Grant's [and Ord's] opening guns [to the north] by this time." To this the colonels offered an astonishing reaction, "Maybe [Grant] is waiting for you to begin." "Not so," Rosecrans insisted. "The main attack should begin on the Railroad [from the north] to attract the enemy's attention and enable me to surprise his left flank and get the roads in his rear."[32]

By his own admission, Colonel Dickey wrote soon after, "Colonel Lagow and I were sent by General Grant to visit General Rosecrans and explain to him the plan of operations." Rather than actually doing so, the two officers left the strategy meeting "and rode with [Rosecrans] to the head of his [advancing] column," having explained nothing of Ord's revised instructions to attack only after Rosecrans opened the

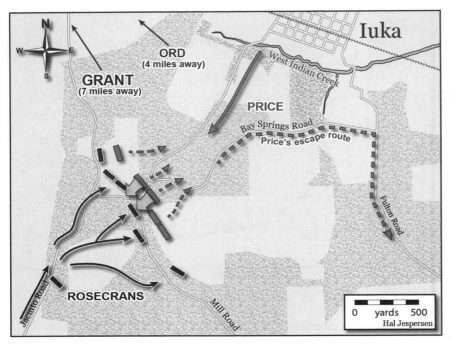

Positions of Grant, Rosecrans, and Ord at Iuka, September 19, 1862.

fighting.[33] As such, Rosecrans rode into battle confident that Ord would
have already drawn Confederate strength north of Iuka, leaving the Bay
Springs Road intersection unprotected, an easy prize for him to prevent
the Confederates from retreating.

Meeting strong enemy resistance, Rosecrans, to his bewilderment,
found the Bay Springs Road junction defended by some 11,000 Confederates and eight cannon. "During all this time," he later wrote his wife,
"not a shot was heard from the forces of Ord."[34] To make matters worse,
Dickey and Lagow delayed their return, "witnessing the battle for half an
hour [before they] set out for . . . Grant[']s Head Quarters . . . to report
the state of affairs and have Ord's army push on in the morning."[35] They
failed to reach Grant in time, however. As the colonels rode for help, they
lost their way in the woods, tumbled into a ravine, and, injured, built a
fire to wait for daylight.[36] Meanwhile, Rosecrans absorbed assaults until nightfall, fully aware that the rebels blocked him from cutting their
escape route, the Fulton Road, which remained open to Price's rear.

The following morning, September 20, Rosecrans's battered force awoke to find that the Confederates had indeed fled to the southeast down the Fulton Road. The general's men entered Iuka uncontested, and still Ord was nowhere to be found. Moreover, Rosecrans had not received a fresh message from Grant for more than thirty-six hours. Now, faced with the consequences of the failed operation, an infuriated Rosecrans turned to his colleague Brigadier General David Stanley and roared, "Where, in the name of God is Grant!"[37] Back at Grant's headquarters in Burnsville, at 8:30 A.M., about the same time his "trusted couriers" Dickey and Lagow finally stumbled out of the woods, a message sent directly from Rosecrans the previous evening arrived, having traveled up the line of cavalry vedettes. This proved to be Grant's first knowledge that a battle had even been fought.[38]

To his credit, Grant immediately sent word to Ord of this "notice that Rosecrans had a fight" and ordered his divisions to push into Iuka in force.[39] Sometime after 10:00 A.M., Ord's infantry came marshaling into the village, "with drums beating and banners flying." At this sight Rosecrans personally rode to the head of the inbound column, where he found Ord. "Why did you leave me in the lurch?" he growled. Ord, without saying a word, handed Rosecrans the dispatch written in Lagow's handwriting ordering that he suspend his advance. One brigade commander, Colonel John Fuller, witnessed the exchange and later remembered that "this miscarriage was the beginning of a misunderstanding which grew into positive dislike between Grant and Rosecrans—a breach that never healed."[40] It was indeed the genesis of endless conflict between the two men.

Historians have never fully diminished the mystery and controversy that surrounds the failure of the Federal pincer movement at Iuka. A phenomenon widely referred to as an "acoustic shadow," or more scientifically "sound refraction," created by winds and terrain, seems to have prevented Ord's force from hearing the sounds of battle just four miles to the south.[41] At 4:00 P.M. on September 19, as Rosecrans's advanced guard made contact with Price's rebels, Ord received word from Brigadier General Leonard Ross, who from a forward position misinterpreted "dense smoke rising from the direction of Iuka" as nothing more than "the enemy . . . evacuating and destroying [their supply] stores" there.[42] Yet, larger questions remained unanswered. As late as 1880 Arthur Ducat, who had served there as a "senior officer to Ord," labored to piece together why that general had not attacked. While preparing a lecture on Iuka for the Military Order of the Loyal Legion of the United States that year, Ducat wrote Rosecrans in search of answers. "Why did not Ord attack *with* or *before* you at Iuka? Why was not Grant [updated] on the actual situation the day of your attack?" he inquired.[43] Rosecrans had posed the same questions for years and seems never to have received satisfactory answers. The actions of Grant at Iuka also remain a mystery. Why did he alter the battle plan and fail to send a written dispatch to Rosecrans alerting him to the changes? Why did his staff officers say nothing of the revised timetable while spending hours with Rosecrans as he rode toward waiting Confederates at Iuka? These questions remain as perplexing today as they were in 1862.

Immediately following the battle, fingers began to point back and forth across Grant's department. "God gave us victory," Rosecrans admitted, "but the failure of proper cooperation unfortunately lost us the capture of Price and his entire army which would have been inevitable had the attack from [Ord] been duly made."[44] Grant took no ownership over the operation's failure. To his colleague Major General Benjamin Hurlbut, he wrote simply, "couriers lost dispatches sent [to] me by General Rosecrans," a statement that has proven untrue.[45] To his sister Mary, he answered, "where you ask me the part I played at . . . Iuka . . . I had no more to do with troops under Gen. Ord than I had with those under Rosecrans but gave the orders to both. The plan was admirably laid for catching Price and his whole Army but owing to the nature of the ground, direction of the wind and Gen. Rosecrans having been so far behind where he was expected to be on the morning before the attack it failed."[46]

Rosecrans, in contrast, seized the lion's share of glory for the fruitless victory at Iuka. He felt justified in doing so, given that the troops of his wing of the pincer were the only ones committed into the fight. Meanwhile, Grant pined over the fact that Rosecrans's interpretation of the battle was embraced so widely by newspapers. "I do not see my report of the battle of Iuka in print!" he wrote to Representative Washburne seven weeks after the fight. "As the papers in Gen. Rosecrans interest have so much misrepresented that affair I would like to see it in print. I have no objection to . . . [him or] any other Gen. being made a hero of by the press, but I do not want to see it at the expense of a meritorious portion of the Army. I endeavored in that report to give a plain statement of facts, some of which I would never have mentioned had it not become necessary in defense of troops who have been with me in all, or nearly all the battles where I have had the honor to command."[47]

Perhaps no other Union victory created greater internal divisiveness within an army than Iuka. Initially, Grant feared only the perpetuation of bitterness between the enlisted men of Ord's and Rosecrans's commands. In his congratulatory message to the department following the battle, he warranted, "the command of General Ord is entitled to equal credit for their efforts in trying to reach the enemy, and in diverting his attention."[48] Weeks later, in a second departmentwide message, Grant implored that between the army's two wings, "there should be, and I trust are, the warmest bonds of brotherhood. Each was risking life in the same cause, and . . . risking it also to save and assist the other."[49] Rosecrans read the directive with shock. "The part expressing the hope that good feeling will exist between Ord's command and my own amazes me. So far as I know there was nothing even to suggest the thought that it might be otherwise. Under such circumstances," Rosecrans scolded his commander, "the [tone] is to be regretted, because our troops knowing there was no foundation for it in them will be led to imagine there is some elsewhere."[50] Unfortunately for all parties involved, there was trouble brewing elsewhere. As September turned to October, it became clear that a poisonous aftereffect from Iuka began to settle throughout the army and beyond.

For the first time since Shiloh, anti-Grant sentiments became renewed both along the front lines and on the home front. Unsubstantiated speculation argued that the general sat out Iuka at the bottom of a whiskey bottle. One Missouri captain snarled: "General Grant was dead drunk and couldn't bring up his army. I was so mad when I first learned the facts that I could have shot Grant if I would have hung for it the next minute."[51] Within days of Iuka, a hearsay account of a Grant drunk in public reached the desks of the U.S. attorney general as well as the secretary of war and the general in chief. A well-reputed St. Louis attorney, Franklin Dick, brother-in-law to former Republican congressman and now brigadier general Francis Blair, wrote an impassioned note to Attorney General Edward Bates. "Seeing it stated that the late attack by Rosecrans upon Price at Iuka failed, for want of cooperation by Genl Grant, I consider it my duty," Dick wrote, "to state, that General Grant was drunk in St. Louis" seven days after the battle. "I did not see him myself," he admitted, but an associate "met and talked with [Grant] and stated to me, that the Genl was [so drunk that he was] 'as tight as a brick.' Believing, as I do, that much of our ill success results from drunken officers, I intend to do my duty in reporting such crime[s] upon their part,

so that the facts may reach those who have power to apply the remedy.
. . . I make this fact as to Grant known, because I have heard it denied
that he now drinks—If drunk in St. Louis on the 26th, he may be drunk
in command of his army a few days later."[52] The general had indeed been
in St. Louis that week visiting his wife, Julia. He also had with him his
roguish staff officers, Lagow (a known drunkard) and Dickey, but no
solid evidence of Grant being drunk on this occasion has emerged.[53] Even
so, when the news of this report was shared with Grant by General in
Chief Halleck, it could only have further incensed his already defensive
attitude both toward the public uproar against him and against possible
gossips within his own department. The criticism seems to have taken
its toll on Grant, who shortly thereafter was described as having become
"a bitter, ill-natured, ill-mannered" fellow.[54]

Army rumor bled into the ink of the *Cincinnati Commercial,* which
printed scathing accusations of Grant's drunkenness at Iuka. The column's author was William D. Bickham, a former clerk in the Ohio State
Senate and closely associated with Lieutenant Governor Ben Stanton,
a man once described as "Grant's bitterest enemy."[55] Criticism too flew
from the desk of Whitelaw Reid, editor of the *Cincinnati Gazette,* who
had been attacking the general's reputation since Shiloh.[56] Rosecrans, for
better or worse, enjoyed friendships with both newspapermen, harken-
ing back to his years living in Cincinnati. As such, many within the army
suspected him of secretly orchestrating a deliberate smear campaign. As
a result, the officer corps further polarized.

In this melee of rumor and innuendo, some among the army appealed
directly to Grant's staff regarding their suspicions about Rosecrans's ties
to the *Cincinnati Commercial.* To John Rawlins, now Grant's chief of
staff, an impassioned Colonel Mortimer Leggett wrote:

> I have been exceedingly vexed and pained of late, to witness the ap-
> parently determined effort . . . to revive and strengthen an unjust popular
> prejudice, against Major General U. S. Grant. The infamous falsehoods and
> hellish malignity originated against the General just after the battle of
> Shiloh . . . partly to excuse the disgraceful cowardice of poltroon officers,
> and partly to satisfy the popular demand for a victim, have left the public
> mind, both in the army, and among our friends at home, in fit condition to
> be readily excited against Major General Grant. General Grant's army were
> winning laurels, even before the late battles. . . . [A]nd when our arms . . .
> [throughout the north Mississippi campaign] . . . had uniformly proved so

successful, it was a gross outrage for the minions of [the] newly fledged Major General [Rosecrans], not only to attempt an exclusive appropriation (or rather absorption) of all the honors, but, by irresponsible assertions, and mysterious insinuations, to attempt to awaken and deepen, former prejudices against the General to whom naturally and rightfully the first honors belonged. Major General Rosecrans, is undoubtedly an excellent officer—and I hope, for his honor, and the honor of his state, that he is not a party in this hellish attempt to ruin General Grant, but the evidence is such, that I cannot rid my mind of the conviction that he must be, at least, *privy* to the whole devilish scheme. It *may* be, that the sin is *only* at the door of the *Cincinnati Commercial* Correspondent . . . William D. Bickham. . . . [I]f so, Major General Rosecrans will yet do partial justice by dismissing said Bickham from his confidence and army. But I fear that the inordinate ambition of Rosecrans, leads him to seek the downfall of Grant, hoping that thereby he may succeed to the command of the department—a position for which he is not, and never can be, fitted:—for while he is a brave, dashing officer, a good fighter, and well calculated to inspire his men with enthusiasm, yet he lacks the business talent, and comprehensiveness of judgment, needed in command of a department. Major [Rawlins] cannot that thing be crushed?

In closing, Leggett sought to resolve the matter and possibly usher in a lasting peace between the two. "It would seem that a friendly note to General Rosecrans from you would bring the subject sufficiently before him, to induce his sense of justice to repair a *wrong* which at least he has *permitted*."[57]

Instead, Rawlins brought the matter to, of all people, Mrs. Grant. Speaking with the general's wife, the chief of staff plead that he wanted to "reach the General's ear through you. In justice to General Grant—in fact, in justice to ourselves—General Rosecrans ought to be relieved."[58] And while Grant then gently and confidentially defended Rosecrans to his wife, he had become increasingly hostile with his rival directly. Two days after Leggett wrote out his note to Rawlins, Grant personally lashed out against Rosecrans. To which the stunned subordinate directly rebutted the mounting accusations: "I am amazed at the tenor of your dispatch. You have had no truer friend no more loyal subordinate under your command than myself. Your dispatch does me the grossest injustice. I now say to you if you have any suspicions at variance with this declaration, or if my position towards you is to receive a shade of coloring different from this, either from the influences, the suspicions or jealousies of mischief-makers, wine sellers or mousing politicians, or from any other cause, I ask you to tell me so frankly and [at] once, as a favor to myself and the service."[59]

The dispute could not have come at a worse time. Two weeks earlier, in a ferocious series of battles on October 3–5, Rosecrans drove Confederate armies under Major General Earl Van Dorn and Price from the gates of Corinth into a crippling retreat to Holly Springs, sixty miles to the southwest. With only a routed and demoralized enemy force between the Federals and the Mississippi River, Rosecrans wanted to mount an early winter offensive against Vicksburg and assail the city from the northeast before the rebels had time to regroup. The Confederate's chief engineer there, Brigadier General Martin Luther Smith, had hardly begun the soon-to-be-redoubtable fortifications around the city. Within the year, though, Vicksburg would become the second-most heavily fortified city in the Confederacy, a prize that eventually cost Grant another nine months and thousands of lives to capture. After Corinth, conversely, Rosecrans thought his army could perhaps take hold of the city within a few weeks.

Grant was not happy with Rosecrans's initially slow pursuit of Price immediately after Corinth. Once he started, however, it seemed Rosecrans would not stop. While pursuing the retreating Confederates southward, Rosecrans received orders from Grant to halt his unwarranted and seemingly reckless advance and to return his troops to Corinth. Yet Rosecrans remained vocal about his desire to strike Vicksburg by contesting these instructions. The signs of their eroding friendship played out openly. Grant accused him of "ignoring higher authority" in the way Rosecrans had begun to parole Confederate prisoners, while adding one further accusation. "The leaky lecture of some in your staff or in confidential relation to you as evidenced by newspaper correspondents and their attempt to keep up an invidious distinction between" the two wings of the department "are detrimental to the good feeling that should exist between officers and men as well as improper and should not be allowed."[60] The dispute finally came to a head. Frustrated by the weeks of accusations rumored against him, Rosecrans sought to quash the debate once and for all:

> That part of your dispatch which refers to newspaper reporters and leaky members of my staff showing the existence of any desire or even any sentiment at these headquarters of keeping up a distinction in feeling and spirit between the troops of my command or the rest of your troops as if they were not an integral part thereof, I answer: That no such feeling

has ever existed at these headquarters—no countenance either directly or indirectly has been given to such an idea nor was I aware that such an idea was abound until I saw indications of it from members of *your* staff and in *your* own orders. I regarded it as the offspring of other sentiments than those of a desire for justice or the good of the service and subsequently hope that you do not participate therein. There are no headquarters in these United States less responsible for what newspaper correspondents and paragraphists say of operations than mine. This I wish to be understood to be distinctly applicable to the affairs of Iuka and Corinth.

After this declaration I am forced to say that if you do not meet me frankly with a declaration that you are satisfied I shall consider my power to be useful in this department ended.[61]

To each man's relief, Rosecrans's time in Mississippi was nearly at its end. For his performance at Iuka, Rosecrans was promoted to major general of volunteers. For his victory at Corinth two weeks later, he was summoned east, where he would finally be out from under Grant's shadow, as commander of the XIV Corps, soon to be rechristened the Army of the Cumberland.

On receiving word of this, Grant recalled being "delighted." By then the collaborative rapport between the two was clearly ruined. "As a subordinate," Grant later lamented in his *Personal Memoirs,* "I found that I could not make him do as I wished." As a result he could not be rid of Rosey fast enough and stood "determined to relieve him from duty that very day."[62] On sharing the development with Sherman, Colonel William S. Hillyer of Grant's staff noted simply, "this is greatly to the relief of [Grant], who was very much disappointed in him. This matter the General will explain to you when he sees you."[63] As would become evident in time, this or other explanations irrevocably soured Sherman's own feelings toward Rosecrans. To Rawlins, Sherman wrote, "I note the General[']s allusion to Rosecrans and was somewhat surprised, though convinced."[64] Though far from concrete implications, such "allusions" could only serve to poison future interactions.

En route to his new command, Rosecrans stopped at Grant's headquarters at Jackson, Tennessee, to say goodbye. Years later he revisited this final exit interview in a letter to Grant. Then, just as he had done in person, Rosecrans defended himself against the accusations proliferated by Mortimer Leggett and others. "When parting with you at Jackson . . . on learning that men for selfish ends, had been leading you to believe that which I knew to be wholly false," he charged, "I asked and gave explanations which you declared, as I considered them, 'perfectly satisfactory.'"[65] At the time, Rosecrans may have thought the matter closed and behind the two forever. Yet as he departed Grant's company that day, he left behind a rift that had failed to close.

Somewhere along the road to Iuka, peculiar events mutated the Grant-Rosecrans friendship. The operation forever altered the culture of the Federal high command in the western theater, creating a dangerous rivalry and disloyalty between the two generals as well as those loyal to either man.

For a brief moment that winter, it seemed as if Rosecrans had emerged as the preeminent Union general in the West. Iowa governor Samuel Kirkwood praised him thus:

> The eyes of the people of Iowa, General, are on you and their hearts are with you. They believe and they rejoice in the belief that in you they have an active, earnest, "fighting" soldier, they know that the salvation of the country depends upon having such at the head of our armies, they confidently trust your glorious and gallant deeds at Iuka and Corinth will be equaled (they cannot be surpassed) in your new command and that your example will stimulate others to like action.
>
> Never in the history of our people have they prayed for the "coming man" as they have for many months past and now [I] believe they have found him.[66]

Even Grant received fan mail praising Rosecrans, as in the case of Illinois senator Lyman Trumbull, who wrote: "I have had a conversation with the President from which I gather that he expects great successes from the armies commanded by you and Gen Rosecrans—to a remark of mine that if let alone from Washington, you two commanders would soon clean out the South West and open the Mississippi river, he replied that you would be let alone except to be urged forward. . . . [T]he Government and the country look especially to you and Gen. Rosecrans and the armies under your commands to crush the rebellion and save the Union."[67] Perhaps also to Grant's chagrin, his close friend and political patron Elihu Washburne warmed up to Rosecrans, praising him for his service in Mississippi, telling Rosey, "If I can at anytime serve you here at the Capitol, in any way, please call on me."[68] Adding great din to the already loud praise, some even bantered Rosecrans's name about as a possible War Democrat presidential candidate for 1864.

Soon after arriving in Tennessee, Rosecrans increased his ever-widening circle of renown. Launching an aggressive winter offensive, he defeated the Army of Tennessee along the banks of Stones River on January 2, 1863. Through the battle, Rosecrans rode along the front lines, personally exhorting his soldiers to hold their ground. Placing himself in almost constant danger, his chief of staff, Julius Garesché, was beheaded by solid shot while riding at the general's side. Despite being bloodied, the Army of the Cumberland held the field, offering the North its only victory in a winter that elsewhere saw Union offensives sink at Chickasaw Bayou, Mississippi, and fail against the heights of Fredericksburg, Virginia. Stones River was of salient value to the Lincoln administration, coming just one day after the Emancipation Proclamation went into effect. The president offered "the Nation's gratitude" for the "skill, endurance, and da[u]ntless courage" exhibited by the army, a message Lincoln reiterated months later. "I can never forget, whilst I remember anything . . . , [that] you gave us a hard earned victory which, had there been a defeat instead, the nation could scarcely have lived over."[69]

After this it seemed as if even Rosecrans's detractors might offer applause. "Your star is decidedly in the ascendant now," wrote an officer from the War Department. "I have repeatedly told the Secretary of War that you would belie his opinion [of you] if he would give you half a chance. He [has] a senseless but strong prejudice against you."[70] In the wake of Stones River, one voice did not join in the chorus of praise. A journalist with the *Cincinnati Gazette* alerted Treasury Secretary Salmon Chase that Grant had grown "shamefully jealous of Rosecrans," adding that his staff "would chuckle to see Rosecrans cut to pieces."[71]

Then in March, on the eve of the 1863 spring campaign season, Secretary of War Stanton dangerously pitted Grant and Rosecrans in direct competition against one another. "There is a vacant Major Generalcy in the Regular Army," wired General in Chief Halleck, "and I am authorized to say that it will be given to the General in the field who first wins an important and decisive victory."[72] There was no ambiguity about the rank being offered as a trophy. "The Secretary decided that he would not fill the vacancy," Halleck admitted, "till some general could claim it as a reward for a complete and decisive victory."[73] Rosecrans, angered at the bribe, brazenly dismissed such a promotion as an "auctioneering of honors." Whichever of the two western-theater candidates was awarded the promotion would then outrank the other, a possibility that must have lingered with menacing dread between Grant and Rosecrans.

In a fit, Rosecrans demanded that his major general of volunteers rank, granted him after Iuka, be backdated to his 1861 successes under McClellan in western Virginia. Such a move would then rank him above Grant for the time being. The demand did but little more than irritate the War Department. President Lincoln personally intervened to both assuage Rosecrans's rage over the promotion offer and quell his rival bearing against Grant. "Truth to speak, I do not appreciate this matter of rank on paper, as you officers do," the president affirmed. "The world will not forget that you fought the battle of 'Stone[s] River' and it will never care a fig whether you rank General Grant on paper or he so ranks you."[74]

As spring turned to summer, Rosecrans further disaffected himself from both Grant and Stanton. By May, the Tennessee roads were temporarily dried out after the spring rains, and the War Department insisted that Rosecrans begin his march on Chattanooga, a circuitous route of some 200 miles to the south. For weeks he contended that further armaments and fresh mounts were needed to ensure a successful campaign. To some historians today, Rosecrans may smell of George McClellan, an officer characterized by irresolution and inaction, but such is not an accurate portrayal. Rosecrans's new chief of staff for the campaign, Brigadier General James Garfield, noted: "General Rosecrans thinks rapidly and strikes forward into action with the utmost confidence in his own judgment. In this he is perfectly unlike McClellan, who rarely has a clear-cut, decisive opinion, and dare[s] not trust it when he has." What the War Department considered loitering, Rosecrans defended as basic necessity, and the Army of the Cumberland supported him, as Garfield went on to note: "The officers who I have met since I came here seem to have the most unbounded confidence in Rosey and are enthusiastic in his praise."[75] Yet a livid Grant feared that Confederate strength in Tennessee could be siphoned away to attack his rear in Mississippi. Despite immense pressure from both Grant and Stanton, Rosecrans did not allow himself to be, as he saw it, blundered into the campaign ill equipped and waited until June 23 to begin his move south.

By July 1, Rosecrans had captured Tullahoma and forced the Army of Tennessee into a general retreat back to Chattanooga, relinquishing all of Middle Tennessee to Federal control. He had done so, however, without being able to bring the rebels to battle. Then on July 4, Grant captured Vicksburg, the Confederate Gibraltar on the Mississippi River, following a six-month campaign and forty-seven-day siege. The promotion to major general within the Regular Army went to Grant. As such, he would indisputably outrank Rosecrans if their commands ever merged. If Rosecrans felt leery at this prospect, his anxiety was well founded. In June Grant had removed from command one subordinate, Major General John McClernand. Though arguably his most successful corps commander during the overland march and initial attacks against Vicksburg, McClernand had long held an uneasy and at times vitriolic relationship with Grant. For McClernand publishing his General Orders No. 72, a self-congratulatory message of himself as well as the rank and file of his corps for their victorious conduct through the opening phases of the Vicksburg Campaign, Grant ordered his removal, replacing him with Major General Ord; such communiqués had to be read and authorized by the War Department prior to publication. To some historians, it seems that Grant seized upon a petty technicality to purge an officer with whom he did not match well, justifying the measure by calling McClernand's conduct an act of insubordination. At its face, this misstep hardly seemed worthy of eliminating a successful corps commander. McClernand, a War Democrat and congressman with presidential ambitions, however, presented a clear threat to the Republican administration, and Secretary Stanton did nothing to stop his removal.[76]

Sitting in Tullahoma, Rosecrans received news of the Union triumphs at Gettysburg and Vicksburg. "You and your noble army now have the chance to give the finishing blow to the rebellion," Stanton asserted. "Will you neglect the chance?" To this Rosecrans rebuked: "You do not appear to observe the fact that this noble army has driven the rebels from Middle Tennessee. . . . I beg in behalf of this army that the War Department may not overlook so great an event because it is not written in showers of blood."[77] Without the recognition to which he felt his army entitled, the general received little more than an order to "push on" to Chattanooga. Others were not impressed with any part of his Tullahoma achievement. On July 5, the day after capturing Vicksburg, Sherman, noting the threat from Robert E. Lee's movements into Maryland and Pennsylvania, wrote, "I read of Washington, Baltimore and Philadelphia being threatened and Rosecrans sitting idly by, and writing for personal fame in the newspapers."[78]

In mid-July Rosecrans halted his army at Winchester, Tennessee. There, he regrouped and refitted before the final great push over the Cumberland Mountains. Again, Washington saw only idleness. "The patience of the authorities here has been completely exhausted," Halleck wired Rosecrans, "and the pressure for your removal has been . . . strong." Rosecrans immediately made his case for the campaign's progress to President Lincoln, who gently wrote back, offering "kind feeling and confidence" in the general. On August 1 Lincoln did not mask his discontent for the slow march but added: "Do not misunderstand . . . I do not cast blame on you. . . . I am not watching you with an evil eye."[79] On August 16 the advance renewed, and Rosecrans shepherded his army safely across the Cumberland Plateau.

Meanwhile, the War Department did keep a close eye on Rosecrans, one that some may have come to regard as an evil eye. On September 11 an unsolicited visitor joined Rosecrans's headquarters, then in Chattanooga, nearing the banks of West Chickamauga Creek. Secretary Stanton, feeling that he could not control the general, dispatched his assistant secretary of war, Charles Anderson Dana, to serve as a mole inside the Army of the Cumberland and report candidly on the progress of the campaign. Lincoln held Dana in high esteem and regarded him as "the eyes of the Government at the front."[80] Though kicked out of Harvard and fired from the *New York Tribune,* Dana, a published poet, had a way with words and could, when required, be charismatic.[81] He won over Rosecrans's trust, a confidence the general would live to regret.

Contrary to what scholars have argued, it is clear that Rosecrans did not manage to see Dana for the operative he was. Notions of him as a "loathsome pimp" or an "interloper, a marplot, [and] a spy upon rival generals" emerge only in letters written after the campaign and recollections published long after the war.[82] After all, Dana had just spent three months in Mississippi, riding with Grant on the Vicksburg Campaign and had done that general no harm. It may be that Rosecrans viewed Dana's presence in the West as an emissary in search of the War Department's next general in chief or perhaps a new commander to take the helm of eastern-theater forces for the next "On to Richmond" expedition. In retrospect, Dana's presence certainly was far more Machiavellian than Rosecrans knew.[83]

From his headquarters at the Gordon-Lee mansion on the eve of the Battle of Chickamauga, Rosecrans revealed his affection for Dana in a letter to his wife: "Mr. Dana . . . is with me. I am very glad of it he is doing well for us."[84] Dana remained at the commander's side to personally witness the Confederate breakthrough that routed the Army of the

Cumberland's right wing, forcing it from the battlefield on September 20. Swept up in the retreat, Rosecrans's headquarters staff, with Dana in company, retreated toward Chattanooga without intimate knowledge of Major General George Thomas's successful stand at Snodgrass Hill with the army's left wing. Arriving at Rossville, Garfield convinced Rosecrans to ride into the safety of Chattanooga while he would return to Thomas. At 3:40 P.M. the general and Dana arrived at Brigadier General George Wagner's Chattanooga headquarters, where an exhausted Rosecrans had to be helped down from his horse. Some said he began to cry, others that he prayed, but within minutes Rosecrans dashed messages out over the telegraph, securing his pontoon crossing at Bridgeport, dispatching troops to hold Missionary Ridge, and sending ammunition to Thomas in preparation for a defense of Rossville Gap the following morning. In secret dispatches to Stanton, however, Dana portrayed the army commander as a cowardly incompetent who abandoned Thomas's command to the enemy. "I know the reasons [for the defeat] well enough," scoffed the secretary of war. "Rosecrans ran away from his fighting men and did not stop for thirteen miles."[85] Stanton set himself "on the war path," an alarmed White House secretary confided, "his hands are red and smoking with the scalping of Rosey."[86]

Unlike the War Department, the army never lost faith in their commander. Even when reeling from retreat on the day after Chickamauga, one Illinois lieutenant scrawled in his diary, "The Army has the greatest confidence in 'Old Rosey' and are confident that there are not men enough in the Rebel army to whip them."[87] Two days later the same officer further illustrated this spirit from within the Chattanooga trench lines, noting:

> About dusk our boys set up cheering in rear of the Forts and going to a little hill I could see troops standing massed in column and a general and his staff riding among them. It soon occurred to me that the general must be Rosecrans, reviewing the troops about the main work. Gen. Rosecrans and staff rode along our line and stopped to chat with our men. "Boys I want you to reserve your fire till you can all tell a black eye from a blue one then fire and your front will be like the Irishman's pocket which was full and there was nothing in it. Do you understand how that was? Why the pocket was full of holes." The men roared and cheered him and he rode on down the line with his staff. There is no question as to the hold Rosecrans has on the affections and confidence of his men. They thoroughly believe in him.[88]

Dana knew the effect Rosecrans maintained over his army's officers and enlisted men. What he did not know was whether a policy shift loomed at the War Department, so on September 27 he tested the waters by audaciously suggesting, "If it be decided to change the chief commander [Rosecrans] . . . , I would take the liberty of suggesting that some Western general of high rank and great prestige, like Grant, for instance, would be preferable as his successor."[89] This mendaciousness went unrecognized by Rosecrans, who the following day, September 28, wrote his wife: "Mr. Dana . . . has been with us during and since the battle. . . . He has been of great service to us. I am very glad he came."[90]

Then on September 30, Dana received a telegram that further altered the character of his own dispatches and behavior.[91] Secretary Stanton stated that once reinforcements were sent to Chattanooga's relief, "all that the Army of the Cumberland can need will be a competent commander. The merit of General Thomas and the debt of gratitude the nation owes to his valor and skill are fully appreciated here, and I wish you to tell him so." He then closed with a very telling statement: "It was not my fault that he was not in chief command months ago." With this prejudicial nod from his boss, Dana continued to secretly ramp up the criticism against Rosecrans while enjoying the general's "personal hospitality, sitting at the same table, and sleeping in the same building" as his target. In retrospect, one eyewitness later lamented how Dana "deliberately drew the general in confidential communications [discussions], the substance of which he used against him," in addition to wielding gossip collected from disgruntled officers.[92]

In his own telegram exchanges with Washington, Rosecrans did little to further the War Department's confidence in him. On October 3 he sent Lincoln a bizarre suggestion to offer legal amnesty to all Confederate officers who surrendered to Federal troops. It seems the general thought that Confederate military authority might collapse overnight if key rebel leaders gave themselves up, turning officers and enlisted men against one another. The president replied that he might one day pursue such a strategy, but with an army under siege, it might seem like "a confession of weakness and fear."[93] Rosecrans's further communiqués sounded more and more distressed. He also confessed fear that the Confederates might construct a pontoon bridge and cut the army's supply route into Chattanooga.

For Lincoln, it was unthinkable to remove Rosecrans during that first week of October. The Ohio gubernatorial election would not be decided until October 9. In that race Republican John Brough faced off against Democrat Clement L. Vallandigham, a true antiwar Copperhead. Given Rosecrans's uneroded popularity within his home state at large, Lincoln felt that the general's pledged support for Brough promised to deliver both massive Democratic support to the Republican as well as the votes of his Ohio soldiers. This proved the case as Brough decisively defeated Vallandigham with 97 percent of the Army of the Cumberland's votes.[94]

With the arrival of October, the supply situation in Chattanooga did indeed become dire and was made worse by the autumn rains. In the coming weeks Dana watched as Rosecrans implemented meticulous plans for the now-besieged and nearly stranded Army of the Cumberland to supply and defend Chattanooga. He sat through councils with the army's quartermasters and engineers that prepared the way for a new, shorter Tennessee River supply route, soon to be christened the "Cracker Line," which in the coming weeks would feed the hungry army.[95] After Dana saw to it that the War Department removed Major Generals Thomas Crittenden and Alexander McCook from their corps commands, he watched as Rosecrans personally restructured the army, consolidating these two corps under Major General Gordon Granger. Being privy to all of these improvements as well as Rosecrans's fighting resolve to hold Chattanooga at any cost, the assistant secretary still sketched a very different picture for Lincoln and Stanton.

On October 15 he telegraphed Washington that "it will soon become necessary for all persons except soldiers to leave here," meaning sutlers, laundresses, civilians, and the like, to make for fewer mouths to feed. Dana then accused Rosecrans of being "obstinate and inaccessible to reason" as well as "irresolute, vacillating, and inconclusive." He alleged that the general squandered his days "employed in pleasant gossip" and laboring over "a long report to prove the fact that the Government is to blame for his failure." Then on October 16, Dana hurled one final barb at the army's commander. "In the midst of all these difficulties General Rosecrans seems to be insensible to the impending danger, and dawdles with trifles in a manner which can scarcely be imagined," he lambasted. Even though the army still possessed "plenty of zealous and energetic officers ready to do whatever can be done, all this precious time is lost because our dazed and mazy commander cannot perceive the catastrophe that is close upon us, nor fix his mind upon the means of preventing it. I never saw anything which seemed so lamentable and hopeless. . . . Nothing can prevent the retreat of the army from this place within a fortnight." As a point of fact, however, there is no evidence that at any time did Rosecrans actually consider abandoning Chattanooga or forsake a personal assurance he made to the president on October 27, promising "that he could hold Chattanooga against double his number" and declaring that the city "could not be taken [unless] after a great battle."[96]

Aside from Dana, another, more unlikely informant rode at Rosecrans's side: his chief of staff and Republican congressman-elect, James Garfield. The previous July, while venting over the campaign's slow progress and halt at Winchester, Tennessee, this future U.S. president surreptitiously mailed a damning letter to his political ally, Treasury Secretary Salmon P. Chase. For Garfield, the note seems a kind of effort to martyr himself as the only general officer within the army who wanted a continual, rapid advance on Chattanooga and certainly the only one who initially thought the campaign had a late start. Therein he "confidentially" spoke of his "regret" regarding "delay" and "inaction."[97] Why had Garfield done this? The widely accepted explanation is that he recognized that Rosecrans was in poor graces with much of the Lincoln administration, and with this secret letter, "Garfield placed himself in a position to jump in either direction," according to scholar Frederick D. Williams.[98] If Rosecrans failed, Garfield stood distanced, with his political fortunes secured. If Rosecrans succeeded, he would likely never learn of his chief of staff's backbiting.

The letter, now two months old, was far from an authentic assessment of how Garfield felt regarding the present defense of Chattanooga. At Rosecrans's side on September 25, Garfield wrote his wife that the Army of the Cumberland had no thought of retreat. "The campaign is successful and *Chattanooga will be held*," he contended, "thus the great end of our movement has been accomplished, even if the battle [of Chickamauga] be considered lost."[99] The administration had no means of attaining an authentic appraisal of the Chattanooga siege, either through their mole Dana or through Garfield's July letter. But both were all Lincoln had when he convened a cabinet meeting on October 16 to discuss solutions. After a review of Dana's frantic telegrams, Secretary Chase supposedly read Garfield's letter. The impression made by the document cannot be understated. It was said to have had "the effect of a casting vote."[100] Stanton insisted that Rosecrans be replaced with Thomas. But the president resisted, if for no other reason than perhaps he felt that he and his cabinet had viewed the history of the past several weeks through dark glass. Lincoln stated that he regarded Rosecrans as "a true, and very able man," and the general's fate would have to wait. Instead, he sought to fix several problems at once. The president consolidated the western theater, merging the Army of the Cumberland; the Army of the Tennessee; and Major General Ambrose Burnside's rogue command, the Army of the Ohio, into one massive army group, the Military Division of the Mississippi, all united under one commander, Ulysses S. Grant. In addition to these troops, Major General Joseph Hooker and two corps of the Army of the Potomac would ride rails westward from Virginia as reinforcements. In short, the full force of Federal military prowess would be brought to bear in a relief effort at Chattanooga. The meeting broke up, and the word went out over the telegraph at 9:00 P.M. that Grant was to meet with "an officer of the War Department" at the Galt House Hotel in Louisville to receive new orders. Receiving the directive in Cairo, Illinois, the following day, Grant boarded a steamboat and set out almost immediately. He knew something great was at hand in part because he was directed to bring his entire staff with him "for immediate operations in the field." What the general could not have anticipated was the identity of the courier en route to meet him.[101]

As if to leave nothing to chance, Secretary Stanton personally en-trained for Louisville. Arriving in Indianapolis on October 18, he learned that Grant's train was also in the station. Stanton walked over to the general's car, and the two met for the first time. As the train rolled toward Louisville, they got down to business. Stanton handed Grant two orders, from which he was asked to choose one. They were nearly identical. Both outlined the new Military Division of the Mississippi and named Grant its commander. But one retained William S. Rosecrans in command of the Army of the Cumberland, while the other replaced him with George Thomas. The decision literally lay in Grant's hands.

What exactly was said between Grant and Stanton is not known, though the secretary of war certainly delivered the message face to face for a reason. Any personal bias he could have added to the conversation would not have aided Rosecrans. For Grant, the decision was clear— Rosecrans would have to go. John Rawlins soon after described that Grant "could not in justice to himself or the cause of his country think of again commanding" Rosecrans, in part because of "his general spirit of insubordination toward Grant, although to his face he professed for him the highest regards both as a man and an officer."[102] Grant never directly addressed his reasons for removing Rosecrans, though his per-sonal feelings were certainly omnipresent at this time. Less than three weeks earlier, he betrayed a lingering bias in a letter to his confidant, William T. Sherman. "I may be wrong and judge Rosecrans from rather a prejudicial view instead of impartially as I would like, and try to do," he admitted.[103]

Before the war, Sherman had cultivated a mutual admiration with Rosecrans. In April 1860 he floated Rosecrans's name to serve as chair of engineering at the illustrious Louisiana State Seminary of Learning and Military Academy, where Sherman presided as superintendent.[104] That same spring Rosecrans offered Sherman employment with his kerosene-refinery firm in Cincinnati.[105] Though neither accepted the other's offer, they continued to hold each other in high regard. By 1863, however, Sherman had clearly come to loath the idea of serving alongside Rosecrans.

From of all places, Sherman awaited news of the Louisville trip at headquarters in Iuka. Perhaps more than any other figure, and writing without knowledge of the removal, he defined the gravity of feeling toward Old Rosey. "Grant don't like Rosecrans—He found great fault with him here at Iuka a year ago," Sherman wrote his brother-in-law. "Rosecrans may be Grant's superior in intellect, but not in sagacity, purity of character and singleness of purpose. Rosecrans is selfish and vainglorious. Grant not a bit so," he continued. "[Grant] would never appropriate the just fame of another. . . . I would rather serve under Grant than Rosecrans, for in an extended country like this any one of us may be worsted, Grant would stand by his friend, but Rosecrans would sacrifice his brother if he stood in the way of his popular renown."[106] In a second letter that day, Sherman further explained that "Rosey is ambitious and notoriety seeking, and Grant is the very reverse." Betraying an air of uncertainty if not rumor, Sherman confessed, "*I am told* that Rosecrans is jealous of the reputation of all his subordinates." He then concluded his thoughts, stating: "Of course I will have nothing to do with such personalities—Grant is an honest plain sensible well meaning officer and I like that style of man better than Rosecrans—the former tries to have genteel folks near him, whereas Rosecrans is surrounded by detectives and newspaper sneaks."[107]

As Stanton and Grant arrived in Louisville, the situation in Chattanooga appeared to grow worse by the hour. Late on the evening of October 18 at the Galt House Hotel, Stanton received yet another frenzied telegraph from Dana. This one spoke of impending starvation and "immediate retreat of this army" that, according to Dana, was about to abandon Chattanooga "like a rabble."[108] Grant replied with equal fervor, instructing Thomas to hold Chattanooga "at all hazards," adding that he "would be at the front as soon as possible."[109]

"I well remember the receipt of that telegram, and the surprise and indignation with which Thomas and I viewed it," Rosecrans contended years later. "We regarded it as an aspersion on the Army of the Cumberland and its commander, founded either in ignorance or malice. We had as little idea of abandoning Chattanooga as anybody in the world." Thomas's reply would become one of the noted telegrams of the entire war, stating simply, "we will hold the town until we starve," though also calling Grant's attention to the fact that the army's wagon trains were already "hauling rations from Bridgeport."[110]

If the tone of Grant's cable was truly surprising, then the word received the following day must have been a striking jolt. That day, October 19, Rosecrans continued to micromanage the reopening of the Tennessee River supply route and even found time to visit his wounded at a hospital. Then, returning to headquarters that evening, he found General Orders No. 337 from the War Department: Thomas was to replace him at the head of the army. A witness at headquarters said that Rosecrans "took it coolly and composedly, exhibiting neither surprise nor chagrin." Well into the evening, he "laughed and talked with those who came in and had faces as if they were mourning the death of a near kin." Thomas then stayed up past midnight with his predecessor, going over supply and defense plans. In his final act Rosecrans wrote out a parting address to his beloved troops. There would be neither a farewell review nor a speech. There was not time for either, and Rosecrans did not want the Confederates to know that he would be traveling overland, leaving the city. At first light on October 20, with only a small cavalcade of officers and his spiritual confidant, Father Patrick Treacy, Old Rosey slipped away, disappearing into the morning mist. Some officers openly wept as he rode off. Within hours a "deep and almost universal regret" settled over his former army.[111]

As fate would have it, Grant and Rosecrans crossed paths. On the night of October 21, at the Army of the Cumberland's remote forward-supply depot hollowed beneath the Alabama mountains at Stevenson, Grant's train rolled in to learn that "Rosecrans was there on his way north," having just ridden the treacherous sixty-mile roundabout supply route from Chattanooga.[112] The two generals, who had not seen each other in almost a year, met for what must have been an awkward conference. "The meeting," Colonel James H. Wilson remembered, "was brief and courteous but not effusive. They were far from sympathetic with each other."[113] According to Rosecrans biographer William M. Lamers, "Grant gave Rosecrans the impression that he had played no part in his removal."[114] Whatever actually was said, a postbellum war of words was fought between the two over the exchange. In 1885 Grant recounted the strategy discussed at the meeting in his widely read *Personal Memoirs,* stating that Rosecrans "came into my car and we held a brief interview, in which he described very clearly the situation at Chattanooga, and made some excellent suggestions as to what should be done. My only wonder was that he had not carried them out."[115] Rosecrans later refuted this recollection, arguing that "doubtless they were 'excellent suggestions,' for they were precisely the ones which General Grant followed." These being instructions already drawn up and left with Thomas for "establishing communication" between the Chattanooga garrison and Hooker's divisions (then to the west of Lookout Valley), an undertaking in which, according to Rosecrans, "every effort had been made to that end." Continuing his defense, Rosecrans further stated: "Yet he says, 'My only wonder was that he had not carried them out.' I think the intelligent reader will wonder whether it was stupidity or malice which dictated this foolish expression, and will himself feel no wonder that as yet they had not been carried out."[116]

The next morning, October 22, amid a driving rainstorm, Rosecrans boarded a train homeward to Cincinnati and an uncertain future, while Grant mounted up to begin the overland trek into Chattanooga. On his journey Grant witnessed the severity of the supply situation. "The roads were strewn with the debris of broken wagons and the carcasses of thousands of starved mules and horses," he later remembered. He arrived in Chattanooga just before dark on October 23 and found his way to Thomas's headquarters. There, it seems, Grant replaced one animosity for another. He already had no special love for Thomas and by one account was rudely greeted by that general upon his arrival. Grant was in a battered condition. He had suffered a fall from his horse in New Orleans weeks earlier, which had rendered him lame. The general had to rely on crutches and, during his punishing ride from Stevenson, "had to be carried over places where it was not safe to cross on horseback."[117] According to eyewitness Colonel Wilson (who with Charles Dana published one of the first biographies of Grant in 1868), the injured Grant hobbled into Thomas's headquarters "wet, hungry, and covered with mud." Soon after, Wilson and Dana entered and found him "sitting on one side of the [fireplace] over a puddle of water that had run out of his clothes," whereas "Thomas, glum and silent, was sitting on the other [side]" while staff officers "were scattered about in disorder."[118] Evidently, the general had offered Grant nothing in the way of dry clothes, hot food, or even a blanket. It is true that Thomas was not an especially warm person. One Illinois lieutenant later described his characteristic temperament, or rather lack thereof: "His face is passive and I don't believe any man can read it at all, or get any intimation of his thoughts."[119] But it is also true that others described Thomas as having been fuming over Rosecrans's removal for the past several days. Colonel Wilson noted that "the situation was embarrassing," and he ended the silence at the fireside, saying, "General Thomas, General Grant is wet, hungry, and in pain; his wagons and camp equipage are far behind; can you not find quarters and some dry clothes for him, and direct your officers to provide the party with supper?"[120] Thomas replied with acts of hospitality. The ice was thus broken, but subsequent historians have pointed to this moment as the reinstitution of a never-ending enmity that Grant felt for Thomas, with the removal of Rosecrans marking Thomas's reciprocation of similar sentiment.

As the evening progressed, however, "conversation began" between the two men, and "it was not long till a glow of warmth and cheerfulness prevailed," Wilson observed. With the arrival of more officers, the evening's exchange turned to the impending siege operations. This discussion also later became a point of contention between Grant and Rosecrans. In his *Personal Memoirs,* Grant claimed that Army of the Cumberland officers rolled out a map and "pointed out . . . [a] line, marked with a red or blue pencil, which Rosecrans had contemplated falling back upon. If any of them had approved the move they did not say so to me."[121] To this charge, Rosecrans heatedly contested: "Poor man! No officer of the Army of the Cumberland ever told him that I contemplated falling back. The line, if any, which was pointed out to him, was the line of communication by way of Brown's Ferry, to be established between the troops in Chattanooga" and Hooker's command then pushing "into Lookout Valley . . . and had no reference whatever to a line of retreat."[122]

Grant's recollections of the conference then turned to praise for the army's newly arrived chief engineer, Brigadier General William F. "Baldy"

Smith, for building a sawmill to aid in corduroying the roads and construction of much-needed pontoons to bridge the Tennessee River at the head of the new supply route. To this Rosecrans exhorted that it was he alone "who established the sawmill long before Smith's arrival." Similarly, Smith was commended by Grant for the construction of a steamboat at Bridgeport, Alabama, that would soon be able to navigate the Tennessee and greatly expedite feeding the hungry army. In truth, this vessel, the *Chattanooga,* was but the first of five steamers that Rosecrans ordered constructed back in September when his army was still at Bridgeport. All of these boats were prefabricated vessels, the components of which the army had carried on the march from Middle Tennessee that summer. Lastly, in his *Personal Memoirs,* Grant took one more strike at Rosecrans. He contended that on the following night, October 24, he "issued orders for opening the [supply] route to Bridgeport—*a cracker line,* as the soldiers appropriately termed it."[123] While Grant, Smith, and others indeed can be credited for clearing this new route of a modest Confederate presence, there could have been no cracker line without the pontoons made at the sawmill and without the steamboats floating out of Rosecrans's dry dock at Bridgeport. Indeed, with regard to the October 24 order, Rosecrans later contended that "all the preliminaries" for this directive "had been detailed to [Grant] by me at Stevenson," adding that Grant sought to give "the public the impression that it was his genius which conceived the plan."[124]

Moreover, the longer, initial Federal supply route over Walden Ridge was still open for business, and by the end of October, it had been cleared of Confederate interference. Brigadier General Charles Cruft's division, for example, had received orders that very day to march over this trail to Bridgeport to protect the supply stores there. Setting out the following morning, October 25, Cruft's soldiers dishearteningly passed dead and starving horses and mules along much of the route, but they were never contested by enemy forces and safely completed the muddy sixty-mile march, carrying their own rations as they went.[125] Some of Cruft's units even passed the steamboat *Paint Rock* on October 30, "showing that the river was free and open as a line over which to supply Chattanooga."[126]

Opening the Tennessee River supply route already had been in rapid progress before Rosecrans's removal. By mid-October, two pontoon bridges spanned the Tennessee and a supply depot and steamboat landing being developed at Williams Island. Rosecrans had also ordered the acquisition of enough rope and chain to ferry further supplies across

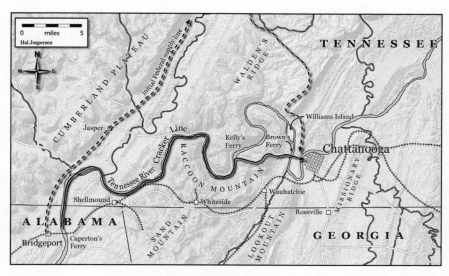

Federal Supply Lines, Siege of Chattanooga.

the river.[127] Shocked to see Grant take credit for the cracker line in 1885, Rosecrans stated vehemently that "no intelligent reader can fail to see that the intention of General Grant is to have it pass for history that his was the plan, and his the orders which opened the [supply] route from Chattanooga to Bridgeport. . . . This fraud, this lie, has been floating before the public for twenty-odd years." In the opening lines of his 1864 official report of the Chattanooga Campaign, General Thomas credited Rosecrans for being the architect of the cracker line supply route. "This statement," Rosecrans later wrote, only "won for [Thomas] the undying dislike of General Grant."[128] For the two rivals, the devil was certainly in the details.

During the last weeks of October 1863, the world beyond the Chatta-nooga siege lines gradually learned of the cashiering of Rosecrans. Still in Iuka, Mississippi, even Sherman seemed stunned at the news. "The Change in the Commands is radical," he conceded to his wife. "I don't pretend to understand all the secrets of Rosecrans position," but just as before, Sherman pointed to the history of the previous year. "I know that [Rosecrans] and Grant had sharp words and feelings over at Corinth and here [at Iuka] a year ago, and that Grant does not like him, besides Rosecrans has all along had a set of flunkeys about him, pouring out the oil of flattery that was sickening to all true men."[129] The news was met with astonishment by the Army of the Potomac. "I notice by the papers that General Rosecrans has been displaced and Grant put in his place," observed a Pennsylvania captain on October 22. "Well, the Western field of action is too far away for me to rightly and clearly understand the situation. . . . [But] Rosecrans has always done so well, until very recently, that I considered him an able man. I don't want to criticize, but really the Government takes great chances in its numerous changes of commanders."[130] Even President Lincoln's secretary, John Hay, was taken aback. One evening Hay noted in his diary, "Rosecrans is all right though somewhat bothered about his supplies," only to wake up the next morning to learn of the dismissal.[131] Secretary Chase absorbed criticism under his own roof when his daughter Kate "spoke a little spitefully about Rosecrans' removal."[132] Another Lincoln loyalist declared, "Though one of the firmest of firm Republicans I cannot justify the act."[133]

Defending the decision back at the White House on October 24, President Lincoln quipped his now-famous adage that Rosecrans had behaved "confused and stunned like a duck hit on the head." But he only said so in response to when "asked what *Dana* thought about Rosecrans," implicating that it was Dana who directly imparted unto the president the notion that "Rosecrans was for the present completely broken down."[134] Further distancing himself from the decision, Lincoln affirmed to White House staff that "it was because of *Grant's* opposition that Rosecrans is not in [command of] the Army of the Cumberland."[135] When later asked by a reporter about the removal, Lincoln allegedly admitted, "I think Stanton had got a pique against him, but Chickamauga showed Rosecrans was not equal to the occasion."[136]

Arriving at home in Cincinnati, "Old Rosey" was greeted by a cheering crowd. He magnanimously entreated them "to remember that whenever we hear the voice of government it is our duty to yield to it with prompt obedience [cheers], to recognize its right to issue orders, and to presume it has good reason for what it does until we know to the contrary."[137] Writing from Washington, D.C., Rosecrans's old West Point chum Abner Doubleday, himself reeling from removal of a temporary corps command at Gettysburg, reassured him that "no one who knows you believes for a moment the accusations which are floating about in a certain class of newspapers. I have no doubt you are perfectly able to vindicate yourself from all these charges."[138] His former chief of military police, William Truesdail, alluded to a wider disdain for Rosecrans as the cause of his capitulation. "O[h] General, the conspirators long at work [have] accomplished their end in your case and removal," he lamented. "True and just causes could not be found. Hence false wicked and imaginary causes must be trumped up. . . . I saw General, one hundred days ago, this conspiracy against you at work. Some men who stooped low with uncovered heads before your popular person and smiled in your face were engaged in this unholy work. I did not dare speak of my observations to you. . . . I feared their success much more than I feared any Confederate success against you and your command."[139]

James Garfield, on his way to Washington, D.C., had passed through Cincinnati just prior to Rosecrans's arrival. Calling on the general's wife, he left a consolatory note: "I need not assure you that the action of the War Department fill [*sic*] upon me like the sound of a fire bell. I am sure it will be the verdict of the people that the War Dept has made a great mistake and have done you a great wrong."[140] Garfield remained a rising star. For his service at Chickamauga, he received a brevet promotion to major general of volunteers just days before taking his seat in Congress. Rosecrans may have considered Representative Garfield a future force of vindication, yet it seems his former chief of staff wasted no time in publicly distancing himself from the general and the disasters of the campaign. Garfield scholar Frederick Williams argues that during these early days in Washington, Garfield "in interviews with a number of people, including Stanton and the president, made derogatory statements about Rosecrans' qualifications to lead an army."[141] Privately, however, he continued to console his former commander. "You are a power among the people—which no act of the War Department can destroy," he doted. Yet to cover the existence and influence that his correspondence with Secretary Chase had had over the general's removal, Garfield lied through his teeth, claiming, "The change in commanders of the Army of the Cumberland was made without consulting [Chase] and he did not know the reasons for it."[142] Further covering his tracks, and following an alleged meeting with President Lincoln, he advised Rosecrans that "it was the tone of your dispatches from Chattanooga several days after [Chickamauga] that led him to fear that you did not feel confident that you could hold the place; and hence the consolidation of the three armies [was ordered] to make Chattanooga" secure. What Garfield told him next could only have rekindled a perpetual sense of whatever animosity he felt toward Grant. "It was still at that time [Lincoln's] intention to keep you at the head of the Army of the Cumberland as before, with Grant, the ranking officer in command of the whole, but Grant made it a condition of accepting the command that you should be removed."[143] While this statement is not exactly true, the damage it must have wrought on Rosecrans's understanding of the matter is immeasurable.

             ✦

The Chattanooga siege dragged on through the end of November 1863. Throughout, Grant kept at his side his increasingly controversial staff officer Colonel Lagow. Even at this point in the war, Lagow offered some of the best proof that Grant's headquarters held Rosecrans in contempt. In mid-November the former commander received a telling letter from William Truesdail, who cut to the heart of the acrimony against Rosecrans. "I have with me here an esteemed friend," Truesdail wrote, "who spent two months in New York with Lago[w] of Grant's staff and up to but a few days since he offered me some strange things and sayings at Grant's Head Quarters touching you and your command and running back to the Battle [of] Iuka. O[h] dear. O[h] dear," he concluded, "I am fearful of the future of this country. May God be with us."[144]

  Ironically, at Chattanooga Lagow's career met with an end far more disgraceful than that of Rosecrans. Almost as soon as Charles Dana was back in the colonel's presence for the first time since Vicksburg, he recommended to Stanton that "Lagow . . . be mustered out," recognizing that Grant "wishes to get rid of him." Dana went on to rank him among "worthless fellows who earn no part of their pay."[145] Despite the dire realities of the surrounding siege, one eyewitness at Grant's headquarters, William Wrenshall Smith, noted in his diary that Lagow spent his nights visiting friends at other commands, where "poker and cold punch fills in the time." Then on the evening of November 14 at Grant's headquarters, Smith recorded: "Quite a disgraceful party—friends of Colonel Lagow, stay up nearly all night. . . . [Grant] breaks up the party himself about 4 o'clock this morning."[146] Rawlins hated Lagow and "wanted him off the staff, and after the unfortunate spree that [Grant] himself broke up," the colonel, according to Smith, felt "that he was treeted [sic] coldly by" the general.[147] With Union victory at the end of November and the siege broken, Lagow resigned his commission. He never again served in the army and died in 1867 at the age of thirty-nine.[148]

Following the Chattanooga Campaign, in January 1864 Grant and Rose-crans met for a final wartime reunion. As guests of honor at a public dinner at the Lindell Hotel in St. Louis, the two shared a stage and an evening together.[149] They were now on permanently separate paths, with Grant about to take the helm of the overall Union war effort, and Rosecrans conversely settling into a self-perceived exile as commander of the Department of the Missouri. The Army of the Cumberland con-tinued to miss its former commander, in whom the men had *never* lost faith. "My glorious general," wrote one soldier convalescing at home in Kentucky, "the soldiers are with you, we love you, you are our idol and I will never serve a country which has acted so meanly to her truest and noblest chief."[150] While marching on Atlanta in June, one Illinois lieuten-ant lamented, "Poor 'old Rosey' where are you now? . . . no officer ever more completely had the confidence and love of his army. We thought ourselves invincible and the intensity of our belief in him and ourselves is shown by the terrible list of Chickamauga dead. His conduct of that field [is] in no [way, however,] lessened [by] the slaughter."[151] The same officer also mourned, "Chickamauga killed Rosey . . . as dead as any of those [soldiers] killed there."[152]

Grant, as the newly minted victor of Chattanooga, was promoted to lieutenant general within the Regular Army, a rank last held by George Washington. Not surprisingly, the promotion was fiercely contested in Congress by Democrats who bitterly disagreed with Rosecrans's removal. The promotion bill survived passage, "notwithstanding the opposition of the Rosecrans interests."[153]

A few weeks after this political skirmish, Grant loyalists on Capitol Hill returned the minds of the Northern public back to Iuka. In the *New York Herald,* Grant published his version of events as "called for by Con-gress." A year and a half after the battle, his slanted account laid blame for the Union fiasco at Iuka solely on Rosecrans's shoulders. "The coun-try never before had an opportunity to know who was responsible for the escape of Price," alleged the *Herald.* "A careful perusal of this report shows conclusively that the failure to destroy or capture Price's army at Iuka resulted from two causes: First—The failure of Rosecrans to bring up his forces at the time appointed. Second—The failure of Rosecrans to occupy the Fulton road as he had been ordered by Grant to do, and in his last dispatch previous to the fight assured Grant he would do."[154] Neither of these belated points offered full justice to the true events of Iuka and served only to add public insult to injury for Rosecrans.

That spring, as Grant went on to lead a series of brilliant campaigns against Robert E. Lee and his Army of Northern Virginia, Rosecrans re- mained in St. Louis, where in his new department command, he managed to alienate the War Department and the Lincoln administration even fur- ther as well as neighboring commands in the Trans-Mississippi West. The general refused to spare troops to send to the relief of the Colorado's gov- ernor John Evans, who sought cavalry to contest hostile plains Indians and to protect the overland-mail route through the territory.[155] He even intercepted combat units passing through St. Louis en route to Sherman and the Georgia front, claiming them for his own. At this Grant blasted, "If Rosecrans does not send forward the regiments belonging to Sherman as ordered arrest him by my order unless the President will authorize him relieved from command altogether." Without a go ahead from the War Department to remove Rosecrans, Grant sent his chief of staff, John Rawlins, out to St. Louis in early November with instructions to rein in the rogue department commander. Surprisingly, Rawlins's assessment was of a Rosecrans who seemed "to appreciate fully the condition of af- fairs on the Mississippi and Tennessee Rivers, and will use every exertion, I have no doubt, to forward troops there."[156] This did not satisfy Grant.

From his siege lines around Petersburg, Virginia, that winter, the Union general in chief began to lobby Secretary Stanton in earnest that Rosecrans's name "be submitted to the President for dismissal from service." In a move eerily similar to the elimination of Major General McClernand from his command, Grant asserted that Rosecrans had violated General Orders No. 151 by "permitting the publication of Major General [Alfred] Pleasonton's report" of successful operations against rebels in Missouri without first clearing it with the War Department. In McClernand's case Grant only went so far as to remove him from combat command; in contrast, he called for Rosecrans to face a full dismissal from the army.[157] When asked where best to shelf the general, Grant freely told Stanton that "Rosecrans will do less harm doing nothing than on duty. I know of no department or any commander deserving such punishment as the infliction of Rosecrans upon them."[158]

That same winter Grant also sought the sacking of George Thomas, then locked in a bitter siege for Nashville with the rebels of John Bell Hood's Army of Tennessee. Grant's communications during this time "show that he had a good memory for injuries, real or fancied, with an utter lack of sympathy or active friendship for Thomas, dating possibly . . . [to] Thomas' coldness and inhospitality at Chattanooga," James Wilson later surmised. Such communiqués "also disclose a willingness, if not a settled purpose, on Grant's part to cause Thomas' removal and downfall, provided the authorities at Washington could be induced to take the responsibility for such radical action," he continued. "When told plainly by Halleck that if he wished Thomas removed he would have to do it himself and take the sole responsibility, he hesitated and, while not abandoning his purpose, he drafted orders to that end, but, fortunately for Thomas and the country, they were not sent."[159] Unknown to Thomas, he survived dismissal by mere hours after winning a stunning battle that drove the Confederates from the Tennessee capitol.[160]

Rosecrans did not have recent successes to buoy his commission, and on December 9, 1864, he received General Orders No. 294 relieving him of department command. At word of his removal, Rosecrans's former aide-de-camp Calvin Goddard wrote him: "I cannot refrain from expressing my sympathy for you in the relentless persecution to which you are subjected by the malice of your enemies. . . . You have certainly proved the truth of the saying 'Republics are ungrateful.' If justice had been done you in Tennessee you would now have been where Sherman is. . . . Yet as long as Secretary Stanton remains at the head of the War Department and Grant at the head of the Army you will be kept as much in the background as possible."[161] One St. Louis man, regarding the War Department as the nation's despotic "rulers," adjured, "may Heaven protect our country and people from such malignant men."[162] Others, such as Emil Pontonius, a secretary to Missouri governor Thomas Fletcher, were not so kind. "To me the reasons of your removal are as plain as can be," he railed. "You are personally obnoxious to Mr. Lincoln, the Secretary of War, Genl. Halleck and Grant—enough to kill (in the official sense of the word) any rising man in this country on the political as well as the military field."[163] Once again, Rosecrans boarded a train for home in Cincinnati, departing the army in shame. This trip, however, marked a permanent departure from military service.

Congressman Garfield consoled his bygone commander: "You bear the distinguished honor of being the only General in the history of the world who had planned and executed three vast and dangerous campaigns with almost unparallel[ed] success—and, at the end of each, suddenly and without allegation of cause [was] removed by his government and sent into a kind of military banishment, at a time when all the military force of the country is needed for its defense." In January 1865 Garfield used his seat in Congress to prompt the Committee on the Conduct of the War to initiate an investigation into Rosecrans's wartime performance and two command removals in an effort to exonerate him. "Indeed I have no doubt myself that the whole cause of your removal is to be found in the War Department," he empathized. "Mr. Stanton has by degrees forgotten nearly all his obligations to law and I have no reservation in saying that next to the rebellion our greatest danger is from the tyranny of the War Department."[164] The April 1865 committee hearings went nowhere and failed to shed new light on the matter.

That same month, in the week following Lee's surrender at Appomattox Court House, it seemed Grant could not keep Rosecrans far removed from his mind. On April 14 President Lincoln convened his final cabinet meeting just hours before his fateful trip to Ford's Theater. Grant attended, in company with Treasury Secretary Hugh McCulloch, Postmaster General and former Ohio governor William Dennison, and Secretary of the Navy Gideon Welles. Before this audience Grant censured the president's notions of Rosecrans's wartime record. During the now-famous meeting, the president digressed into describing a recurring "dream which he had preceding nearly every great and important event of the War." Generally, the dream foreran Union victories. When citing that the dream came on the eve of Rosecrans success at Stones River, Grant interrupted, admonishing that the battle "was no victory,—that a few such fights would have ruined us." Lincoln reportedly "looked at Grant curiously and inquiringly," replying that he would have to "differ on that point." As Grant biographer William S. McFeely describes: "Gideon Welles was fascinated by this intrusion by Grant into Lincoln's personal reverie and saw it as a sign of Grant's envy of other generals. Lincoln appears to have judged it both as an expression of jealousy and as an appealing instance of candor."[165] The awkward moment lingered in Welles's memory. "This was the first occasion I had to notice Grant's jealous nature," he later footnoted in his private diary. "In turning it over in my mind at a later period, I remembered that [John] Rawlins had been sent to Washington to procure action against General McClernand at Vicksburg. Later there was jealousy manifested towards General Thomas and others."[166]

"Immediately after the war," according to Rosecrans biographer William M. Lamers, the now-deposed Rosey sought to "get his finances in order and then bring charges of conduct unbecoming an officer against Grant" but could not do so, due to his own economic struggles."[167] In 1865, when endorsing a list of 218 officers for promotion to brevet rank (one of them his disgraced former staff officer Clark Lagow, whom he promoted to brigadier general), Grant removed the names of seven officers, including Rosecrans.[168] Then in 1867, he expunged Rosecrans's commission entirely. Still an officer in the Regular Army, Rosecrans for the past two years had been on an official leave of absence to await a new command assignment that never came. Yet he refused to quit the army, even after his paid leave ended. "As Gen. Rosecrans' resignation has not been received," Grant cabled Stanton, "I respectfully recommend that this communication be regarded as a tender of resignation, and that it be accepted to date from the expiration of his leave of absence."[169] Rosecrans was thus ousted from the army forever. Meanwhile, Grant's meteoric rise continued unfettered.

In 1868 Grant accepted the Republican nomination for president to run against the Democratic candidate, former New York governor Horatio Seymour. In a race as vicious as any political election in American history, Democrats argued against the black vote and the right of freedmen to serve in public office. Republicans countered that Seymour would pander to an unreconciled former Confederacy and dodge support for civil rights to former slaves, in doing so effectively undermining the Union war victory. To achieve moral suasion over the question, William Rosecrans went south. In August, while working as a manager for Seymour's campaign, Rosecrans traveled to the White Sulphur Springs resort in the mountains of West Virginia. A known summer retreat for influential Confederate political and military leaders, the former general held meetings with Robert E. Lee, Pierre Gustave Toutant Beauregard, and Alexander H. Stephens among others. Most reaffirmed the signed commitment of their loyalty oaths that they would support the reunited Union and offer justice to the freed blacks of the South. Seeking proof of reconciliation to buttress Seymour's campaign, Rosecrans went so far as to secure a public letter from Lee confirming as much. Despite these efforts, Grant won the election, becoming the eighteenth president of the United States.[170]

Just before the election and in the closing months of the Johnson administration, Rosecrans left the country, having secured an appointment as minister to Mexico from the president. In September 1868 Grant's personal secretary, Adam Badeau, wrote a telling letter to Cayetano Romero, with instructions to share it with his brother, Matias Romero, the leading American emissary for Mexican president Benito Juarez. "General Rosecranz [*sic*] has been ever since 1862 the enemy of General Grant," Badeau stated bluntly, "especially since his great defeat at Chikamauga [*sic*], and the success of General Grant immediately afterwards." Pointing to other Grant derogators, namely Democrats in Congress, he argued that Rosecrans's "nomination to his present position was undoubtedly due to this fact; just as General McClernand was certainly nominated for the same reason. Since his [Rosecrans's] confirmation I *know* of his using language in regard to General Grant, which indicates the most decided personal hostility. His behavior in visiting the rebel generals lately in [West] Virginia, with the avowed intention of thwarting the success of the republican party and of General Grant shows in what spirit he is ready to administer his functions at Mexico. Everything he does will be affected doubtless by his hostility to the general."[171] No more-scathing an introduction could have been provided the Mexican government.

As president, Grant terminated Rosecrans's appointment. Left adrift in Mexico, "Old Rosey" pursued a forlorn effort to promote and engineer a transcontinental railroad across that country, connecting the Pacific Ocean with Tampico. In addition to squabbling with superiors, he struggled against corrupt local officials, malarial jungles, and uncooperative weather. Rosecrans ultimately resigned from the abortive project and returned to the United States in 1873.[172]

Having sunk into relative obscurity, he continued to be haunted by the lingering shadow of his wartime service and the Battle of Iuka. In 1874, reeling from dysentery and suffering from rotting, aching teeth, a "poverty stricken" Rosecrans wrote his wife from the silver fields of Nevada: "Yesterday was the 12th anniversary of the Battle of Iuka. Last evening I vividly recalled all its incidents, and among that of Grant's not getting into the fight with his troops and of all his subsequent lying and rascality on the subject, and of the positions we now occupy. He President of the U.S., and I sub-superintendent of an old mine and mill."[173] The following summer Rosecrans received a letter from a former colleague, Brigadier General Francis Darr, warning him, "Sherman goes for your scalp about Iuka and Corinth."[174] Apparently Sherman, an early protector of Grant's legacy, had already begun to help shape the memory of those battles, though he had not himself been present at either. General John Fuller, who had been present in those fights, argued that the "unworthy [and] unfortunate" narrative of Iuka and Corinth, as offered by "my friend . . . Sherman in his [1875] 'memoirs' contain substantial falsifications of the truth."[175] Darr encouraged Rosecrans to strike back from within the pages of the *New York Tribune,* whose editor was eager to come to Rosey's rescue and print his firsthand rebuttal. To this offer of retaliation, Rosecrans wrote his wife quite simply, "My time is not yet."[176] With patience, his critics would be within reach.

Elected to Congress in 1880, Rosecrans found himself centrally placed to oppose Grant, then in political retirement in New York. While serving as chairman of the House Military Affairs Committee in 1882, Rosecrans vehemently opposed a bill designed to save the Grant family from destitution after the ex-president had sunk his family's savings in failed Wall Street investments. The "Grant Retirement Bill," as it became known, sought to reinstate Grant's lieutenant-general rank and backdate his pay to 1869, when he resigned his commission to serve as president. As chairman, Representative Rosecrans held great sway over the committee. As his swansong at the end of his last term, the congressman spoke out against the bill. Considered by many to be a public retaliation against Grant, he argued that the pension's purpose was to "reward Grant for his distinguished military service," which he argued, "when true history is written," Grant would not remain deserving of *any* reward.[177] To this, one Philadelphia man praised him: "Thousands here understand you, and applaud your courage. . . . Regarding Grant you have dared to say what many, many have thought."[178]

At a time when Wall Street corruption seemed unbridled, Rosecrans also urged that Grant's affiliation with his son's underhanded banking firm Grant and Ward ought not to be rewarded with fiscal salvation. The financial "failure of the Grant family," charged one of Rosecrans's allies, "is given as the excuse for the passage of this aid. . . . Congress now proposes to make itself a party to this swindle by pensioning the man in whose name it was perpetuated."[179] These inclinations aside, it had proven difficult for Congress to justify paying financial restitution of any kind to impoverished public figures under any circumstances. It was not until 1870, for example, that former first lady Mary Todd Lincoln had secured a pension from the government, fully five years after her husband's assassination. Even still, the retirement bill survived passage in 1885, arriving just five months before Grant's death.

Rosecrans paid a dear price for attempting to thwart the bill. In an anonymous letter from someone within the Grand Army of the Republic (GAR), the largest of all Union veterans' organizations, he became aware

of the degree to which he had embittered untold thousands of former
comrades:

> You made a cowardly indecent and wholly unwarranted attack on Gen-
> eral Grant, full of mean innuendoes on his personal integrity and luring
> depreciation of his military ability and achievements, which *cannot fail* to
> subject *you* to the contempt of the *patriotic people* of our whole country,
> especially 9/10th of our *noble GARs* (*it will not be forgotten by us*).
>   Your very utterances showed that your opposition was the outgrowth of
> *malignant vindictiveness* which is discreditable to you as a man and *dis-*
> *reputable in a soldier.* Go on with your dirty work with your *Rebel Friends—*
> more the better for you. . . .
>   —G.A.R.[180]

During the pension battle, Grant had sought other means to provide
for his family. Completing his *Personal Memoirs* in the final weeks of
his life, he hoped that book sales might ensure financial security for his
wife and children. In the wake of the retirement dispute, Grant did not
go to his grave without taking a parting shot at Rosecrans. With his pen
strokes, the old general may have permanently perpetuated the image of
Rosecrans as a troublesome subordinate during the Corinth Campaign
and an irresolute and incompetent soldier whose mind was adrift during the Chattanooga siege, a stigma that has been embraced by perhaps
most Civil War scholars. Grant died on July 23, 1885, but the animosity
that Rosecrans felt would diehard.

Five months after Grant's death, William Rosecrans made one final
plea to history. Publishing a lengthy treatise in the *North American Re-*
view, he carefully dissected passages from Grant's *Memoirs* relating to
the campaign for Chattanooga and Rosecrans's 1863 removal from army
command.[181] The article, entitled "The Mistakes of Grant," sought "to
warn readers and students of military history of the war that [Grant's
narrative] abounds in inaccurate, misleading, and untruthful statements . . . [wherein] General Grant misstated facts to gratify dislikes of
others and to glorify himself."[182] This scathing criticism of the former
president's wildly popular and widely read *Personal Memoirs* fell on the
deaf ears of an American public who seemed to revere him even more
in death than in life.[183] Yet Rosecrans besought posterity that "truth
and justice require that, upon historical events especially within my
cognizance, I should not in silence permit insatiable and conscienceless

egotism, under the shadow of a great name, to masquerade as the muse of history."[184] With Grant no longer alive to defend himself, this publication marks the final word and a close to the protracted rivalry.

Rosecrans went on to serve in various other government offices and outlived Grant by eleven years, dying on March 11, 1897, at his ranch near Redondo Beach, California. With him, so too died the enmity. Yet the controversy over what really happened at Iuka and how much personal malice prompted Rosecrans's removal at Chattanooga continues to this day.

In the last decades of his life, Rosecrans became all too aware of his assured obscurity in American memory. Nine months after his defeat at Chickamauga, the general received a frankhearted letter from his former corps commander Gordon Granger. Still stinging from his own removal from command at Grant's hands at the end of the Chattanooga Campaign, Granger foretold of their destined anonymity:

> I have been extremely anxious to visit you and talk over the memories of the glorious past—compare ideas and opinions of the present and future, the acts of the present drama and the actors. . . . After three years of fiddling and piddling the government has finally brought every man (private soldiers and politicians) to the front under Grant and Sherman. How different the policy was towards them from what it was with you. . . . Such has been the injustice and caprice of the War Dept and the political demagogues controlling public affairs for the last three years. You and I have been sacrificed to their venom and vindictiveness while many others [have] shared a similar fate.
>
> If Grant and Sherman squelch out the rebellion they will be the heroes and we will be forgotten and sink into oblivion.[185]

For William Starke Rosecrans, these words proved all too prophetic, as his name and legacy now befit little more than a footnote in American history.

ACKNOWLEDGMENTS

I wish to single out the late Professor John Y. Simon, editor of the *Papers of Ulysses S. Grant* at Southern Illinois University, who graciously shared with me his extended thoughts on this subject. Alan Jutzi and Olga Tsapina at the Henry E. Huntington Library, as well as archivists at the Charles E. Young Library at UCLA, and the Hubert H. Bancroft Library at UC Berkeley proved invaluable toward completing this research. Thanks also to Gordon Cotton, Pete Ronayne, Wiley Sword and James Torrance in addition to all of the contributing authors of this book for providing insight and assistance throughout this project.

NOTES

1. Wiley Sword, "Where in the Name of God Is Grant? Ulysses S. Grant's Field Order at Iuka, Miss., Creates Confusion and Also a Bitter Rival—William S. Rosecrans," *Blue and Gray Magazine* 22, no. 4 (Fall 2005): 22.

2. For more on Grant's relationship with the *New York Herald* during this time, see William A. Blair, "Grant's Second Civil War: The Battle for Historical Memory," in Gary W. Gallagher, ed., *The Spotsylvania Campaign* (Chapel Hill: University of North Carolina Press, 1998), 237.

3. Grant, interview with the *New York Herald,* July 6, 1878, Hamburg, Germany, in Grant, *The Papers of Ulysses S. Grant,* ed. John Y. Simon, John F. Marszalek, et al., 31 vols. to date (Carbondale: Southern Illinois University Press, 1967–), 28:422.

4. John Hay, *Inside Lincoln's White House: The Complete Civil War Diary of John Hay,* ed. Michael Burlingame and John R. Turner Ettlinger (Carbondale: Southern Illinois University Press, 1997), 98–99 (Oct. 24, 1863).

5. To date, the only biography of William Starke Rosecrans remains William M. Lamers, *The Edge of Glory: A Biography of William S. Rosecrans, U.S.A.* (New York: Harcourt, Brace, and World, 1961). While Lamers's treatment is still considered balanced and capacious, a new biography of Rosecrans is past due. For a recent and fresh look at Ulysses S. Grant, see Joan Waugh, *U. S. Grant: American Hero, American Myth* (Chapel Hill: University of North Carolina Press, 2009), in addition to Ronald C. White Jr., whose promising biography of Grant is forthcoming from Random House.

6. While Rosecrans and Grant actually received their brigadier appointments at later dates, their commissions were backdated to May 16 and 17, 1861, respectively. In actuality, Rosecrans received his promotion in June, and it was confirmed on August 3, whereas Grant obtained his later in August. As such, Rosecrans *technically* outranked Grant for the time being. See Ezra J. Warner, *Generals in Blue: Lives of the Union Commanders* (Baton Rouge: Louisiana State University Press, 1964), 184, 410.

7. James Garfield, *The Wild Life of the Army: The Civil War Letters of James A. Garfield,* ed. Frederick D. Williams (East Lansing: Michigan State University Press, 1964), 226.

8. Rosecrans and Meagher were the only two *practicing* Roman Catholic Union generals of the war. In his youth William T. Sherman had been baptized Roman Catholic but, according to biographer John Marszalek, "refused to call himself Catholic or practice that creed." See Marszalek, *Sherman: A Soldier's Passion for Order* (New York: Free Press, 1993), 10. Other Union generals who were raised Roman Catholic include James Negley and Phillip Sheridan. Evidence suggests, however, that like Sherman, neither practiced that religion in adult life.

9. Catholic Americans during this era were, by and large, members of the Democratic Party, in part because the Republican Party had absorbed the anti-Catholic "Know Nothing" movement into its ranks and even elected a Know-Nothinger, New Jersey congressman William Pennington, speaker of the House in 1860.

10. See "Noble Letter from General Rosecrans," in *A Savory Dish for Loyal Men* (Philadelphia, 1863), original tract at Henry E. Huntington Library, San Marino, Calif. (repository hereafter cited as HEH).

11. For a superb investigation of Catholic American Democrats and the culture of war dissent, see Frank L. Klement, "Catholics as Copperheads during the Civil War," *Catholic Historical Review* 80, no. 1 (Jan. 1994): 36–57.

12. See Brooks D. Simpson, "After Shiloh: Grant, Sherman, and Survival," in Steven E. Woodworth, ed., *The Shiloh Campaign* (Carbondale: Southern Illinois University Press, 2009), 150.

13. Grant to Julia Dent Grant, Apr. 30, 1862, in Grant, *Papers,* 5:102–103.

14. For a superb examination of Grant and the political consequences of Shiloh, see Simpson, "After Shiloh," 142–58.

15. In addition to Sherman, Grant was good friends with Major General John Pope, alongside whom he also served at this time. Pope was among the first officers in the nation to defend Grant against rumors of drinking but was far from being as tenacious a supporter as Sherman. This was perhaps partly because Pope was not present at Shiloh and subsequently did not have to answer to charges regarding the battle's prosecution.

16. Grant to Julia Dent Grant, May 4, 1862, in Grant, *Papers,* 5:110–11.

17. Ibid., 213n.

18. John Rawlins, Memorandum, n.d., in ibid., 9:298.

19. Rosecrans Annie Rosecrans, Aug. 24, 1862, Iuka, Miss., William Starke Rosecrans Papers, Charles E. Young Research Library, University of California, Los Angeles (collection hereafter cited as Rosecrans Papers, UCLA), Box 55, Folder 50.

20. Edward Betty to Rosecrans, Feb. 7, 1863, Frankfort, Ky., ibid., Box 8, Folder 30.

21. Telegraph, Charles Dana to Edwin Stanton, Nov. 1, 1863, in Grant, *Papers,* 9:328.

22. Edward G. Longacre, *From Union Stars to Top Hats: A Biography of the Extraordinary General James Harrison Wilson* (Harrisburg, Pa.: Stackpole, 1972), 62.

23. Maj. William R. Rowley to Rep. Elihu Washburne, Nov. 20, 1862, in Grant, *Papers,* 7:32. Rowley complains that Colonels "Lagow, Regan, and Hillyer" were guilty of chronic drunkenness.

24. Grant to Henry W. Halleck, Aug. 9, 1862, in ibid., 5:276.

25. To date, the best researched and most comprehensive in-depth study of the 1862 northern Mississippi campaign remains Peter Cozzens, *The Darkest Days of the War: The Battles of Iuka and Corinth* (Chapel Hill: University of North Carolina Press, 1997). See also Timothy B. Smith, *Corinth 1862: Siege, Battle, Occupation* (Lawrence: University Press of Kansas, 2012).

26. Grant to Jesse Root Grant, Sept. 17, 1862, in Grant, *Papers,* 6:62.

27. Grant, *Personal Memoirs of U. S. Grant* (reprint, New York: Penguin, 1999), 222.

28. Dispatch, Grant to Edward O. C. Ord, Sept. 19, 1862, Wiley Sword Collection, Suwanee, Ga.

29. Grant, *Personal Memoirs,* 411.

30. Grant, *Papers,* 6:172.

31. Ibid., 65n.

32. Rosecrans, *Rosecrans's Campaigns* (Washington, D.C., 1865), 19, copy at HEH. See also Cozzens, *Darkest Days of the War,* 72–73.

33. Col. Theophilus Lyle Dickey to his wife, Oct. 19, 1862, in Grant, *Papers,* 6:178.

34. Rosecrans to Annie Rosecrans, Sept. 22, 1862, Jacinto, Miss., Rosecrans Papers, UCLA, Box 59, Folder 55.

35. Dickey to his wife, Oct. 19, 1862, in Grant, *Papers,* 6:178.

36. Ibid., 177–78. Dickey's letter states:

[O]ur route [back to Burnsville] lay through a deep forest—over steep hills and low bottoms—with a blind winding path—It soon became pitch dark—and although clear star-light night—in the woods it was very dark. In our progress we lost the road and traveled a mile by the north star our only guide through grape vines—briers and fallen trees brush piles, etc, at length my horse which was ahead halted and putting his nose down refused to go forward—I told Col Lagow that my horse refused to go—that we had doubtless come to some obstruction—He said "Let me try it" and spurred his horse past me and to his surprise plunged horse and man down a perpendicular bank five feet high into the bed of a creek—The horse fell flat on his side and caught Lagow's leg under him—They both grunted and got up again and found that they were not seriously hurt—We could find no crossing and had to build a fire—tie our horses and lie down in the woods till daylight—At day-light we mounted and galloped seven miles to Burnsville. Couriers sent by a more circuitous, had reached Gen Grant about 3 o'clock A.M. Saturday giving him word of the engagement—and Gen Grant had ordered Ord to advance at day-light and attack the enemy from the north.

37. Sword, "Where in the Name of God Is Grant?" 24.

38. Dispatch, U. S. Grant to Maj. Gen. Edward O. C. Ord, 8:30 A.M., Sept. 20, 1862, Burnsville, Miss., Edward Otho Cresap Ord Papers, Bancroft Library, University of California, Berkeley (collection hereafter cited as Ord Papers, UC Berkeley). This item also describes another "dispatch just received from Rosecrans," which brought notice that a battle had been underway the previous evening.

39. Ibid. The back of the dispatch reads, "Sept 20—Notice that Rosecrans had a fight. Recd, 20th, 9AM." These words, likely written by Grant or someone on his staff, help confirm that this report marked Grant's first knowledge that a battle had been fought by Rosecrans the previous night.

40. Cozzens, *Darkest Days of the War,* 126.

41. I am indebted to Brig. Gen. Parker Hills (ret.) of the Mississippi Army National Guard, who, using his intimate knowledge of the Iuka terrain, the battle's history, and GPS technology, has mapped the distances between Ord's forward positions and the epicenter of battle.

42. Dispatch, Brig. Gen. Leonard Ross to Ord, 4:00 P.M., Sept. 19, 1862, Ord Papers, UC Berkeley.

43. Arthur Ducat to Rosecrans, Dec. 29, 1880, New York City, Rosecrans Papers, UCLA, Box 40, Folder 113.

44. Rosecrans to Annie Rosecrans, Sept. 22, 1862, Jacinto, Miss., ibid., Box 59, Folder 55.

45. Telegram, Grant to Maj. Gen. Benjamin Hurlbut, Oct. 3, 1862, in Grant, *Papers,* 6:103.

46. Grant to Mary Grant, Oct. 16, 1862, Jackson, Tenn., in ibid., 154–55.

47. Grant to Rep. Elihu Washburne, Nov. 7, 1862, in ibid., 275.

48. Grant, Headquarters, District of West Tennessee, General Field Orders No. 1, Sept. 20, 1862, Corinth, Miss., Ord Papers, UC Berkeley.

49. Grant, Headquarters, District of West Tennessee, General Orders No. 88, Oct. 7, 1862, Jackson, Tenn., quoted in Henry Coppee, *Grant and His Campaigns: A Military Biography* (New York: Charles E. Richardson, 1866), 129.

50. Rosecrans to Grant, Oct. 10, 1862, Corinth, Miss., Rosecrans Papers, UCLA, Box 45, Folder 1.

51. William S. Stewart to parents, Sept. 23, 1862, William S. Stewart Letters, Western Historical Manuscripts Collection, University of Missouri, Columbia.

52. Franklin A. Dick to Attorney General Edward Bates, Sept. 28, 1862, St. Louis, in Grant, *Papers,* 6:87.

53. *New York Times,* Oct. 5, 1862.

54. Edward Betty to Rosecrans, Feb. 7, 1863, Frankfort, Ky., Rosecrans Papers, UCLA, Box 8, Folder 30.

55. Col. Mortimer Leggett to Maj. John Rawlins, Oct. 19, 1862, in Grant, *Papers,* 6:167.

56. See Simpson, "After Shiloh," 145.

57. Leggett to Rawlins, Oct. 19, 1862, 166–67.

58. Julia Dent Grant, *The Personal Memoirs of Julia Dent Grant,* ed. John Y. Simon (New York: Putnam, 1975), 104.

59. Dispatch, Rosecrans to Grant, Oct. 21, 1862, Corinth, Miss., Rosecrans Papers, UCLA, Box 45, Folder 57.

60. Dispatch, Grant to Rosecrans, Oct. 21, 1862, Jackson, Tenn., in Grant, *Papers,* 6:165.

61. Dispatch, Rosecrans to Grant, Oct. 21, 1862, Corinth, Miss., Rosecrans Papers, UCLA, Box 45, Folder 60.

62. Grant, *Personal Memoirs,* 227.

63. Communiqué, Col. William S. Hillyer to Sherman, Oct. 29, 1862, in Grant, *Papers,* 6:180.

64. William T. Sherman to John Rawlins, Nov. 1, 1862, in ibid.

65. Rosecrans to Grant, Feb. 18, 1865, in ibid., 288.

66. Iowa governor Samuel Kirkwood to Rosecrans, Nov. 4, 1862, Rosecrans Papers, UCLA, Box 7, Folder 138.

67. Sen. Lyman Trumbull to Grant, Nov. 24, 1862, in Grant, *Papers,* 6:288.

68. Rep. Elihu Washburne to Rosecrans, Dec. 3, 1862, Washington, D.C., Rosecrans Papers, UCLA, Box 7, Folder 148.

69. Lincoln to Rosecrans, Jan. 5, Aug. 31, 1863, in Abraham Lincoln, *The Collected Works of Abraham Lincoln,* ed. Roy Basler, vol. 6. (New Brunswick, N.J.: Rutgers University Press, 1954), 424–25. See also James M. McPherson, *Tried by War: Abraham Lincoln as Commander in Chief* (New York: Penguin, 2008), 156.

70. Maj. Gen. George Lucas Hartsuff to Rosecrans, Jan. 8, 1863, Washington, D.C., Rosecrans Papers, UCLA, Box 8, Folder 9.

71. Murat Halstead to Salmon Chase, Apr. 1, 1863, quoted in Lesley J. Gordon, "'I Could Not Make Him Do as I Wished': The Failed Relationship of William S. Rosecrans and Grant," in Steven E. Woodworth, ed., *Grant Lieutenants: From Cairo to Vicksburg* (Lawrence: University Press of Kansas, 2001), 123.

72. Communiqué, General in Chief Henry Wager Halleck to Rosecrans, Mar. 1, 1863, Washington, D.C., Rosecrans Papers, UCLA, Box 8, Folder 38.

73. General in Chief Henry Wager Halleck to Rosecrans, Mar. 13, 1863, Washington, D.C., ibid., Box 8, Folder 44.

74. President Lincoln to Rosecrans, Mar. 17, 1863, Washington, D.C., ibid., Box 8, Folder 138.

75. Garfield, *Wild Life of the Army,* 225–26.

76. For a superb essay on the Grant-McClernand relationship, see Terrence J. Winschel, "John A. McClernand: Fighting Politician," in *Triumph and Defeat: The Vicksburg Campaign, Volume 2* (New York: Savas Beatie, 2006), 49–72.

77. McPherson, *Tried by War,* 192.

78. William T. Sherman to unknown, July 5, 1863, "Camp near Black River," in W. T. Sherman, *Home Letters of General Sherman,* ed. Mark A. DeWolfe Howe (New York: Charles Scribner's Sons, 1909), 271.

79. McPherson, *Tried by War,* 193.

80. Wiley Sword, *Mountains Touched with Fire: Chattanooga Besieged, 1863* (New York: St. Martin's, 1995), 49.

81. For more on Charles Dana's background as a poet and literary figure, see James Harrison Wilson, *The Life of Charles A. Dana* (New York: Harper and Brothers, 1907), 53–55.

82. Maj. Gen. Gordon Granger to Rosecrans, June 6, 1864, New York City, Rosecrans Papers, UCLA, Box 8, Folder 44. William Shanks, *Personal Recollections of Distinguished Generals,* 263, quoted in Peter Cozzens, *This Terrible Sound: The Battle of Chickamauga* (Urbana: University of Illinois Press, 1992), 80. Another postwar source for comment on Dana as an unwelcome meddler within the Army of the Cumberland appears in Smith Atkins to Henry Cist (Chickamauga Campaign veteran and Army of the Cumberland historian), March 18, 1898, Abraham Lincoln Bookshop, Chicago, quoted in ibid.

83. In a personal conversation with the author, the late historian Brian C. Pohanka regarded Dana as a kind of "commissar," being a politically motivated spy working on behalf of Secretary Stanton, much like the Soviet commissars who informed on Red Army commanders to communist leaders during World War II.

84. Rosecrans to Annie Rosecrans, Sept. 16, 1863, Crawfish Springs, Ga., Rosecrans Papers, UCLA, Box, 59, Folder 93.

85. Sword, *Mountains Touched with Fire,* 48. A fascinating view of Rosecrans, as seen by the War Department and the White House, during this time can be followed in Hay, *Inside Lincoln's White House,* 85–108.

86. Benjamin P. Thomas and Harold M. Hyman, *Stanton: The Life and Times of Lincoln's Secretary of War* (New York: Knopf, 1962), 290.

87. Chesley Mosman, *The Rough Side of War: The Civil War Journal of Chesley A. Mosman,* ed. Arnold Gates (Garden City, N.Y.: Basin, 1987), 85 (Sept. 21, 1863).

88. Ibid., 88–89 (Sept. 23, 1863).

89. Sword, *Mountains Touched with Fire,* 46.

90. Rosecrans to Annie Rosecrans, Sept. 28, 1862, Chattanooga, Tenn., Rosecrans Papers, UCLA, Box 59, Folder 96.

91. The September 30 telegraph traffic between Dana and Stanton was done with Dana temporarily in Nashville so that he could engage in a secret wire chat without any possibility of Rosecrans catching wind of the War Department's designs.

92. Sword, *Mountains Touched with Fire,* 48.

93. Ibid.

94. Ibid., 51–52.

95. Both the initial overland supply line and the Tennessee River route were interchangeably referred to the as the "Cracker Line" by Army of the Cumberland soldiers during the siege. My use of the term to denote the river route is in step with a settled postwar designation among veterans on the subject.

96. Sword, *Mountains Touched with Fire,* 49; Hay, *Inside Lincoln's White House,* 86.

97. Brig. Gen. James Garfield to Salmon P. Chase, July 27, 1863, in Garfield, *Wild Life of the Army,* 289–91.

98. Ibid., 220.

99. Garfield to Crete (wife), Sept. 23, 1863, Chattanooga, Tenn., in ibid., 296–97.

100. Sword, *Mountains Touched with Fire,* 50.

101. See Peter Cozzens, *The Shipwreck of Their Hopes: The Battles for Chattanooga.* (Urbana: University of Illinois Press, 1996), 1–6.

102. John Rawlins to Mary Hurlbut, Nov. 23, 1863, John Rawlins Papers, Chicago Historical Society, quoted in ibid., 4.

103. Grant to Sherman, Sept. 30, 1863, in Grant, *Papers,* 9:256.

104. Charles Stone to Rosecrans, Apr. 13, 1860, New York City, Rosecrans Papers, UCLA, Box 7, Folder 13.

105. Philemon Ewing to Rosecrans, Apr. 19, 1860, Lancaster, Ohio, ibid., Box 7, Folder 16.

106. William T. Sherman to Philemon B. Ewing, Oct. 24, 1863, Iuka, Miss., in W. T. Sherman, *Sherman's Civil War: Selected Correspondence of William T. Sherman, 1860–1865,* ed. Brooks D. Simpson and Jean V. Berlin (Chapel Hill: University of North Carolina Press, 1999), 563–64.

107. William T. Sherman to John Sherman, Oct. 24, 1863, Iuka, Miss., in ibid., 566–67.

108. Sword, *Mountains Touched with Fire,* 54.

109. William S. Rosecrans, "The Mistakes of Grant," *North American Review* (Dec. 1885).

110. Ibid.; Sword, *Mountains Touched with Fire,* 54.

111. Sword, *Mountains Touched with Fire,* 55–56.

112. Grant, *Personal Memoirs,* 329.

113. James Harrison Wilson, *Under the Old Flag: Recollections of Military Operations in the War for the Union, the Spanish War, the Boxer Rebellion, etc.,* 2 vols. (New York: D. Appleton, 1912), 1:265.

114. Lamers, *Edge of Glory,* 398.

115. Grant, *Personal Memoirs,* 329.

116. Rosecrans, "Mistakes of Grant."

117. Grant, *Personal Memoirs,* 329–30.

118. Benson Bobrick, *Master of War: The Life of General George H. Thomas* (New York: Simon and Schuster, 2009), 198–99. For another eyewitness account, see Wilson, *Under the Old Flag,* 1:273–76.

119. Mosman, *Rough Side of War,* 266–67 (entry for Aug. 28, 1864).

120. Bobrick, *Master of War,* 198–99. Another eyewitness, Horace Porter, who grew to idolize Grant, wrote of this meeting in detail in his 1897 memoirs, *Campaigning with Grant,* and made no mention of Thomas's poor treatment of Grant. Yet the authenticity of Wilson's account is without question. By the time he wrote of this meeting, in 1912, Wilson had grown to idolize Thomas. Moreover, his close friendship with Grant had ended bitterly. A series of disagreements between the two during Grant's White House years caused bad blood, and

by 1881, according to historian Edward Longacre, the two "could not tolerate each other's presence." See Longacre, *From Union Stars to Top Hats,* 243–45.

121. Grant, *Personal Memoirs,* 330.

122. Rosecrans, "Mistakes of Grant."

123. Grant, *Personal Memoirs,* 331.

124. Rosecrans, "Mistakes of Grant."

125. Mosman, *Rough Side of War,* 106–13 (Oct. 25–31, 1863).

126. Ibid., 112 (Oct. 30, 1863).

127. Dispatch, Maj. Frank S. Bond, army headquarters aide-de-camp, to Lt. .Col. Andrew Jackson MacKay, chief quartermaster, Oct. 18, 1863, Wiley Sword Collection, Suwanee, Ga. I am indebted to Wiley Sword for sharing this document and his personal notes regarding its importance with me.

128. Rosecrans, "Mistakes of Grant."

129. William T. Sherman to Ellen Ewing Sherman, Oct. 28, 1863, Iuka, Miss., in Sherman, *Sherman's Civil War,* 569.

130. Capt. Francis Donaldson to brother, Oct. 22, 1863, "Camp near Baltimore, Va.," in Francis Adams Donaldson, *Inside the Army of the Potomac: The Civil War Experience of Captain Francis Adams Donaldson,* ed. J. Gregory Acken (Mechanicsburg, Pa.: Stackpole, 1998), 371.

131. Hay, *Inside Lincoln's White House,* 94 (Oct. 18, 19, 1863).

132. Ibid., 97 (Oct. 21, 1863).

133. Lewis Ashmead to Rosecrans, Nov. 9, 1863, Philadelphia, Pa., Rosecrans Papers, UCLA, Box 9, Folder 12.

134. Hay, *Inside Lincoln's White House,* 98–99 (Oct. 24, 1863).

135. Ibid., 107 (Nov. 2, 1863).

136. James Gilmore to Rosecrans, May 23, 1864, Boston, Rosecrans Papers, UCLA, Box 9, Folder 148.

137. Lamers, *Edge of Glory,* 401.

138. Abner Doubleday to Rosecrans, Oct. 25, 1863, Washington, D.C., Rosecrans Papers, UCLA, Box 8, Folder 151.

139. William Truesdail to Rosecrans, Nov. 1, 1863, ibid., Box 9, Folder 3.

140. James Garfield to Rosecrans, Oct. 23, 1863, Cincinnati, Ohio, ibid., Box 8, Folder 148.

141. Garfield, *Wild Life of the Army,* 219 (chapter introduction). For a firsthand account of Garfield slandering Rosecrans to the Washington political elite, see Hay, *Inside Lincoln's White House,* 103 (Oct. 29, 1863).

142. James Garfield to Rosecrans, Nov. 2, 1863, Washington, D.C., Rosecrans Papers, UCLA, Box 9, Folder 4.

143. James Garfield to Rosecrans, Dec. 18, 1863, Washington, D.C., ibid., Box 9, Folder 44.

144. William Truesdail to Rosecrans, Nov. 19, 1863, Cincinnati, Ohio, ibid., Box 9, Folder 4.

145. Telegraph, Charles Dana to Edwin Stanton, Nov. 1, 1863, in Grant, *Papers,* 9:328.

146. William Wrenshall Smith, "Holocaust Holiday," *Civil War Times Illustrated* (Oct. 1979): 31 (Nov. 14, 1863). This seems to be the only place where Smith's diary has been published in its entirety.

147. Ibid., 40 (Nov. 20, 1863).

148. Sword, "Where in the Name of God Is Grant?" 24.

149. John McHowe to Rosecrans, Jan. 28, 1864, St. Louis, Rosecrans Papers, UCLA, Box 9, Folder 74.

150. John H. Kingston to Rosecrans, Oct. 24, 1863, Covington, Ky., ibid., Box 8, Folder 150.

151. Mosman, *Rough Side of War,* 226 (June 26, 1864).

152. Ibid., 175 (Apr. 2, 1864).

153. James Harrison Wilson to Grant, Feb. 25, 1864, in Grant, *Papers,* 10:142.

154. *New York Herald,* Apr. 13, 1864, Rosecrans Papers, UCLA, Box 80, Folder 33.

155. Grant, *Papers,* 12:104. See also Lamers, *Edge of Glory,* 415–39.

156. Ulysses S. Grant to Henry W. Halleck, Sept. 29, 1864; and John Rawlins to Ulysses S. Grant, Nov. 4, 1864, quoted in Gordon, "'I Could Not Make Him Do as I Wished,'" 125.

157. Grant to Edwin Stanton, Jan. 1, 1865, in Grant, *Papers,* 13:199. The provocation for Rosecrans's dismissal, General Orders No. 151, reads: "If any officer shall hereafter, without proper authority, permit the publication of any official letter and report, or allow any copy of such document to pass into the hands of persons not authorized to receive it, his name will be submitted to the President for *dismissal.* This rule applies to all official letters and reports written by an officer himself." U.S. War Department, *The War of the Rebellion: A Compilation of the Official Records of the Union and Confederate Armies,* 128 vols. (Washington, D.C.: GPO, 1880–1901), ser. 3, 2:649.

158. Quoted in Gordon, "'I Could Not Make Him Do as I Wished,'" 126.

159. Wilson, *Under the Old Flag,* 2:66–67.

160. For insight into the complex circumstances surrounding the decision to remove George Thomas from army command during the 1864 Tennessee Campaign, see Wiley Sword, *Embrace an Angry Wind: The Confederacy's Last Hurrah: Spring Hill, Franklin, and Nashville* (New York: Harper Collins, 1992), 308–19, 345–47, 402, 412–13.

161. Calvin Goddard to Rosecrans, Dec. 27, 1864, Rosecrans Papers, UCLA, Box 10, Folder 122.

162. E. Stone to Rosecrans, Jan. 9, 1865, St. Louis, ibid., Box 10, Folder 129.

163. Emil Pontonius to Rosecrans, Jan. 2, 1865, St. Louis, ibid., Box 10, Folder 126.

164. James Garfield to Rosecrans, Jan. 22, 1865, ibid., Box 10, Folder 139.

165. William S. McFeeley, *Grant: A Biography* (New York: W. W. Norton, 1981), 223.

166. Gideon Welles, *Diary of Gideon Welles,* ed. Howard K. Beale and Alan W. Brownsword, 3 vols. (Boston, 1909–11), 2:282–83.

167. Lamers, *Edge of Glory,* 440.

168. See Grant, *Papers,* 15:220n; and Sword, "Where in the Name of God Is Grant?" 24.

169. Telegraph, Grant to Edwin Stanton, Feb. 25, 1867, in Grant, *Papers,* 17:410–11.

170. Rosecrans to Robert E. Lee, published in *The Rosecrans-Lee Correspondence* (Democratic State Executive Committee of Ohio, 1868), copy at HEH. For more on Rosecrans's meeting with Lee and other former Confederate leaders, see Alan T. Nolan, *Lee Considered: General Robert E. Lee and Civil War History* (Chapel Hill: University of North Carolina Press, 1991), 143–45; and Douglas Southall Freeman, *R. E. Lee: A Biography,* 4 vols. (New York: Charles Scribner's Sons, 1947), 4:373–78.

171. Adam Badeau to Cayetano Romero, Sept. 13, 1868, Galena, Ill., in Grant, *Papers,* 19:282–83. For more on the relationship between the Grant administration and Mexican diplomat Matias Romero, see Blair, "Grant's Second Civil War," 240.

172. See David M. Pletcher, "General William S. Rosecrans and the Mexican Transcontinental Railroad Project," *Mississippi Valley Historical Review* 38, no. 4 (Mar. 1952): 657–78.

173. Rosecrans to Annie Rosecrans, Sept. 20, 1874, Egan, Nev., Rosecrans Papers, UCLA,
Box 62, Folder 14.

174. Rosecrans to Annie Rosecrans, June 11, 1875, Egan, Nev., ibid., Box 62, Folder 35.

175. John Wallace Fuller to Rosecrans, Sept. 19, 1878, San Francisco, ibid., Box 48,
Folder 30.

176. Rosecrans to Annie Rosecrans, June 11, 1875, Egan, Nev.

177. Lamers, *Edge of Glory,* 445–46. Also see Horace Green, *General Grant's Last Stand*
(New York: Charles Scribner's Sons, 1936), 268–75.

178. Ferdinand S. Sarmiento to Rosecrans, Mar. 2, 1885, Philadelphia, Rosecrans Papers,
UCLA, Box 43, Folder 65.

179. John McDonald to Rosecrans, May 14, 1884, Washington, D.C., ibid., Box 43,
Folder 46.

180. Author unknown (signed "G.A.R." [Grand Army of the Republic]) to Rosecrans,
Mar. 1884, Toledo, Ohio, ibid., Box 43, Folder 44.

181. The *North American Review* initially asked Rosecrans to write a rebuttal to Grant's
Personal Memoirs just a few weeks after Grant's death. Rosecrans decided to wait five months
before publishing his criticism and thereby let a period of national mourning pass.

182. Rosecrans, "Mistakes of Grant."

183. See Joan Waugh, "Pageantry of Woe: The Funeral of U. S. Grant," *Civil War History* 51, no. 2 (June 2005).

184. Rosecrans, "Mistakes of Grant."

185. Maj. Gen. Gordon Granger to Rosecrans, June 6, 1864, New York City, Rosecrans
Papers, UCLA, Box 8, Folder 44.

CHAPTER 8

"OUR FIRESIDE IN RUINS"

Consequences of the 1863 Chattanooga Campaign

WILEY SWORD

The broad panoply of Chattanooga's rugged mountain ranges stretch in an endless scene of breathtaking grandeur. To Sergeant Lyman S. Widney of the 34th Illinois Infantry: "The valley [was] so far, far down that I could scarcely believe it was not a picture. I have often tried to imagine how the earth would appear to a person elevated thousands of feet. [Yet] as I stood on the mountain looking down into the valley I realized what imagination had failed to paint in true colors." Another wide-eyed observer considered that he could see forty or fifty miles, including three states. It was a most impressive display for the beginning of events that seemed to prophesy a compelling tale of grandeur and adventure.[1]

Instead, it turned out to be a chronicle of grim and often ugly despair. The events at Chattanooga, Tennessee, in the fall of 1863 determined much in the outcome of a war that had promised in 1861 a destiny either divided or united. Indeed, the protracted and stunning series of battles around Chattanooga from September through November 1863 proved to be an enormous blow to the Southern Confederacy's chances of survival. Initially, there had been the bright hope for a major, course-of-the-war-altering victory there in the wake of the stunning Confederate victory at Chickamauga. Only weeks later, however, following the November 25 disaster on Missionary Ridge, the euphoria of September 20 had given way to stark reality for the South—impending total defeat. A luring gateway had been opened for the enemy into the Deep South, beyond which lay the prospect of invasion of the core Confederate heartland, economic ruin, diminishing resources, and irreplaceable manpower losses. Abraham Lincoln had thoughtfully regarded Chattanooga with extreme importance, referring to the permanent Union occupation and control of the city as "a thorn in its [the Confederacy's] vitals." He foresaw events there as crucial to the existence of both the United States and the Confederacy. Lieutenant General Ulysses S. Grant later added to the assessment, suggesting that Chattanooga was "the heaviest blow they [the rebels] have received during the war," the Union army having thus driven "a big nail in the coffin of rebellion."[2]

Remarkably, due to the press of new and rapidly occurring war developments, an enduring public perspective about the critical events at Chattanooga seemed to be quickly lost. Amid the overriding publicity generated from the more populous eastern regions, which were long considered to be the seat of the war, popular scrutiny of the West abated for several months until the spring 1864 campaign for Atlanta began. In fact, with Grant going east in 1864 to command the key Union forces that had so often failed to cope successfully with Robert E. Lee's magnificent army, many future headlines were devoted to the eastern theater.

What significantly remained in the West was the campaign that, according to prominent historians such as Albert Castel, resulted in "the [final] decision." This, of course, was the crucial Atlanta Campaign, which many regarded as the primary event that saved the Lincoln administration from defeat in the 1864 election. Ironically, this circumstance involved a personnel issue that defined the essential thinking of the new overall Union commander, U. S. Grant, which further reveals another key aspect of the decisive 1863 events at Chattanooga.

With Grant going east in the spring of 1864 to manage the war there, the huge command void to be filled in the western theater became a critical question: who would be the new commander in the West? Leadership of the combined Federal armies that were gathering to invade Georgia loomed as a major component of the overall war effort. Yet there were a multitude of competent, successful generals who seemed worthy of higher responsibility, particularly George H. Thomas and William Tecumseh Sherman (also, to a lesser extent, James B. McPherson, Phil Sheridan, and William F. "Baldy" Smith). All had many stellar qualities that bespoke of their ability to wage successful warfare.

George H. Thomas was the senior-ranking Union major general and seemed to have earned promotion, especially on the basis of his recent performances at Chickamauga and Chattanooga. The "Rock of Chickamauga" was already a popular hero, and he had contributed the most to

Union successes in the late battles. Thomas also had the strong support of his men, who revered his reputation as never having lost a battle.

William Tecumseh Sherman had always been Grant's right-hand man. From Shiloh to Chattanooga, the hard-fighting and aggressive Sherman had been everything from an obedient subordinate to a consoling mentor. He had also made big mistakes, especially at Shiloh. His performance at Chattanooga was distressing in the inability to defeat Major General Patrick Cleburne's relatively few troops on North Missionary Ridge with his own massive forces—all due to the want of coordinated attacks. Yet most importantly, Sherman and Grant thought alike. Grant knew Sherman's will, and Sherman regarded Grant with awe: "he is a great general, he makes his plans and goes ahead, cares nothing for what he cannot see, while some things I cannot see at times scare me like hell." Thomas and Grant clashed in personality and demeanor. Thus, "Old Slow Trot" Thomas would not do. It was Sherman Grant selected, despite the differences in combat performance between Sherman and Thomas.[3]

Grant made this unique decision personally and, coming in the aftermath of the key events at Chattanooga, was attributable to the sour relationship he had with Thomas. Grant's masterminding of the overall Union war effort thus was one of the highly crucial consequences of the Chattanooga Campaign. Now called upon to head the offensive against Robert E. Lee in the East, Grant would trust only Sherman to take over in the West. Despite Sherman's ultimate strategic victory in capturing Atlanta, his costly attacks at Kennesaw Mountain and elsewhere revealed an underlying weakness for tactical warfare. Also, in the aftermath of losing that city, the rag-tag Confederate Army of Tennessee was allowed to recoup and refit since Sherman failed to press, crush, or disperse the badly defeated and depleted Southern force. Had Thomas been in command, according to historian Castel, "almost surely the Union victory at Atlanta would have been easier, quicker, and more complete."[4]

Of course, Thomas's enormous contribution to the Union war effort would continue later in 1864 when, with his makeshift army, he won the greatest major victory of the war at Nashville—largely destroying Hood's valiant but overwhelmed army in the process. That Thomas, a native Virginian, had such a profound practical influence on the war later became one of its more overlooked aspects. At Missionary Ridge his troops had assumed the key role in the enormous Chattanooga victory and were the battle's deciding factor. Indeed, today Thomas rightfully remains as one of the nation's premiere soldiers, despite the relative lack of popular approbation.

Despite the absence of Thomas in the top Union hierarchy, soon in place was the extraordinary military command triumvirate of Grant, Sherman, and Sheridan. That this was a direct consequence secured in the aftermath of Chattanooga was all but overlooked in the initial 1864 rush of events. These strong and mutually supportive primary relationships, later so highly publicized in the newspapers, created a popular conception that the three were the guiding lights who virtually won the war by masterminding the concluding military events. Yet in truth, beginning with the fighting at Chattanooga, the nature of the war had basically changed. The overall conflict had transitioned into a "grinding war" of attrition, and 1864 soon saw the top Union commanders marshaling the North's vast resources to overwhelm a weaker opponent.

While the hierarchy of the Union top command was firmly established by the events at Chattanooga, the Confederacy afterward continued to struggle in its quest for an effective commander in the West. It is well recorded that Braxton Bragg, who many regarded as the South's most obnoxious general, was replaced as commander of the Army of Tennessee in the aftermath of Chattanooga. But what is not so well publicized is the extent of turmoil and downright incompetence that was allowed to continue in the wake of the defeat on Missionary Ridge.

Bragg's admission of a crushing defeat, his request to resign from command, and his petition for a court of inquiry led to his temporary replacement by Lieutenant General William J. Hardee on November 30, 1863. Yet Bragg's role in the war was far from complete. His plaintive, fawning letter to Jefferson Davis in the aftermath of his removal asked that he again "be allowed to participate in the struggle" so as to allow him "to restore his character, prestige, and lost territory." In fact, following a three-month retirement, Bragg was called to the president's side as his "special military adviser." Ultimately, he became in essence the de-facto chief of staff, with responsibility for the conduct of military operations throughout the Confederacy. Jefferson Davis simply would not allow himself to be proven wrong in his personal judgments. Soon, he was flaunting Bragg's prominence and allowed the acerbic North Carolinian to exert influence even over command decisions.[5]

Of particular importance in the aftermath of Chattanooga were the succession of openings for corps commanders that occurred in the Army of Tennessee. First, Lieutenant General D. H. Hill was removed after an intense post-Chickamauga controversy. Then Lieutenant General Leonidas Polk was killed at Pine Mountain during the Atlanta Campaign. Another corps commander, the controversial Lieutenant General John Bell Hood, was later promoted. Also, General Hardee was transferred again from corps command in Atlanta's aftermath. Four assignments to corps command in the Army of Tennessee occurred in 1864, yet the army's best fighting general, the man acknowledged to be the "Stonewall Jackson of the West," was never promoted and given the opportunity he had so well earned. Patrick R. Cleburne remained on the sidelines in the top command echelon as the result of a bizarre sequence of events that had as its roots in the Confederate defeat at Chattanooga.[6]

Most important as a result of the stunning events at Chattanooga was a full awareness among the leaders of the Army of Tennessee that the war was being lost. The Confederacy's best blood had been spilled in more than two years of hard fighting, and there was nothing to show for it but the long lists of dead and mangled. An estimated 350,000 Southern casualties had occurred from the war's beginning in 1861 through the end of December 1863, and Confederate-controlled territory had shrunk by about two-thirds. Union armies with increasing numbers were poised to invade the deep interior heartland and ravage what remained of the Confederacy's critical food and supply resources. Morale among Southern soldiers had plummeted, creating a "fatal apathy" in the wake of an endless series of defeats and hardships, and desertion had become rife. Much of the South was in ruins, supplies were faltering, and unless some drastic, significant measure was quickly enacted, the Confederacy would be conquered.[7]

In essence, it was a time of emergency that required immediate and radical measures. Thus, to "save the Confederacy," the new post-Bragg senior commanders of the Army of Tennessee prepared a memorial within several weeks of Hardee taking command. Twenty-nine senior officers signed it, and at its heart was an innovative concept to take back the initiative rather than passively react to the enemy's movements. Specifically, this memorial of December 17, 1863, was a petition to the Confederate Congress asking to increase the military with all white males (involuntarily enlisted) between the ages fifteen to eighteen and fifty to sixty and to add directly to the Confederate army many noncombatant "able-bodied negroes and mulattoes, bond and free," to serve as "cooks, laborers, teamsters, and hospital attendants." The significant increase in troop strength from this action would allow Hardee's army to consolidate manpower resources in the West and retake the offensive.[8]

Among those signing the petition were Lieutenant General Hardee, Major General Cleburne, and Major Generals A. P. Stewart, John C. Breckinridge, Benjamin F. Cheatham, and Thomas C. Hindman. Yet the inspiration for this concept was William J. Hardee himself. Simultaneously, he wrote a letter to Adjutant General Samuel Cooper that this measure would enable offensive operations in Kentucky and Tennessee. He was emphatic that the Army of Tennessee must not remain passive in waiting for the enemy to resume their march south. Yet Hardee's letter was referred to President Davis, who essentially tabled it.[9]

While this memorial to Congress was favorably received by the Confederate legislature in Richmond, and laws were enacted enabling the use of free blacks and slaves in noncombat roles, it proved to be merely a de-facto measure. More significantly, the response from the Davis administration was far different. The president's reply to Hardee was essentially that additional men for the Army of Tennessee was dependent on its units recovering deserters and absentees rather than using radical means to tap general resources. Soon afterward, Hardee was removed from army command and replaced by the controversial General Joe Johnston, a popular choice among the soldiers.[10]

This little-known Hardee initiative came as a direct result of the defeat at Chattanooga and concurrently inspired the more famous, more radical proposal authored by Major General Cleburne, perhaps the Army of Tennessee's most outstanding combat commander. Indeed, Cleburne's proposal of January 2, 1864, came only two weeks later and appears to be a *direct outgrowth* of Hardee's memorial. That evening, at a meeting organized by Hardee at Johnston's headquarters in Dalton, Cleburne addressed the army's corps and division commanders. Few, including the new army commander, had any idea as to the purpose of the gathering. Introduced by Hardee, Cleburne stood before his colleagues and reflected on the army's recent failures. "Through some lack in our system the fruits of our struggles and sacrifices have invariably slipped away from us and left us nothing but long lists of dead and mangled," the general noted. "Our soldiers can see no end to this state of affairs except in our own exhaustion; hence, instead of rising to the occasion, they are sinking into a fatal apathy, growing weary of hardships and slaughters which promise no results." Looking to the future, Cleburne outlined the aftereffects of further Confederate failures and a total capitulation:

The consequences of this condition are showing themselves more plainly every day; restlessness of morals spreading everywhere . . . , desertion spreading to a class of soldiers it never dared to tamper with before; [respect for] military commissions sinking in the estimation of the soldier; our supplies failing; our fireside in ruins. If this state continues much longer we must be subjugated. Every man should endeavor to understand the meaning of subjugation before it is too late. We can give but a faint idea when we say it means the loss of all we now hold most sacred—slaves and all other personal property, lands, homesteads, liberty, justice, safety, pride, manhood. It means that the history of this heroic struggle will be written by the enemy; that our youth will be trained by Northern school teachers; will learn from Northern school books their version of the war; will be impressed by all the influences of history and education to regard our gallant dead as traitors, our maimed veterans as fit objects for derision. It means the crushing of Southern manhood, the hatred of our former slaves.[11]

To the white South, the prospectus of consequences could not be greater. To prevent them, Cleburne then outlined the most controversial measure of the war to date by which Confederate independence might be achieved; a program to enroll slaves as fighting men in the Southern army. The enlistment of blacks as combat soldiers was necessary, said Cleburne, due to three major reasons:

1—The Confederacy's armies were far outnumbered by those of the enemy.

2—There was not enough remaining unused white manpower to replenish the great losses already sustained.

3—Liberated slaves were being fully utilized by the enemy. In fact, as a source of enemy soldiers, vital information, and cooperation with the Yankees, blacks had now become a military liability to the South.

As an untapped resource, the black population of the South represented about 4 million individuals, more than a third of the South's total population. Perhaps a million among these might be considered males of military age, and of that number, according to a later Confederate study, perhaps 680,000 were fit for combat service. Thus, a potential addition of perhaps a half-million men for the Confederacy's armies (which

An image of what could have been. Armed to the teeth, Chickamauga veteran
Andrew Chandler poses with his slave Silas. With the rejection of Major General
Patrick Cleburne's proposal, the latter never had the opportunity to fight as a
Confederate soldier and instead continued to serve as Andrew's body servant
until the end of the war. Andrew Chandler Battaile Collection.

had dwindled to less than that very number) would mark a significant
influx of fighting strength. Despite his great adoration for the troops he
now commanded, Cleburne was willing to relinquish those brigades in
exchange for the promise to train and command an entire division of
black troops. But would slaves fight for the South? If offered freedom, as
well as the freedom of his family so they would have the prospect after
the war of living amid familiar homes and a warm agricultural climate,
Cleburne reasoned that they would be faithful and reliable soldiers. Yet
the idea was so incendiary, so unthinkable in terms of the Southern aristocracy, that it not only came to naught but also seemingly cost Cleburne
the prospect of promotion. Joe Johnston, unlike Hardee, was opposed
to the idea. Moreover, Jefferson Davis, the final arbiter in the matter,
was outraged to learn that such a proposal had been uttered at all.[12]

The president chastised Cleburne in a letter sent to Major General W. H. T. Walker, who had secretly forwarded a copy of the proposal to Richmond, although specifically ordered by Johnston not to do so. Wrote Davis of the Cleburne proposal: "Deeming it to be injurious to the public service that such a subject should be . . . entertained by persons in the public confidence, I have concluded that the best policy will be to avoid all publicity. . . . If kept out of the public journals its ill effect will be much lessened."[13]

That was it. Despite the compelling lessons and dire results from Chattanooga, there would be no last, best resort, at least not until the actual end was at hand. The Cleburne proposal was suppressed, and even discussion of it was prohibited.

Controversy among historians over the years has centered on the idea that arming slaves as soldiers was unacceptable to the white population of the South and thus not a realistic option. Cleburne asserted in his Dalton argument that, "As between the loss of independence and the loss of slavery, we assume that every patriot will freely give up the latter—give up the Negro slave rather than be a slave himself." Having examined many Confederate letters and Southern newspaper accounts on the subject, both pro and con, it is my opinion that the unwillingness of rebel soldiers to accept blacks in the army and fight alongside them is greatly overstated. If Jefferson Davis and the Confederate government had then accepted the idea, supported by the endorsement of well-respected leaders such as Robert E. Lee (who in 1865 urged this policy), there is reason to believe that the program would have succeeded. In the North, for example, there were many men who opposed the introduction of blacks into the Union armies after the Emancipation Proclamation, yet it gave rise to few defections. The prevailing sentiment reflects that many might complain about it and not particularly like it, but collectively they would support the cause as the central government officially directed. That a similar situation would have occurred in the Confederate armies upon the introduction of blacks as soldiers appears likely despite the strong societal implications. Indeed, this very aspect involved heavy irony, for in the early spring of 1865, with certain defeat imminent, reconsideration of using slaves as soldiers in the Southern armies resulted in even Davis endorsing the idea. On March 13 approval by a narrow margin of the Confederate Congress led to active recruitment of blacks as soldiers, and a few black companies were organized in Richmond in early April.[14]

Of course, it already was far too late. By that time Pat Cleburne was dead, technically the victim of a bullet at the Battle of Franklin, Tennessee, but more essentially of the gross inability of the Confederate administration to properly recognize and reward its brilliant if outspoken personnel. As noted historian Joseph T. Glatthaar has observed, in May 1866 journalist Peter W. Alexander suggested that had the Confederacy adopted blacks as soldiers merely a year earlier than they did, the Southern republic might have survived. Even among the most ardent critics of Cleburne's proposal present at the Dalton meeting, his own chief of staff, Major Calhoun Benham, publicly pleaded in 1889 that had the Confederacy embraced the idea, the ensuing "movement . . . doubtless would . . . have changed the destiny of the southern people. The southern people were like the Roman denizens of Utica," he contended, "all for the cause, but unwilling to emancipate and arm their slaves, as Cato wished them to do."[15]

What many have regarded as forward thinking, a military means of survival following the revealing disaster at Chattanooga had turned instead into the bitter ashes of defeat. Cleburne himself had long endorsed a higher power in his humane attitude about the plight of the black man. His personal comments, found in the recently discovered private diary he kept in mid-October 1864, reveal an ingrained compassion for all humanity. Speaking of the black Union troops captured at Dalton and also in blockhouse forts during the Army of Tennessee's post-Atlanta foray into northern Georgia, Cleburne wrote: "Our men were very bitter on the negroes and their [white] officers, hollering to the latter [in jest] to kiss their [black] brothers. A great many of the men think that negroes ought not to be taken prisoner, and in case of a fight I think they [the blacks] will catch it. I told several [that] if the universally acknowledged principle that to a higher scale of intelligence was attached a heavier weight of responsibility be true, [then] . . . whites, who employ, incite, and almost drive these poor creatures into their [Union] armies, are a thousand times more guilty than they [the blacks]." In Cleburne's case, despite his compassion for humanity suffering at the hands of others, it was a pyrrhic victory in April 1865 when his proposal for the widespread use of blacks was finally implemented.[16]

Other results as a consequence of Chattanooga became extremely significant and strongly influenced the course of the war. Of particular significance was the revision in concepts about the exchange of prison-

An irrefutable illustration of the true and immutable role of "black Confederates" as cooks, laborers, teamsters, and servants within rebel armies. These white soldiers, the junior-officer corps of Company H, 57th Georgia Infantry, embodied the rationale for ending the prisoner-exchange system. All three were surrendered to Grant at Vicksburg only to be paroled and subsequently exchanged. They then served with the Army of Tennessee until the end of the war. Bonner Collection, Special Collections, Georgia College Library, Georgia College.

ers of war. After Chattanooga, the ever-observant and tough-minded Ulysses Grant carefully scrutinized the various means for the South to replenish its increasingly severe manpower losses, just as Cleburne did. Accordingly, his strategic concepts involved denying the Confederacy the means of gaining military prowess in its much-depleted armies. Aware that the North could replace its manpower losses far better than the South, in Chattanooga's aftermath he sought to implement a policy that would deny prisoner exchanges as a means of limiting replenishment of the Confederate armies.

His comments to Secretary of State William Seward are revealing: "We ought not to make a single exchange nor release a prisoner on any pretext whatever until the war closes. We have got to fight until the military power of the South is exhausted, and if we release or exchange prisoners

captured it simply becomes a war of extermination." For justification
of his views, Grant only had to cite the Vicksburg prisoner exchanges,
which restored about 30,000 soldiers to the South in the aftermath of
their capture and declared (by Confederate authorities) exchange the
following September. In breaking the Chattanooga siege, Grant's Federals faced eight regiments of Vicksburg veterans at Lookout Mountain,
commanded by the likewise recently exchanged Major General Carter
Stevenson and Brigadier Generals John Moore and Edmund Pettus. At
Missionary Ridge the following day, November 25, those same units,
driven off Lookout Mountain, fought alongside the four regiments of
Brigadier General Alfred Cumming's former Vicksburg POWs. There,
the Cherokee Light Artillery, which lost its guns at Vicksburg, bitterly
defended the ridge with new cannon with which the unit had been out-
fitted a few weeks earlier. The Vicksburg exchange therefore had only
resulted in more dead Union troops. Consequently, in response to pleas
for exchange on the basis of humanitarian issues, Grant wrote in 1864: "It
is hard on our men held in Southern prisons not to exchange them, but
it is humanity to those left in the ranks [who have] to fight our battles.
Every man we hold, when released on parole or otherwise, becomes an
active soldier against us at once, either directly or indirectly. If we commence a system of exchange which liberates all prisoners taken, we will
have to fight on until the whole South is exterminated. If we hold those
caught, they amount to no more than dead men."[17]

Grant's insistence on not releasing enemy prisoners, which prevented
recovery of starving Confederate-held POWs at Andersonville and elsewhere, led to severe criticism and even outrage in the North. Yet his
bulldog determination to exhaust the military resources of the South as
a means of more rapidly ending the war was self-evident. His strength of
character prevailed, and he did not buckle under the enormous pressure
brought to bear upon him on this issue. War is hell, as his friend Sherman
proclaimed, and with the war's end in sight, as witnessed by the events at
Chattanooga, Grant continued to hold fast to his discipline of purpose.

That a crucial point in diminishing resources had been reached by the
South in its ability to fight an effective war was plainly evident within
the Army of Tennessee in December 1863. Initially, it was the enormous
losses of manpower, military equipment, and ordnance that was primarily in view. Official casualties in the Confederate army at Chattanooga
were reported at 361 killed, 2,160 wounded, and 4,146 missing, a total of
6,667 men, about 15 percent of the entire army. Together with their re-

cent personnel loss at Chickamauga of 2,312 killed, 14,674 wounded, and 1,468 missing, a total of 18,454 men, the combined cumulative casualty count of 25,121 represented a crucial manpower decline. In contrast to their reported capture at Chickamauga of sixty-six Union artillery pieces and 23,281 various enemy small arms, the stated Confederate losses at Chattanooga numbered forty cannon and some 6,175 small arms (many of which were largely Enfield rifled muskets and very hard to obtain, being first-class arms run through the Union blockade from England).[18]

This combined loss in manpower, together with shortages of artillery and ordnance, was particularly worrisome and critical to the Confederacy. The ability to replace good weapons became increasingly restricted due to the South's ever-diminishing manufacturing facilities, vastly depleted raw materials, and a lack of experienced personnel to make good quality weapons. Also, the debacle at Chattanooga further exacerbated supply deficiencies of all types. The operational core of the Army of Tennessee, from its prowess to speed of maneuverability, had been greatly diminished. Railroad rolling stock, wagons, and horses (in particular) were in very short supply. Furthermore, the extent of despair and grief within the gray ranks had increased enormously after Vicksburg and Chattanooga. Morale had plummeted due to a lack of food, supplies, and any viable prospect for military success. Some 60,000 deserters and absentees were missing from the Confederacy's armies, and less than 40,000 effectives were present in the Army of Tennessee in January 1864.[19]

Even the turmoil in the Army of Tennessee's command structure after Chattanooga resulted in a sustained crisis that played out during the forthcoming Atlanta Campaign. As a result of Chattanooga, General Johnston, when he assumed command at the end of 1863, found his army so ill prepared for an offensive that he quickly became involved in major controversy with President Davis. Arguments over a viable strategy and despair about the lack of adequate communications created a bitter relationship between the two, which ultimately led to Johnston's replacement by the aggressive John Bell Hood. Even in the public spectrum, the humiliating defeat at Chattanooga led to additional woes, higher taxes to support the war effort, and increased inflation that became rife throughout the Confederacy. Moreover, the prospect of one's family being so deprived of food and sustenance as to face starvation weighed heavily on the attitude of many gray soldiers.

The Chattanooga disaster further affected the popular will to continue with the war for Southern independence, affecting recruiting and the total effort expended by the populace. Even more insidiously, the western theater now loomed increasingly as the area of final decision. The question of Southern independence was being inexorably shaped in the West despite the political attention given to the East.[20]

Indeed, that the western regions continued to remain subordinate in the administration's perspective finally became a crucial aspect in the South's ultimate defeat. Davis's concern that the war turned primarily on events in the East resonated from his central perception that Virginia was involved in the "main shock" of the war.[21]

While the disaster at Chattanooga, from Davis's viewpoint, was an aberration, blamable on the lack of valor by a few critically positioned troops, the essential reality was far different. The whole cloth of the Confederacy was at this point woven of a weakened fabric despite the brilliance of a few subordinate commanders. At the root of the matter was the Confederacy's real deficit—the lack of a winning perspective on the part of key leaders.[22]

In the final analysis, the Confederacy's failure to incorporate the lessons and meaningful results of the Chattanooga Campaign had created both a strategic and practical disaster. While many of the physical losses at Chattanooga had been easy to enumerate in the aftermath—a loss of territory with its abundance of supplies and resources, along with the loss of vital military equipment and ordnance captured or abandoned— what had more significantly occurred was the yielding of an important staging area, allowing the enemy to concentrate its forces and supplies as a springboard for further invasion of the Deep South.

Despite Hardee's earnest pleas, as reflected in his memorial of December 17, 1863, the Army of Tennessee remained after Chattanooga on the strategic defensive, except for Hood's desperation-inspired and ill-fated 1864 raid into Tennessee. Thus, the strategic war inevitably turned, as it then seemed, on the hope of the South prolonging the conflict by stalemate so as to destroy the will of the Northern populace to continue with the enormous losses in both lives and money. Considering that the U.S. presidential election of 1864 was in the offing, this was the South's great last hope—a public referendum on the war that would deny prolonged, attrition-oriented combat. Lincoln's subsequent reelection thus turned, in large measure, on the military success of Union arms within a specific time frame.

Yet the best opportunity for the Confederacy to crush a major Union army—following the huge victory at Chickamauga—had been allowed to dissipate. This had virtually reversed the tide of warfare in the West. Instead of adding to the war weariness in the North, the crowning victory at Chattanooga proved to be an enormous psychological turning point in the struggle. The wasting war of defense, of depleting resources in an ever-constricted territory, and irreplaceable manpower losses had ensured that the key battles around Chattanooga were ultimately ruinous to the South.

It is not that the Atlanta Campaign of 1864 was anticlimatic, but rather that the die had been cast. The impending result of overwhelming numbers and resources was apparent following Chattanooga. The one great shining moment of the Confederacy in the West at Chickamauga had been squandered in ineptitude. The Army of Tennessee was one of the two major military pillars sustaining the Confederacy. The survival of Southern independence depended upon it remaining a viable and effective force. That Chattanooga had thrust a fatal thorn in the South's vital organs is only apparent in retrospect. But the seeds of defeat and despair had been inevitably sewn, and with the fruition of these defects came ultimate despair. As Jefferson Davis admitted at the very end: "If the Confederacy falls, there should be written on its tombstone, 'Died of a theory.'" That theory was all too apparent at Chattanooga, for whereas Abraham Lincoln had replaced William S. Rosecrans with Grant because the former commander did not win, Davis had essentially maintained a "losing" status quo and deferred to Bragg's ultimate influence. The Southern president had ignored a fundamental tenet in the course of human endeavor. Warfare is the means to an end only if successful, for wars are inevitably political in consequence.[23]

At Chattanooga the politics of independence depended on the South being victorious in this key, important battle. They had to turn the military tide and not engage in a war of practical resources—a contest they could not win. After Chattanooga, the grinding, wasting war of attrition prevailed, and the prospects for Confederate independence flickered ever lower, like a solitary candle in a gathering breeze.

APPENDIX A

MEMORIAL

Army of Tennessee, Dec. 17, 1863.

To the Congress of the Confederate States:

In the existing condition of affairs, it is hoped your honorable bodies will pardon the variance from the custom of addressing you from the army. It is done in no spirit of dictation, but under the conscientious conviction that the necessities of the country demand the voices and labors of all, and that delay, even for 30 days, in enacting proper measures may make the present disorders incurable, and the dangers of the moment omnipotent for our destruction.

In our opinion, it is essential to retain, for the term of during the war, without reorganization, the troops now in service; to place in service, immediately, for the same term, all other white males between eighteen and fifty years of age, able to perform any military duty; to provide for placing in service, at the discretion of the president, for the same term, all white males between fifteen and eighteen, and between fifty and sixty years of age; to prohibit substitutions; to prohibit exemptions, except for the necessary civil offices and employments of the Confederate States and of the several States; to prohibit details, except for limited times, and for carrying on works essential to the army; to prohibit discharges, except in cases of permanent disability from all duty; to prohibit leaves and furloughs, except under uniform rules of universal application based, as far as practicable, on length of service and meritorious conduct; to prohibit, to the greatest possible extent, the detail of able bodied officers and men to post, hospital, or other interior duty; and to place in service as cooks, laborers, teamsters, and hospital attendants, with the army and elsewhere, able bodied negroes and mulattoes, bond and free.

These measures, we think, if promptly enacted as laws, so as to give time for organizing and disciplining the new material, would make our armies invincible at the opening of the campaign of next year, and enable us to win back our lost territory, and conquer a peace before that campaign shall be ended.

We further suggest that, in our opinion, the dissatisfaction, apprehended or existing, from short rations, depreciated currency, and the retention of old soldiers in service, might be obviated by allowing bounties, with discriminations in favor of the retained troops, as increase pay, the commutation to enlisted men of rations not issued, and rations, or the value thereof, to officers.

We have the honor to be,

Very respectfully, your obedient servants,

W. J. Hardee, Lieut. General

B. F. Cheatham, Maj. General, C.S.A.

C. L. Stevenson, Maj. General

John C. Breckinridge, Maj. General

John C. Brown, Brig. General

Edm'd W. Pettus, Brig. General

A. W. Reynolds, Brig. General

John R. Jackson, Brig. General

I sign this with the reservation that I approve the President's proposed system of permanent consolidation.

P. R. Cleburne, Maj. General

T. C. Hindman, Maj. General

Jos. H. Lewis, Brig. General

D. C. Govan, Colonel 2d N.C. Regiment,

Commanding Liddell's Brigade

I approve the above, except that portion which has reference to exemptions, and the proposition to place in service those under the age of eighteen and over fifty years of age. I believe the old men and boys would be of more service to the country at home, and that ministers of the gospel, a necessary number of physicians and teachers should be exempt.

M. P. Lowrey, Brig. General

B. J. Hill, Colonel comd'g 35th and 48th

Tenn. Regt's and Polk's Brigade

H. B. Granbury, Colonel comd'g Texas

Brigade, Cleburne's Division

Patton Anderson, Brig. General

A. M. Manigault, Brig. General

J. G. Coltart, Colonel 50th Ala. Reg't

Commanding Deas' Brigade

A. J. Vaughn, Jr. Brig. General

Wm. A. Quarles, Brig. General

Approved, but would favor consolidation of regiments, and no increase of pay.

J. H. Sharp, Col. comd'g Anderson's Brig.

T. Burton Smith, Colonel commanding

Bates' Brig., Breckinridge's Div.

J. J. Finley, Brig. General

Wm. B. Bate, Brig. General

Alex. P. Stewart, Maj. General

H. D. Clayton, Brig. General

O. F. Strahl, Brig. General

R. L. Gibson, Col., comd'g Adams' Brigade

The term "without reorganization" relates to re-election of company and regimental officers only, and not to consolidation of skeleton commands.

T. C. Hindman, Maj. General

[See a letter simultaneously sent by Lieutenant General William J. Hardee to Adjutant General Samuel Cooper in Richmond on December 17, 1863, about the need for offensive operations to regain the lost initiative (*Official Records of the War of the Rebellion,* ser. 1, 31[3]:839–41). These offensive operations were dependent on large numbers of reinforcements for the Army of Tennessee, reported Hardee, who suggested partly stripping other locations and consolidating those troops in northern Georgia.]

PROPOSAL TO MAKE SOLDIERS OF SLAVES AND GUARANTEE
FREEDOM TO ALL LOYAL NEGROES
ADDRESS BY P. R. CLEBURNE, JANUARY 2, 1864
COMMANDING GENERAL, THE CORPS, DIVISION, BRIGADE,
AND REGIMENTAL COMMANDERS
OF THE ARMY OF TENNESSEE

GENERAL: Moved by the exigency in which our country is now placed, we take the liberty of laying before you, unofficially, our views on the present state of affairs. The subject is so grave, and our views so new, we feel it a duty both to you and the cause that before going further we should submit them for your judgement and receive your suggestions in regard to them. We therefore respectfully ask you to give us an expression of your views in the premises. We have now been fighting for nearly three years, have spilled much of our best blood, and lost, consumed, or thrown to the flames an amount of property equal in value to the specie currency of the world. Through some lack in our system the fruits of our struggles and sacrifices have invariably slipped away from us and left us nothing but long lists of dead and mangled. Instead of standing defiantly on the borders of our territory or harrassing those of the enemy, we are hemmed in to-day into less than two-thirds of it, and still the enemy menacingly confronts us at every point with superior forces. Our soldiers can see no end to this state of affairs except in our own exhaustion; hence, instead of rising to the occasion, they are sinking into a fatal apathy, growing weary of hardships and slaughters which promise no results. In this state of things it is easy to understand why there is a growing belief that some black catastrophe is not far ahead of us, and that unless some extraordinary change is soon made in our condition we must overtake it. The consequences of this condition are showing themselves more plainly every day; restlessness of morals spreading everywhere, manifesting itself in the army in a growing disregard for private rights; desertion spreading to a class of soldiers it never dared to tamper with before; military commissions sinking in the estimation of the solder; our supplies failing; our fireside in ruins. If this state continues much longer we must be subjugated. Every man should endeavor to understand the meaning of subjugation before it is too late. We can give but a faint idea when we say it means the loss of all we now hold most sacred—slaves and all other personal property, lands, homesteads, liberty, justice, safety, pride, manhood. It means that the history of this heroic struggle will be written by the enemy; that our youth will be trained by Northern school teachers; will learn from Northern school books their version of the war; will be impressed by all the influences of history and education to regard our gallant dead as traitors, our maimed veterans as fit objects for derision. It means the crushing of Southern manhood, the hatred of our former slaves, who will, on a spy system, be our secret police. The conqueror's policy is to divide the conquered into factions and stir up animosity among them, and in training an army of negroes the North no doubt holds this thought in perspective. We can see three great causes operating to destroy us: First, the inferiority of our armies to those of the enemy in point of numbers; second, the poverty of our single source of supply in comparison with his several sources; third, the fact that slavery, from being one of our chief sources of strength at the commencement of the war, has now become, in a military point of view, one of our chief sources of weakness.

The enemy already opposes us at every point with superior numbers, and is endeavoring to make the preponderance irresistible. President Davis, in his recent message, says the enemy "has recently ordered a large conscription and made a subsequent call for volunteers, to be followed, if ineffectual, by a still further draft." In addition, the President of the United States announces that "he has already in training an army of 100,000 negroes as good as any troops," and every fresh raid he makes and new slice of territory he wrests from us will add to this force. Every soldier in our army already knows and feels our numerical inferiority to the enemy. Want of men in the field has prevented him from reaping the fruits of his victories, and has prevented him from having the furlough he expected after the last reorganization; and when he turns from the wasting armies in the field to look at the source of supply, he finds nothing in the prospect to encourage him. Our single source of supply is that portion of our white men fit for duty and not now in the ranks. The enemy has three sources of supply: First, his own motley population; secondly, our slaves; and thirdly, Europeans whose hearts are fired into a crusade against us by fictitious pictures of the atrocities of slavery, and who meet no hindrance from their Governments in such enterprise, because these Governments are equally antagonistic to the institution. In touching the third cause, the fact that slavery has become a military weakness, we may rouse prejudice and passion, but the time has come when it would be madness not to look at our danger from every point of view, and to probe it to the bottom. Apart from the assistance that home and foreign prejudice against slavery has given to the North, slavery is a source of great strength to the enemy in a purely military point of view, by supplying him with an army from our granaries; but it is our most vulnerable point, a continued embarrassment, and in some respects an insidious weakness. Wherever slavery is once seriously disturbed, whether by the actual presence or the approach of the enemy, or even by a cavalry raid, the whites can no longer with safety to their property openly sympathize with our cause. The fear of their slaves is continually haunting them, and from silence and apprehension many of these soon learn to wish the war stopped on any terms. The next stage is to take the oath to save property, and they become dead to us, if not open enemies. To prevent raids we are forced to scatter our forces, and are not free to move and strike like the enemy; his vulnerable points are carefully selected and fortified depots. Ours are found in every point where there is a slave to set free. All along the lines slavery is comparatively valueless to us for labor, but of great and increasing worth to the enemy for information. It is an omnipresent spy system, pointing out our valuable men to the enemy, revealing our positions, purposes, and resources, and yet acting so safely and secretly that there is no means to guard against it. Even in the heart of our country, where our hold upon this secret espionage is firmest, it waits but the opening fire of the enemy's battle line to wake it, like a torpid serpent, into venomous activity.

In view of the state of affairs what does our country propose to do? In the words of President Davis, "no effort must be spared to add largely to our effective force as promptly as possible. The sources of supply are to be found in restoring to the army all who are improperly absent, putting an end to substitution, modifying the exemption law, restricting details, and placing in the ranks such of the able-bodied men now employed as wagoners, nurses, cooks, and other employes, as are doing service for which the negroes may be found competent." Most of the men improperly absent, together with many of the exempts and men having substitutes, are now without the Confederate lines and cannot be calculated on. If all the exempts capable of bearing arms were enrolled, it will give us the boys below eighteen, the men above forty-five, and those persons who are left at home to meet the wants of the country and the army, but this modification of the exemption law will remove from the fields and manufactories most of the skill that directed agriculture and mechanical labor, and, as stated by the President, "details will have to be made to meet the wants of the country," thus sending many of the men to be derived from this source back to their homes again. Independently of this, experience proves that striplings and men above conscript age break down and swell the sick lists more than they do the ranks. The portion now in our lines of the class who have substitutes is not on the whole a hopeful element, for the motives that created it must have been stronger than patriotism, and these motives added to what many of them will call breach of faith, will cause some to be not forthcoming, and others to be unwilling and discontented soldiers. The remaining sources mentioned by the President have been so closely pruned in the Army of Tennessee that they will be found not to yield largely. The supply from all these sources, together with what we now have in the field, will exhaust the white race, and though it should greatly exceed expectations and put us on an equality with the enemy, or even give us temporary advantages, still we have no reserve to meet unexpected disaster or to supply a protracted struggle.

Like past years, 1864 will diminish our ranks by the casualties of war, and what source of repair is there left us? We therefore see in the recommendation of the President only a temporary expedient, which at best will leave us twelve months hence in the same predicament we are in now. The President attempts to meet only one of the depressing causes mentioned; for the other two he has proposed no remedy. They remain to generate lack of confidence in our final success, and to keep us moving down hill as heretofore. Adequately to meet the causes which are now threatening ruin to our country, we propose, in addition to a modification of the President's plans, that we retain in service for the war all troops now in service, and that we immediately commence training a large reserve of the most courageous of our slaves, and further that we guarantee freedom within a reasonable time to every slave in the South who shall remain true to the Confederacy in this war. As between the loss of independence and the loss of slavery, we assume that every patriot will freely give up the latter—give up the negro slave rather than be a slave himself. If we are correct in this assumption it only remains to show how this great national sacrifice is, in all human probabilities, to change the current of success and sweep the invader from our country.

Our country has already some friends in England and France, and there are strong motives to induce these nations to recognize and assist us, but they cannot assist without helping slavery, and to do this would be in conflict with their policy for the last quarter of a century. England has paid hundreds of millions to emancipate her West India slaves and break up the slave trade. Could she now consistently spend her treasure to reinstate slavery in this country? But this barrier once removed, the sympathy and the interests of these and other nations will accord with our own, and we may expect from them both moral support and material aid. One thing is certain, as soon as the great sacrifice to independence is made and known in foreign countries there will be a complete change of front in our favor of the sympathies of the world. This measure will deprive the North of the moral and material aid which it now derives from the bitter prejudices with which foreigners view the institution, and its war, if continued, will henceforth be so despicable in their eyes that the source of recruiting will be dried up. It will leave the enemy's negro army no motive to fight for, and will exhaust the source from which it has been recruited. The idea that it is their special mission to war against slavery has held growing sway over the Northern people for many years, and has at length ripened into an armed and bloody crusade against it. This baleful superstition has so far supplied them with a courage and constancy not their own. It is the most powerful and honestly entertained plank in their war platform. Knock this away and what is left? A bloody ambition for more territory, a pretended veneration for the Union, which one of their own most distinguished orators (Doctor [Henry Ward] Beecher in his Liverpool speech) openly avowed was only used as a stimulus to stir up the anti-slavery crusade, and lastly the poisonous and selfish interests which are the fungus growth of war itself. Mankind may fancy it a great duty to destroy slavery, but what interest can mankind have in upholding this remainder of the Northern war platform? Their interests and feelings will be diametrically opposed to it. The measure we propose will strike dead all John Brown fanaticism, and will compel the enemy to draw off altogether, or in the eyes of the world to swallow the Declaration of Independence without the sauce and disguise of philanthropy. This delusion of fanaticism at an end, thousands of Northern people will have leisure to look at home and to see the gulf of despotism into which they themselves are rushing.

The measure will at one blow strip the enemy of foreign sympathy and assistance, and transfer them to the South; it will dry up two of his three sources of recruiting; it will take from his negro army the only motive it could have to fight against the South, and will probably cause much of it to desert over to us; it will deprive his cause of the powerful stimulus of fanaticism, and will enable him to see the rock on which his so-called friends are now piloting him. The immediate effect of the emancipation and enrollment of negroes on the military strength of the South would be: To enable us to have armies numerically superior to those of the North, and a reserve of any size we might think necessary; to take the offensive, move forward, and forage on the enemy. It would open to us in prospective another and almost untouched source of supply, and furnish us with the means of preventing temporary disaster, and carrying on a protracted struggle. It would instantly remove all the vulnerability, embarrassment, and inherent weakness which result from slavery. The approach of the enemy would no longer find every household surrounded by spies; the fear that sealed the master's lips and the avarice that has, in many cases, tempted him practically to desert us would alike be removed. There would be no recruits awaiting the enemy with open arms, no complete history of every neighborhood with ready guides, no fear of insurrection in the rear, or anxieties for the fate of loved ones when our armies moved forward. The chronic irritation of hope deferred would be joyfully ended with the negro, and the sympathies of his whole race would be due to his native South. It would restore confidence in an early termination of the war with all its inspiring consequences, and even if contrary to all expectations the enemy should succeed in overrunning the South, instead of finding a cheap, ready-made means of holding it down, he would find a common hatred and thirst for vengeance, which would break into acts at every favorable opportunity, would prevent him from settling on our lands, and render the South a very unprofitable conquest. It would remove forever all selfish taint from our cause and place independence above every question of property. The very magnitude of the sacrifice itself, such as no nation has ever voluntarily made before, would appall our enemies, destroy his spirit and his finances, and fill our hearts with a pride and singleness of purpose which would clothe us with new strength in battle. Apart from all other aspects of the question, the necessity for more fighting men is upon us. We can only get a sufficiency by making the negro share the danger and hardships of the war. If we arm and train him and make him fight for the country in her hour of dire distress, every consideration of principle and policy demand that we should set him and his whole race who side with us free. It is a first principle with mankind that he who offers his life in defense of the State should receive from her in return his freedom and his happiness, and we believe in acknowledgement of this principle. The Constitution of the Southern States has reserved to their respective governments the power to free slaves for meritorious services to the State. It is politic besides. For many years, ever since the agitation of the subject of slavery commenced, the negro has been dreaming of freedom, and his vivid imagination has surrounded that condition with so many gratifications that it has become the paradise of his hopes. To attain it he will tempt dangers and difficulties not exceeded by the bravest soldiers in the field. The hope of freedom is perhaps the only moral incentive that can be applied to him in his present condition. It would be preposterous then to expect him to fight against it with any degree of enthusiasm, therefore we must bind him to our cause by no doubtful bonds; we must leave no possible loop-hole for treachery to creep in. The slaves are dangerous now, but armed, trained, and collected in an army they would be a thousand fold more dangerous; therefore when we make soldiers of them we must make free men of them beyond all question, and thus enlist their sympathies also. We can do this more effectually than the North can now do, for we can give the negro not only his own freedom, but that of his wife and child, and can secure it to him in his old home. To do this, we must immediately make his marriage and parental relations sacred in the eyes of the law and forbid their sale. The past legislation of the South concedes that a large free middle class of negro blood, between the master and slave, must sooner or later destroy the institution. If, then, we touch the institution at all, we would do best to make the most of it, and by emancipating the whole race upon reasonable terms, and within such reasonable time as will prepare both races for the change, secure to ourselves all the advantages, and to our enemies all the disadvantages that can arise, both at home and abroad, from such a sacrifice. Satisfy the negro that if he faithfully adheres to our standard during the war he shall receive his freedom and that of his race. Give him as an earnest of our intentions such immediate immunities as will impress him with our sincerity and be in keeping with his new condition, enroll a portion of his class as soldiers of the Confederacy, and we change the race from a dreaded weakness to a position of strength.

Will the slaves fight? The helots of Sparta stood their masters good stead in battle. In the great sea fight of Lepanto where the Christians checked forever the spread of Mohammedianism over Europe, the galley slaves of portions of the fleet were promised freedom, and called on to fight at a critical moment of the battle. They fought well, and civilization owes much to those brave galley slaves. The negro slaves of Saint Domingo, fighting for freedom, defeated their white masters and the French troops sent against them. The negro slaves of Jamaica revolted, and under the name of Maroons held the mountains against their masters for 150 years, and the experience of this war has been so far that half-trained negroes have fought as bravely as many other half-trained Yankees. If, contrary to the training of a lifetime, they can be made to face and fight bravely against their former masters, how much more probable is it that with the allurement of a higher reward, and led by those masters, they would submit to discipline and face dangers.

We will briefly notice a few arguments against this course. It is said Republicanism cannot exist without the institution. Even were this true, we prefer any form of government of which the Southern people may have the moulding, to one forced upon us by a conqueror. It is said the white man cannot perform agricultural labor in the South. The experience of this army during the heat of summer from Bowling Green, Ky., to Tupelo, Miss., is that the white man is healthier when doing reasonable work in the open field than at any other time. It is said an army of negroes cannot be spared from the fields. A sufficient number of slaves is now administering to luxury alone to supply the place of all we need, and we believe it would be better to take half the able-bodied men off a plantation than to take the one master mind that economically regulated its operations. Leave some of the skill at home and take some of the muscle to fight with. It is said slaves will not work after they are freed. We think necessity and a wise legislation will compel them to labor for a living. It is said it will cause terrible excitement and some disaffection from our cause. Excitement is far preferable to the apathy which now exists, and disaffection will not be among the fighting men. It is said slavery is all we are fighting for, and if we give it up we give up all. Even if this were true, which we deny, slavery is not all our enemies are fighting for. It is merely the pretense to establish sectional superiority and a more centralized form of government, and to deprive us of our rights and liberties. We have now briefly proposed a plan which we believe will save our country. It may be imperfect, but in all human probability it would give us our independence. No objection ought to outweigh it which is not weightier than independence. If it is worthy of being put in practice it ought to be mooted quickly before the people, and urged earnestly by every man who believes in its efficacy. Negroes will require much training; training will require time, and there is danger that this concession to common sense may come too late.

P. R. CLEBURNE, major-general, commanding division;

D. C. GOVAN, brigadier-general;

JOHN E. MURRAY, colonel Fifth Arkansas;

G. F. BAUCUM, colonel Eighth Arkansas;

PETER SNYDER, lieutenant-colonel, commanding Sixth and Seventh Arkansas;

E. WARFIELD, lieutenant-colonel, Second Arkansas;

M. P. LOWREY, brigadier-general;

A. B. HARDCASTLE, colonel Thirty-second and Forty-fifth Mississippi;

F. A. ASHFORD, major Sixteenth Alabama;

JOHN W. COLQUITT, colonel First Arkansas;

RICH J. PERSON, major Third and Fifth Confederate;

G. S. DEAKINS, major Thirty-fifth and Eighth Tennessee;

J. H. COLLETT, captain, commanding Seventh Texas;

J. H. KELLY, brigadier-general, commanding Cavalry Division.

[While not present at the Dalton meeting, Major General Benjamin Franklin Cheatham and Brigadier General Lucius E. Polk had previously offered Cleburne their spoken word of support for the proposal.]

ACKNOWLEDGMENTS

For the generous assistance of various individuals, I am particularly grateful. Evan Jones provided the inspiration and much-needed editing. He is to be commended for the significant effort he has made in making this project a reality. William Lee White's generosity in making available portions of the recently discovered Patrick Cleburne diary of October 5–16, 1864, reflects the true spirit of sharing valuable information that is so important in the attempt to record and interpret our historical heritage. Lee's forthcoming publication of this Cleburne material should be welcomed by all. Various books and publications on the events at and around Chattanooga have been consulted, and many are listed in the endnotes. The effort to study and publicize the significant story of Chattanooga continues, and with each new project, we are more aware of the components of a truly remarkable and fascinating story. Thanks are due to all who perpetuate this process.

NOTES

1. Lyman S. Widney, 34th Illinois Infantry, letter, Nov. 10, 1863, Chickamauga and Chattanooga National Military Park Library, Ft. Oglethorpe, Ga.; Cecil Fogg, 36th Ohio Infantry, letter, Aug. 23, 1863, Wiley Sword Collection, Suwanee, Ga.

2. U.S. War Department, *The War of the Rebellion: A Compilation of the Official Records of the Union and Confederate Armies,* 128 vols. (Washington, D.C.: GPO, 1880–1901), ser. 1, 30(1):148 (hereinafter cited as *OR;* all citations to series 1 unless otherwise specified); U. S. Grant, *The Papers of Ulysses S. Grant,* ed. John Y. Simon, John F. Marszalek, et al., 31 vols. to date (Carbondale: Southern Illinois University Press, 1967–), 9:480, 491.

3. D. R. Lucas, *New History of the 99th Indiana* (Rockford, Ill., 1900), 162.

4. Albert Castel, *Decision in the West: The Atlanta Campaign of 1864* (Lawrence: University Press of Kansas, 1992), 565.

5. *OR,* 31(2):681,682,774,775,799 31(3):754,764,767. For a consolidated view of the Bragg-Davis relationships in late 1863–early 1864, see Wiley Sword, *Mountains Touched with Fire: Chattanooga Besieged, 1863* (New York: St. Martin's, 1995), 353ff.

6. Howell Purdue and Elizabeth Purdue, *Pat Cleburne, Confederate General* (Hillsboro, Tex.: Hill College Press, 1973), 267ff.

7. This estimate of 350,000 casualties is based on the figures reported in Thomas L. Livermore, *Numbers and Losses in the Civil War in America, 1861–65* (1900; reprint, Bloomington: Indiana University Press, 1957), 48; Army of Tennessee, memorial, Dec. 17, 1863, original printed copy in Wiley Sword Collection, Suwanee, Ga. Livermore compiles the Confederate losses for two years at 286,981 based upon 94,000 killed and mortally wounded, 59,297 dead from disease, 82,922 desertions, and 57,762 discharged. The memorial was prepared under Lt. Gen. William J. Hardee's lead and signed by twenty-nine senior Confederate commanders.

8. Army of Tennessee, memorial, Dec. 17, 1863.

9. Ibid.

10. Ibid. For a comprehensive view of this document, see Wiley Sword, *Courage under Fire* (New York: St. Martin's, 2007), 249–60; and also *Blue & Gray Magazine* 23, no. 5 (Winter 2007): 29ff.

11. Purdue and Purdue, *Pat Cleburne,* 267–83, 453–61.

12. In a speech Confederate secretary of state Judah Benjamin estimated that blacks in the South could offer 680,000 fresh troops to Confederate arms. See *Richmond Daily Examiner,* Feb. 10, 1865; Purdue and Purdue, *Pat Cleburne,* 267–83, 453–61; and Sword, *Courage under Fire,* 252, 257.

13. Purdue and Purdue, *Pat Cleburne,* 272–77.

14. Ibid., 457. For a profound discussion of the consequences of the Confederacy arming slaves, see William W. Freehling, *The South vs. The South: How Anti-Confederate Southerners Shaped the Course of the Civil War* (New York: Oxford University Press, 2001), 188–96. Another equally fascinating study is Bruce Levine, *Confederate Emancipation: Southern Plans to Free and Arm Slaves during the Civil War* (New York: Oxford University Press, 2007). For a superb look at slaves training to be soldiers in the Army of Northern Virginia, see Joseph T. Glatthaar, *General Lee's Army: From Victory to Collapse* (New York: Free Press, 2008), 452–55.

15. Peter Wellington Alexander, "The State of the Confederate Cause," May 17, 1866, Peter Wellington Alexander Papers, Columbia University Rare Book and Manuscript Library, New York, used in Glatthaar, *General Lee's Army,* 454. Alexander had a unique perspective on the downward spiral of Confederate fortunes. Throughout the conflict, he had traveled the frontlines of Confederate movements, covering important military campaigns in both the eastern and western theater. Calhoun Benham, *Kennesaw Gazette,* May 15, 1889.

16. Patrick R. Cleburne Diary, Oct. 14, 1864, William Lee White Collection, Villanow, Ga.

17. *OR,* ser. 2, 7(1):607, 614, 615.

18. *OR,* 31(1):228, 233, 31(2):40–43, 99, 100, 682–84; Livermore, *Numbers and Losses,* 105–108.

19. Livermore, *Numbers and Losses,* 45–47; E. C. Dawes, "The Confederate Strength in the Atlanta Campaign," in Robert Underwood Johnson and Clarence Clough Buel, eds., *Battles and Leaders of the Civil War,* 4 vols. (1887; reprint, New York: Castle, 1956), 4:281–82. For another marvelous study of the strength of the army during this time, see Keith S. Bohannon, "'Witness the Redemption of the Army': Reenlistments in the Confederate Army of Tennessee, January–March 1864," in Lesley J. Gordon and John C. Inscoe, eds., *Inside the Confederate Nation: Essays in Honor of Emory M. Thomas* (Baton Rouge: Louisiana State University Press, 2005).

20. Sword, *Mountains Touched with Fire,* 357–59.

21. Dunbar Rowland, ed., *Jefferson Davis, Constitutionalist, His Letters, Papers, and Speeches,* vol. 6 (Jackson: Mississippi Department of Archives and History, 1923), 529–31.

22. Ibid., 95–96.

23. Jefferson Davis, *The Rise and Fall of the Confederate Government,* 2 vols. (1881; reprint, New York: D. Appleton, 1958), 1:518.

CHAPTER 9

AMBROSE BIERCE, CHICKAMAUGA, AND WAYS TO WRITE HISTORY

STEPHEN CUSHMAN

Valor, *n.* A soldierly compound of vanity, duty, and the gambler's hope.

"Why have you halted?" roared the commander of a division at Chickamauga, who had ordered a charge; "move forward, sir, at once."

"General," said the commander of the delinquent brigade, "I am persuaded that any further display of valor by my troops will bring them into collision with the enemy."

— *The Devil's Dictionary* (1911)

Writing on August 17, 1892, to Blanche Partington, one of his many disciples, from St. Helena, California, the Napa Valley town where he sought relief from chronic asthma (and where one can stay where he did, now the Ambrose Bierce House Bed and Breakfast, a structure built on Main Street in 1872), Ambrose Bierce, at the age of fifty, responded to the young woman's request for a list of books to read with, among others, this sentence: "Read Longinus, Herbert Spencer on Style, Pope's 'Essay on Criticism' (don't groan—the detractors of Pope are not always to have things their own way)[, and] Lucian on the writing of history—though you need not write history."[1] Even this small sample of recommended works reveals much about Bierce's literary sensibility, its layers of neo-classicism and admiration for British models, the latter fueled in part by his residence in England from 1872 to 1875 and the former the impressive result of his autodidactic exertions, which led him to brandish his familiarity with Latin, though not with Greek. Although any one of the authors in his list could lead productively to discussion of Bierce the writer, the last name, Lucian, offers the swiftest access to Bierce's complicated dual relation as both participant in and subsequent chronicler of the events of September 19 and 20, 1863, near Chickamauga Creek in North Georgia.

Footnotes to the contrary notwithstanding, Lucian was not a Greek, though he wrote in Greek, nor was he merely a satirist anymore than Alexander Pope or Bierce himself, if by "satirist" one means a writer who only attacks and lampoons.[2] Born in Syria in the second century A.D., Lucian of Samosata lived in the Roman Empire at its height under Marcus Aurelius. The work to which Bierce refers in his letter to Partington—its transliterated Greek title is *PÇs dei historian syngraphein,* which means literally "How it is binding to write history together" or "How one must compose history," though usually translated "How to Write History" or "The Way to Write History"—considers the writing of history in the context of recent warring with the Parthians over Armenia. The history of historiography around the Mediterranean shows it to be the offspring of war, and the conflict with the Parthians, according to Lucian, uncorked a spate of new histories of the fighting, so many of which were bad that he must first show his addressee, Philo, in what ways they offend and then give his prescriptions for writing good history: *"Well,* I may be told, *you have now a clear field; the thorns and brambles have all been extirpated, the débris of others' buildings has been carted off, the rough places have been made smooth; come, do a little construction yourself, and show that you are not only good at destroying, but capable of yourself planning a model, in which criticism itself shall find nothing to criticize."*[3]

"Come, do a little construction yourself, and show that you are not only good at destroying." This is the ethos of true satire, as practiced by Lucian and his student Ambrose Bierce, and it explains much of what readers of Bierce describe under the heading of his contradictions. If in his writings, epistolary, journalistic, or fictional, he was a fierce and feared destroyer, he was also a tirelessly productive builder. But this congruence of Lucian and Bierce as constructive satirists is not the only one. When it comes to presenting the ingredients of good history, Lucian not only prescribes ingredients Bierce uses but also describes traits Bierce embodies. Although no one who has published a book on Bierce seems to have taken his advice to Partington and read Lucian's twenty-five pages on the writing of history in order to understand Brigadier General William B. Hazen's young topographical officer at the Battle of Chickamauga, not to mention the older man who later wrote about that battle in a number of ways, Lucian's short work contains passage after

passage that resonates sonorously with Bierce's historical outlook and
authorial credo. Let three brief examples suffice:

> Well then, my perfect historian must start with two indispensable quali-
> fications; the one is political insight, the other the faculty of expression;
> the first is a gift of nature, which can never be learnt; the second should
> have been acquired by long practice, unremitting toil, and loving study of
> the classics. . . .
>
> "He must not be weak either at understanding or at making himself un-
> derstood, but a man of penetration, a capable administrator—potentially,
> that is,—with a soldierly spirit (which does not however exclude the civil
> spirit), and some military experience; at the least he must have been in
> camp, seen troops drilled or manoevred, know a little about weapons and
> military engines, the differences between line and column, cavalry and
> infantry tactics (with the reasons for them), frontal and flank attacks; in
> a word, none of your armchair strategists relying wholly on hearsay. . . .
>
> "For history, I say again, has this and this only for its own; if a man will
> start upon it, he must sacrifice to no God but Truth; he must neglect all
> else; his sole rule and unerring guide is this—to think not of those who are
> listening to him now, but of the yet unborn who shall seek his converse."[4]

Bierce's qualification that Partington should read Lucian "though you
need not write history" suggests that, for her, the value of reading the
ancient author would reside in his exhortations to seek truth, to ignore
the self-interested responses of a contemporary audience, and to cul-
tivate the faculty of expression, especially important to Bierce, who in
1909 published a little book entitled *Write It Right: A Little Blacklist of
Literary Faults.* All these exhortations would speak to him too, of course,
but Lucian's requirement that the historian also have some military
experience would exclude Bierce's young female correspondent and en-
dorse her mentor's own soldierly credentials. Bierce liked to flash those
credentials, as we shall see shortly, and many of his biographers and
literary critics have been somewhat hypnotized by them, as though his
presence as a Union staff officer near the northern end of Poe Field on
the long afternoon of Saturday, September 19, 1863, and on Snodgrass
Hill during the even longer afternoon of the following day sufficed to
put his various representations of Chickamauga beyond the reach of
the kind of exacting historical cross-examination to which Lucian, like
Bierce himself, put so many other historical writings. But if we are to
honor the rigorous historiographic ethic that Lucian urges and Bierce

Ambrose Bierce in California shortly after the Civil War.
Elkhart County Historical Museum.

endorses, then we must sacrifice to no god but truth, even when truth complicates the image of Bierce as unimpeachably truthful witness.

A little more than two weeks before he wrote her to recommend Lucian, Bierce wrote Partington from Angwin, California, also in Napa County, to lecture her on the difference between literature as art, in which he firmly believed, and literature as an instrument of social reform, which he just as firmly rejected. His lecture includes this Lucian-worthy declaration: "The love of truth is good enough motive for me when I wrote of my fellow men."[5] As it subsequently turned out, Bierce's unapologetic identification of his own motives with truthfulness anticipated that of Archibald Gracie, whose painstakingly meticulous study *The Truth about Chickamauga* appeared in December 1911. What makes these two versions of self-proclaimed truthfulness more than coincidental is that Bierce corresponded with Gracie during the writing of his book, and their correspondence, from which only one item has received any appreciable attention from Bierce scholars, is worth a closer look.

Son of Brigadier General Archibald Gracie Jr., who commanded Gracie's Brigade of Preston's Division of Buckner's Corps of Longstreet's Left Wing of Bragg's Army of Tennessee at Chickamauga and was later killed at Petersburg, the younger Gracie made clear from the outset that he was a man on a mission, which was to "show how the history of Chickamauga has ever since the day it was fought been made a conspiracy for the silencing and suppression of the truth."[6] According to Gracie, this historiographic conspiracy included "the fact that the Confederate soldier's testimony was thus thrown out and no attempt made to reconcile his statements with the truth." In his opening chapter, which bears the title "Elimination of False History," he continued, "and (*hinc illae lachrymae* ['hence those tears': quotation from Roman playwright Terence]) it was due thereto that my work was undertaken, and an effort made to find the truth, first, from the Federal reports themselves, then from the Confederate, and reconcile the two."[7] As Ralph Waldo Emerson proclaimed in 1841 in his essay "Self-Reliance," "If I know your sect I anticipate your argument," and anyone reading only this far in Gracie's book could be excused for anticipating that an author lamenting the suppression of Confederate testimony, who was also the son of a Confederate general, probably wrote a book devoted to tipping the balance back toward a Southern perspective, especially when the reader finds, twenty-five pages later, that "the heart of this hydra-headed monster of untruth . . . comes from the newspaper writings and similar publications of Colonel Henry V. Boynton," who at Chickamauga commanded the 35th Ohio, Third Brigade (Van Derveer), Third Division (Brannan), XIV Corps (Thomas).[8]

But Gracie turned out to be a truer student of the truth, and his book, which contains fold-out maps that anticipated Peter Cozzens's later designation of the three hills comprising Horseshoe Ridge as "Numbers One, Two, and Three," undertook to correct Boynton, author of *The National Military Park, Chickamauga-Chattanooga, An Historical Guide* (1895) and later "called upon to fill the office of Historian of the Park Commission," not to promote a Confederate perspective but rather to clean up the "awful mess" the colonel made because of his desire to promote the importance of the 35th Ohio on Horseshoe Ridge.[9] Furthermore, in the process of making such an awful historiographic mess, Boynton distracted attention from units that actually deserved credit, as Gracie proposed to demonstrate by careful examination of *The War of the Rebellion: A Compilation of the Official Records of the Union and Confederate Armies,* recently completed in 1901.[10] According to him, the colonel's chief fault as historian was that he did not bother to consult the *Official Records.*

Among the units receiving considerable attention from Gracie were the 9th Indiana (Suman), Bierce's own original regiment in the Second Brigade (Hazen), Second Division (Palmer), XXI Corps (Crittenden); and the 18th Battery (Aleshire), Ohio Light Artillery, belonging to the First Brigade (Whitaker), First Division (Steedman), Reserve Corps (Granger).[11] This battery included Lieutenant Albert Sherwood Bierce, Ambrose's immediately older sibling in a family of thirteen children, the last three of whom did not survive childhood. In his preface Gracie thanked "surviving comrades of the Army of the Cumberland with whom I have had an exhaustive correspondence," to which the two Bierce brothers contributed.[12] A portion of a letter from Albert appeared among the endnotes to Gracie's book, and Ambrose wrote the author a letter, dated March 9, 1911, that only found its way to publication in 1998, though subsequently reprinted in two other books.[13] It is to this letter that we now turn.

At first glance, and considered out of context as it appears in the books that contain it, the letter to Gracie would seem to offer champions of Bierce many familiar satisfactions, for the veteran who had read Lucian undertook to set the younger historian straight without troubling to do so gently. Including in his first sentence the bold opening gambit, "I infer

that you are really desirous of the truth," Bierce proceeded to deliver
that truth, in the process condescending to admonish Gracie about the
need for good historiographic sportsmanship: "The historians who have
found, and will indubitably continue to find, general acceptance are those
who have most generously affirmed the good faith and valor of their enemies. All this, however, you have of course considered. But consider it
again."[14] Many readers of Bierce know him as so dazzlingly offensive, in
both senses of that word, that they may not always consider how sometimes his aggressive offensiveness also may have functioned to defend
his own limitations and shortcomings. Examined a little more closely,
and in conjunction with other documents, his letter to Gracie turns out
to be not a shining moment of historical instruction, but something of
an embarrassment.

First, if ever there has been a military historian who needed no lecture
on how to affirm the good faith and valor of his enemies generously, it
is Archibald Gracie. We do not know the nature of all his consultations
with Bierce, and Bierce probably would not have read everything Gracie
wrote about Chickamauga before he published it, but subsequent letters
from Gracie to Bierce clearly show the former working strenuously to
give full credit where credit was due, as does this representative sentence
from his book: "This, my first volume, while intended to preserve the
truth and record of great deeds, is also devoted to doing justice to the
memories of those Federal soldiers whose records have suffered by most
undeserved aspersions cast upon their conduct and character."[15] Bierce
saw things differently, however, and warning Gracie against history
written by "bad losers" (his phrase), he continued, "your strange views
of Thomas, Granger, and Brannan, and some of the events in which they
figured, are (to me) so obviously erroneous that I find myself unable to
account for them on the hypothesis of an entirely open mind."[16]

But the mind not entirely open appears to have been Bierce's, when
one considers, for one example, that Gracie thought enough of his enemies to use a photograph of Thomas as the frontispiece to his book
and that, for another, with respect to the question of Granger's presence
or absence on Horseshoe Ridge during the afternoon of September 20,
Gracie worked diligently to supplement the *Official Records* with extensive correspondence documented in long endnotes.[17] Furthermore,
more-recent accounts of Granger's behavior, after marching his troops
to Thomas's support, suggest that this balanced statement by Gracie is
wholly justified: "After General Granger had performed his great service

in saving the army under Thomas by his timely arrival, it does not appear from our study of the Records and from our information from authoritative sources, that his subsequent services were at all creditable."[18]

This kind of criticism of Granger could have posed problems for Bierce. For one thing, not only was the general Albert Bierce's corps commander, but, according to Cozzens, the general also helped Albert's battery "place his pieces and then set to work aiming and firing them."[19] With his own commanding general eagerly pitching in to the same gritty work he was doing, how could Albert avoid the conclusion in his unpublished letter to his brother, dated March 29, 1911, "I believe there were some officers in high command who did not do their whole duty at Chickamauga but Thomas, Granger, and Brannan were not in that class surely."[20] That Granger might have been better employed closer to his own troops extending the precarious Union right on Horseshoe Ridge does not seem to have occurred to either Bierce. For another thing, criticism of Granger could have taken some of the shine off Ambrose's "happy distinction of a discoverer" of Granger's approach toward Snodgrass Hill (Bierce was the only person on Snodgrass Hill to notice the approach of Steedman's two-brigade division—or amid so many intensities, could be sure he was the first to do so?), a distinction he later represented in the "little unmilitary sketch" he lent Gracie, "A Little of Chickamauga," first published in the *San Francisco Examiner* (April 24, 1898).[21] To be sure, it is a far better distinction to discover an approaching hero, or to claim that one has, than it is to discover an approaching commander whose record later turns out to be mixed.

A second questionable aspect of Bierce's letter involves place names and topography, the veteran's specialty, as he was quick to remind Gracie with his credentials: "I passed almost the entire afternoon at and near the Snodgrass house, with nothing to do but look on, and, as a topographical officer, with some natural interest in, and knowledge of, 'the lay of the land.'" The point in question was the identification of the three-hill ridge to the south and west of the Snodgrass house: "Hazen's fire was at no time directed toward what I think you call Horse-shoe Ridge," then after an intervening sentence, "The ridge immediately south of the Snodgrass house (I do not know if that is the one that you call Horse-shoe Ridge) was at no time, until after nightfall, occupied by the Confederates, nor was any other part of the ridges that our forces had held."[22]

What these two sentences show is that Bierce's credentials as a witness to events on Snodgrass Hill did not also make him a thorough reader of writings about those actions. In fairness to him, the ridge now designated as Horseshoe Ridge on most recent maps of the battle did not have that name at the time of the fighting, or Bierce most certainly would have known it. It was the Battle of Chickamauga that christened this particular topographic feature, as so many other battles produced so many other capitalized names of topographic features on other fields in both the eastern and western theaters. But when did the name emerge? Cozzens comments, "From the Snodgrass hill west to the Dry Valley road was a series of hills and ridges that after the battle become known collectively as Horseshoe Ridge."[23] But how long after? Was it in 1911, when Gracie took a long paragraph's worth of pains to warn his reader against "the pitfalls of nomenclature": "Let him not be misled by any such general terms as 'Snodgrass Hill,' or the 'Snodgrass Hill Line.'" Instead, "Let him use the term '*Horseshoe Ridge*.'"[24] If this moment marked the birth of the name, certainly Bierce could be excused for not knowing it. But it did not.

The name "Horseshoe Ridge" appeared in Granger's reports of the battle, dated September 30, 1863, and his handling of it with quotation marks shows the freshness of the designation:

> At about 1 P.M. I reported to General Thomas. His forces were at that time stationed upon the brow of and holding a "horseshoe ridge." The enemy were pressing him hard in front and endeavoring to turn both of his flanks.
>
> To the right of this position was a ridge running east and west, and nearly at right angles therewith. Upon this the enemy were just forming. They also had possession of a gorge in the same, through which they were rapidly moving in large masses, with the design of falling upon the right flank and rear of the forces upon the Horseshoe Ridge.[25]

We cannot know for sure, though perhaps we can imagine, when the first soldier or officer pointed to the ridgeline and compared it to a horseshoe, but we can and do know that the name was in official circulation ten days after the battle. Again in fairness to Bierce, he could not have had access to Granger's reports in the *Official Records* until 1890, but that date still would have given him twenty-one years until his correspondence with Gracie. Meanwhile, Granger need not have been Bierce's only source for the name. Brigadier General John B. Turchin, Third Brigade, Fourth Division, XIV Corps, used it throughout his 1888 book, *Chickamauga,* for example, and seven years later it appeared in Boynton's historical guide to the newly created national military park.[26]

Whatever the written antecedents of the name "Horseshoe Ridge," one cannot help wondering what a self-described topographical officer, "with nothing to do but look on" in the vicinity of two generals, Thomas and Granger, was doing with his "natural interest in, and knowledge of, 'the lay of the land,'" if he was not seizing immediately on every scrap of newly minted nomenclature adhering to that lay of the land. But behind this wondering looms a larger question about Bierce and his ways of writing, and judging the writing of, history: Is it enough to have been there? In his letter to Gracie, he assumed the posture of affirming that it is, and many of his readers and critics seem to concur, if their ready acceptance of his versions of events is any indication. But Bierce himself has written one of the great passages on the limitations that inevitably circumscribe the perceptions of an eyewitness during a Civil War battle. The passage appeared in the piece that follows "A Little of Chickamauga" in his *Collected Works,* "The Crime at Pickett's Mill," first published in the *San Francisco Examiner* on May 27, 1888. This long passage ends with the summary sentence, "It may be said, generally, that a soldier's knowledge of what is going on about him is coterminous with his official relation to it and his personal connection with it; what is going on in front of him he does not know at all until he learns it afterward."[27]

To think otherwise would be naive, and there was something uncharacteristically naive about Bierce's response to Gracie, who clearly had read much more about Chickamauga than he had. How did a Civil War soldier learn afterward about what had gone on in front of him? He read. Bierce read too, of course, but his letter to Gracie showed that he read rather selectively. One of the things he did read, which he mentioned twice in his letter, was Lieutenant General Hill's "Chickamauga—The Great Battle of the West," first published in *Century Magazine* in April 1887 and reprinted in the third volume of *Battles and Leaders of the Civil War* (1888). In his first reference to Hill's account, Bierce pointed to the Confederate general as an example of "the 'good loser'" of the war "and, with reference to the battle of Chickamauga, the good winner," someone who pays the "tribute of admiration to some of the men whom he fought."[28] In the second reference, he concurred with Hill on the time of Granger's arrival as about two hours later than the 1:00 P.M. stated in Granger's official report. But although Hill's account contains much of undisputed value for the student of Chickamauga, Bierce again appears to have been somewhat naive in holding him up as the standard of judicious and accurate historiography. Moreover, a closer look at this account sheds some light on Bierce's own writings about Chickamauga.

Whatever else one can say of Hill's battlefield record, which included his leadership in Bloody Lane at Sharpsburg (Antietam), one cannot say that the Chickamauga was his shining hour, and whatever else one can say about his account of that battle, one cannot say that it was free from all taint of bad losing.[29] In the case of his contribution to *Century Magazine,* Hill did not come across as a bad loser of the war; he came across as a bad loser to Braxton Bragg, who after the battle requested that Hill be relieved from duty, as subsequently happened. For all its other virtues as a piece of historical narrative, some of which clearly impressed Bierce, "Chickamauga—The Great Battle of the West" was about blaming the Army of Tennessee's commander: "As the failure of Bragg to beat Rosecrans in detail has been the subject of much criticism, it may be well to look into the causes of the failure."[30]

Not surprisingly, Hill's account did not receive much attention in Gracie's book, which mentioned the general only once in 450 pages and cited his article only four times, once to correct it, since Gracie's judgment of Bragg's performance differed markedly from Hill's: "In the course of my study, however, I have awakened to the fact that, whatever may have been his faults before or immediately after the Battle of Chickamauga, there is no evidence contained in the Official Reports of any action or order of his, particularly on September 20, which I can find deserving of anything but the greatest of praise. The worst that can be said against him is that he was unfortunate,—therefore unsuccessful as a leader."[31] Some may feel that this assessment lets Bragg off too easily, but recent historians of the battle confirm that having Hill as a subordinate was among the commander's misfortunes. Tucker asserts that Bragg was "poorly served" by Hill, who before the battle failed, in Bragg's judgment, to "bag Negley in McLemore's Cove."[32] Cozzens judges that "Bragg erred both in giving Polk only oral attack orders on the night of the nineteenth and then in failing to see they were implemented." Although he gives Hill's account the last word in his book, he also paints the general throughout as a sulker who carried out his orders "with the energy of a sloth."[33]

Although students of Chickamauga may apportion blame to Bragg and Hill in different proportions, if blaming is what they incline toward, no informed student of the battle now can see Hill, in his capacity as general, as trustingly as Bierce did. But in his capacity as writer, Hill deserves more attention, particularly with respect to the visible effects of his writing on Bierce's own treatments of Chickamauga, the first of which, "On Chickamauga," appeared in the *San Francisco Examiner* on November 11, 1888, or just nineteen months after the general's piece in magazine form. Then, two months later came the famous story "Chickamauga," to which we shall turn soon.

One can make different arguments about the timing of Bierce's Civil War writings—in 1888 he published eight pieces, in 1889 six, which rank first and second in his annual output of material about the war.[34] In a letter of August 13, 1887, to Sergeant Abe Dills, he expressed gratitude for an invitation to a reunion of the 9th Indiana, which he did not accept, and then continued, "Your letter has called up all manner of memories—men and things that had not for years been in my mind."[35] Exerting itself throughout the United States in the 1880s, the memory-stirring power of reunions corresponded to copious publication of Civil War writings as well, and the timing of Bierce's contributions certainly reflected this larger trend. Another stimulus could have been Boynton's visit to the Chickamauga battlefield with Ferdinand Van Derveer, his former brigade commander, in June 1888, a visit about which Boynton, Washington correspondent of the *Cincinnati Commercial Gazette* at the time, wrote a series of letters published in the newspaper. According to Boynton, these letters represented the first step toward development of the national military park.[36] Meanwhile, one reader of Bierce has linked his story "Chickamauga" to coverage by the *San Francisco Examiner* of the volatile situation in Samoa.[37] Biographical pressures may have been driving Bierce as well, with the winter of 1888–89 bringing separation from his wife, Mollie, after his discovery of what he took for love letters from another man.[38] But whatever the promptings that pushed him to write about Chickamauga at a particular moment, Bierce still needed to figure out the way to write his versions of history, and it appears that Hill helped him do so.

In "The Way to Write History," Lucian advised the historian that "his attention should be for the generals first of all."[39] Despite a contemporary countercurrent of attention paid to common soldiers—in, for example, Walt Whitman's *Memoranda during the War* (1875) or Sam Watkins's *"Co. Aytch"* (1882)—and despite moments in his own Civil War writings when he did focus on soldiers below the rank of general, Bierce certainly took this advice, especially in his nonfiction about Chickamauga. In particular, these writings show that he paid special attention to how generals talked and wrote. In "On Chickamauga," for example, Bierce attended

to his division commander, Major General John M. Palmer, whose "perfectly ghastly frankness" clearly impressed him and whose honesty in
admitting error, in the general's later writing, clearly distinguished him
in Bierce's mind.[40] In "A Little of Chickamauga" he singled out, through
indirect discourse, the incivility, and implicit cowardice, of Brigadier
General James S. Negley, commander of the Second Division, XIV Corps,
and by contrast the tough single-mindedness of Brigadier General Hazen, whom Bierce admired.[41] In a piece published in 1882, he quoted
Brigadier General Thomas J. Wood's command, delivered "with marked
impatience": "'General, send a couple of regiments and your battery out
there and put an end to that fighting.'"[42] In attending so closely to the
utterances of generals, Bierce appears to have been fascinated not only
by what they said and the consequences of their utterances—many of his
war writings, fictional and nonfictional, pivot on the giving and following
of particular orders—but also by how they said the things they said, by
the tones, phrases, and formulas that reflect individual character and
sensibility.

The only generals Bierce would have heard during Chickamauga
would have been Union ones, but twenty-five years later he read Hill's
narrative, and in it he would have heard the tones of a kindred spirit,
one who admired many of the same qualities he did and taught him
ways to show his admiration in the manner of a West Point professional.
Take, for example, Hill's description of Longstreet's breakthrough at the
Brotherton Farm during the late morning of September 20: "Discovering,
with the true instinct of a soldier, that he could do more by turning to
the right, he disregarded the order to wheel to the left and wheeled the
other way."[43] Hill's reference to "the true instinct of a soldier" not only
praised and endorsed Longstreet, a fellow member of the West Point class
of 1842, it also consolidated his own authority as someone in a position
to recognize and determine what constitutes true soldierly instinct in a
commander.

Neither a general, nor a professional, nor even a college graduate,
Bierce struggled, according to one biographer, with feelings of inferiority
in relation to West Pointers, and Hill's rhetorical move still reverberates
with a confidence and authority Bierce apparently coveted.[44] In his depic-
tions of Granger marching toward Snodgrass Hill, he used versions of
Hill's formula twice, first in "A Little of Chickamauga" and next in "War
Topics," published in the *San Francisco Examiner* two weeks later, on
May 8, 1898. In the former he described Granger as "moving soldier-like

toward the sound of heavy firing," and in the latter the phrasing was even closer to Hill's: "As to who saved the army there can be no two intelligent opinions: it was saved by the superb obstinacy of Thomas and the soldierly instinct of Gordon Granger in marching toward the sound of cannon."[45] Necessarily limited by his relatively low rank in the chain of command, and consequently by the restricted scope of his understanding, a young lieutenant's opinion of his corps commander would not necessarily carry on its own the same ring of unquestionable authority that Bierce established here with the help of Hill's professional tone, as though like Hill on Longstreet, Bierce were praising his peer rather than his superior.

Hill's narrative contains many other tones and rhetorical flourishes that anticipated Bierce's war writings and may sound familiar to many of his readers. There was, for example, the drily civil understatement of "My interview with General Bragg at Chattanooga was not satisfactory"; the praise for coolness under fire, specifically with reference to Bushrod Johnson; and moments of amused irony, such as this description of Crittenden, which appeared to consist of more praise for coolness but turned into subtle mockery of the kind Bierce came to master: "Surely in the annals of warfare there is no parallel to the coolness and nonchalance with which General Crittenden marched and counter-marched for a week with a delightful unconsciousness that he was in the presence of a force of superior strength."[46]

As for the faculty of expression extolled by Lucian, Hill's narration also provided models of compelling rhythmic variations, whether in the use of short sentences or clauses to puncture and deflate—a technique Bierce also employed (compare Hill's "but Bragg had other plans" with Bierce's "Chickamauga was a fight for possession of a road")—or in the alternation of specific details of battle with sweeping, authoritative-sounding generalizations about leadership in warfare, such as a sentence by Hill beginning, "The one thing that a soldier never fails to understand is victory," or the sentence, "The great commander is he who makes his antagonist keep step with him."[47] With such magisterial pronouncements as these, compare Bierce's dicta to Gracie about good historians or the statement about eyewitness perspectives in "The Crime at Pickett's Mill." Given the blind spots we have discovered in Bierce's view of Chickamauga, we might think a more circumspect, qualified tone appropriate for his letter to Gracie, but a circumspect, qualified tone would not have become the voice of military professionalism he admired in Hill, and this was the voice, or one of the voices, Bierce worked to develop in his war writings.

Hill's narrative of Chickamauga may also have influenced Bierce's fictional treatment of the battle, but before leaving the letter to Gracie and turning to that fiction on the way toward conclusion, we can glance fruitfully at two other sets of unpublished documents, one that illuminates Bierce's fascination with the giving of orders, and one that raises some more questions about his accuracy as an historical witness.

On September 25, 1908, when he lived in Washington, D.C., Bierce wrote a letter to the adjutant general of the army, a letter the adjutant general then referred to Brigadier General William Wallace Wotherspoon, president of the Army War College. Wotherspoon's side of the correspondence soon makes it clear that "Major Bierce," as the general addressed him (Bierce was commissioned brevet major as of March 13, 1865, "for distinguished service during the war," the commission signed by Andrew Johnson and Edwin M. Stanton on August 3, 1866), had written seeking an opportunity "to explain and illustrate" his "theory and system of giving oral commands." In his letter of September 29, 1908, Wotherspoon invited Bierce "to come to the War College at 1:30 P.M., Saturday, October 3rd, and either lecture or explain and illustrate before the officers connected therewith, your theory and system." In a letter of October 1, 1908, the general expressed gratification at Bierce's acceptance of the invitation, invited him to "a very simple luncheon which we have daily at 12:30," and told him his talk could be "just as informal as you please." Subsequently, in a letter dated October 16, 1908, answering a letter of Bierce's dated three days earlier, Wotherspoon summed up the apparently successful visit: "both I and the officers who listened to you were so convinced of the correctness of your position in all respects as to deem a field demonstration as unnecessary."[48]

According to biographer Walter Neale, "Bierce said that he thought oral commands in the field should be given slowly, in rolling tones, as carrying several times farther than sharp and crisp orders."[49] From this information, which Neale gives in the course of illustrating Bierce's sense of inferiority with respect to West Point officers, one may infer that Major Bierce went to the Army War College to demonstrate the giving of orders in slow, rolling tones. One might hear in Wotherspoon's third letter either the genuine endorsement of someone wholly persuaded by this demonstration or the polite but firm refusal to humor the old veteran any further (Bierce was then sixty-six). Either way, what is significant and revealing about this incident is that late in his life, Bierce identified so clearly with the army, the officers of the army, and the giving of orders that is their responsibility and power. Where did this identification come from? Did it spring from the single year he spent at the Kentucky Military Institute at Franklin Springs, beginning in the fall of 1859? Did it come from admiration of his uncle, Lucius Verus Bierce, who went by the title "general" and who, according to Roy Morris Jr., on December 3, 1838, "led a contingent of volunteers across Lake Erie aboard a captured passenger steamer and set fire to the British barracks at Windsor," Ontario?[50] Or did it come from his own experiences as sergeant and lieutenant in Company C, 9th Indiana before his appointment to Hazen's staff, after which he would have had fewer opportunities to give orders than to execute them? Wherever it came from, his identification with order-giving officers challenges any reductive description of Bierce as so embittered and appalled by his Civil War service that his attitudes toward the military, and toward its war-waging function, turned wholly toward revulsion and cynicism.[51]

The second set of unpublished documents, those that raise more questions about Bierce's accuracy as historical witness, return us to his correspondence with Archibald Gracie, specifically to Gracie's side of that correspondence. In a letter of July 1, 1911, written not quite four months after Bierce's corrective letter to him, Gracie asked him to examine a photograph of Brigadier General James Steedman with his staff "and state whether you recognize the members of the Staff and can give me their names. If so, please simply mark on the back of the picture, designating each Staff officer and whether he was with Steedman in the battle of Chickamauga." The painstaking carefulness reflected in this letter was typical of Gracie's procedure, and in a subsequent letter of July 22, 1911, he questioned Bierce's identification of himself in a photograph because Isaac Suman, colonel of the 9th Indiana at Chickamauga, had said "you are mistaken." In his reply of July 24, 1911, Bierce admitted his error: "If you are in correspondence with Suman kindly make to him my acknowledgment of my error and convey my greeting. (Confidentially, I may say to you that he and I never loved each other as all are commanded by your Holy Scriptures to do.)"

A letter from Suman to Bierce, dated March 25, 1894, and addressed to "My Esteemed Capt. A. G. Bierce," was perfectly friendly and cordial,

This photograph has been identified for many years as an image of Lieutenant Ambrose Gwinnett Bierce during the Civil War. It is signed, however, "Yours truly A.S. Bierce" and is almost certainly Ambrose's brother, Lieutenant Albert Sherwood Bierce, who at Chickamauga served with the 18th Ohio Battery. Archibald Gracie published this photograph in his 1911 book *The Truth about Chickamauga* after consulting with Ambrose. In it Gracie labeled the image "A. S. Bierce" of the 18th Ohio Battery. Moreover, unlike the subject of this picture, Ambrose Bierce had blond hair, by all accounts. Elkhart County Historical Museum.

even nostalgic, in tone, culminating in the closing, "Your comrade in the Ninth," so it remains unclear what animosity toward his old commander Bierce was still nursing seventeen years later in the summer of 1911.[52] What is clear is that, once again, his status as participant in the Battle of Chickamauga did not guarantee the reliability of his testimony. This episode of his mistaken identification of himself in a photograph becomes especially interesting when one turns to page 318 of Gracie's *The Truth about Chickamauga* and recognizes the familiar and widely reproduced picture of the mustachioed Bierce in uniform but then reads the caption "Jun. 1st Lieut. A. S. Bierce" and, at the bottom of the page, "18th Ohio Battery Officers." Is this a photograph of Ambrose Bierce or his brother Albert? The Elkhart County Historical Museum, in Bristol, Indiana, claims the former, as does everyone else who has reproduced the photograph with the exception of Gracie, who sought Bierce's help in identifying the subjects of photographs he used. But even with an allowance for the indeterminacy of black-and-white contrast, the man in this photograph does not look blond, as Bierce has been described so frequently as being. Did he commit another error, mistaking his own young face for his brother's? Did Gracie make a mistake once Bierce had made the correct identification? Is the photograph really one of Albert, despite its wide dissemination as an image of Ambrose?[53]

The mystery here, with its tantalizing evasion of verifiable factuality, leads easily and finally to Bierce's other way to write history, his short fiction. In many discussions of his story "Chickamauga," Bierce's readers have felt called upon, for reasons of their own, to describe it as one of his two greatest Civil War stories, the other being "An Occurrence at Owl Creek Bridge." This judgment, which is unnecessary, risks foreclosing full appreciation of the thirteen other stories in the "Soldiers" section of the second volume of Bierce's *Collected Works,* but it does testify to the power of his story of a deaf-mute boy wandering the edges of the Chickamauga battlefield during the fighting, as does the decision of French director Robert Enrico to make a film of the story, released in black and white in 1962. (Enrico also made films of Bierce's stories "The Mocking-Bird" and "An Occurrence at Owl Creek Bridge," the latter airing in the United States as an episode of *The Twilight Zone,* on February 28, 1964.) Somewhat less predictable but still common are attempts by both professional and amateur readers of "Chickamauga" to identify the factual aspects of Bierce's fiction. In a letter of July 18, 1975, for example, one visitor to the Chickamauga and Chattanooga National Military Park wrote the superintendent, Robert L. Deskins, to ask about "parallels between the story and fact," anticipating by many years the interest of professional readers of Bierce in the same parallels.[54]

In his reply of July 24, 1975, Deskins summarized several facts that one could construe as connected to Bierce's story:

> Mr. George W. Snodgrass who lived on Chickamauga Battlefield, had two sons, Charles and Joh[n]. Charles was killed during the battle, but John managed to survive the battle and the war as he was a cripple.
>
> At the time of the Battle in 1863, there were 24 families living on the land which was to become Chickamauga Battlefield. The Glenn and Poe houses were destroyed by direct shell fire. It is possible that most of the other houses were destroyed or damaged by shell or musketry fire. This area in 1863 suffered one of the worse droughts that the State has ever had. The fields and woods were literally tinderboxes. Hot shot from the cannon set the woods afire and many soldiers burned to death.[55]

Deskin misread the ending of Bierce's story—he opened his letter by referring to "the death of the child" in it, though the deaf-mute child does not die—but he did point his correspondent to James A. Sartain's *History of Walker County, Georgia* (1932), also a source for Tucker and Cozzens (whose bibliography mistakes the author's name as "Sartrain") and those who have relied on them.

The section of Sartain's book devoted to the families living on the battlefield in fact was not written by Sartain; it was, according to his headnote, a reprint of an article by Charles W. Lusk, first published in the *Chattanooga Times* in September 1923. Lusk's article apparently provided Deskins with several of the details he gave his correspondent, such as the severe drought and the burning of the Poe and Glenn houses. But Lusk also provided details that Deskins did not mention: that the Poe house was burned by Confederate shells, not Union ones; that more than sixty local people left their houses at the start of the battle and spent eight days in a ravine northwest of the Snodgrass house; that these people suffered greatly both from overnight frost and from lack of water until the Union retreat, since they were behind Union lines and had no access to Chickamauga Creek; that the death of Charles Snodgrass was not that of a civilian since he was a Confederate soldier who fought in the battle; that in addition to the two sons mentioned in Deskins's letter, the Snodgrass family included six younger children also at home when the battle began.[56]

Bierce had no access to Lusk's article, of course, and to the extent that he drew on real topographic features, conditions, and events in writing "Chickamauga," he may have drawn on his own observations. Did he have any contact with local civilians before they withdrew to the ravine beyond the Snodgrass house? If so, did he encounter John Snodgrass and reimagine his disability as deaf-muteness? Did he see the Glenn or Poe house burning and use it as a model for the child's burning house at the end of the story? Perhaps so, but he could not have been omnipresent along a battle front of several miles, and two details in Hill's narrative suggest that it is just as likely that Bierce may have drawn on that article for some of his material. One detail appears in this sentence: "Wood's (Confederate) brigade on the left had almost reached Poe's house (the burning house) on the Chattanooga road, when he was subjected to a heavy enfilading and direct fire, and driven back with great loss." The second appears in a caption beneath an image reproduced from a photograph of the sink-hole near the Glenn house: "This sink-hole contained the only water to be had in the central part of the battle-field. Colonel Wilder's brigade of mounted infantry at one time gained the pool after a hard contest and quenched their thirst. In the water were lying dead men and horses that had been wounded and had died while drinking."[57] A burning cabin and wounded men drowning while drinking from a water source (a creek in "Chickamauga," not a sinkhole) are two vivid images from a story full of them.[58] Bierce could have encountered these images elsewhere, either in oral reportage or in print, if he did not see such sights himself, which would have been unlikely in the case of the men drinking at the sinkhole since presumably he would have been with Hazen near the Kelly house when Wilder was fighting at Bloody Pond around midday on September 20. But since we know that he read and admired Hill's narrative, it makes sense that Hill would have been, if not his only source for these images, then at least the most recent stimulus in recollecting them for his story.

The drawing of parallels between Bierce's story and the facts of the Chickamauga battlefield is not a trivial exercise, particularly for those interested in how writers of historically based fiction go about the business of shaping their materials. That a few years after the publication of his story Bierce became acquainted with Elizabeth "Lily" Walsh, a young deaf-mute woman in whose life and writing he took keen interest before her early death in 1895, might make some wish that chronology would permit the drawing of this parallel too.[59] But to become preoccupied with drawing parallels between selected realities of Chickamauga and Bierce's fictionalization of Chickamauga is to risk missing at least one important point of that fictionalization: it is not realistic, and the ways in which it is not suggest that it never was intended to be.[60]

Bierce's departures from the realities of the battle are many and obvious: all the families had left the battlefield by the time the fighting erupted around their houses; the gradual arrival in the vicinity of more than 135,000 soldiers—a number exceeding that of the 1860 population of Chicago—with all their horses, mules, artillery, and wagons, could have taken no one by surprise, and no child would have been left alone to gambol through the woods during the gathering of the opposing armies; deafness does not preclude sensitivity to vibration, so the child's sleeping through the concussions of artillery fire, the advance of soldiers who "had almost trodden on him as he slept," and the fighting of a battle almost "within a stone's throw of where he lay" suggests the magical sleep of Rip Van Winkle rather than the real sleep of a real child; and finally, the topography of Bierce's plot does not agree at all with the real events of the fighting since the only army that could have advanced and retreated near a creek would have been Bragg's, and any Confederate unit that both advanced and retreated did so well to the west of Chickamauga Creek.[61]

Then there are all the details of the real conditions at Chickamauga about which Bierce's story is completely and inscrutably silent, such as the tinderbox dryness caused by drought, the resulting fires and immolation of wounded soldiers as at Shiloh and the Wilderness (Bierce had written about the burning of soldiers at Shiloh in "What I Saw of Shiloh" [1881]), and the local families thirsting and shivering in the ravine northwest of the Snodgrass house.[62] Given so many omissions, one might incline toward questioning, or at least in the case of "Chickamauga" toward qualifying, the claims of those who have praised Bierce's realistic treatment of war, H. L. Mencken among them.[63] The one aspect of his story that some might associate with realism could be its graphic description of maimed bodies, especially those of a wounded soldier with "a face that lacked a lower jaw" and of the child's dead mother, whose forehead has been torn away by a shell: "from the jagged hole the brain protruded, overflowing the temple, a frothy mass of gray, crowned with clusters of crimson bubbles."[64] But do such graphic descriptions necessarily point toward realism? Some might call them pornographic instead. In itself,

Ambrose Bierce, depicted in this portrait by J. H. E. Partington,
reinforced his proud self-image as a master of gothic and macabre literature
in the years following the Civil War. Library of Congress.

gory ghoulishness, a streak of which Bierce began showing early in his
life, does not necessarily promote realism; it may lead instead toward
violent fixation and gothic fantasy.[65]

If in "Chickamauga" Bierce was not trying to write realistically about
the battle, what was he trying to do, and how does the story constitute a
way of writing history? We can begin to answer these questions by looking at Bierce's little book *Write It Right,* his blacklist of literary faults,

among which he included the mistaken use of "novel" for "romance": "In a novel there is at least an apparent attention to considerations of probability; it is a narrative of what might occur. Romance flies with a free wing and owns no allegiance to likelihood. Both are fiction, both works of imagination, but should not be confounded. They are as distinct as beast and bird."[66] According to his own definitions, "Chickamauga" is closer to the realm of romance than to that of the novel, and with "no allegiance to likelihood," it would seem to be the opposite of history. But the title, originally set in large bold type at the top of the leftmost column of the front page of the special Sunday section of the *San Francisco Examiner* for January 20, 1889, insisted to its first readers, as it still does, recalcitrant and unyielding, on linkage to a particular historical event.

One way to understand this insistence would be to say that for all his admiration of Lucian and Daniel Harvey Hill, for all his attentiveness to the words of generals and all his eagerness to correct Archibald Gracie's version of the truth about Chickamauga, for Bierce something about the battle clearly remained unspoken, both in the writings of others and in his own nonfictional efforts, which have furnished recent histories with colorful quotations.[67] In fact, the professional way of writing history, as exemplified by Hill, not only left much unspoken but also demonstrated that the true professional necessarily treated real aspects of war with a particular kind of decorous restraint, as when Hill described a wounded man, "his head partly supported by a tree," as "shockingly injured."[68] This was not a lie or an untruth. In its way it even may have been, and still be, more effectively suggestive, to some readers, than Bierce's graphic descriptions of wounds in "Chickamauga." But suggestive or not, it reflected the rhetorical code of an insider, someone who knew the reality of historical events so well that he could represent them adequately to other insiders, such as Bierce, with this kind of shorthand. Those insiders, in turn, knew how to interpret the code.

But what about those who were not insiders? In Bierce's hands the decorous restraint of the military professional threatened to turn into, or converge with, what Edmund Wilson, in an ambivalent appraisal of Bierce's Civil War writing, called his "marble correctitude."[69] What Wilson may have missed, as in the case of the entry for "valor" in *The Devil's Dictionary,* is that "marble correctitude" also provided Bierce with a target for mockery, especially in the context of combat. In other words, he too found something unsatisfactory about such phrasings, particularly when it came to trying to convey to noncombatants, such as most readers of the *San Francisco Examiner,* the truth about the massive indecorousness of battle. In helping him get at this indecorous truth, neither Lucian of Samosata nor Daniel Harvey Hill could have been of much use. He needed something beyond the conventional codes of either the ancient historian or the professional general.

That something was fiction, by means of which Bierce also tried to write history from the opposite extreme of unlikely romance. In titling his unlikely romance "Chickamauga," Bierce in effect titled it "History" or "Real Historical Event." It is easy to say that fiction can tell truth in ways that nonfiction cannot, but it is not always so easy to say how. In his story about the battle, with "about" meaning both "with reference to" and "around," Bierce attempted to get at the truth—or another truth—of this historical event by disrupting the familiarity of conventional codes often used to represent it. The adjective "strange" appears five times in the story, piling up repetitions a stickling editor might question. But Bierce was severe in his self-justifying response to an early instance of editorial second guessing: "Everything I send you is constructed with the utmost care; most of it being written three times over, and all of it twice."[70] If he used the word "strange" five times, he did so because he wanted to hammer a sense of strangeness into a reader's awareness, something nowhere to be found in, for example, Hill's account of Chickamauga, which worked to manage and contain strangeness with decorous professionalism and correctitude.

In choosing to filter a little of Chickamauga through the sensibility of a deaf-mute child, Bierce imagined a sensibility at the opposite end of the spectrum from that of a commanding general engaged in the battle. One, an insider, would have known as much about the battle as any one person could know; the other, an outsider, would have known as little. Again and again in the story, Bierce represented these extremes by using the child's point of view to make strange what would be familiar to a veteran of Chickamauga and then dispelling the strangeness with a short, simple, matter-of-fact sentence, clause, or phrase: "They were men"; "He was dead"; "But that was blood"; "They were drowned"; "the work of a shell"; "The child was a deaf mute."[71] The last of these, "The child was a deaf mute" ("He was a deaf mute" in the *Examiner*), is the penultimate sentence of the story and springs a surprise ending, which some readers admire, while some do not. But the surprise of the ending cannot be separated from the chain of smaller surprises the story forges all along, those of strange and unfamiliar things suddenly turned comprehensible, even if awfully so. Admittedly, surprise is not altogether foreign to the language of warfare, which includes the phrase "surprise attack." But the language of military history, whether written by a participant in events treated by that account or by someone narrating those events one hundred years later, tends to promote explanation over surprise. In doing so, however, it may be forfeiting a crucial connection to the strange and unprofessional, the inexplicable and indecorous, which also formed part of the historical truth—at least for Ambrose Bierce—of Chickamauga.

<hr>

APPENDIX

Albert Bierce to Ambrose Bierce, March 29, 1911 (Albert and Shirley Small Special Collections Library, University of Virginia, MSS 5992, Box 1, Item 41)

Montesano [California]

My dear Brother

This is my story of Chickamauga, all of which is true to the best of my recollection.

On the evening of the 18 of Sept. 1863 Whitaker's brigade to which Aleshires battery was attached was on the Ringgold road, probably about a mile east of McAfee's church where, first at dusk, we met the enemy and engaged in a sharp but short artillery duel in which infantry [p. 2] took no part. After dark the brigade was withdrawn to McAfee's church where Granger was, with the rest of his command. My section of the battery was left on picket-duty about a quarter of a mile in advance of this position with instructions to remain awake all night and take note of any sound which might indicate a movement of the enemy, for, as the staff officer said to me, they will either leave our front tonight or attack us in the morning. In the latter case [p. 3] when I was sure of his advance I was to fire one gun as a signal to prepare to receive the advance and then fall back to the main line near the church. At about daybreak I heard the rumble of his artillery in motion but waited till I saw him coming, fired the one shot and fell back as ordered and reported to Granger. The attack was made and repulsed, renewed about an hour later with the same result. In this attack Lieut. Roseburg of the battery was wounded. During the rest of the day there was only a [p. 4] succession of skirmishes. We remained in this position until the following day.

Now this brings us to the morning of the 20th[.] Historians tell us that Gen Rosecrans was overwhelmed and carried from the field in the rout at about 11 a.m. Rosecrans thinking his whole army in retreat would of course hasten to order Granger to fall back by the Rossville and Ringgold road which order he promptly sent and which was promptly disregarded by Granger. Whitaker and Mitchell were soon in column on [p. 5] their way to Thomas. This was, to my best recollection, about 12 m. The distance from McAfee's church to the Snodgrass [house or farm] is something like three miles and the column moved with but one short halt. Some of the enemy's cavalry and a battery were seen on our left. The battery opened fire on our column and Granger halted for a few minutes, surveyed them with his field glasses, then ordered the column to advance. My section was detained here probably about twenty minutes by a shell from [p. 6] the enemy's battery on our left which broke the pole to one of my gun carriages. I repaired it by splicing a sapling on to it. This happened but a short distance before you met us. I remember your saying to me that Hazen had left the position that he held when you left him to go for the ammunition train and as you did not know where he was at the time you would stay with the battery. You remember that Granger reported to Thomas not far from the Snodgrass house and the battery went into position at the edge [p. 7] of a cornfield. Was there a cornfield in Hazens front at the Kelly farm? You probably remember that Lieut Chestnut was wounded only a short time before the battery got into position, and it seems to me that this happened near the Snodgrass house—a little east of it. I remember that we were agreeably surprised to find that the battery's position was with Hazen's troops. There were no breastworks of any kind there. The enemy made one assault on Hazen through the cornfield and we harvested the [p. 8] corn with canister. We left this position under the guidance of somebody's chief of artillery to be placed farther to the right, just where we, or at least I, never knew as the officer was wounded or killed before placing us. Aleshire asked me if I thought it possible to get the battery on that hill south of the Snodgrass house. I told him I could get my part of it there, and his reply was "Go ahead[.]" I got it there by taking the hill at an angle and the shoulders of the men at the wheels. On the crest, [p. 9] which was sharp, I found a line of infantry lying flat on their stomachs and a desperate conflict going on at its southern base, almost hand-to-hand. I could have killed an hundred men with one round of canister but some of them would have been wearing the blue. The officer in command of the troops on the hill—a col. whom I did not know—said to me, "This is no place for artillery, you cant do a thing." And he was right. He made no attempt to make room for my guns on the crest so I rode down and told [p. 10] Aleshire the condition of things and he ordered me to bring my guns down. You may remember that when I came down the battery passed near the Snodgrass house—a little to the east of it—and took a position in open ground after making a half circle to the right. In this place we remained until about dark when we got the order to retire by the McFarland Gap road.

You're right in your letter to Gracie when you say that the Confederates did not take possession of this hill till after [p. 11] our forces had withdrawn. I believe there were some officers in high command who did not do their whole duty at Chickamauga but Thomas, Granger and Brannan were not in that class surely.

I think that this whole muddle of placing the battery at the Kelly farm comes about by the mistake of Hazen putting the time of his arrival at the Snodgrass farm about two hours too late. Our loss was, in the three days, two Lieuts wounded, two men killed. [p. 12] Our loss of horses compelled us to abandon one caisson, which we destroyed.

I think that Col Gracie will get little satisfaction from your criticism of his work.

Yes, I have the fifth volume and shall be very glad to get the others; and doubtless you will be glad when your work is finished.

Affectionately
Alberto

March 29, 1911

[p. 13, unnumbered] P.S. On reading this over I find I've made a blunder. When the battery was first moved from Hazens line it was placed farther to the right, near the east base of the ridge, and it was from this position that we were moving when I took my guns up the hill.

[This letter covers thirteen sheets of 5- x 7.75-inch paper, sixteen horizontal blue lines on each page. All spellings are Albert's. His writing is clear and legible, although not all punctuation marks and indentations are clear: for example, some of his commas could be dashes or other marks. I have not included any of his crossings out, which are few.]

ACKNOWLEDGMENTS

The author wishes to thank Gary W. Gallagher for reading an early draft of this essay as well as William Lee White and Diana Zornow for their help gathering research materials.

NOTES

1. Ambrose Bierce, *A Much Misunderstood Man: Selected Letters of Ambrose Bierce,* ed. S. T. Joshi and David E. Schultz (Columbus: Ohio State University Press, 2003), 27 (hereinafter cited as Bierce, *Selected Letters*).

2. Bierce, *Selected Letters,* 27–28.

3. H. W. Fowler and F. G. Fowler, *The Works of Lucian of Samosata,* vol. 2 (Oxford: Clarendon, 1905), 126 (hereinafter cited as Lucian). Although Bierce could have seen this translation late in his life, its publication date shows that it is not the one he would have had in mind for Blanche Partington.

4. Lucian, 126, 127, 128–29.

5. Bierce, *Selected Letters,* 23.

6. Archibald Gracie, *The Truth about Chickamauga* (Boston and New York: Houghton Mifflin, 1911), ix (hereafter cited as Gracie, *Truth*).

7. Ibid., 5.

8. Ibid., 30.

9. Peter Cozzens, *This Terrible Sound: The Battle of Chickamauga* (Urbana: University of Illinois Press, 1992), 418; Gracie, *Truth,* 32–33. Although Cozzens does not credit Gracie with the designation of the hills, he does include Gracie's book in his bibliography of secondary works.

10. For an account of Boynton's role with the 35th Ohio on Horseshoe Ridge that suggests he did have good reason to be proud, see Cozzens, *This Terrible Sound,* 505–509.

11. See, for example, Gracie, *Truth,* 407–409. For a more recent perspective on the credit deserved by the 9th Indiana, see Laurence D. Conley, "The Truth about Chickamauga: A Ninth Indiana Regiment's Perspective," *Indiana Magazine of History* 98 (June 2002): 114–43. I am grateful to Lee White, Chickamauga and Chattanooga National Battlefield Park, for directing me to this essay.

12. Gracie, *Truth,* xii.

13. Ibid., 405–406. Of Albert's letter, Carey McWilliams has written, "'Old Sloots,' as Ambrose called his brother, was rather shy about relating his feats of gallantry, but he finally wrote an account of what he saw of Chickamauga for Mr. Gracie, who was his brother's friend. Ambrose was rather shocked at the document and forwarded it to Mr. Gracie with a world of apology for the style!" *Ambrose Bierce: A Biography* (New York: Albert and Charles Boni, 1929), 50. McWilliams has cited no source for the claim that Bierce was shocked by his brother's style. Meanwhile, Albert must have written at least two accounts of what he saw of Chickamauga, that or either Bierce or Gracie must have rewritten his original account since the one quoted by Gracie is not the same as one dated March 29, 1911, and housed in the Albert and Shirley Small Special Collections Library, University of Virginia (MSS 5992, Box 1, Item 41; see Appendix). Bierce's letter to Gracie appeared first, without salutation or signature, in Ambrose Bierce, *A Sole Survivor: Bits of Autobiography,* ed. S. T. Joshi and David E. Schultz (Knoxville: University of Tennessee Press, 1998), 34–35. It was subsequently reprinted the same way in Ambrose Bierce, *Phantoms of a Blood-Stained Period: The Complete Civil War Writings of Ambrose Bierce,* ed. Russell Duncan and David J. Klooster (Amherst: University of Massachusetts Press, 2002), 202–204. It then appeared with salutation and signature in *Selected Letters,* which is my text here.

14. Bierce, *Selected Letters,* 210, 211.

15. Gracie, *Truth,* x–xi.

16. Bierce, *Selected Letters,* 210.

17. See Gracie, *Truth,* 228–29, 428–37, 448–49.

18. Ibid., 157. See also Cozzens, *This Terrible Sound,* 450; Glenn Tucker, *Chickamauga: Bloody Battle in the West* (1961; reprint, Dayton, Ohio: Morningside, 1984), 368; and William Glenn Robertson, "The Chickamauga Campaign: The Battle of Chickamauga, Day 2, September 20, 1863," *Blue and Gray* 25, no. 2 (Summer 2008): 46.

19. Cozzens, *This Terrible Sound,* 450.

20. See Appendix to this chapter.

21. Bierce, *Selected Letters,* 211; Ambrose Bierce, *Collected Works of Ambrose Bierce,* 10 vols. (New York: Neale, 1909), 1:275–76.

22. Bierce, *Selected Letters,* 211.

23. Cozzens, *This Terrible Sound,* 417–18.

24. Gracie, *Truth,* 33.

25. U.S. War Department, *The War of the Rebellion: A Compilation of the Official Records of the Union and Confederate Armies,* 128 vols. (Washington, D.C.: GPO, 1880–1901), ser. 1, 30(1):855.

26. See, for example, Henry V. Boynton, *The National Military Park, Chickamauga-Chattanooga: An Historical Guide, with Maps and Illustrations* (Cincinnati: Robert Clarke, 1895), xvi, 53, 55.

27. Bierce, *Collected Works* 1:281.

28. Bierce, *Selected Letters,* 211.

29. For a full-length study of Hill's generalship, see Hal Bridges, *Lee's Maverick General: Daniel Harvey Hill* (1961; reprint, with an introduction by Gary Gallagher, Lincoln: University of Nebraska Press, 1991). For Lee's shrewd appraisal of Hill as a general, see especially ibid., 148–50.

30. Daniel H. Hill, "Chickamauga—The Great Battle of the West," in Robert Underwood Johnson and Clarence Clough Buel, eds., *Battles and Leaders of the Civil War,* vol. 3 (New York: Century, 1888), 641 (hereafter cited as "Great Battle").

31. Gracie, *Truth,* 31–32.

32. Tucker, *Chickamauga,* 67, 214.

33. Cozzens, *This Terrible Sound,* 309–310, 489.

34. Bierce, *Phantoms of a Blood-Stained Period,* 344–46.

35. Bierce, *Selected Letters,* 20.

36. For Boynton's narrative of the creation of the park at Chickamauga, see Boynton, *National Military Park,* 219–50.

37. Donald T. Blume, *Ambrose Bierce's Civilians and Soldiers in Context* (Kent, Ohio: Kent State University Press, 2004), chap. 7 passim. Although suggestive, Blume's argument becomes heavy handed as it reduces the story "Chickamauga" to an allegory of the situation in Samoa. It is also marred by mistakes, such as the confusing of Archibald Gracie, author of *The Truth about Chickamauga,* with his father, the general (370n23), and the shortening of the battle to only one day, September 20 (142).

38. For this version of Bierce's separation from his wife, see McWilliams, *Ambrose Bierce,* 189–90. For a very different version, which puts Bierce in the wrong ("when he rashly unbosomed himself to the wife of his bosom and sang of another's charms"), see Walter Neale, *Life of Ambrose Bierce* (New York: Walter Neale, 1929), 132–36.

39. Lucian, 131.

40. Bierce, *Sole Survivor,* 35–36.

41. Bierce, *Collected Works* 1:275–77.

42. Bierce, *Sole Survivor,* 64.

43. Hill, "Chickamauga," 655.

44. See Neale, *Life of Ambrose Bierce,* 73.

45. Bierce, *Collected Works* 1:276; Bierce, *Sole Survivor,* 33–34.

46. Hill, "Chickamauga," 639, 655n, 643.

47. Ibid., 639, 651; Bierce, *Collected Works,* 1:271.

48. Wotherspoon's letters to Bierce are in the Albert and Shirley Small Special Collections Library, University of Virginia, MSS 5992, Box 1, Items 35, 36, 37. Bierce's commission to brevet major is Item 12 in the same box. Item 14 is his commission to second lieutenant, 5th U.S. Infantry, dated April 3, 1867.

49. Neale, *Life of Ambrose Bierce,* 73.

50. Roy Morris Jr., *Ambrose Bierce: Alone in Bad Company* (New York: Crown, 1995), 16.

51. For example, Morris endorses another reader's assessment of Bierce's Civil War stories as "enduring peace tracts." Ibid., 63. Although Bierce's war experiences certainly disabused him of any romantic illusions about war making, saying so is not at all the same thing as projecting an oversimplified and undifferentiated pacifism onto those stories. In his study *On Killing: The Psychological Cost of Learning to Kill in War and Society* (Boston: Little, Brown, 1995), Dave Grossman quotes this telling statement from Gen. Douglas MacArthur: "The soldier above all other people prays for peace, for they [*sic*] must suffer and bear the deepest wounds and scars of war" (xxiv). A soldier's prayer for peace differs from that of a Quaker or a conscientious objector. The latter believe war making to be morally wrong and refuse to participate in it; the former, if he (or she) is a professional, recognizes that war is an inevitable component of human affairs, that it must not be undertaken rashly, and that it must be anticipated with thorough training and preparation, for when it does come, as it always has, he or she will have to participate in it. Bierce's life and work show that his inclinations toward peacefulness belong to the soldier's category, not the Quaker or conscientious objector's. See also H. L. Mencken, "Ambrose Bierce," *Critical Essays on Ambrose Bierce,* ed. Cathy N. Davidson (1927; reprint, Boston: G. K. Hall, 1982), 61–62.

52. Gracie's letters to Bierce are in Albert and Shirley Small Special Collections Library, University of Virginia, MSS 5992, Box 1, Items 43 and 44; Bierce's reply is Item 45; Suman's letter to Bierce is Item 28.

53. I am grateful to Diana Zornow of the Elkhart County Historical Museum for a photocopy of Item AB 22, a print of this photograph, identified in the museum records as "Haussler, photographer, San Francisco." The photo is signed, "Yours truly / A. S. Bierce," but Zornow has pointed out that the signature looks similar to one reading "Lieut. A. G. Bierce" in Ambrose Bierce's field book. I am not a handwriting expert, but even if the same person wrote the two signatures, it is perfectly possible that Bierce penned the signature for his brother, perhaps to send the photograph on to Gracie for use in his book or for some other reason. In any case, I see no reason to distrust the signature "Yours truly / A. S. Bierce."

54. See Paul O. Hardt to Superintendent, Chickamauga National Battlefield, July 18, 1975, Ambrose Bierce File, Chickamauga and Chattanooga National Military Park, Ft. Oglethorpe, Ga. I am grateful to Lee White for providing me with copies of this letter and the one from Robert L. Deskins responding to it. For recent examples of those who draw parallels between the facts of Chickamauga and Bierce's story, see David M. Owens, *The Devil's Topographer: Ambrose Bierce and the American War Story* (Knoxville: University of Tennessee Press, 2006), 93–99; and Sharon Talley, *Ambrose Bierce and the Dance of Death* (Knoxville: University of Tennessee Press, 2009), 94–95. For a discussion of both the battle and the story, see Morris, *Ambrose Bierce,* 56–64. Morris does not insist on specific parallels between fact and Bierce's fiction beyond pointing out that "the child's experiences ironically mirror those of the Union army during the battle." Ibid., 62.

55. Robert L. Deskins to Paul O. Hardt, July 24, 1975, Bierce File.

56. James Alfred Sartain, *History of Walker County, Georgia,* vol. 1 (Dalton, Ga.: A. J. Showalter, 1932), 100–101.

57. Hill, "Chickamauga," 656.

58. Bierce, *Collected Works* 2:55.

59. Bierce, *Selected Letters,* 41, 45–48, 50, 54. For biographical background on Bierce's interest in and care for Lily Walsh, see, for example, McWilliams, *Ambrose Bierce,* 250–51;

M. E. Grenander, *Ambrose Bierce* (New York: Twayne, 1971), 64–65; and Morris, *Ambrose Bierce*, 215. During 1895, until her death in October, Walsh wrote Bierce approximately forty letters, which are in the Bancroft Library, University of California at Berkeley.

60. The best account of Bierce's complicated relationship to literary realism is Howard W. Bahr, "Ambrose Bierce and Realism," *Southern Quarterly* 1 (1963): 309–31 (reprinted in Davidson, *Critical Essays*, 150–68).

61. Cozzens, *This Terrible Sound*, 154; Bierce, *Collected Works* 2:48–49, 54. See also Christopher Krentz, *Writing Deafness: The Hearing Line in Nineteenth-Century American Literature* (Chapel Hill: University of North Carolina Press, 2007), 127. In light of Bierce's connection with Walsh, Krentz's argument that Bierce subscribed to negative stereotypes of his fictional character's deafness may need reconsideration.

62. Bierce, *Collected Works* 1:261–62.

63. H. L. Mencken wrote, "Bierce, I believe, was the first writer of fiction ever to treat war realistically." "Ambrose Bierce," 61.

64. Bierce, *Collected Works* 2:52, 57. Cathy N. Davidson refers to "the mangled body of his probably raped ('the clothing deranged') and definitely murdered mother." *The Experimental Fictions of Ambrose Bierce: Structuring the Ineffable* (Lincoln: University of Nebraska Press, 1984), 43. The story is quite clear that the mother has been hit by a shell or a shell fragment, the impact of which would certainly have been sufficient to derange her clothing as it knocked her to the ground. She was definitely not murdered, unless Davidson means that the accidental killing of a civilian caught on a battlefield is a form a murder, and the mother hardly could have been raped by any soldier amid the shelling, not to mention one who somehow managed to derange her clothing, violate her, and continue unhurt at the very moment the shell fragment killed her before she could rearrange her clothing. Davidson frames her commentary on "Chickamauga" by labeling it "one of the most gruesome and arresting antiwar tales ever written." Ibid., 36. See also note 15.

65. For an account of a bloody fantasy from Bierce's childhood, see Paul Fatout, *Ambrose Bierce: The Devil's Lexicographer* (Norman: University of Oklahoma Press, 1951), 22.

66. *Write It Right: A Little Blacklist of Literary Faults* (1909; reprint, New York: Union Library Association, 1934), 46.

67. See, for example, Tucker, *Chickamauga*, 206; and Cozzens, *This Terrible Sound*, 257, chap. 13 (title).

68. Hill, "Chickamauga," 659.

69. Edmund Wilson, *Patriotic Gore: Studies in the Literature of the American Civil War* (New York: Oxford University Press, 1962), 632.

70. Bierce, *Selected Letters*, 5.

71. Bierce, *Collected Works* 2:50, 51, 55, 57. The technique of making the familiar strange, which twentieth-century Russian Formalist critics called *ostranie* (usually translated "making strange" or "defamiliarization"), was, according to them, the essence of the literary. Bierce's technique of defamiliarizing and then dispelling the unfamiliarity corresponds to what Ian Watt, in a discussion of Joseph Conrad (born fifteen years after Bierce) calls "delayed decoding." See Watt, *Conrad in the Nineteenth Century* (Berkeley: University of California Press, 1979), 175–79.

CHAPTER 10

NO "SICKLY SENTIMENTAL GUSH"

Chickamauga and Chattanooga National Military Park
and the Limits of Reconciliation

CAROLINE E. JANNEY

For nearly two decades in the late nineteenth century, September 18–20 had been set aside as the annual reunion for the Society of the Army of the Cumberland. The date was no random selection; it marked the anniversary of the veterans' most fierce battle, their most sustained loss: the Battle of Chickamauga. In 1895, however, these days would serve not merely as an opportunity for Union veterans to recall their role in the battle but also for the entire nation to come together and dedicate the first national military park in the name of all Americans. As all had expected, the three-day festivities had been overwhelmingly reconciliatory in nature. The planning commission had exerted tremendous effort into ensuring that both Union and Confederate interests were equally represented in the processions and dedication services. The orators had, for the most part, abided by this guiding sentiment, emphasizing the courage of soldiers who wore the blue and gray and stressing the fraternity and unity evident upon the field. Most had likewise remained silent on the divisive issues of the war's causation and the tumultuous aftermath of Reconstruction. But not all were willing to forget or ignore the cause for which they had fought. Even at an event specifically planned and carefully orchestrated to emphasize reconciliation, the lingering power of the Lost Cause, the Union Cause, and the Emancipationist Cause could not be entirely suppressed.

In recent years scholars of Civil War memory have pointed to Blue-Gray reunions and the establishment of battlefield parks as evidence of the reconciliation sentiment that washed over the nation between the

1880s and early 1900s. The accepted narrative suggests an increasing momentum toward amicable relations between Union and Confederate veterans beginning in the 1880s based on shared ideas about bravery, honor, and white supremacy. According to many recent scholars, central to this reconciliationist memory was a willingness to forget. By the 1890s, they argue, the Union Cause, with its emphasis on preserving the Republic and ending slavery, had been largely forgotten. In order to secure sectional harmony, Union veterans had agreed to remain silent on divisive issues such as emancipation and secession. To bind up the nation's wounds, the victors had ignored both the war's causation and its outcome. Alternatively, these scholars observe, the Lost Cause had triumphed by locking arms with sentiments that extolled the battlefield bravery and valor of all (white) soldiers. Reconciliation thus offered both a whitewashed memory of the war and a vision of sectional healing on Confederate terms.[1]

Since the establishment of Chickamauga and Chattanooga National Military Park, veterans and historians have continued to tout it as a symbol of the golden age of reconciliation.[2] But even here the vision of sectional harmony described recently by historians did not prevail. On this hallowed site of national reunion, reconciliation was precarious and certainly did not mean that either side had forgotten—or was willing to forget—what they had fought for. Even if they failed to invite veterans of the U.S. Colored Troops to participate, white Union veterans had certainly not forgotten that slavery had been abolished by the war.[3] Reconciliatory rhetoric and sentiment certainly gained popularity during the closing decades of the nineteenth century, but it was never so linear, without contention, or as dominant as historians have described. Instead, as the creation of a national park at Chickamauga and Chattanooga reveals, the veterans of each side steadfastly maintained that their respective causes had been righteous and just. They might gather on the former fields of battle and shake hands over the proverbial bloody chasm, but they remained resolute that reconciliation had its limits.

In late April 1865, the men who had waged war on the fields around Chickamauga Creek and high above the clouds at Lookout Mountain ceased fighting on the field at Durham Station, North Carolina. Over the next few days, members of the defeated Army of Tennessee took oaths of amnesty and began the journey home. In the months that followed, most of the men who had fought with Major General William Tecumseh Sherman's combined armies marched on to Washington, D.C., for a grand review before being mustered out and returning to their own homes. But numerous veterans of the Army of the Cumberland who had fought to secure Chattanooga in 1863 and remained in the city for two years of occupation chose not to venture back to their antebellum homes. Instead, men like Brigadier General John T. Wilder, Hiram Chamberlain, and H. Clay Evans elected to remain in the city. Recognizing the region's potential, they purchased sawmills, waterworks, and rolling mills built during the Union army's occupation. Working alongside native Unionists who began returning to East Tennessee after the war, they mined the rich coal and iron deposits, built steel plants, and extended the railroad system, transforming the city into a Southern industrial stronghold.[4]

Even as the seventy-seven former officers and countless other Union veterans who remained in Chattanooga by 1868 sought to rebuild the region, they also worked hard to ensure that the city they had captured and defended with so much blood might serve as a shrine to the Union Cause.[5] Immediately after the war, members of the U.S. Colored Troops stationed there had constructed a large national cemetery between the Tennessee River and Missionary Ridge to honor the Union dead.[6] Like their counterparts throughout the nation, Unionists in Chattanooga gathered in the cemetery each May 30 for Memorial Day to pay tribute to their fallen heroes. The city's Union veterans, both white and black, joined fraternal organizations such as the Grand Army of the Republic (GAR) that provided opportunities to socialize with other veterans as well as support for less-fortunate comrades and their dependents.[7]

In each of these endeavors, Unionists reminded the nation that the war had been fought to preserve the Republic from secessionist fanatics who threatened the Founding Fathers' vision and, therefore, the future viability of democracy. As a member of the 1st Ohio Light Artillery reminded his comrades only months after the war ended, "The preservation of the government was paramount to all other objects."[8] But they had done more than that. "To save the Union was the single purpose of the people," observed another Union veteran. But "what statesmen had prophesied, what ourselves had surmised, we learned in the hard school of war—the perpetuity of the Union could be secured only through the freedom of the slave." Slavery had undermined the nation, and only slavery's demise could ensure its survival. For Northern veterans, the task of saving the Union could not be separated from slavery.[9] The four regiments of African Americans who had enlisted in Chattanooga during the war no doubt agreed.[10] But for them and their abolitionist supporters, universal freedom had been the most important cause and accomplishment of the war, and as such, espoused an emancipationist memory.[11] For them, the war would always be much more than merely the "War between the States." Instead, it had been the "Slavery War," the "Freedom War."[12]

Confederates in Chattanooga and elsewhere crafted their own memory of the war in these years. The Lost Cause, as it became known, was a romanticized interpretation of the war in which Confederate defeat was presented in the most favorable terms. This explanation began to take shape even before the Army of Northern Virginia had stacked its weapons and signed paroles at Appomattox. On April 10, 1865, General Robert E. Lee read his General Order No. 9 to his men. In it he lauded the loyalty, valor, and "unsurpassed courage and fortitude" of "the brave survivors of so many hard-fought battles" and assured his men that the surrender was through no fault of their own. Instead, he insisted that the army had been "compelled to yield to overwhelming numbers and resources."[13] By the 1870s, through the efforts of elite white Southern women of the Ladies' Memorial Associations, who helped establish Confederate cemeteries and the first Memorial Days, as well as such former Confederate leaders as Jubal A. Early, most white Southerners had embraced the Lost Cause. Its defenders repeatedly maintained that states' rights, not slavery, had caused the war and insisted that most slaves remained faithful to their masters even after emancipation. They claimed that Confederate soldiers had fought honorably and bravely and that the South had not been defeated but overwhelmed by insurmountable odds (and therefore was destined to lose). They maintained that throughout the war, Southern white women remained loyal and devoted to the cause. Finally, they heralded Robert E. Lee as the epitome of a Southern gentleman and the greatest military leader of the war.[14] By the late 1860s, there were three clear memories of the war: the Lost Cause, the Union Cause, and the Emancipationist Cause.

After U.S. troops began withdrawing from occupation duties in the South in the 1870s, a fourth memory of the war appeared, "Reconciliation," in which veterans of both sides found common ground often built around shared wartime hardships, exaggerated accounts of fraternization on the field of battle, and Lieutenant General Ulysses S. Grant's

magnanimous terms at Appomattox. Chattanoogans proudly declared
their city a symbol of this emerging spirit of cooperation among former
foes. Although not the first Union veteran to be elected mayor, John T.
Wilder's victory in 1871 offered an opportunity for former Confederates
to affirm the lessening of sectional acrimony. "It was deemed appropriate
that he should be elected mayor of the free choice of the people of Chattanooga to show that no bitterness engendered by the war remains in our
hearts," observed one self-proclaimed rebel.[15] Five years later the city's
former Confederate and Federal contingents came together for a centen-
nial celebration, prompting the newspaper to proclaim that "Chattanooga
knows no North, no South, no East, no West," but only "one indivisible
country."[16] Perhaps the most impressive showing of intersectional harmony occurred the following year, when Union and Confederate veterans
joined each other's respective Memorial Day services. On May 10, the anniversary of Lieutenant General Thomas J. "Stonewall" Jackson's death,
the "boys in blue" accompanied a procession of those clad in gray to the
Confederate cemetery. Wishing to reciprocate, on May 30 the "boys in
gray" agreed to appear without their rebel uniforms or battle flags in the
Federal Memorial Day services. Marching together, the former enemies
passed beneath a Gothic arch that read simply "Peace" before proceeding
to the national cemetery, where the city's women had decorated 12,000
graves. "Unity of sentiment, and oneness of action," observed a special
edition of the *Chattanooga Times,* "marked our characters on these days
in which the Gray blended with the Blue, and *vice versa.*"[17]

In the 1880s and 1890s, this spirit of reconciliation peaked on the
national stage. Throughout the country, Union and Confederate veterans
commenced participating in joint Blue-Gray reunions while popular
magazines such as *The Century* increasingly valorized the battles and
leaders of the war. When the former foes met at Blue-Gray reunions, they
agreed to remain silent on the divisive political issues that had caused
the conflict as well as the turmoil of Reconstruction. Instead, they com-
miserated on the severity of camp life and marches while commending
each other for their bravery on the field of battle. For reconciliation to
flourish, the North and South had to reach a compromise predicated
upon the exaltation of military experience and the insistence that the
causes of the war as well as the postwar consequences, namely Reconstruction, be ignored.

But this reverence for reconciliation had not supplanted the other
memories of the conflict for veterans. They had not lost sight of what

they had fought for—or against. When Union veterans met on their own at monument dedications and Memorial Days, they continued not only to espouse their allegiance to the Union Cause but also maintained that theirs was the only good and noble cause. Such was the case at an 1883 meeting of the Society of the Army of the Cumberland in Cincinnati. Although Major General Smith D. Atkins acknowledged that "southern soldiers were no cowards," he insisted theirs had been a wrong cause. He reminded his comrades that the rebels "were defending . . . a false and narrow civilization, and they ought to have been whipped." Neither had he nor his comrades forgotten emancipation. "It was a war for mastery of this continent between freedom and slavery," Atkins declared. "Freedom was the victory, and slavery is dead forever."[18] Former Confederates likewise continued to espouse the Lost Cause in Southern periodicals, reunions, and Memorial Days. Speaking before the Tennessee Association of Confederate Veterans in 1888, Peter Turney, chief justice of the state supreme court, fervently defended the Southern position. "We retract nothing, and believe the cause in which our comrades fell was just." He assured his fellow veterans that "they and we were not traitors or rebels against the authorized action of that government from which we seceded. Otherwise," he admitted, "it would be unlawful and immoral to keep alive and perpetuate the memories of those who fell."[19]

Even Blue-Gray reunions did not mean that animosity between the former foes had vanished, as attempts to plan the first gathering at Gettysburg revealed. In 1887, veterans of Major General George E. Pickett's division agreed to meet with some of their former adversaries in Brigadier General Alexander S. Webb's brigade. But tensions among the veterans nearly thwarted the proposed reunion. Not only did some Virginians question the loyalty of their brethren who agreed to attend, but reports that the former rebels would place a memorial behind Union lines at the so-called High Water Mark of the Confederacy caused a ruckus among Northerners. John Bachelder of the Gettysburg Battlefield Memorial Association received "bushels of letters" opposing any such memorial, while Governor Joseph B. Foracker threatened to use the Ohio National Guard "to prevent such sacrilege."[20] Lucius Fairchild, the one-armed commander in chief of the GAR, adamantly denounced the reunion. Given such animosity, in May the Virginians unanimously agreed not to attend. Only an open letter from the Philadelphia Brigade Association and a concession to mark the spot reached by Pickett's men during their now-famous charge convinced them otherwise.[21]

Despite the apparent success of the reunion, many Northerners were unwilling to embrace reconciliation. As veterans of the 15th Massachusetts observed, no "sickly sentimental gush of reconciliation" could make them forget that the principles their comrades died for "were right, and those against which they fought were deeply wrong."[22] Although Union veterans had invited Southerners to attend the twenty-fifth anniversary of the battle, most Confederates elected not to attend. Some, including Major General Daniel E. Sickles, nonetheless extolled the common brotherhood that all Americans had found on the field, but the absence of their foes pleased at least a few Northerners.[23] One Union veteran counseled former Confederates that "the hallowed field of Gettysburg is no place to vaunt treason and glorify rebellion." He was perfectly content that the ex-rebels "stay at home and gnaw the file of discontent in obscurity."[24] General J. P. S. Gobin, addressing members of a GAR post atop Little Round Top, likewise declared that he was "tired of this gush and pretense for the glorification of the veteran simply because he wore a gray uniform with a Southern flag printed on his badge. That badge meant treason and rebellion in 1861, and what it meant then it means now." "I want it to be distinctly understood, now and for all time," he bellowed, "that the men who wore the gray were everlastingly and eternally wrong."[25]

Perhaps it was such acerbic sectionalism that compelled Union veterans Henry Van Ness Boynton and Ferdinand Van Derveer to call for the preservation of another battlefield, one that would be established on the premise of national reconciliation. In their telling, the idea occurred to the Army of the Cumberland veterans as they traversed the battlefield of Chickamauga that same summer, electing to remember the silver anniversary of their army's bloodiest action. In late August Boynton, a lieutenant colonel in the 35th Ohio Infantry during the battle, penned a series of articles in the *Cincinnati Commercial Gazette* imploring his former comrades to preserve the notable field. "Why should it not, as well as the Eastern fields, be marked by monuments, and its lines accurately preserved for history?" Chickamauga was exceptional, he claimed. "There was no more magnificent fighting during the war than both armies did there." Hoping to move beyond the sectional bitterness that still seemed to hold sway at Gettysburg, he suggested that at Chickamauga "both sides might well unite in preserving the field where both, in a military sense, won such renown."[26]

In September Boynton and Van Derveer presented their idea at the annual meeting of the Society of the Army of the Cumberland. The society found the notion compelling and appointed a committee to report back the following year. Enlivened by the support, Boynton worked tirelessly on his propaganda campaign. As the Washington correspondent for the *Cincinnati Commercial Gazette,* he continued to send articles to Ohio. But he also reached out to former Confederates, requesting individual officers to support the endeavor and appealing to their principal periodical, the *Southern Historical Society,* to publish his appeal. Gettysburg had been established exclusively by (and many argued for) Northerners. Only the positions of the Army of the Potomac had been marked, while the marble, granite, and bronze statuary erected on the field in the 1870s and 1880s served as poignant reminders that Gettysburg was an exclusively Union memorial park.[27] Chickamauga would be different. Not only would it honor both sides equally, but men like Boynton hoped, it would be funded and directed by the national government rather than a private corporation or a handful of states. This park, unlike Gettysburg, would honor Union and Confederate veterans "with equal satisfaction."[28]

Plans for the proposed military park continued to gain momentum throughout 1889. In mid-February the committee appointed by the Society of the Army of the Cumberland held its first meeting in Washington with several members of the War Department. Within hours the committee had agreed upon the necessity of inviting former Confederates who had served at Chickamauga and now sat in Congress to join their effort. The next day these men, including Senator John Tyler Morgan and Representative Joseph Wheeler, gathered alongside Union veterans in the room of the Senate Committee of Military Affairs. Together with the aid of one hundred influential veterans from both sides, the committee would move forward for the creation of the intersectional Chickamauga Memorial Association.[29]

The association held its first official meeting at Chattanooga on September 19, 1889, during the Society of the Army of the Cumberland's annual reunion. For several months prior to this, newspapers from around the country had beseeched veterans from both sides to attend the festivities. "Come, you who wore the gray and those who wore the blue, and have a frolic on the field where you fought and lend your aid to the preservation of that field as a model memorial of your own and your countrymen's valor," they implored. And come they did. More than 12,000 veterans descended upon Chattanooga, Tennessee, for the first meeting of the bisectional Chickamauga Memorial Association. Gathered under a large tent, they listened intently to speeches by former Union major general William Rosecrans and former Confederate major general John B. Gordon emphasize unity and laud the idea for a national park at Chickamauga as a symbol of the nation's healed wounds.[30]

Heralded by his comrades as the man responsible for the proposed park, Boynton likewise took the stage that day. Like the others, he reminded his audience of Chickamauga's importance, of its astronomical casualty rate, and of the heroics of its assaults—attacks far more daring and commendable than Pickett's Charge at Gettysburg. "There is no other field of the war which more fully illustrates the indomitable courage and all the varied qualities of the American veteran," he asserted. As such, the Chickamauga Memorial Association hoped to preserve the field and surpass Gettysburg's efforts, where only the Union lines had been marked. Here, the lines of both armies would be equally marked along with monuments from each of the states that had men in the fight. "We meet here, surviving veterans of that field," he declared, "under one flag, citizens of one country, to celebrate and take measures to perpetuate the memory of the fighting which will cause Chickamauga to take first rank among the battles of the world."[31]

Like his fellow veterans, Boynton sought a spirit of sectional cooperation and comradeship. This was indeed a significant part of the impetus behind the park movement. But such did not mean that he had forgotten why they had waged such a bloody battle twenty-six years earlier. "I yield to no man an iota of my convictions," he firmly stated. "They are as dear to me, as clear in my mind, as when we fought for them." He had not forgotten the Union Cause. But neither did he expect the Confederates to forget theirs. Instead, he insisted that these were differences that need not be discussed. Questions of politics and blame did not belong. Such might threaten the very premise of national reconciliation that was central to the proposed park. Instead, the park project should emphasize "American fighting" and "the achievements of American manhood" performed by each side on the field at Chickamauga.[32] This was to be a national park established on the premise of sectional reunion.

The following day even more arrived for a grand barbeque in nearby Crawfish Springs, Georgia. Serving perhaps as many as 25,000 people, thirty tables had been piled high with meat, loaves of bread, and "pickles in abundance." But that would have to wait. First the ravenous crowds would have to elect the officers of the Chickamauga Memorial Association, appoint incorporators from each state, and listen to more speeches espousing reconciliation.[33]

By early 1890, a bill proposing the establishment of a military park that would include the battlefields at both Chickamauga and Chattanooga had been introduced in Congress. The House Committee on Military Affairs heartily endorsed the plan, noting that the eastern armies had a semipreserved battlefield at Gettysburg, but the western armies had no such memorial. The committee reminded the House that the fighting had been especially bloody, "if not the bloodiest," and strategically significant. "Some of the most remarkable tactical movements and the deadliest fighting of the war of the rebellion" had occurred on these fields. As such, the committee tacked on an additional justification for the creation of a *national military* park: the lines of battle should be preserved for professional study by both historians and the military. Despite this pragmatic rationale, the committee unequivocally held that "the political questions which were involved in the contest do not enter into this view of the subject, nor do they belong to it." Instead, the creation of the park would be in all aspects "purely a military project."[34] In other words, the park would be the epitome—the shining national emblem—of reconciliation. Everyone agreed to ignore the causes and consequences of the war and concentrate instead on the heroics and valor of the field's "American veterans."

On August 20, 1890, President Benjamin Harrison, the last Union general to hold the presidency, signed the bill into law, thus establishing the nation's first military park. The enabling legislation, like the battlefield itself, was to be a joint effort between Union and Confederate veterans. Three commissioners would be appointed by the secretary of war, one a Union veteran of the battle (Brevet Brigadier General Joseph S. Fullerton), who would also serve as chairman of the commission; one a Confederate veteran of the battle (Lieutenant General Alexander P. Stewart); and finally a Union veteran still on active duty (Captain Sanford C. Kellogg). Boynton, who had precipitated the whole idea, would serve as the commission's historian and secretary.

During the next five years, the work of restoring the field to its 1863 appearance progressed steadily. Once the land had been obtained, either through the willing sale by owners or more often through condemnation, the park's burgeoning staff cleared undergrowth that had appeared since the battle, opened more than forty miles of roads, and marked the battle lines. Under Boynton's direction, the commission began placing tablets on the field marking unit positions and headquarters and erecting cannonball pyramids on the sites where general officers had fallen. By 1894,

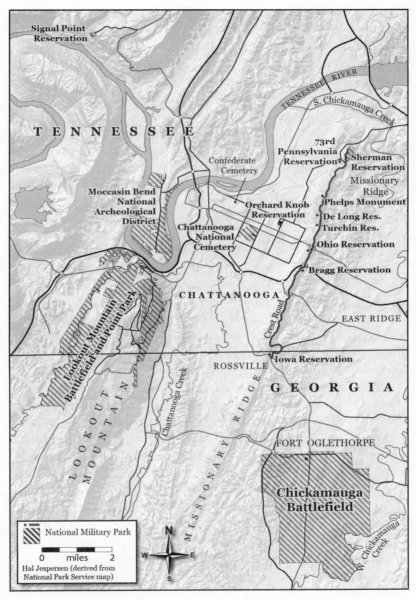

Chickamauga and Chattanooga National Military Park, Present Day
(2013 Boundary).

twenty-one states had organized commissions charged with raising funds to erect monuments, tablets, and markers for their various units. The park was developing just as its proponents had hoped—so much so that other battlefields were following in its lead, with commissions established at Shiloh and Gettysburg.[35] But before Americans could turn their attention to these other parks, the nation's first national military park would host a grand dedication ceremony.

In mid-September 1895 the crowds began flocking to Chattanooga. Thousands of Union veterans made their way south from Louisville, where they had attended the annual GAR encampment—the first ever south of the Ohio River. Others, both Union and Confederate, came from every direction of the compass by rail, wagon, or carriage. Flags had been unfurled to the breeze, and colorful bunting in the national colors decorated the homes and businesses of every town along the route. "This bubbling spirit of pleasure and exuberant feeling of patriotism seems to have penetrated every community in this section," observed a journalist from Atlanta, transforming the surrounding countryside into "one solid streak of red, white, and blue."[36] Chattanooga welcomed the expected crowd of 50,000 with open arms. The city had spent the better part of the previous year upgrading roads and securing accommodations, food, and care for their guests. It was prepared for the throngs who descended to consecrate the blood-bought field in the name of reunion.[37]

Not everyone looked forward to the impeding Blue-Gray love fest. "I am in for a rather conspicuous part in the Chattanooga Park dedication—though I did my best to dodge it," Senator Edward Cary Walthall, a former Confederate general from the Army of Tennessee, wrote to a friend in early September 1895. "I am a poor hand at Blue and Gray *gush,* but the occasion will require a little of that," he confessed. "My idea is to do enough in that direction to save my distance, but to set the Confederate before the world, briefly, as eating no dirt but still bowing to the inevitable—but raising his head afterward and keeping it up ever since—& to show too, that a Southern soldier & a Mississippian took the lead in bringing about the state of things that makes the justification possible." He then wondered, "Have I said the Confederate stuff *stiff* enough & not too much so?"[38] Clearly, Walthall recognized the precarious balancing act required of him. How would he find the right tone, the right mix of "gush" without denouncing his own cause? One can only imagine how many other veterans from both sides kept such sentiments to themselves.

The three-day celebration opened on September 18, an unseasonably

hot day and the thirty-second anniversary of the first clashes at Chickamauga. Throughout the first day, eight states (all Northern) dedicated
regimental and state monuments scattered across the battlefield, ultimately turning over ownership to the federal government.[39] The following day, September 19, crowds gathered for the formal dedication of the
Chickamauga portion of the park. Along the crescent of Snodgrass Hill, a
crowd of 40,000–50,000 spectators gathered for a forty-four-gun salute
promptly at noon commencing the service. After a stirring rendition
of "America," Senator (and former general) John M. Palmer of Illinois
spoke on behalf of the Union veterans, followed by Senator (and former
Confederate general) John B. Gordon of Georgia, commander in chief
of the United Confederate Veterans. Neither President Harrison nor
Secretary of War Daniel S. Lamont could attend. Instead, Vice President
Adlai E. Stevenson provided the keynote address, then various other
generals and state governors offered a few words.[40] On September 20
the ceremonies shifted to Chattanooga, where the veterans gathered to
dedicate that section of the park. A slight relief from the previous days'
oppressive heat convinced many city residents to join in the festivities,
which began with a parade by soldiers of the U.S. Army and Civil War
veterans. Again, veterans from both sides offered dedicatory addresses.[41]

In keeping with the park's mission, the spirit of reconciliation carried the day. Unionists and former Confederates greeted each other with
warm embraces, marched together under the Stars and Stripes in great
processions, and heralded the bravery and honor of their former foes.
In his keynote address, Vice President Stevenson reminded the crowds
that this day was truly auspicious. Thirty-two years after the great battle,
the honored survivors had gathered once more on the heights. "They
meet, not in deadly conflict," he noted, "but as brothers—under one flag,
fellow-citizens of a common country."[42] Reporters from across the nation
echoed these sentiments. "The Mason and Dixon line has been wiped off
the map," observed a Los Angeles newspaper. "The friendly, brotherly
feeling that has been displayed here this week . . . proves that the bitter
sectionalism that so long divided the Union no longer exists." Its reporter
declared, "There is no 'North and South.'" On this blood-stained field,
the aging warriors had "signed a compact by which the last vestige of
venom caused by the civil war was blotted out."[43]

At least a handful of Union veterans, however, disagreed, taking the
opportunity to remind their listeners that there had been a right cause
and a wrong cause. Speaking at the Illinois monument dedication, Major

James A. Connolly intoned that "the men of the blue and the men of the gray fell and slept together in death on this field, where armed Right and armed Wrong met in their giant struggle for mastery."[44] Colonel Henry M. Duffield of Michigan was not opposed to honoring Confederates for their bravery, but he adamantly refused to acknowledge that their cause had been just. "Upon this field hallowed by the bravery and sanctified by the blood of the men who saved the Union," he implored, "no mawkish sentiment should confuse the right or palliate the wrong." Someday, he believed, the South would recognize that "the cause of secession was wrong and the cause of the Union was right."[45] Charles H. Grosvenor, a congressman and former general from Ohio who had sponsored the park's legislation, observed that Confederates "were terribly wrong," though he admitted that they had "stood ready to die for the errors they espoused."[46] U.S. Senator (and former general) Charles F. Manderson of Nebraska perhaps expressed such sentiments most succinctly. Paraphrasing Grant after Appomattox, he asserted, "we, who fought to save, were forever right and they, who fought to destroy, were eternally wrong."[47]

Governor John P. Altgeld of Illinois was more pointed in explaining precisely what "armed Wrong" implied. "The principle these men fought for meant the perpetuation of human slavery," he declared, "they were fighting for a condition against which the humanity of the age protested."[48] Ohio governor William McKinley likewise acknowledged that slavery had been abolished, and thus the cause of conflict removed.[49] Even at the Chickamauga dedication services on September 19, Senator Palmer of Illinois reminded the crowd of both Union and Confederate veterans that African slavery had been "the root of sectional bitterness." It was not merely that slavery had caused the war, but rather Union veterans lauded their role in emancipation. As Palmer noted, Union victory had ensured that "the flag of our country became at once the emblem of freedom and the symbol of National power."[50] In a bit of revisionist history, or selective memory at the least, Altgeld went so far as to suggest that most U.S. soldiers had been motivated from the outset by abolitionist sentiment. "More than a million of men [sic] in all came down from the North, shouting as they marched, 'This Union forever and equal rights for all,'" he proclaimed.[51] And some exceptional figures, such as Major General O. O. Howard, former commissioner of the Freedmen's Bureau, recognized the long-term implications of emancipation, pointing out that "black men are advancing; the schools are almost universal; his home is being improved."[52]

Veterans such as these sternly defended the Union Cause as the *only* righteous cause, refusing to overlook the fact that slavery had precipitated the war. Nor were they willing, even in the name of white supremacy, to forget that their actions had helped secure freedom.[53] They left no doubt that they were the victors, commemorating the Union soldiers who had so bravely ensured that slavery would never again tear the nation asunder. Although U.S. Colored Troops veterans, including the two local colored GAR posts, were not present at the dedication, white veterans had not forgotten the twin achievements of the Northern war effort: preservation of the Union and universal freedom. The dedication may have been premised on reconciliation, but emancipation would not be forgotten.

Even those who appeared to espouse reconciliation were more accurately invoking the Union Cause. Speaking at Ohio's dedication services, McKinley elaborated on the fruits of Union victory. What had it all been for, he asked. What had the war meant? "A Union stronger and freer than ever before," he answered. "A reunited people, a reunited country, is the glorious reward." This was not merely reconciliationist rhetoric devoid of any blame. Instead, what he offered was the very essence of the Union Cause. Northern soldiers had fought to preserve the democratic principles established by the Founding Fathers that set the United States apart from other nations. They had fought to prevent secession. They had fought to reunite a nation shattered by slavery. And they had won. "The bond of union shall not be broken," the governor observed. Union victory had ensured "that the Constitution is and shall remain the supreme law over all."[54] General Grosvenor invoked a similar point. He too argued that the victorious Union army had "prevented the overthrow of the union of States" and "fought to restore the Constitution as the supreme law of the land." But something even grander had occurred in the war's aftermath. "The American Union is today firmly reestablished," he observed, "in the affection, and in the loyalty of all her citizens, North and South. This is the result which makes us happy today. It is that we are no longer enemies, but brothers. Brothers in loyalty; brothers in the devotion to the Union."[55] Reunion and reconciliation *was* the Union Cause.

Central to this message of reunion was an emphasis on the "American soldier." Speaker after speaker, whether Union or Confederate, lauded "American traits" of courage and honor to dedicate the field where "American met American" in bloody struggle.[56] On one hand, this was vital to the sentiment of reconciliation. During the war, both Northerners and

Southerners had conceived of themselves as the true Americans perpetuating the Founding Fathers' legacy. Both had maintained that they were Americans either of the United States or the Confederate States (it was their foe whom they described as decidedly "un-American").[57] By the 1890s, focusing on the common "American" heritage allowed veterans and politicians to avoid the divisive political issues of the conflict, including slavery, while commemorating the best of white Northern and Southern society—that is, remembering a war of brotherly camaraderie rather than one of senseless bloodshed. On the other hand, in embracing the American soldier, Confederate veterans were buying into—consciously or not—at least part of the Union Cause. After all, Union soldiers had fought for the perpetuation of the United States of America—and they had won.

The Union Cause, however, was not the only one that would be remembered and even celebrated during the dedication. Perhaps the most ostentatious display of the Lost Cause, indeed of continuing sectional rancor, appeared on the night of September 20. The evening had been reserved for a reunion between veterans of the Army of the Potomac and their former foes from the Army of Northern Virginia who had fought at Chickamauga. Meeting under at great canvas tent at Orchard Knob, the occasion began typically enough. General Walthall (who had lamented his distaste for "Blue and Gray *gush*" a few weeks prior), a senator-elect from Mississippi, provided a brief overview of the battle, while Colonel Lewis R. Stegman of New York discussed the battles around Chattanooga.[58]

Alabama governor William C. Oates took the stage next, with complete disregard for the spirit of reconciliation that had dominated the proceedings thus far. His address began with an account of Chickamauga replete with references to his "humble" but "conspicuous" role in it. But he soon shifted tone. As he had done in countless other speeches over the years, Oates turned to an exposition on the causes of the war filled with venom and acrimony. He condemned the North for its Puritan ancestry and suggested that the Southern cavalier represented a substantially superior culture. The Puritans and their "aggressive fanaticism," he intoned, had "caused an ocean of tears to be shed, drenched the land in blood, and sacrificed the lives of a million men and untold millions of treasure." Expecting the usual Blue-Gray rhetoric, the veterans must have been stunned into rapt silence.[59]

Still Oates continued. Unlike so many other Lost Cause orators, he did not shy away from slavery. On the contrary, he argued that it had

long been the Pandora's box of American politics. It had been a lawful
state institution, and the responsibility for its continuance belonged to
the states alone. In the tradition of the Lost Cause, he described a land
of benevolent masters and faithful slaves. It was Lincoln and his "band
of fanatics" who had incited "the slaves to insurrection, arson, and indis-
criminate murder of white people" and who had martyred such figures
as John Brown. Recalling the speeches of Illinois governor Altgeld and
others, the Alabama governor challenged the notion that abolition had
been one of the grand objects of the Northern soldier. In race-baiting
language he asserted that such was the revisionist interpretation of the
Radicals. "You could not more deeply offend a Union soldier than tell him
he was fighting for the freedom of the negroes," he shouted. Wrapping up
his diatribe, he informed the veterans that the white South "awakened
to common danger—not about slavery alone, but that their ancient and
well defined right to govern their own internal affairs in their own way
would be denied and destroyed . . . under the guise of law and consti-
tutional administration." Finally, having endured enough, the Union
veterans jumped to their feet in protest. Those gathered had expected
to hear the by-now-predictable lines about reconciliation, not an attack
on their sacred cause.[60]

Antagonistic accusations were not uncommon at Confederate-only
occasions, yet seldom did speakers employ such discordant language at
Blue-Gray reunions, especially not at such events on the national stage.
Oates's divisive remarks were more than a rejection of the reconciliatory language—they were a rejection of the Union Cause. As soon as the
recalcitrant rebel made his way back to his seat, several Northern governors leapt at the opportunity to respond. Vermont governor Urban A.
Woodbury took the stage first. Assuring the veterans that he harbored
no ill will toward those who had worn the gray, he observed that he was
willing to admit that Confederates had fought for what they believed
right. "But," he proclaimed, "we cannot teach our children but that they
were wrong." Incensed, Governor Peter Turney of Tennessee, a former
Confederate colonel, strode to the podium, offering what appeared at
first to be a more reconciliatory tone. "We fought this fight together. This
is our common country," he bellowed. But he would not denounce his
cause. "I was on the losing side. I believed I was right. . . . It has been said
that our children should be taught that we were wrong," he observed. "I
stand before you as one who does all in his power to persuade his children . . . that their father was no traitor, that he acted from an honest

conviction . . . and expects to stand by his convictions." With that, the
Confederate veterans in the audience erupted in applause.[61] Just as Union
veterans accepted the "sentimental gush" of reconciliation on their own
terms, so would former Confederates. Reconciliation had its place. It
also had its limitations.

As the dedication of the nation's first national military park came to a
close, the crowds again boarded the trains and wagons that had brought
them to Chattanooga only days earlier. Many headed back to their homes
throughout the nation, but others would continue their trek southward
to attend the Atlanta Cotton States and International Exposition. With
them, many would take images of a reunited nation. "The general trend
of sentiment, apparently, of all those who participated," reported one
Northern periodical, "was that the war is over; the Union preserved;
the nationality established; slavery destroyed; and that we are to be
henceforth one people with one flag; and that we are so far and so fast as
possible to ignore the past and set our faces toward the future, to work
out together our manifest destiny."[62] In other words, the Union Cause of
reunion had been secured.

At least a few left the battlefield-turned-park with lingering doubts
about the extent of sectional reconciliation, uncertainties prompted in
large part by Governor Oates. Horatio King, a former officer in the Army
of the Potomac, forwarded copies of Oates's speech to John P. Nicholson,
a commissioner for the newly appointed Gettysburg National Military
Park. "The joyful exercises," he wrote, "were marred . . . by the discordant
notes of General and Governor Oates of Alabama[,] who . . . declared
that their (the Confederate) cause was just and that . . . the peaceable
separation of the North and South would have been both wise and desirable." Alabamians, however, relished their leader's fiery words, writing
to Oates to request copies of his decidedly unreconciliatory speech.[63] For
its part, the *Confederate Veteran,* the principle organ for all Confederate
organizations, neglected to print Oates's address, although it did feature
Governor Woodbury's response. For those who had not read the newspapers or heard of Oates's inflammatory speech, they must have surely
thought that Woodbury had initiated the sectional acrimony.[64]

Former Confederates who read the *Veteran* may have simply been
primed to see attacks on their sacred Lost Cause. In the aftermath of
the GAR's annual encampment at Louisville only a month earlier, the
magazine had seethed at the pompous behavior of the Union veterans
invited to hold their reunion in the Southern-sympathizing city. Former

GAR commander-in-chief John Palmer, claimed the *Veteran,* was not nearly as "magnanimous" in his remarks in relation to the causes of the war as he should have been (foreshadowing his address at the Chickamauga dedication). But the magazine was particularly irritated that the attendees had elected to wear their uniforms rather than civilian clothes. "The array of blue and tinsel was quite similar to that worn South . . . [a] third of a century ago," one article grumbled. "These things excited memories which did not increase our admiration for 'Old Glory,' as they call the flag of the United States, made sacred by the blood of our fathers. Many evidently did not consider the proprieties on becoming guests."[65] Neither Confederate nor Union veterans were willing to forget.

Despite the lingering evidence of sectional hostility, in the years after the dedication of Chickamauga and Chattanooga National Military Park, many veterans continued to join together in the name of reconciliation. Following the model established at Chickamauga of Union and Confederate cooperation, four more battlefields were authorized as national military parks: Antietam (1890), Shiloh (1894), Gettysburg (1895), and Vicksburg (1899). At each of these, veterans gathered for dedication ceremonies that highlighted the reunited and reconciled nation.[66] Speakers such as John B. Gordon continued to espouse the "American brotherhood" that held such a predominant place at the 1895 dedication.[67] Veterans continued to attend Blue-Gray reunions, perhaps most famously in 1913, when 53,407 former soldiers and possibly as many spectators descended on Gettysburg to mark the fiftieth anniversary of the battle.[68]

For many of the men who had fought at Chickamauga and Chattanooga, there would be additional opportunities to celebrate the battlefield's reconciliatory spirit. In 1898 the park served as a staging area for the Spanish-American War. Once again, Northern and Southern soldiers descended upon the field, but this time they would do so under one flag united against a common enemy.[69] In September 1899, veterans of the blue and gray gathered to dedicate the Wilder Tower, an observation tower erected upon the site where John T. Wilder's famed Lightening Brigade had fought on the second day of Chickamauga. Chief among those who attended the celebration were members of the Nathan Bedford Forrest Post of the United Confederate Veterans. Colonel Tomlinson Fort, attired in his Confederate uniform, commended Wilder's brigade for their courage, observing that "there were no better fighters in the Federal Army." But like Oates and other ex-rebels only five years earlier, he refused to abandon the Lost Cause even when speaking at a predominantly

Union occasion. The war had been over the constitution, he maintained. In other words, the Confederate cause had been as just as righteous as that for which his former enemies had laid down their lives.[70]

If neither side was willing to forget its cause, perhaps some other grand gesture might at least serve as a testament to the reunited nation in the wake of the Spanish-American War. In December 1899 Ohio congressman Grosvenor, a former Union brigade commander, drafted legislation requesting three hundred thousand dollars from the federal government to construct an "Arch of Nationality" at Chickamauga. In the style of the Arc de Triomphe in Paris and constructed of massive granite blocks, the monument was to "commemorate the heroism of the American soldier, and the complete union which has resulted from the joint military service of all sections in the war with Spain." Others had proposed that such a memorial be placed in Washington, D.C., but Secretary of War Elihu Root and Henry Boynton, now chairman of the Chickamauga Commission, thought the battlefield a better option. Not only had troops mobilized at the park prior to the war with Cuba but also the fields were centrally located midway between Maine and Texas. Perhaps more importantly, they noted, nearly every state east of the Rocky Mountains had troops that had fought on these fields. "The military history of the United States can be more appropriately symbolized at Chickamauga than at any other point within our national boundaries."[71] But like other attempts to construct national peace memorials with federal funds later in the century, the arch never materialized.[72]

The national government never succeeded in erecting a memorial of stone to the reunited nation, but the state of New York fared better. In November 1910, fifty years after the election of President Abraham Lincoln had precipitated the bitter war, New York veterans unveiled their Peace Monument upon Lookout Mountain. The tallest memorial in the park, the white marble shaft was crowned with a Union and Confederate veteran clasping hands in peace and standing beneath the Stars and Stripes. The bronze group by sculptor Hinton Perry had been titled "Reconciliation." But the inscription on one façade, bearing the words of President McKinley, suggested that perhaps this was a monument to the Union Cause rather than merely reconciliation. "Reunited—One Country Again and Forever," it declared.[73] Three years later the GAR hosted a reunion for the battle's fiftieth anniversary. As was expected, GAR commander Alfred B. Beers focused on the spirit of cooperation that now existed between the former foes. Confederate veterans were even invited to don their gray uniforms in the parade. But no one could have misunderstood the event's theme: "One People, One Nation, One Flag."[74] The Union Cause had been the victorious one.

Here, fifty years after one of the war's bloodiest battles, was evidence that the nation finally had reunited. Not only could veterans come together for reunions but at Chickamauga they also revealed that they could work together to preserve a field drenched with their blood only thirty years prior. Yet the story of the first military park reveals that even though reconciliationist sentiment might have reached its apex in the 1890s, it was never complete nor was it the dominant interpretation of the war. Instead, veterans and civilians from both sides tenaciously clung to their own cause, whether that was the Union, Lost , or Emancipationist Cause. . . It likewise reminds us that reconciliation was not solely based upon a whitewashed memory of the war, as historians have argued. In this case, as in countless others, Northerners had not forgotten (or agreed to forget) that slavery had caused the war. They had not capitulated to the Lost Cause. Nor were Confederates willing to concede that they had been wrong. The war had been too bloody, too long, and too costly to forget. Reconciliation might be wonderfully successful in establishing national military parks, but everyone understood that it had its limits.

ACKNOWLEDGMENTS

I would like to thank Keith Bohannon, Tim Smith, Evan Jones, and William Lee White for sharing some of their research regarding Chickamauga and Chattanooga with me. I would also like to thank Gary Gallagher and Darren Dochuck for reading and commenting on earlier versions of this essay.

NOTES

1. For historians who have emphasized reunion and reconciliation, see Paul H. Buck, *Road to Reunion, 1865–1900* (Boston, 1937); David Blight, *Race and Reunion: The Civil War in American Memory* (Cambridge: Harvard University Press, 2001), 2–5, 65, 198, 265; Nina Silber, *Romance of Reunion: Northerners and the South, 1865–1900* (Chapel Hill: University of North Carolina Press, 1993); and Timothy B. Smith, *The Golden Age of Battlefield Preservation: The Decade of the 1890s and the Establishment of America's First Five Military Parks* (Knoxville: University of Tennessee Press, 2008). For discussion of the complexities of reconciliation and the persistence of sectional animosities, see John R. Neff, *Honoring*

the Civil War Dead: Commemoration and the Problem of Reconciliation (Lawrence: University Press of Kansas, 2005); and John Coski, *The Confederate Battle Flag: America's Most Embattled Emblem* (Cambridge: Harvard University Press, 2005), 67.

2. Timothy Smith, in particular, touts Chickamauga and Chattanooga as well as the other four military parks created in the 1890s as "the chief symbols of this reconciliatory and commemorative era." *Golden Age,* 5.

3. Union veterans heralded emancipation among their achievements (along with preserving the Union) from 1865 well into the twentieth century. See Gary W. Gallagher, *The Union War* (Boston: Harvard University Press, 2011); and Barbara Gannon, *The Won Cause: Black and White Comradeship in the Grand Army of the Republic* (Chapel Hill: University of North Carolina Press, 2011). Race was another matter. Noting that white Union soldiers continued to celebrate their role in emancipation is not meant to suggest that they did not harbor attitudes of white supremacy.

4. Charles Stuart McGehee, "Wake of the Flood: A Southern City in the Civil War, Chattanooga, 1838–1873" (Ph.D. diss., University of Virginia, 1982), 141–48; Steven Cox, "Chattanooga Was His Town: The Life of General John T. Wilder," unpublished paper presented at the Chattanooga Area Historical Association, Jan. 24, 2004, Chickamauga and Chattanooga National Military Park Library.

5. For historians who have discussed the Union Cause at length, see Gallagher, *Union War;* Joan Waugh, *U. S. Grant* (Chapel Hill: University of North Carolina Press, 2009); Gary W. Gallagher, *Causes Won, Lost, & Forgotten: How Hollywood and Popular Art Shape What We Know about the Civil War* (Chapel Hill: University of North Carolina Press, 2008); and Neff, *Honoring the Civil War Dead,* 8–10. Neff refers to the Northern myth as the "Cause Victorious."

6. McGehee, "Wake of the Flood," 147–52.

7. Wallace Even Davies, *Patriotism on Parade: The Story of Veterans' and Hereditary Organizations in America, 1783–1900* (Cambridge: Harvard University Press, 1955), 31–33, 74; Stuart McConnell, *Glorious Contentment: The Grand Army of the Republic, 1865–1900* (Chapel Hill: University of North Carolina Press, 1992), 24–25.

8. H. M. Davidson, *History of Battery A, First Regiment of Ohio Vol. Light Artillery.* (Milwaukee: Daily Wisconsin Steam Printing House, 1865), 139–40.

9. "Memorial Day Oration of William H. Lambert at the National Cemetery, Arlington, Va., May 30, 1883" (Philadelphia: Grant, Faires, & Rodgers, 1883), 7–8; Gannon, *Won Cause.*

10. The four regiments that enlisted in Chattanooga were the 14th, 16th, 42nd, and 44th U.S. Colored Troops. McGehee, "Wake of the Flood," 137.

11. For discussion of how emancipation—and the preservation of the Union—remained integral to Northern memories of the war well into the twentieth century, see M. Keith Harris, "'The Unending Work of the Republic': Emancipation and the National Commemorative Ethos, 1885–1915," unpublished conference paper, presented at the Southern History Association meeting, Oct. 2008. For discussion of emancipation as a separate category, see Gallagher, *Causes Won, Lost, & Forgotten,* 2; and Blight, *Race and Reunion,* 2–3.

12. Kathleen Ann Clark, *Defining Moments: African American Commemoration & Political Culture in the South, 1863–1913* (Chapel Hill: University of North Carolina Press, 2005), 15. Despite threats from whites, there was very little violence at the Evacuation Day and Surrender Day ceremonies. But on April 16, 1866, when freedmen and women gathered in Norfolk for a procession to mark the passage of the Civil Rights Bill, a shootout left two white people dead, one black youth stabbed in the stomach, and countless others wounded.

William A. Blair, *Cities of the Dead: Contesting the Memory of the Civil War in the South, 1865–1914* (Chapel Hill: University of North Carolina Press, 2004), 41–42.

13. William Marvel, *Lee's Last Retreat: The Flight to Appomattox* (Chapel Hill: University of North Carolina Press, 2002), 189; Robert E. Lee, *Wartime Papers of R. E. Lee,* ed. Clifford Dowdey and Louis H. Manarin (Boston: Little, Brown, 1961), 934–35.

14. On the Lost Cause, see, for example, W. Fitzhugh Brundage, *The Southern Past: A Clash of Race and Memory* (Cambridge: Harvard University Press, 2005); Alice Fahs and Joan Waugh, eds., *The Memory of the Civil War in American Culture* (Chapel Hill: University of North Carolina Press, 2004); Blair, *Cities of the Dead;* Blight, *Race and Reunion;* Gary Gallagher and Alan T. Nolan, eds., *The Myth of the Lost Cause and Civil War History* (Bloomington: Indiana University Press, 2000); Grace Elizabeth Hale, *Making Whiteness: The Culture of Segregation in the South, 1890–1940* (New York: Vintage, 1998), 47–49, 79–80; and Gaines M. Foster, *Ghosts of the Confederacy: Defeat, the Lost Cause and the Emergence of the New South, 1865–1913* (New York: Oxford University Press, 1988).

15. McGehee, "Wake of the Flood," 152, 190, 195; newspaper quoted in Gilbert E. Govan and James W. Livingood, *The Chattanooga Country, 1540–1975: From Tomahawks to TVA,* 3rd ed. (Knoxville: University of Tennessee Press, 1977), 286. Wilder resigned within eight months, citing business reasons.

16. Unnamed Chattanooga newspaper, July 6, 1876, quoted in Govan and Livingood, *Chattanooga Country,* 306–307.

17. Ibid., 306–308.

18. *New York Times,* Oct. 25, 1883.

19. Peter Turney, "They Wore the Gray.—The Southern Cause Vindicated," *Southern Historical Society Papers* 16 (1888), 319–38. Interestingly, this speech is printed immediately ahead of Boynton's essay calling for a reconciliationist national military park (see note 28 below).

20. Bachelder served as the superintendent of tablets and legends beginning in 1883. It was he who suggested the criteria for inscribing and positioning monuments. That is, monuments were to mark points from which units launched their attack—the so-called battle-line regulations. Jim Weeks, *Gettysburg: Memory, Market, and an American Shrine* (Princeton, N.J.: Princeton University Press, 2003), 24–25.

21. Carol Reardon, *Pickett's Charge in History and Memory* (Chapel Hill: University of North Carolina Press, 1997), 91–95; *Maine Farmer,* Apr. 21, 1887. The marker would ostensibly mark the spot where Confederate general Lewis A. Armistead fell, thus not overriding the battle-line regulations.

22. Reardon, *Pickett's Charge,* 92.

23. Edward T. Linenthal, *Sacred Ground: Americans and Their Battlefields* (Urbana: University of Illinois Press, 1991), 95. Only about three hundred former Confederates attended. Reardon, *Pickett's Charge,* 111.

24. Reardon, *Pickett's Charge,* 110.

25. Linenthal, *Sacred Ground,* 95.

26. Henry Van Ness Boynton, *Chattanooga and Chickamauga: General H. V. Boynton's Letters to the* Cincinnati Commercial Gazette (Washington, D.C.: Geo. R. Gray, Printer, 1891). The article originally appeared on August 17, 1888.

27. The first Confederate monument was erected by the 2nd Maryland in 1885.

28. [H. V. Boynton], "The Blue and the Gray United," *Southern Historical Society Papers* 16 (1888), 339–48.

29. Timothy B. Smith, *A Chickamauga Memorial: The Establishment of America's First Civil War National Military Park* (Knoxville: University of Tennessee Press, 2009), 19–20.

30. *Galveston Daily News,* Aug. 27, 1889; Smith, *Chickamauga Memorial,* 20–21; Chickamauga Memorial Association, *Proceedings at Chattanooga, Tenn., and Crawfish Springs, Ga., September 19 and 20, 1889* (Chattanooga Army of Cumberland Reunion Entertainment Committee, 1889), 7, 15–20. For the most comprehensive account of the creation of Chickamauga and Chattanooga National Military Park, see Smith, *Chickamauga Memorial.* For an equally compelling and thorough account of the first five national military parks, see Smith, *Golden Age.*

31. Chickamauga Memorial Association, *Proceedings at Chattanooga,* 136–41; Smith, *Chickamauga Memorial,* 22.

32. Chickamauga Memorial Association, *Proceedings at Chattanooga,* 136–41.

33. *St. Paul Daily News,* Sept. 21, 1889; *Los Angeles Times,* Sept. 21, 1889; *Chicago Daily Inter Ocean,* Sept. 21, 1889; Chickamauga Memorial Association, *Proceedings at Chattanooga,* 29–31; Smith, *Chickamauga Memorial,* 20.

34. House Committee on Military Affairs, *House Reports,* 51st Cong., 1st sess., Mar. 5, 1890, H. Rep. 643, 1–6; Smith, *Chickamauga Memorial,* 26–31.

35. Smith, *Chickamauga Memorial,* 37–39, 43–51.

36. *Los Angeles Times,* Sept. 15, 1895; *Atlanta Constitution,* Sept. 17, 1895.

37. *Los Angeles Times,* Sept. 20, 1895; Smith, *Golden Age,* 66–67; Smith, *Chickamauga Memorial,* 53–57.

38. Edward C. Walthall [ex-C.S. general, Army of Tennessee] to Robert W. Banks [ex-C.S. regimental adjutant and staff officer to Walthall], Grenada, Miss., Sept. 4, 1895, in "Letters of Senator Edward Cary Walthall to Robert W. Banks," ed. George C. Osborn, *Journal of Mississippi History* 9 (July 1949): 191. Thanks to Keith Bohannon for bringing this letter to my attention.

39. The eight states were Michigan, Missouri, Ohio, Wisconsin, Indiana, Illinois, Minnesota, and Massachusetts.

40. *New York Times,* Sept. 20, 1895.

41. *Atlanta Constitution,* Sept. 21, 1895; Smith, *Chickamauga Memorial,* 67.

42. Henry Van Ness Boynton, *Dedication of the Chickamauga and Chattanooga National Military Park* (Washington, D.C.: GPO, 1896), 27–28.

43. *Los Angeles Times,* Sept. 19, 20, 1895.

44. Boynton, *Dedication,* 245.

45. Ibid., 304.

46. Ibid., 75.

47. Ibid., 89.

48. Ibid., 239–40.

49. Ibid., 346.

50. *New York Times,* Sept. 20, 1895; Boynton, *Dedication,* 36.

51. Boynton, *Dedication,* 239.

52. Ibid., 123.

53. The 1890s witnessed a heightened effort among Southern whites to forestall black economic advancement, institute state-sanctioned segregation, and implement disenfranchisement. Where disenfranchisement and segregation efforts proved inadequate measures to keep blacks in their subservient position, white Southerners turned to the extralegal

method of lynching. Just a year after the Chickamauga and Chattanooga dedication, the U.S. Supreme Court would support state-sanctioned segregation in *Plessy v. Ferguson*. On the era of segregation, see Edward L. Ayers, *The Promise of the New South: Life after Reconstruction* (New York: Oxford University Press, 1992), 132–59; and C. Vann Woodward, *Strange Career of Jim Crow* (New York: Oxford University Press, 1955).

54. *New York Times,* Sept. 19, 1895; Boynton, *Dedication,* 346.

55. Boynton, *Dedication,* 69, 72.

56. See, for example, the speech of Governor McKinley in Boynton, *Dedication,* 341.

57. For discussions of Confederates comparing themselves to the revolutionaries of 1776, see Emory M. Thomas, *The Confederacy as a Revolutionary Experience* (Englewood Cliffs, N.J.: Prentice-Hall, 1970), 44–46; Reid Mitchell, *Civil War Soldiers* (New York: Viking, 1988), 1–2, 12, 20, 23, 24; and James M. McPherson, *For Cause and Comrades: Why Men Fought in the Civil War* (New York: Oxford University Press, 1997), 20–22.

58. *New York Times,* Sept. 21, 1895.

59. Ibid.; Boynton, *Dedication,* 181–83; Glenn W. LaFantasie, *Gettysburg Requiem: The Life and Lost Causes of Confederate Colonel William C. Oates* (New York: Oxford University Press, 2006), 246–47.

60. *New York Times,* Sept. 21, 1895; Boynton, *Dedication,* 181–83; LaFantasie, *Gettysburg Requiem,* 246–47.

61. *Confederate Veteran* 3, no. 10 (Oct. 1895), 292–93.

62. *The Watchman,* Oct. 3, 1895.

63. LaFantasie, *Gettysburg Requiem,* 246–48.

64. *Confederate Veteran* 3, no. 10 (Oct. 1895), 292.

65. Ibid., 289.

66. Smith, *Golden Age,* 36–37, 48, 211. The momentum to preserve the heroic fields continued, with bills for seventeen proposed parks reaching Congress by 1904. But as Timothy Smith points out, no new Civil War parks were established until the mid-1920s.

67. *The Atlanta,* July 20, 1900.

68. Blight, *Race and Reunion,* 6–12.

69. Smith, *Chickamauga Memorial,* 79.

70. [Lawson S. Kilborn], *Dedication of the Wilder Brigade Monument on Chickamauga Battlefield on the Thirty-Sixth Anniversary of the Battle, September 20, 1899* (Marshall, Ill.: Herald, 1900), 22; Samuel C. Williams, *General John T. Wilder: Commander of the Lightning Brigade* (Bloomington: Indiana University Press, 1936), 49.

71. *House Reports,* 56th Cong., 1st sess., Dec. 5, 1899, H. Rept. 869; *New York Times,* Dec. 5, 1899; *Washington Post,* Feb. 8, 1900; Smith, *Chickamauga Memorial,* 101–102.

72. For an account of the failed attempts to construct a peace memorial at Appomattox, see Caroline E. Janney, "War over the Shrine of Peace: The Appomattox Peace Monument and Retreat from Reconciliation," *Journal of Southern History* 77, no. 1 (2011): 91–120. There was also an effort to erect a peace memorial at Chickamauga or Chattanooga in the wake of Boynton's death. But like the "Arch of Nationality," it was never constructed. Smith, *Chickamauga Memorial,* 107.

73. *Washington Post,* July 8, 1906; *New York Times,* Nov. 16, 1910; *Monuments and Markers of the 29 States Engaged at Chickamauga and Chattanooga* (Collegedale, Tenn.: College Press, n.d.).

74. Smith, *Chickamauga Memorial,* 120.

CONTRIBUTORS

Russell S. Bonds is a graduate of the Georgia Institute of Technology and the University of Georgia School of Law. He is the author of *War Like the Thunderbolt: The Battle and Burning of Atlanta.* His book *Stealing the General: The Great Locomotive Chase and the First Medal of Honor* won the 2007 Richard B. Harwell Award of the Atlanta Civil War Round Table and is now in development as a feature film.

Stephen Cushman is the Robert C. Taylor Professor of American Literature and Poetry at the University of Virginia. He completed his undergraduate work at Cornell University and Ph.D. at Yale University. His books include *Bloody Promenade: Reflections on a Civil War Battle.*

Caroline E. Janney is associate professor of American history at Purdue University and holds a Ph.D. from the University of Virginia. She is the author of *Burying the Dead but Not the Past: Ladies' Memorial Associations and the Lost Cause* as well as *Remembering the Civil War: Reunion and the Limits of Reconciliation.*

Evan C. Jones is a graduate of the University of Virginia. Before leaving the National Park Service, he worked at the Vicksburg National Military Park, the Fredericksburg and Spotsylvania National Military Park, the Appomattox Court House National Historical Park, and the Chickamauga and Chattanooga National Military Park. He is presently writing a book about life in the American South immediately after the Civil War.

David A. Powell is a graduate of the Virginia Military Institute. He is the author of the campaign atlas *The Maps of Chickamauga.* His book *Failure in the Saddle: Nathan Bedford Forrest, Joe Wheeler, and the Confederate Cavalry in the Chickamauga Campaign* won the 2011 Richard B. Harwell Award of the Atlanta Civil War Round Table.

Gerald J. Prokopowicz is chair of the Department of History at East Carolina University. He completed a law degree at the University of Michigan and received his Ph.D. from Harvard University, where he studied under David Herbert Donald. He is a member of the advisory board to the Abraham Lincoln Bicentennial Commission and the Lincoln Forum. His books include *All for the Regiment: The Army of the Ohio, 1861–62.*

William Glenn Robertson is director emeritus of the U.S. Army's Combat Studies Institute at the Combined Arms Center at Fort Leavenworth, Kansas. Dr. Robertson completed his undergraduate work at the University of Richmond and Ph.D. at the University of Virginia, where he studied under Willie Lee Rose. For more than a decade he taught a semester-long course on the Chickamauga Campaign at the U.S. Army Command and General Staff College. In 1983 he resurrected the Army Staff Ride to deepen instruction on the Battle of Chickamauga. His books include *The Bermuda Hundred Campaign* and *The Battle of Old Men and Young Boys.* He is presently working on the book-length study *River of Death: The Campaign of Chickamauga.*

Wiley Sword is the author of eight books, including *Mountains Touched with Fire, Chattanooga Besieged, 1863* and *Embrace an Angry Wind,* for which he received the 1992 Fletcher Pratt Award. His book *President Washington's Indian War* was nominated for the Pulitzer Prize, Bancroft Prize, Parkman Prize, and Western Heritage Prize. He was educated at the University of Michigan.

Craig L. Symonds is professor emeritus of American history at the U.S. Naval Academy. Dr. Symonds completed his undergraduate work at UCLA and Ph.D. at the University of Florida, where he studied under John K. Mahon. He is the editor of nine books and the author of thirteen others, including *Lincoln and His Admirals,* for which he received the 2009 Lincoln Prize. His other works have been awarded the Barondess Lincoln Prize, the Daniel and Marilyn Laney Prize, the S. A. Cunningham Award, the Theodore and Franklin D. Roosevelt Prize, and the John Lyman Prize. His teaching experience includes semesters as professor of strategy and policy at the Britannia Naval College and the Naval War College. Symonds is a member of the advisory board to the Abraham Lincoln Bicentennial Commission and the Lincoln Forum.

INDEX

Abolition, 288, 298, 301

Acoustic shadow, 183

Adams, Gen. Dan, 80, 141

African Americans, 9, 19, 24, 53, 54, 59n61, 116, 175, 213, 232–37, 244–50, 252, 287, 288, 298, 306. *See also* Slavery; Slaves

Alexander, Peter W., 236, 252

Alexander's Bridge, 72, 74, 76, 86, 132, 133, 135, 137, 138, 139, 140

Alexander's Bridge Road, 76, 140

Allegheny Mountains, 21

Alpine, AL, 73

Anderson, Lt. Col. Archer, 132, 133, 134, 137, 138, 154, 156n

Anderson, Maj. Charles W., 85

Anderson, J. B., 48

Anderson, Gen. James Patton, 243

Anderson House, 73

Andrews, James J., 1, 29, 41; "Andrews's Raid," 3, 29

Antietam, Battle of, 37, 264

Antietam National Military Park, 303

Appalachian Mountains, 1, 3, 17, 34n, 39

Appomattox Court House, VA, 212, 288, 289, 298

Armstrong, Gen. Frank, 67, 69, 70, 71, 73, 77, 80, 89

Armstrong, Sgt. Gilbert, 105, 106, 108

Armstrong, John, 19

Army of Mississippi, 160

Army of Northern Virginia, 2, 4, 68, 111, 163, 210, 252n, 288, 300

Army of Tennessee (Confederate)

—Corps: Buckner's, 64, 67, 68, 74, 258; First (Longstreet's/Hood's), 68, 72, 73, 76, 77, 130; Hardee's, 127n; Cavalry (Forrest's), 62, 63, 67, 70, 76, 79, 88, 89, 91n; Cavalry (Wheeler's), 63, 65, 66, 69, 70, 71, 73, 77; Hill's, 73, 79, 80, 132, 133, 135, 138, 139, 140; Left Wing (Longstreet's), 79, 81, 130, 131, 258; Polk's, 131, 133, 134, 139; Reserve Corps (Walker's), 73, 75, 77, 134; Right Wing (Polk's), 79, 81, 92n, 130, 131, 132, 133, 140

—Divisions: Breckinridge's, 80, 132, 133, 134, 135, 137, 138, 141, 147; Cleburne's, 133, 135, 138; Preston's, 164, 258; Wharton's, 66, 69, 73, 91n

Army of the Cumberland

—Corps: XIV (Thomas's), 71, 77, 80, 81, 89, 131, 141, 142, 143, 144, 146, 147, 148, 149, 189, 195, 259, 260, 262, 266; XX (McCook's), 68, 89, 106, 109, 112, 118, 142, 143, 144, 146, 150, 152; XXI (Crittenden's), 65, 69, 70, 71, 77, 89, 106, 109, 112, 130, 142, 143, 144, 145, 146, 150, 152, 259; Cavalry (Stanley's), 101, (Mitchell's), 142, 143, 278n; Reserve (Granger's), 72, 81, 142, 143, 259, 260, 261, 263, 266, 267, 278, 279

—Divisions: Brannan's, 77, 81, 145, 146, 147, 148, 149, 150, 152, 259; Negley's, 80, 81, 141, 143–48

—Route from Chickamauga, 4, 81–83, 89, 130, 152, 161, 173, 194–95, 272, 278

Army of the Mississippi, 177, 178

Army of the Ohio, 3, 4, 5, 7, 36, 39, 40, 43, 44, 47, 49, 50, 51, 52, 53, 199

Army of the Potomac, 4, 36, 38, 48, 111, 117, 175, 199, 206, 292, 300, 302

Army of the Tennessee (Federal), 4, 41, 57n, 111, 199

Athens, AL, 48, 49, 50; sack of, 53

Atkins, Gen. Smith D., 290

Atlanta, GA, 5, 15, 17, 19, 21, 23, 26, 30, 40, 41, 45, 68, 85, 87, 159, 165, 166, 296, 302; Sherman's campaign, 45, 114, 118, 124, 209, 228, 229, 231, 236, 239, 241

Augusta, GA, 23, 24, 26

Baird, Gen. Absalom, 143

Barnes, Col. Sidney M., and his brigade, 146, 152

Barnett's Crossroads, MS, 180

Bartleson, Col. Frederick A., 147

Bate, Gen. William B., 243

Bates, Edward, 185

Baton Rouge, LA, 27

"Battle above the Clouds." *See* Lookout Mountain

Battle Creek, TN, 48

Bay Springs Road, 180, 182

Beatty, Gen. John, and his brigade, 144, 145

Beatty, Col. Taylor, 83

Beauregard, Gen. P. G. T., 165, 170, 213

Benham, Maj. Calhoun, 236

Benjamin, Judah P., 252n

Bickham, William D., 186, 187

Bierce, Lt. Albert, 259, 261, 270, 271, 278, 280, 281n

Bierce, Lt. Ambrose, 10, 123, 128n51, 254–79, 280n–284n

Big South Railroad, 101

Blair, Francis, 185

Blockade, 239

Bloody Pond, 273

Blue Ridge Mountains, 1, 21

Bond, Maj. Frank S., 149, 150, 153, 154, 158n

Bonds, Russell S., 5, 6, 10

Bowling Green, KY, 31, 40, 45, 250

Boynton, Lt. Col., Henry V. N., 259, 265, 281n, 291, 292, 293, 294, 304, 307n, 309n

Bragg, Gen. Braxton, 3, 4, 5, 7, 12n, 30, 31, 35n, 44, 52, 63, 64, 65, 66, 67, 68, 69, 70, 71, 72, 73, 74, 77, 78, 79, 80, 81, 82, 83, 84, 85, 86, 87, 88, 89, 94, 101, 111, 116, 129, 130, 131, 132, 133, 134, 135, 137, 138, 139, 140, 141, 153, 159, 160, 161, 169, 170, 230, 231, 258, 264, 267, 274; enmity with other generals, 8, 82, 83, 84, 85, 86, 87, 88, 89, 159, 160, 161, 162, 163, 164, 165, 166, 167, 168, 169, 170, 264, 267; and Jefferson Davis, 159, 160, 162, 164, 165, 166, 167, 168, 169, 170, 230, 241, 251n; opinion of Forrest, 83, 84, 85, 86, 87, 88; poor health and spirits, 164, 165

Brannan, Gen. John, 148, 260, 261, 279; and his division, 77, 81, 145, 146, 147, 148, 149, 150, 152, 259

Breckinridge, Gen. John C., 80, 132, 133, 134, 135, 137, 138, 139, 159, 164, 166, 232, 242; and his division, 80, 132, 133, 134, 135, 137, 138, 141, 147

Bridgeport, AL, 24, 42, 46, 47, 48, 57n, 64, 66, 118, 119, 120, 195, 201, 204, 205

Brock Field, 112, 114

Brotherton Cabin, 146, 147

Brotherton Farm, 146, 147, 152, 266

Brotherton Field, 81

Brough, Gov. John, 197

Brown, John, 247, 301

Brown, Gen. John C., 164, 242

Brown, Gov. Joseph, 166

Brown's Ferry, 120, 203

Buckner, Gen. Simon B., 64, 67, 68, 69, 74, 131, 132, 164, 167, 168, 169, 170, 258

Buell, Maj. Gen. Don Carlos, 3, 7, 29, 30, 31, 36–41, 43–54, 54n, 55n, 56n, 57n, 58n, 59n, 98, 117, 118; and McClellan, 36, 38, 40, 41, 53, 59n; and Mitchel, 3, 7, 41, 43, 44, 46–51, 56n, 58n

Buell, Col. George P., 146, 147, 152

Buell Commission, 7, 36, 37, 38, 52, 54n, 57n

Cleveland, TN, 21, 28
Coleman, Capt. Thaddeus, 135, 137
Colquitt, Col. John W., 250
Colt revolving rifles, 99, 104, 105
Confederate Congress, 132, 231, 232, 235, 241
Confederate Nitre and Mining Bureau, 11, 24, 25, 26, 34n; epsom salts caves, 26; mines, 11, 24, 25, 26; potash works, 24; resources, 24, 31, 40; saltpeter caves, 24, 40
Confederate Powder Works, 23, 24
Confederate Veteran (magazine), 302
Congressional Committee on the Conduct of the War, 212
Connell, Col. John M., and his brigade, 146, 148
Connelly, Thomas, 25, 169
Cooper, Gen. Samuel, 232, 243
Cooper Iron Works, 23
Corinth, MS, 3, 21, 27, 28, 30, 36, 41, 43, 44, 45, 46, 47, 48, 49, 55n, 57n, 176, 178, 188; battle of, 188, 189, 190, 205, 214, 216
Corse, Gen. John, and his brigade, 112
Cowan, Dr. James B., 86; account of confrontation between Bragg and Forrest, 86, 87, 88
Cozzens, Peter, 5, 11, 156n, 259, 261, 262, 264, 272, 281n
"Cracker Line," 35n, 120, 197, 204, 205, 223n; postwar controversy over, 204, 205
Crawfish Springs, GA, 12n, 142, 293
Crittenden, Gen. Thomas L., 47, 67, 69, 70, 71, 142, 144, 149, 150, 152, 197, 267
Croxton, Col. John T., 77, 78, 148
Cruft, Gen. Charles, 204
Crutchfield House, 18, 27
Cumberland Gap, 3, 29, 40, 41, 44
Cumberland Mountains, 1, 21, 193, 194
Cumberland River, 49

Dalton, GA, 1, 70, 74, 232, 235, 236, 251
Dalton's Ford, 74, 135
Dana, Charles A., 4, 149, 194, 195, 196, 197, 198, 200, 203, 206, 208, 222n

Darr, Gen. Francis, 214, 215
Davidson, Col. Henry B., 69, 73, 77, 80, 83
Davis, Pres. Jefferson, 3, 6, 8, 18, 27, 87, 88, 98, 159, 160, 162–70, 230, 232, 234, 235, 239, 240, 241, 245, 246, 251n
Davis, Gen. Jefferson C., 143, 146, 150, 152
Davis, Varina, 33n
Davis, William C. "Jack," 167, 170
Decatur, AL, 41, 42, 44, 46, 47, 48, 50, 56n
DeCredico, Mary A., 27
Democratic Party, 38, 39, 175, 176, 191, 193, 197, 209, 213, 214, 218n, 219n
Dennison, William, 212
Department of East Tennessee, 31, 56n, 64
Department of Mississippi, 176
Department of the Cumberland, 97, 98, 115. *See also* Army of the Cumberland
Department of the Missouri, 209
Department of the Ohio, 38
Department of the Pacific, 38
Desertion, 63, 231, 232, 233, 239, 244, 252n
Dibrell, Col. George, 65, 66, 69, 77, 78, 79, 83
Dick, Franklin, 185
Dickey, Col. Theophilus, 178, 180, 181, 182, 186, 219n, 220n
Die Presse, 1
Dodge, William Sumner, 117
Dry Valley Road, 262
Ducat, Arthur C., 183, 184
Duck River, 48
Ducktown, TN, 24
Durham Station, NC, 286
Dyer Field, 147, 148, 150, 152

Early, Jubal A., 288
East Tennessee, 2, 13, 14, 15, 17, 18, 19, 24, 28, 30, 34n, 40, 41, 46, 56n, 86, 116, 169, 287; Unionism, 2, 3, 14, 18, 19, 28, 40
East Tennessee and Georgia Railroad, 17, 21, 28
East Tennessee and Virginia Railroad, 17, 28
Eastport, MS, 44
Ector, Gen. Matthew D., 76, 78, 79
Elk River, 50, 51, 56n